Perceptrons

The MIT Press
Massachusetts Institute of Technology
Cambridge, Massachusetts, and London, England

Marvin Minsky and Seymour Papert

Perceptrons

An Introduction to Computational Geometry

Expanded Edition

In memory of Frank Rosenblatt

Third printing, 1988

This book was set in Photon Times Roman by The Science Press, Inc., and printed and bound by Halliday Lithograph in the United States of America.

Library of Congress Cataloging-in-Publication Data

Minsky, Marvin Lee, 1927–
Perceptrons : An introduction to computational geometry.

Bibliography: p.
Includes index.
1. Perceptrons. 2. Geometry—Data processing.
3. Parallel processing (Electronic computers)
4. Machine learning. I. Papert, Seymour. II. Title.
Q327.M55 1988 006.3 87-30990
ISBN 0-262-63111-3 (pbk.)

CONTENTS

Prologue: A View from 1988

This book is about perceptrons—the simplest learning machines. However, our deeper purpose is to gain more general insights into the interconnected subjects of parallel computation, pattern recognition, knowledge representation, and learning. It is only because one cannot think productively about such matters without studying specific examples that we focus on theories of perceptrons.

In preparing this edition we were tempted to "bring those theories up to date." But when we found that little of significance had changed since 1969, when the book was first published, we concluded that it would be more useful to keep the original text (with its corrections of 1972) and add an epilogue, so that the book could still be read in its original form. One reason why progress has been so slow in this field is that researchers unfamiliar with its history have continued to make many of the same mistakes that others have made before them. Some readers may be shocked to hear it said that little of significance has happened in this field. Have not perceptron-like networks—under the new name *connectionism*—become a major subject of discussion at gatherings of psychologists and computer scientists? Has not there been a "connectionist revolution?" Certainly yes, in that there is a great deal of interest and discussion. Possibly yes, in the sense that discoveries have been made that may, in time, turn out to be of fundamental importance. But certainly no, in that there has been little clear-cut change in the conceptual basis of the field. The issues that give rise to excitement today seem much the same as those that were responsible for previous rounds of excitement. The issues that were then obscure remain obscure today because no one yet knows how to tell which of the present discoveries are fundamental and which are superficial. Our position remains what it was when we wrote the book: We believe this realm of work to be immensely important and rich, but we expect its growth to require a degree of critical analysis that its more romantic advocates have always been reluctant to pursue—perhaps because the spirit of connectionism seems itself to go somewhat against the grain of analytic rigor.

In the next few pages we will try to portray recent events in the field of parallel-network learning machines as taking place within the historical context of a war between antagonistic tendencies called *symbolist* and *connectionist*. Many of the participants in this history see themselves as divided on the question of strategies for thinking—a division that now seems to pervade our culture, engaging not only those interested in building models of mental functions but also writers, educators, therapists, and philosophers. Too many people too often speak as though the strategies of thought fall naturally into two groups whose attributes seem diametrically opposed in character:

symbolic	connectionist
logical	analogical
serial	parallel
discrete	continuous
localized	distributed
hierarchical	heterarchical
left-brained	right-brained

This broad division makes no sense to us, because these attributes are largely independent of one another; for example, the very same system could combine symbolic, analogical, serial, continuous, and localized aspects. Nor do many of those pairs imply clear opposites; at best they merely indicate some possible extremes among some wider range of possibilities. And although many good theories begin by making distinctions, we feel that in subjects as broad as these there is less to be gained from sharpening boundaries than from seeking useful intermediates.

The 1940s: Neural Networks

The 1940s saw the emergence of the simple yet powerful concept that the natural components of mind-like machines were simple abstractions based on the behavior of biological nerve cells, and that such machines could be built by interconnecting such elements. In their 1943 manifesto "A Logical Calculus of the Ideas Immanent in Nervous Activity," Warren McCulloch and Walter Pitts presented the first sophisticated discussion of "neuro-logical networks," in which they combined new ideas about finite-state machines, linear threshold decision elements, and logical representations of various forms of behavior and memory. In 1947 they published a second monumental essay, "How We Know Universals," which described network architectures capable, in principle, of recognizing spatial patterns in a manner invariant under groups of geometric transformations.

From such ideas emerged the intellectual movement called cybernetics, which attempted to combine many concepts from biology, psychology, engineering, and mathematics. The cybernetics era produced a flood of architectural schemes for making neural networks recognize, track, memorize, and perform many other useful functions. The decade ended with the publication of Donald Hebb's book *The Organization of Behavior,* the first attempt to base a large-scale theory of psychology on conjectures about neural networks. The central idea of Hebb's book was that such networks might learn by constructing internal representations of concepts in the form of what Hebb called "cell-assemblies"—subfamilies of neurons that would learn to support one another's activities. There had been earlier attempts to explain psychology in terms of "connections" or "associations," but (perhaps because those connections were merely between symbols or ideas rather than between mechanisms) those theories seemed *then* too insubstantial to be taken seriously by theorists seeking models for mental mechanisms. Even after Hebb's proposal, it was years before research in artificial intelligence found suitably convincing ways to make symbolic concepts seem concrete.

The 1950s: Learning in Neural Networks

The cybernetics era opened up the prospect of making mind-like machines. The earliest workers in that field sought specific architectures that could perform specific functions. However, in view of the fact that animals can learn to do many things they aren't built to do, the goal soon changed to making machines that could learn. Now, the concept of learning is ill defined, because there is no clear-cut boundary between the simplest forms of memory and complex procedures for making predictions and generalizations about things never seen. Most of the early experiments were based on the idea of "reinforcing" actions that had been successful in the past—a concept already popular in behavioristic psychology. In order for reinforcement to be applied to a system, the system must be capable of generating a sufficient variety of actions from which to choose and the system needs some criterion of relative success. These are also the prerequisites for the "hill-climbing" machines that we discuss in section 11.6 and in the epilogue.

Perhaps the first reinforcement-based network learning system was a machine built by Minsky in 1951. It consisted of forty electronic units interconnected by a network of links, each of which had an adjustable probability of receiving activation signals and then transmitting them to other units. It learned by means of a reinforcement process in which each positive or negative judgment about the machine's behavior was translated into a small change (of corresponding magnitude and sign) in the probabilities associated with whichever connections had recently transmitted signals. The 1950s saw many other systems that exploited simple forms of learning, and this led to a professional specialty called adaptive control.

Today, people often speak of neural networks as offering a promise of machines that do not need to be programmed. But speaking of those old machines in such a way stands history on its head, since the concept of programming had barely appeared at that time. When modern serial computers finally arrived, it became a great deal easier to experiment with learning schemes and "self-organizing systems." However, the availability of computers also opened up other avenues of research into learning. Perhaps the most notable example of this was Arthur Samuel's research on programming computers to learn to play checkers. (See Bibliographic Notes.) Using a success-based reward system, Samuel's 1959 and 1967 programs attained masterly levels of performance. In developing those procedures, Samuel encountered and described two fundamental questions:

Credit assignment. Given some existing ingredients, how does one decide how much to credit each of them for each of the machine's accomplishments? In Samuel's machine, the weights are assigned by correlation with success.

Inventing novel predicates. If the existing ingredients are inadequate, how does one invent new ones? Samuel's machine tests products of some preexisting terms.

Most researchers tried to bypass these questions, either by ignoring them or by using brute force or by trying to discover powerful and generally applicable methods. Few researchers tried to use them as guides to thoughtful research. We do not believe that any completely general solution to them can exist, and we argue in our epilogue that awareness of these issues should lead to a model of mind that can accumulate a multiplicity of specialized methods.

By the end of the 1950s, the field of neural-network research had become virtually dormant. In part this was because there had not been many important discoveries for a long time. But it was also partly because important advances in artificial intelligence had been made through the use of new kinds of models based on serial processing of symbolic expressions. New landmarks appeared in the form of working computer programs that solved respectably difficult problems. In the wake of these accomplishments, theories based on connections among symbols suddenly seemed more satisfactory. And although we and some others maintained allegiances to both approaches, intellectual battle lines began to form along such conceptual fronts as parallel versus serial processing, learning versus programming, and emergence versus analytic description.

The 1960s: Connectionists and Symbolists

Interest in connectionist networks revived dramatically in 1962 with the publication of Frank Rosenblatt's book *Principles of Neurodynamics,* in which he defined the machines he named perceptrons and proved many theories about them. (See Bibliographic Notes.) The basic idea was so simply and clearly defined that it was feasible to prove an amazing theorem (theorem 11.1 below) which stated that a perceptron would learn to do anything that it was possible to program it to do. And the connectionists of the 1960s were indeed able to make perceptrons learn to do certain things—but not other things. Usually, when a failure occurred, neither prolonging the training experiments nor building larger machines helped. All perceptrons would fail to learn to do those things, and once again the work in this field stalled.

Arthur Samuel's two questions can help us see why perceptrons worked as well as they did. First, Rosenblatt's credit-assignment method turned out to be as effective as any such method could be. When the answer is obtained, in effect, by adding up the contributions of many processes that have no significant interactions among themselves, then the best one can do is reward them in proportion to how much each of them contributed. (Actually, with perceptrons, one never rewards success; one only punishes failure.) And Rosenblatt offered the simplest possible approach to the problem of inventing new parts: You don't have to invent new parts if enough parts are provided from the start. Once it became clear that these tactics would work in certain circumstances but not in others, most workers searched for methods that worked in general. However, in our book we turned in a different direction. Instead of trying to find a method that would work in every possible situation, we sought to find ways to understand why the particular method used in the perceptron would succeed in some situations but not in others. It turned out that perceptrons could usually solve the types of problems that we characterize (in section 0.8) as being of low "order." With those problems, one can indeed sometimes get by with making ingredients at random and then selecting the ones that work. However, problems of higher "orders" require too many such ingredients for this to be feasible.

This style of analysis was the first to show that there are fundamental limitations on the kinds of patterns that perceptrons can ever learn to recognize. How did the scientists involved with such matters react to this? One popular version is that the publication of our book so discouraged research on learning in network machines that a promising line of research was interrupted. Our version is that progress had already come to a virtual halt because of the lack of adequate basic theories, and the lessons in this book provided the field with new momentum—albeit, paradoxically, by redirecting its immediate concerns. To understand the situation, one must recall that by the mid 1960s there had been a great many experiments with perceptrons, but no one had been able to explain why they were able to learn to recognize certain kinds of patterns and not others. Was this in the nature of the learning procedures? Did it depend on the sequences in which the patterns were presented? Were the machines simply too small in capacity?

What we discovered was that the traditional analysis of learning machines—and of perceptrons in particular—had looked in the wrong direction. Most theorists had tried to focus only on the mathematical structure of what was common to all learning, and the theories to which this had led were too general and too weak to explain which patterns perceptrons could learn to recognize. As our analysis in chapter 2 shows, this actually had nothing to with learning at all; it had to do with the relationships between the perceptron's architecture and the characters of the problems that were being presented to it. The trouble appeared when perceptrons had no way to represent the knowledge required for solving certain problems. The moral was that one simply cannot learn enough by studying learning by itself; one also has to understand the nature of what one wants to learn. This can be expressed as a principle that applies not only to perceptrons but to every sort of learning machine: No machine can learn to recognize X unless it possesses, at least potentially, some scheme for *representing* X.

The 1970s: Representation of Knowledge

Why have so few discoveries about network machines been made since the work of Rosenblatt? It has sometimes been suggested that the "pessimism" of our book was responsible for the fact that connectionism was in a relative eclipse until recent research broke through the limitations that we had purported to establish. Indeed, this book has been described as having been intended to demonstrate that perceptrons (and all other network machines) are too limited to deserve further attention. Certainly many of the best researchers turned away from network machines for quite some time, but present-day connectionists who regard that as regrettable have failed to understand the place at which they stand in history. As we said earlier, it seems to us that the effect of *Perceptrons* was not simply to interrupt a healthy line of research. That redirection of concern was no arbitrary diversion; it was a necessary interlude. To make further progress, connectionists would have to take time off and develop adequate ideas about the representation of knowledge. In the epilogue we shall explain why that was a prerequisite for understanding more complex types of network machines.

In any case, the 1970s became the golden age of a new field of research into the representation of knowledge. And it was not only connectionist learning that was placed on hold; it also happened to research on learning in the field of artificial intelligence. For example, although Patrick Winston's 1970 doctoral thesis (see "Learning Structural Definitions from Examples," in *The Psychology of Computer Vision,* ed. P. H. Winston [McGraw-Hill, 1975]) was clearly a major advance, the next decade of AI research saw surprisingly little attention to that subject.

In several other related fields, many researchers set aside their interest in the study of learning in favor of examining the representation of knowledge in many different contexts and forms. The result was the very rapid development of many new and powerful ideas—among them frames, conceptual dependency, production systems, word-expert parsers, relational databases, K-lines, scripts, nonmonotonic logic, semantic networks, analogy generators, cooperative processes, and planning procedures. These ideas about the analysis of knowledge and its embodiments, in turn, had strong effects not only in the heart of artificial intelligence but also in many areas of psychology, brain science, and applied expert systems. Consequently, although not all of them recognize this, a good deal of what young researchers do today is based on what was learned about the representation of knowledge since *Perceptrons* first appeared. As was asserted above, their not knowing that history often leads them to repeat mistakes of the past. For example, many contemporary experimenters assume that, because the perceptron networks discussed in this book are not exactly the same as those in use today, these theorems no longer apply. Yet, as we will show in our epilogue, most of the *lessons* of the theorems still apply.

The 1980s: The Revival of Learning Machines

What could account for the recent resurgence of interest in network machines? What turned the tide in the battle between the connectionists and the symbolists? Was it that symbolic AI had run out of steam? Was it the important new ideas in connectionism? Was it the prospect of new, massively parallel hardware? Or did the new interest reflect a cultural turn toward holism?

Whatever the answer, a more important question is: Are there inherent incompatibilities between those connectionist and symbolist views? The answer to that depends on the extent to which one regards each separate connectionist scheme as a self-standing system. If one were to ask whether any particular, homogeneous network could serve as a model for a brain, the answer (we claim) would be, clearly, No. But if we consider each such network as a possible model for a *part* of a brain, then those two overviews are complementary.

This is why we see no reason to choose sides. We expect a great many new ideas to emerge from the study of symbol-based theories and experiments. And we expect the future of network-based learning machines to be rich beyond imagining. As we say in section 0.3, the solemn experts who complained most about the "exaggerated claims" of the cybernetics enthusiasts were, on balance, in the wrong. It is just as clear to us today as it was 20 years ago that the marvelous abilities of the human brain must emerge from the parallel activity of vast assemblies of interconnected nerve cells. But, as we explain in our epilogue, the marvelous powers of the brain emerge not from any single, uniformly structured connectionist network but from highly evolved arrangements of smaller, specialized networks which are interconnected in very specific ways.

The movement of research interest between the poles of connectionist learning and symbolic reasoning may provide a fascinating subject for the sociology of science, but workers in those fields must understand that these poles are artificial simplifications. It can be most revealing to study neural nets in their purest forms, or to do the same with elegant theories about formal reasoning. Such isolated studies often help in the disentangling of different types of mechanisms, insights, and principles. But it never makes any sense to choose either of those two views as one's only model of the mind. Both are partial and manifestly useful views of a reality of which science is still far from a comprehensive understanding.

0

0.0 Readers

In writing this we had in mind three kinds of readers. First, there are many new results that will interest specialists concerned with "pattern recognition," "learning machines," and "threshold logic." Second, some people will enjoy reading it as an essay in abstract mathematics; it may appeal especially to those who would like to see geometry return to topology and algebra. We ourselves share both these interests. But we would not have carried the work as far as we have, nor presented it in the way we shall, if it were not for a different, less clearly defined, set of interests.

The goal of this study is to reach a deeper understanding of some concepts we believe are crucial to the general theory of computation. We will study in great detail a class of computations that make decisions by weighing evidence. Certainly, this problem is of great interest in itself, but our real hope is that understanding of its mathematical structure will prepare us eventually to go further into the almost unexplored theory of parallel computers.

The people we want most to speak to are interested in that general theory of computation. We hope this includes psychologists and biologists who would like to know how the brain computes thoughts and how the genetic program computes organisms. We do not pretend to give answers to such questions—nor even to propose that the simple structures we shall use should be taken as "models" for such processes. Our aim—we are not sure whether it is more modest or more ambitious—is to illustrate how such a theory might begin, and what strategies of research could lead to it.

It is for this third class of readers that we have written this introduction. It may help those who do not have an immediate involvement with it to see that the theory of pattern recognition might be worth studying for other reasons. At the same time we will set out a simplified version of the theory to help readers who have not had the mathematical training that would make the later chapters easy to read. The rest of the book is self-contained and anyone who hates introductions may go directly to Chapter 1.

0.1 Real, Abstract, and Mythological Computers

We know shamefully little about our computers and their computations. This seems paradoxical because, physically and logically, computers are so lucidly transparent in their principles of operation. Yet even a school boy can ask questions about them that today's "computer science" cannot answer. We know very little, for instance, about how much computation a job should require.

As an example, consider one of the most frequently performed computations: *solving a set of linear equations*. This is important in virtually every kind of scientific work. There are a variety of standard programs for it, which are composed of additions, multiplications, and divisions. One would suppose that such a simple and important subject, long studied by mathematicians, would by now be thoroughly understood. But we ask, How many arithmetic steps are absolutely required? How does this depend on the amount of computer memory? How much time can we save if we have *two* (or n) identical computers? Every computer scientist "knows" that this computation requires something of the order of n^3 multiplications for n equations, but even if this be true no one knows—at this writing—how to begin to prove it.

Neither the outsider nor the computation specialist seems to recognize how primitive and how empirical is our present state of understanding of such matters. We do not know how much the speed of computations can be increased, in general, by using "parallel" as opposed to "serial"—or "analog" as opposed to "digital"—machines. We have no theory of the situations in which "associative" memories will justify their higher cost as compared to "addressed" memories. There is a great deal of folklore about this sort of contrast, but much of this folklore is mere superstition; in the cases we have studied carefully, the common beliefs turn out to be not merely "unproved"; they are often drastically wrong.

The immaturity shown by our inability to answer questions of this kind is exhibited even in the language used to formulate the questions. Word pairs such as "parallel" vs. "serial;" "local" vs. "global," and "digital" vs. "analog" are used as if they referred to well-defined technical concepts. Even when this is true, the technical meaning varies from user to user and context to context. But usually they are treated so loosely that the species of computing machine defined by them belongs to mythology rather than science.

Now we do not mean to suggest that these are mere pseudo-problems that arise from sloppy use of language. This is not a book of "therapeutic semantics"! For there *is* much content in these intuitive ideas and distinctions. The problem is how to capture it in a clear, sharp theory.

0.2 Mathematical Strategy

We are not convinced that the time is ripe to attempt a very general theory broad enough to encompass the concepts we have mentioned and others like them. Good theories rarely develop outside the context of a background of well-understood real problems and special cases. Without such a foundation, one gets either the vacuous generality of a theory with more definitions than theorems—or a mathematically elegant theory with no application to reality.

Accordingly, our best course would seem to be to strive for a *very thorough* understanding of well-chosen particular situations in which these concepts are involved.

We have chosen in fact to explore the properties of the simplest machines we could find that have a clear claim to be "parallel"—for they have no loops or feedback paths—yet can perform computations that are nontrivial, both in practical and in mathematical respects.

Before we proceed into details, we would like to reassure non-mathematicians who might be frightened by what they have glimpsed in the pages ahead. The mathematical methods used are rather diverse, but they seldom require advanced knowledge. We explain most of that which goes beyond elementary algebra and geometry. Where this was not practical, we have marked as *optional* those sections we feel might demand from most readers more mathematical effort than is warranted by the topic's role in the whole structure. Our theory is more like a tree with many branches than like a narrow high tower of blocks; in many cases one can skip, if trouble is encountered, to the beginning of the following chapter.

The reader of most modern mathematical texts is made to work unduly hard by the authors' tendency to cover over the intellectual tracks that lead to the discovery of the theorems. We have tried to leave visible the lines of progress. We should have liked to go further and leave traces of all the false tracks we followed; unfortunately there were too many! Nevertheless we have occasionally left an earlier proof even when we later found a "better" one. Our aim is not so much to prove theorems as to give insight into methods and to encourage research. We hope this will be read not as a chain of logical deductions but as a mathematical novel where characters appear, reappear, and develop.

0.3 Cybernetics and Romanticism

The machines we will study are abstract versions of a class of devices known under various names; we have agreed to use the name "perceptron" in recognition of the pioneer work of Frank Rosenblatt. Perceptrons make decisions—determine whether or not an event fits a certain "pattern"—by adding up evidence obtained from many small experiments. This clear and simple concept is important because most, and perhaps all, more complicated machines for making decisions share a little of this character. Until we understand it very thoroughly, we can expect to have trouble with more advanced ideas. In fact, we feel that the critical advances in many branches of science and mathematics began with good formulations of the "linear" systems, and these machines are our candidate for beginning the study of "parallel machines" in general.

Our discussion will include some rather sharp criticisms of earlier work in this area. Perceptrons have been widely publicized as "pattern recognition" or "learning" machines and as such have been discussed in a large number of books, journal articles, and voluminous "reports." Most of this writing (some exceptions are mentioned in our bibliography) is without scientific value and we will not usually refer by name to the works we criticize. The sciences of computation and cybernetics began, and it seems quite rightly so, with a certain flourish of romanticism. They were laden with attractive and exciting new ideas which have already borne rich fruit. Heavy demands of rigor and caution could have held this development to a much slower pace; only the future could tell which directions were to be the best. We feel, in fact, that the solemn experts who most complained about the "exaggerated claims" of the cybernetic enthusiasts were, in the balance, much more in the wrong. But now the time has come for maturity, and this requires us to match our speculative enterprise with equally imaginative standards of criticism.

0.4 Parallel Computation

The simplest concept of parallel computation is represented by the diagram in Figure 0.1. The figure shows how one might compute a function $\psi(X)$ in two stages. First we compute *independently* of one another a set of functions $\varphi_1(X)$, $\varphi_2(X)$, ..., $\varphi_n(X)$ and then combine the results by means of a function Ω of n arguments to obtain the value of ψ.

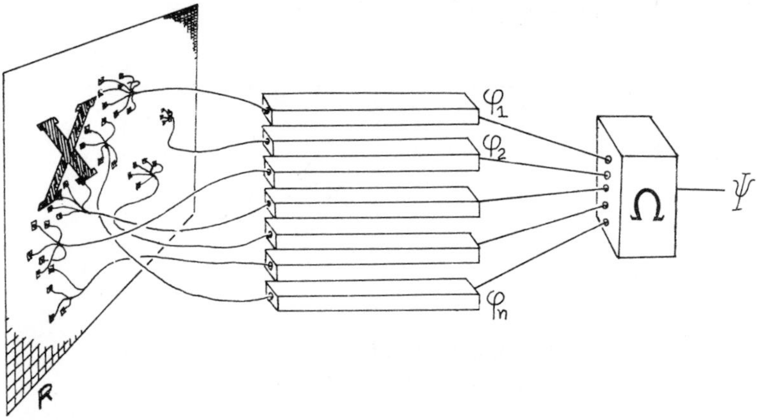

Figure 0.1

To make the definition meaningful—or, rather, productive—one needs to place some restrictions on the function Ω and the set Φ of functions $\varphi_1, \varphi_2, \ldots$. If we do not make restrictions,we do not get a theory: any computation ψ could be represented as a parallel computation in various trivial ways, for example, by making one of the φ's be ψ and letting Ω do nothing but transmit its result. We will consider a variety of restrictions, but first we will give a few concrete examples of the kinds of functions we might want ψ to be.

0.5 Some Geometric Patterns; Predicates

Let R be the ordinary two-dimensional Euclidean plane and let X be a geometric figure drawn on R. X could be a circle, or a pair of circles, or a black-and-white sketch of a face. In general we will think of a figure X as simply a subset of the points of R (that is, the black points).

Let $\psi(X)$ be a function (of figures X on R) that can have but two values. We usually think of the two values of ψ as 0 and 1. But by taking them to be FALSE and TRUE we can think of $\psi(X)$ as a predicate, that is, a variable statement whose truth or falsity depends on the choice of X. We now give a few examples of predicates that will be of particular interest in the sequel.

$$\psi_{\text{CIRCLE}}(X) = \begin{cases} 1 \text{ if the figure } X \text{ is a circle,} \\ 0 \text{ if the figure is not a circle;} \end{cases}$$

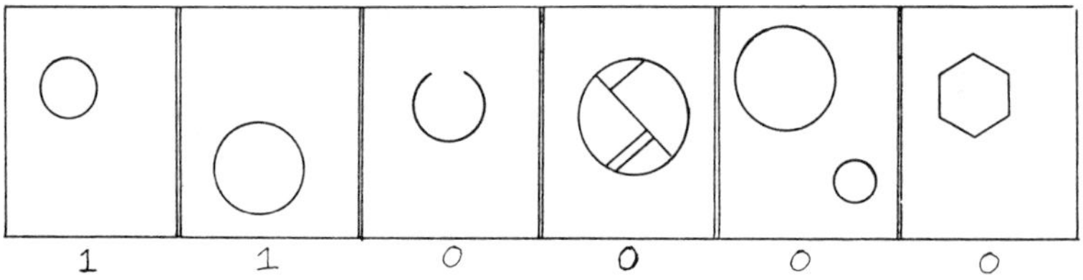

$$\psi_{\text{CONVEX}}(X) = \begin{cases} 1 \text{ if } X \text{ is a convex figure,} \\ 0 \text{ if } X \text{ is not a convex figure;} \end{cases}$$

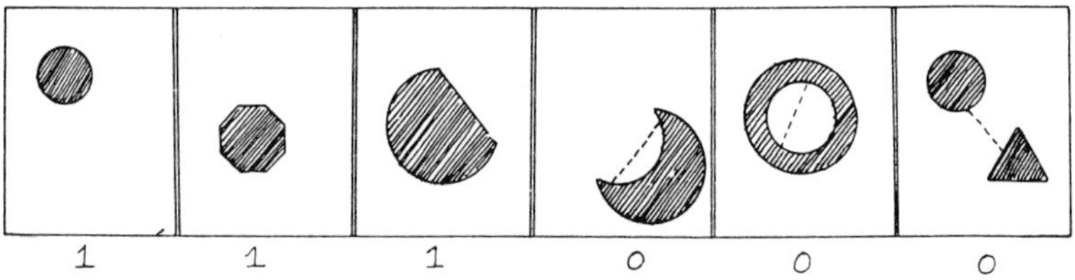

$$\psi_{\text{CONNECTED}}(X) = \begin{cases} 1 \text{ if } X \text{ is a connected figure,} \\ 0 \text{ otherwise.} \end{cases}$$

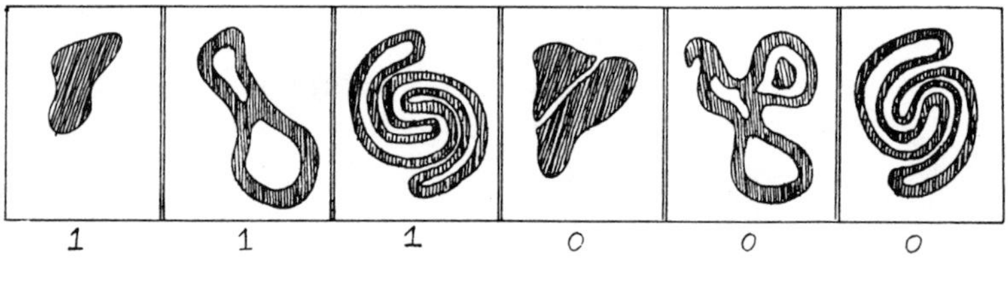

We will also use some very much simpler predicates.* The very simplest predicate "recognizes" when a particular single point is in X: let p be a point in the plane and define

$$\varphi_p(X) = \begin{cases} 1 \text{ if } p \text{ is in } X, \\ 0 \text{ otherwise.} \end{cases}$$

Finally we will need the kind of predicate that tells when a particular set A is a subset of X:

$$\varphi_A(X) = \begin{cases} 1 \text{ if } A \subset X, \\ 0 \text{ otherwise.} \end{cases}$$

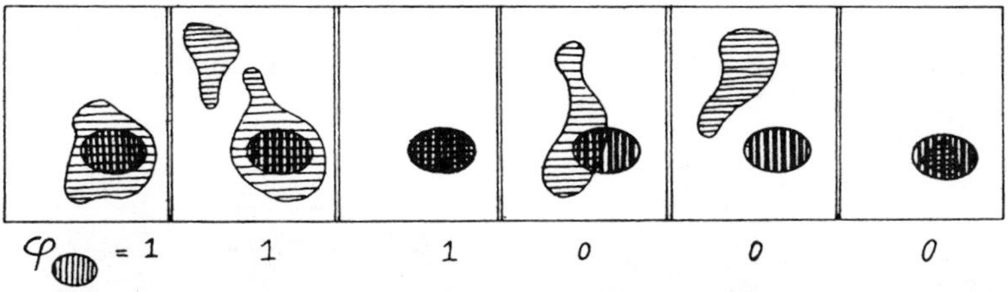

0.6 One simple concept of "Local"

We start by observing an important difference between $\psi_{\text{CONNECTED}}$ and ψ_{CONVEX}. To bring it out we state a fact about convexity:

Definition: A set X fails to be convex if and only if there exist three points such that q is in the line segment joining p and r, and

$$\begin{cases} p \text{ is in } X, \\ q \text{ is not in } X, \\ r \text{ is in } X. \end{cases}$$

Thus we can test for convexity by examining triplets of points. If all the triplets pass the test then X is convex; if any triplet fails (that is, meets all conditions above) then X is not convex. Because all the tests can be done independently, and the final decision made by such a logically simple procedure—unanimity of all the tests—we propose this as a first draft of our definition of "local."

*We will use "φ" instead of "ψ" for those very simple predicates that will be combined later to make more complicated predicates. No absolute logical distinction is implied.

Definition: A predicate ψ is conjunctively local of order k if it can be computed, as in §0.4, by a set Φ of predicates φ such that

$$\begin{cases} \text{Each } \varphi \text{ depends upon no more than } k \text{ points of } R; \\ \psi(X) = \begin{cases} 1 \text{ if } \varphi(X) = 1 \text{ for every } \varphi \text{ in } \Phi, \\ 0 \text{ otherwise.} \end{cases} \end{cases}$$

Example: ψ_{CONVEX} is conjunctively local of order 3.

The property of a figure being *connected* might not seem at first to be very different in kind from the property of being convex. Yet we can show that:

Theorem 0.6.1: $\psi_{\text{CONNECTED}}$ is not conjunctively local of any order.

PROOF: Suppose that $\psi_{\text{CONNECTED}}$ has order k. Then to distinguish between ~~the two figures~~ these two $K+1$ - wide figures —

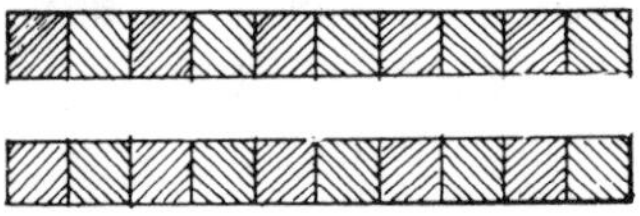

and

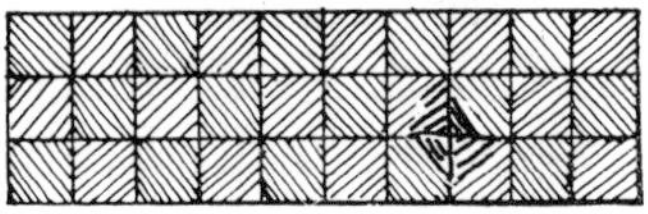

X_0 X_1

there must be some φ_0 ~~which has value 0 on X_0 which~~ such that $\varphi_0(X_0) = 0$, because X_0 is not connected. All φ's have value 1 on X_1, which is connected. Now, φ_0 can depend on at most k points, so there must be at least one middle square, say S_j, that does not contain one of these points. But then, on the figure X_2,

X_2

which is connected, φ_0 must have the same value, 0, that it has on X_0. But this cannot be, for all φ's must have value 1 on X_2.

Of course, if some φ is allowed to look at *all* the points of R then $\psi_{\text{CONNECTED}}$ can be computed, but this would go against any concept of the φ's as "local" functions.

0.7 Some Other Concepts of Local

We have accumulated some evidence in favor of "conjunctively local" as a geometrical and computationally meaningful property of predicates. But a closer look raises doubts about whether it is broad enough to lead to a rich enough theory.

Readers acquainted with the mathematical methods of topology will have observed that "conjunctively local" is similar to the notion of "local property" in topology. However, if we were to pursue the analogy, we would restrict the φ's to depend upon all the points inside small circles rather than upon fixed numbers of points. Accordingly, we will follow two parallel paths. One is based on *restrictions on numbers of points* and in this case we shall talk of predicates of *limited order*. The other is based on restrictions of distances between the points, and here we shall talk of *diameter-limited predicates*. Despite the analogy with other important situations, the concept of local based on diameter limitations seems to be less interesting in our theory—although one might have expected quite the opposite.

More serious doubts arise from the narrowness of the "conjunctive" or "unanimity" requirement. As a next step toward extending our concept of *local*, let us now try to separate essential from arbitrary features of the definition of *conjunctive localness*. The intention of the definition was to divide the computation of a predicate ψ into two stages:

Stage I:
The computation of many properties or features φ_α which are each easy to compute, either because each depends only on a small part of the whole input space R, or because they are very simple in some other interesting way.
Stage II:
A decision algorithm Ω that defines ψ by combining the results of the Stage I computations. For the division into two stages to be meaningful, this decision function must also be distinctively homogeneous, or easy to program, or easy to compute.

The particular way this intention was realized in our example ψ_{CONVEX} was rather arbitrary. In Stage I we made sure that the φ_α's were easy to compute by requiring each to depend only upon a few points of R. In Stage II we used just about the simplest imaginable decision rule; if the φ's are *unaminous* we accept the figure; we reject it if even a single φ disagrees.

We would prefer to be able to present a perfectly precise definition of our intuitive local-vs.-global concept. One trouble is that phrases like "easy-to-compute" keep recurring in our attempt to formulate it. To make this precise would require some scheme for comparing the complexity of different computation procedures. Until we find an intuitively satisfactory scheme for this, and it doesn't seem to be around the corner, the requirements of both Stage I and Stage II will retain the heuristic character that makes formal definition difficult.

From this point on, we will concentrate our attention on a particular scheme for Stage II—"weighted voting," or "linear combination" of the predicates of Stage I. This is the so-called perceptron scheme, and we proceed next to give our final definition.

0.8 Perceptrons

Let $\Phi = \{\varphi_1, \varphi_2, \ldots, \varphi_n\}$ be a family of predicates. We will say that

ψ is linear with respect to Φ

if there exists a number θ and a set of numbers $\{\alpha_{\varphi_1}, \alpha_{\varphi_2}, \ldots, \alpha_{\varphi_n}\}$ such that $\psi(X) = 1$ if and only if $\alpha_{\varphi_1}\varphi_1(X) + \cdots + \alpha_{\varphi_n}\varphi_n(X) > \theta$. The number θ is called the threshold and the α's are called the coefficients or weights. (See Figure 0.2). We usually write more compactly

$$\psi(X) = 1 \text{ if and only if } \sum_{\varphi\in\Phi} \alpha_\varphi \varphi(X) > \theta.$$

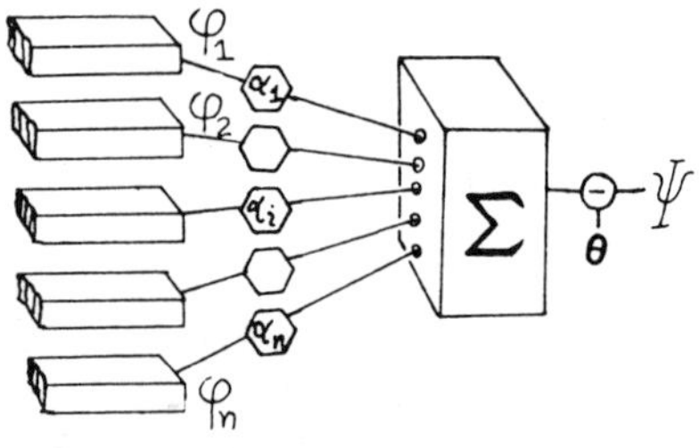

Figure 0.2

The intuitive idea is that each predicate of Φ is supposed to provide some evidence about whether ψ is true for any figure X. If, on the whole, $\psi(X)$ is strongly correlated with $\varphi(X)$ one expects α_φ to be positive, while if the correlation is negative so would be α_φ. The idea of correlation should not be taken literally here, but only as a suggestive analogy.

Example: Any conjunctively local predicate can be expressed in this form by choosing $\theta = -1$ and $\alpha_\varphi = -1$ for every φ. For then

$$\sum (-1)\,\varphi(X) > -1$$

Or one could write (See §1.2.1) $\sum \varphi(x) = 0$, or $\sum \varphi(X) < 1$.

exactly when $\varphi(X) = 0$ for every φ in Φ. (The senses of TRUE and FALSE thus have to be reversed for the φ's, but this isn't important.)

Example: Consider the seesaw of Figure 0.3 and let X be an arrangement of pebbles placed at *some* of the equally spaced points $\{p_1, \ldots, p_7\}$. Then R has seven points. Define $\varphi_i(X) = 1$ if and only if X contains a pebble at the ith point. Then we can express the predicate

"The seesaw will tip to the right"

by the formula

$$\sum (i - 4)\,\varphi_i(X) > 0,$$

where $\theta = 0$ and $\alpha_i = (i - 4)$.

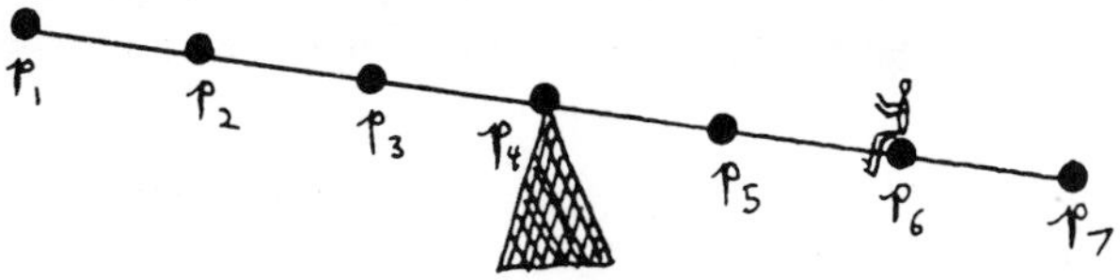

Figure 0.3

There are a number of problems concerning the possibility of infinite sums and such matters when we apply this concept to recognizing patterns in the Euclidean plane. These issues are discussed extensively in the text, and we want here only to reassure the mathematician that the problem will be faced. Except when there is a good technical reason to use infinite sums (and this is sometimes the case) we will make the problem finite by two general methods. One is to treat the retina R as made up of discrete little squares (instead of points) and treat as equivalent figures that intersect the same squares. The other is to consider only bounded X's and choose Φ so that for any bounded X only a finite number of φ's will be nonzero.

Definition: A perceptron is a device capable of computing all predicates which are linear in some given set Φ of partial predicates.

That is, we are given a set of φ's, but can select freely their "weights," the α_φ's, and also the threshold θ. For reasons that will become clear as we proceed, there is little to say about all perceptrons in general. But, by imposing certain conditions and restrictions we will find much to say about certain particularly interesting *families* of perceptrons. Among these families are

1. Diameter-limited perceptrons: for each φ in Φ, the set of points upon which φ depends is restricted not to exceed a certain *fixed diameter* in the plane.

2. Order-restricted perceptrons: we say that a perceptron has order $\leq n$ if no member of Φ depends on more than n points.

3. Gamba perceptrons: each member of Φ may depend on all the points but must be a "linear threshold function" (that is, each member of Φ is itself computed by a perceptron of order 1, as defined in 2 above).

4. Random perceptrons: These are the form most extensively studied by Rosenblatt's group: the φ's are random Boolean functions. That is to say, they are order-restricted and Φ is generated by a stochastic process according to an assigned distribution function.

5. Bounded perceptrons: Φ contains an infinite number of φ's, but all the α_φ lie in a finite set of numbers.

To give a preview of the kind of results we will obtain, we present here a simple example of a theorem about diameter-restricted perceptrons.

Theorem 0.8: No diameter-limited perceptron can determine whether or not all the parts of any geometric figure are connected to one another! That is, no such perceptron computes $\psi_{\text{CONNECTED}}$.

The proof requires us to consider just four figures

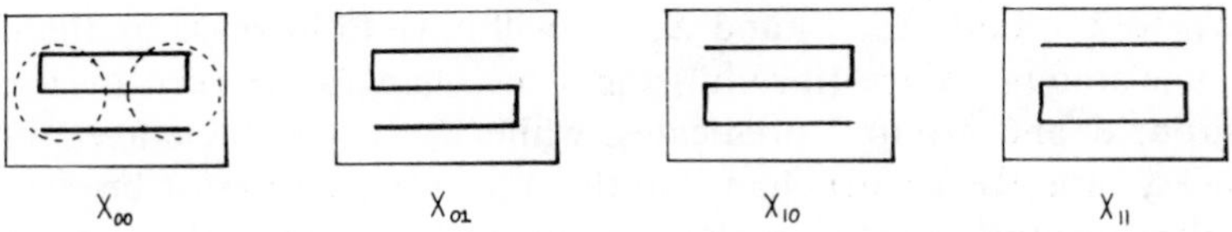

and a diameter-limited perceptron ψ whose support sets have diameters like those indicated by the circles below:

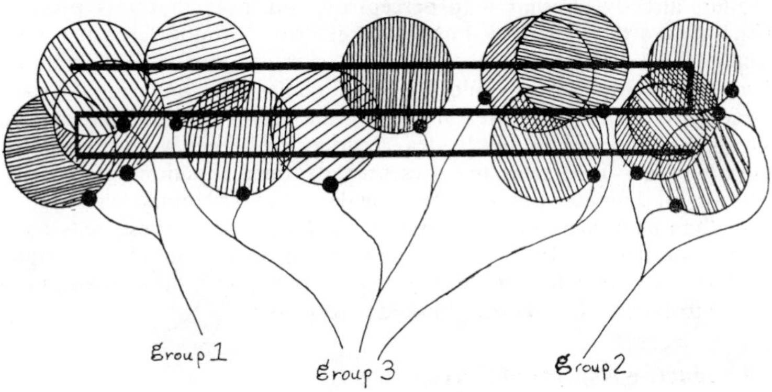

It is understood that the diameter in question is given at the start, and we *then* choose the X_{ij}'s to be several diameters in length. Suppose that such a perceptron could distinguish disconnected figures (like X_{00} and X_{11}) from connected figures (like X_{10} and X_{01}), according to whether or not

$$\sum \alpha_\varphi \varphi > \theta$$

that is, according to whether or not

$$\left[\sum_{\text{group 1}} \alpha_\varphi \varphi(X) + \sum_{\text{group 2}} \alpha_\varphi \varphi(X) + \sum_{\text{group 3}} \alpha_\varphi \varphi(X) - \theta\right] > 0$$

where we have grouped the φ's according to whether their support sets lie near the left, right, or neither end of the figures. Then for X_{00} the total sum must be negative. In changing X_{00} to X_{10} only $\Sigma_{\text{group 1}}$ is affected, and its value must *increase* enough to make the total sum become positive. If we were instead to change X_{00} to X_{01} then $\Sigma_{\text{group 2}}$ would have to increase. But if we were to change X_{00} to X_{11}, both $\Sigma_{\text{group 1}}$ and $\Sigma_{\text{group 2}}$ will have to increase by these same amounts since (locally!) the same changes are seen by the group 1 and group 2 predicates, while $\Sigma_{\text{group 3}}$ is unchanged in every case. Hence, net change in the $X_{00} \rightarrow X_{11}$ case must be even more positive, so that if the perceptron is to make the correct decision for X_{00}, X_{01}, and X_{10}, it is forced to accept X_{11} as connected, and this is an error! So no such perceptron can exist.

Readers already familiar with perceptrons will note that this proof—which shows that diameter-limited perceptrons cannot recognize connectedness—is concerned neither with "learning" nor with probability theory (or even with the geometry of hyperplanes in n-dimensional hyperspace). It is entirely a matter of relating the geometry of the patterns to the algebra of weighted predicates. Readers concerned with physiology will note that—insofar as the presently identified functions of receptor cells are all diameter-limited—this suggests that an animal will require more than neurosynaptic "summation" effects to make these cells compute connectedness. Indeed, only the most advanced animals can apprehend this complicated visual concept. In Chapter 5 this theorem is shown to extend also to order-limited perceptrons.

0.9 Seductive Aspects of Perceptrons

The purest vision of the perceptron as a pattern-recognizing device is the following:

The machine is built with a fixed set of computing elements for the partial functions φ, usually obtained by a random process. To make it recognize a particular pattern (set of input figures) one merely has to set the coefficients α_φ to suitable values. Thus "programming" takes on a pleasingly homogeneous form. Moreover since "programs" are representable as points $(\alpha_1, \alpha_2, \ldots, \alpha_n)$ in an n-dimensional space, they inherit a metric which makes it easy to imagine a kind of automatic programming which people have been tempted to call *learning*: by attaching feedback devices to the parameter controls they propose to "program" the machine by providing it with a sequence of input patterns and an "error signal" which will cause the coefficients to change in the right direction when the machine makes an inappropriate decision. The *perceptron convergence theorems* (see Chapter 11) define conditions under which this procedure is guaranteed to find, eventually, a correct set of values.

0.9.1 Homogeneous Programming and Learning

To separate reality from wishful thinking, we begin by making a number of observations. Let Φ be the set of partial predicates of a perceptron and $L(\Phi)$ the set of all predicates linear in Φ. Thus

$L(\Phi)$ is the repertoire of the perceptron—the set of predicates it can compute when its coefficients α_φ and threshold θ range over all possible values. Of course $L(\Phi)$ could in principle be the set of *all* predicates but this is impossible in practice, since Φ would have to be astronomically large. So any physically real perceptron has a limited repertoire. The ease and uniformity of programming have been bought at a cost! We contend that the traditional investigations of perceptrons did not realistically measure this cost. In particular they neglect the following crucial points:

1. The idea of thinking of classes of geometrical objects (or programs that define or recognize them) as classes of n-dimensional vectors $(\alpha_1, \ldots, \alpha_n)$ loses the geometric individuality of the patterns and leads only to a theory that can do little more than *count* the number of predicates in $L(\Phi)$! This kind of imagery has become traditional among those who think about pattern recognition along lines suggested by classical statistical theories. As a result not many people seem to have observed or suspected that there might be *particular* meaningful and intuitively simple predicates that belong to *no* practically realizable set $L(\Phi)$. We will extend our analysis of $\psi_{\text{CONNECTED}}$ to show how deep this problem can be. At the same time we will show that certain predicates which might intuitively seem to be difficult for these devices *can*, in fact, be recognized by low-order perceptrons: ψ_{CONVEX} already illustrates this possibility.

2. Little attention has been paid to the size, or more precisely, the information content, of the parameters $\alpha_1, \ldots, \alpha_n$. We will give examples (which we believe are typical rather than exceptional) where the ratio of the largest to the smallest of the coefficients is meaninglessly big. Under such conditions it is of no (practical) avail that a predicate be in $L(\Phi)$. In some cases the information capacity needed to store $\alpha_1, \ldots, \alpha_n$ is even greater than that needed to store the whole class of figures defined by the pattern!

3. Closely related to the previous point is the problem of *time of convergence* in a "learning" process. Practical perceptrons are essentially finite-state devices (as shown in Chapter 11). It is therefore vacuous to cite a "perceptron convergence theorem" as assurance that a learning process will eventually find a correct

setting of its parameters (if one exists). For it could do so trivially by cycling through all its states, that is, by trying all coefficient assignments. The significant question is how fast the perceptron learns relative to the time taken by a completely random procedure, or a completely exhaustive procedure. It will be seen that there are situations of some geometric interest for which the convergence time can be shown to increase even faster than exponentially with the size of the set R.

Perceptron theorists are not alone in neglecting these precautions. A perusal of any typical collection of papers on "self-organizing" systems will provide a generous sample of discussions of "learning" or "adaptive" machines that lack even the degree of rigor and formal definition to be found in the literature on perceptrons. The proponents of these schemes seldom provide any analysis of the range of behavior which can be learned nor do they show much awareness of the price usually paid to make some kinds of learning easy: they unwittingly restrict the device's total range of behavior with hidden assumptions about the environment in which it is to operate.

These critical remarks must not be read as suggestions that we are opposed to making machines that can "learn." Exactly the contrary! But we do believe that significant learning at a significant rate presupposes some significant prior structure. Simple learning schemes based on adjusting coefficients can indeed be practical and valuable when the partial functions are reasonably matched to the task, as they are in Samuel's checker player. A perceptron whose φ's are properly designed for a discrimination known to be of suitably low order will have a good chance to improve its performance adaptively. Our purpose is to explain why there is little chance of much good coming from giving a high-order problem to a quasi-universal perceptron whose partial functions have not been chosen with any particular task in mind.

It may be argued that *people* are universal learning machines and so a counterexample to this thesis. But our brains are sufficiently structured to be programmable in a much more general sense than the perceptron and our *culture* is sufficiently structured to provide, if not actual program, at least a rather complex set of interactions that govern the course of whatever the process of self-programming may be. Moreover, it takes time for us to become universal learners: the sequence of transitions from infancy to intellectual maturity seems rather a confirmation of the thesis that the rate of acquisition of new cognitive structure (that is, learning) is a sensitive function of the level of existing cognitive structure.

0.9.2 Parallel Computation

The perceptron was conceived as a parallel-operation device in the physical sense that the partial predicates are computed simultaneously. (From a formal point of view the important aspect is that they are computed independently of one another.) The price paid for this is that *all* the φ_i must be computed, although only a minute fraction of them may in fact be relevant to any particular final decision. The *total amount* of computation may become vastly greater than that which would have to be carried out in a well planned sequential process (using the same φ's) whose decisions about what next to compute are conditional on the outcome of earlier computation. Thus the choice between parallel and serial methods in any particular situation must be based on balancing the increased value of reducing the (total elapsed) time against the cost of the additional computation involved.

Even low-order predicates may require large amounts of wasteful computation of information which would be irrelevant to a serial process. This cost may sometimes remain within physically realizable bounds, especially if a large tolerance (or "blur") is acceptable. High-order predicates usually create a completely different situation. An instructive example is provided by $\psi_{\text{CONNECTED}}$. As shown in Chapter 5, *any* perceptron for this predicate on a 100 × 100 toroidal retina *needs* partial functions that *each* look at many hundreds of points! In this case the concept of "local" function is almost irrelevant: the partial functions are themselves global. Moreover, the fantastic number of possible partial functions with such large supports sheds gloom on any hope that a modestly sized, randomly generated set of them would be sufficiently dense to span the appropriate space of functions. To make this point sharper we shall show that for certain predicates and classes of partial functions, the *number* of partial functions that have to be used (to say nothing of the size of their coefficients) would exceed physically realizable limits.

The conclusion to be drawn is that the appraisal of any particular scheme of parallel computation cannot be undertaken rationally without tools to determine the extent to which the problems to be solved can be analyzed into local and global components. The lack of a *general* theory of what is global and what is local is no excuse for avoiding the problem in particular cases. This study will show that it is not impossibly difficult to develop such a theory for a limited but important class of problems.

0.9.3 The Use of Simple Analogue Devices

Part of the attraction of the perceptron lies in the possibility of using very simple physical devices—"analogue computers"—to evaluate the linear threshold functions. It is perhaps generally appreciated that the utility of this scheme is limited by the sparseness of *linear* threshold functions in the set of *all* logical functions. However, almost no attention has been paid to the possibility that the set of linear functions which are *practically* realizable may be rarer still. To illustrate this problem we shall compute (in Chapter 10) the range and sizes of the coefficients in the linear representations of certain predicates. It will be seen that certain ratios can increase faster than exponentially with the number of distinguishable points in R. It follows that for "big" input sets—say, R's with more than 20 points—no simple analogue storage device can be made with enough information capacity to store the whole range of coefficients!

To avoid misunderstanding perhaps we should repeat the qualifications we made in connection with our critique of the perceptron as a model for "learning devices." We have no doubt that analogue devices of this sort have a role to play in pattern recognition. *But we do not see that any good can come of experiments which pay no attention to limiting factors that will assert themselves as soon as the small model is scaled up to a usable size.*

0.9.4 Models for Brain Function and Gestalt Psychology

The popularity of the perceptron as a model for an intelligent, general-purpose learning machine has roots, we think, in an image of the brain itself as a rather loosely organized, randomly interconnected network of relatively simple devices. This impression in turn derives in part from our first impressions of the bewildering structures seen in the microscopic anatomy of the brain (and probably also derives from our still-chaotic ideas about psychological mechanisms).

In any case the image is that of a network of relatively simple elements, randomly connected to one another, with provision for making adjustments of the ease with which signals can go across the connections. When the machine does something bad, we will "teach" it not to do it again by weakening the connections that were involved; perhaps we will do the opposite to reward it when it does something we like.

The "perceptron" type of machine is one particularly simple version of this broader concept; several others have also been studied in experiments.

The mystique surrounding such machines is based in part on the idea that when such a machine learns the information stored is not localized in any particular spot but is, instead, "distributed throughout" the structure of the machine's network. It was a great disappointment, in the first half of the twentieth century, that experiments did not support nineteenth century concepts of the localization of memories (or most other "faculties") in highly local brain areas. Whatever the precise interpretation of those not particularly conclusive experiments should be, there is no question but that they did lead to a search for nonlocal machine-function concepts. This search was not notably successful. Several schemes were proposed, based upon large-scale fields, or upon "interference patterns" in global oscillatory waves, but these never led to plausible theories. (Toward the end of that era a more intricate and substantially less global concept of "cell-assembly"—proposed by D. O. Hebb [1949]—lent itself to more productive theorizing; though it has not yet led to any conclusive model, its popularity is today very much on the increase.) However, it is not our goal here to evaluate these theories, but only to sketch a picture of the intellectual stage that was set for the perceptron concept. In this setting, Rosenblatt's [1958] schemes quickly took root, and soon there were perhaps as many as a hundred groups, large and small, experimenting with the model either as a "learning machine" or in the guise of "adaptive" or "self-organizing" networks or "automatic control" systems.

The results of these hundreds of projects and experiments were generally disappointing, and the explanations inconclusive. The machines usually work quite well on very simple problems but deteriorate very rapidly as the tasks assigned to them get harder. The situation isn't usually improved much by increasing the size and running time of the system. It was our suspicion that even in those instances where some success was apparent, it was usually due more to some relatively small part of the network, and not really to a global, distributed activity. Both of the present authors (first independently and later together) became involved with a somewhat therapeutic compulsion: to dispel what we feared to be the first shadows of a "holistic" or "Gestalt" misconception that would threaten to haunt the fields of engineering and artificial intelligence as it had earlier haunted biology and psychology. For this, and for a variety of more practical and theoretical goals, we set out to find something about the range and limitations of perceptrons.

It was only later, as the theory developed, that we realized that understanding this kind of machine was important whether or not the system has practical applications in particular situations! For the same kinds of problems were becoming serious obstacles to the progress of computer science itself. As we have already remarked, we do not know enough about what makes some algorithmic procedures "essentially" serial, and to what extent—or rather, at what cost—can computations be speeded up by using multiple, overlapping computations on larger more active memories.

0.10 General Plan of the Book

The theory divides naturally into three parts. In Part I we explore some very general properties of linear predicate families. The theorems in Part I apply usually to all perceptrons, independently of the kinds of patterns considered; therefore the theory has the quality of algebra rather than geometry. In Part II we look more narrowly at interesting geometric patterns, and get sharper but, of course, less general, theorems about the geometric abilities of our machines. In Part III we examine a variety of questions centered around the potentialities of perceptrons as *practical* devices for pattern recognition and learning. The final chapter traces some of the history of these ideas and proposes some plausible directions for further exploration.

To read this book, one does not have to "know" all the mathematics mentioned in it. Most of the "harder" mathematical sections are "terminal"— they can be skipped without losing the sense of later chapters. The best chapters to skip are §4, §5, §7, and §10.

ALGEBRAIC THEORY OF LINEAR PARALLEL PREDICATES

I

Introduction to Part I

Part I (Chapters 1–4) contains a series of purely algebraic definitions and general theorems used later in Part II. It will be easier to read through this material if one has already a preliminary picture of the roles these mathematical devices are destined to play. We can give such a picture by outlining how we will prove the following theorem: We do not expect the reader to really absorb this condensed synopsis.

Theorem 3.1 (Chapter 3) Informal Version: Suppose the retina R has a finite number of points. Then there is no perceptron $\Sigma \alpha_\varphi \varphi(X) > \theta$ that can decide whether or not the "number of points in X is odd" unless at least one of the φ's depends on all the points of R.

Thus no bound can be placed on the *orders* of perceptrons that compute this predicate for arbitrarily large retinas. To realize it a perceptron has to have at the start at least one φ that looks at the whole picture! The proof uses several steps:

Step 1: In §1.1–§1.4, we define "perceptron," "order," etc., more precisely, and show that certain details of the definitions can be changed without serious effects.

Step 2: In §1.3 we define the particularly simple φ functions called "masks." For each subset A of the retina define the mask $\varphi_A(X)$ to have value 1 if the figure X contains or "covers" all of A, value 0 otherwise. Then we prove the simple but important theorem (§1.5) that if a predicate has order $\leq k$ (see §1.3) in *any* set of φ functions, then there is an equivalent perceptron that uses only *masks* of size $\leq k$.

Step 3: To get at the *parity*—the "odd-even" property—we ask: *What rearrangements of the input space R leaves it unaffected?* That is, we ask about the group of transformations of the figure that have no effect on the property. This might seem to be an exotic way to approach the problem, but since it seems necessary for the more difficult problems we attack later, it is good first to get used to it in this simple situation. In this case, the group is the whole permutation group on R—the set of *all* rearrangements of its points.

Step 4: In Chapter 2 we show how to use this group to reduce the perceptron to a simple form. **The group-invariance theorem** (proved in §2.2) is used to show that, for the parity perceptron, all masks with the same support size—that is, all those that look at the same number of points—can be given identical coefficients. Let β_j be the weight assigned to all masks that have support size $= j$.

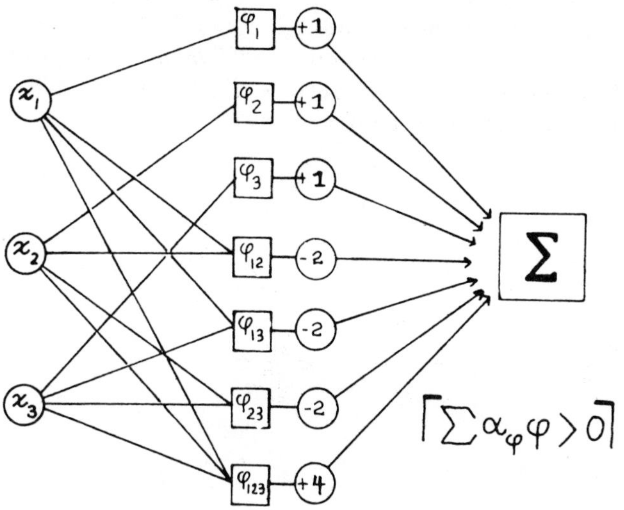

Group-invariant coefficients for $|R| = 3$ parity predicate.

Step 5: It is then shown (in §3.1) that the parity perceptron can be written in the form

$$\sum_{0}^{k} \beta_j \binom{|X|}{j} > 0,$$

In fact, one can use $\beta_j = (-2)^{j-1}$. No smaller numbers will do. See §10.1.

where $|X|$ is the number of points in X, k is the largest support size, and $\binom{|X|}{j}$ is the number of subsets of X that have j elements.

Step 6: Because

$$\binom{n}{j} = \frac{n!}{j!(n-j)!} = \frac{1}{j!} \cdot (n + 1 - \mathbf{1}) \cdot (n + 1 - \mathbf{2}) \cdot \cdots \cdot (n + 1 - \mathbf{j})$$

is a product of **j** linear terms, it is a polynomial of degree j in n. Therefore we can write our predicate in the form

$$P_k(|X|) > 0,$$

where P_k is a polynomial in $|X|$ of algebraic degree $\leq k$. Now if $|X|$ is an odd number, $P_k(|X|) > 0$ while if $|X|$ is even, $P_k(|X|) \leq 0$. Therefore, in the range $0 \leq |X| \leq |R|$, P_k must change its direction $|R| - 1$ times. But a polynomial must have degree $\geq |R|$ to do that, so we conclude that $k \geq |R|$. This completes the proof exactly as it will be done in §3.1.

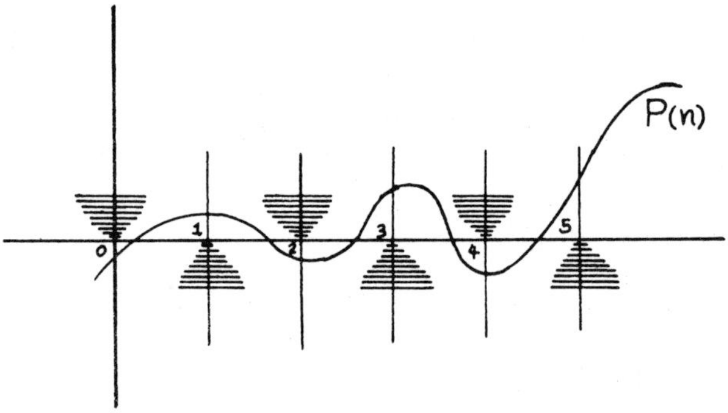

This shows how the algebra works into our theory. For some of the more difficult connectedness theorems of Chapter 5, we need somewhat more algebra and group theory. In Chapter 4 we push the ideas about the geometry of algebraic degrees a little further to show that some surprisingly simple predicates require unbounded-order perceptrons. But the results of Chapter 4 are not really used later, and the chapter could be skipped on first reading.

To see some simpler, but still characteristic results, the reader might turn directly to Chapter 8, which is almost self-contained because it does not need the algebraic theory.

1

1.0

In this chapter we introduce the theory of the linear representation of predicates. We will talk about properties of functions defined on an abstract set of points, without any additional mathematical or geometrical structure. Thus this chapter can be regarded as an extension of ordinary Boolean algebra. Later, the theorems proved here will be applied to sets with particular geometrical or topological structures, such as the ordinary Euclidean plane. So, we begin by talking about sets in general; only later will we deal with properties of familiar things like "triangles."

We shall begin with predicates defined for a fixed base space R. In §1.1–§1.5, whenever we speak of a predicate we assume an R is already chosen. Later on, we will be interested in "predicates" defined more broadly, either entirely independent of any base space, or on any one of some large family of spaces. For example, the predicate

The set X is nonempty

can be applied to *any* space R. The predicate

The set X is connected

is meaningful when applied to many different spaces in which there is a concept of points being near one another. In §1.6 we will introduce the term "predicate scheme" for this more general sense of "predicate." Our main goal is to define the general notion of *order of a predicate* (§1.5) and the notion of *finite order of a predicate-scheme* (§1.6). In later chapters we will use the term predicate loosely to refer also to predicate-schemes, and in §1.7 there are some remarks on making these definitions more precise and formal. But we do not recommend readers to worry about this until after the main results are understood intuitively.

1.1 Definitions

The letter R will denote an arbitrary set of points. We will usually use the lower case letters $a, b, c, \ldots, x, y, z$ for individual points of R and the upper case $A, B, C, \ldots, X, Y, Z$ for subsets of R. Usually "x" and "X" will be used for "variable" points and subsets.

We will often be interested in particular "families" of subsets, and will use small upper-case *words* for them. Thus CIRCLE is the set of subsets of R that form complete circles (as in §0.5). For an abstract family of subsets we will use the bold-face **F**.

It is natural to associate with any family **F** of sets a predicate $\psi_{\mathbf{F}}(X)$ which is TRUE if and only if X is in the family **F**. For example $\psi_{\text{CONVEX}}(X)$ is TRUE or FALSE according to whether X is or is not a convex set. Of course, ψ_{CIRCLE} and ψ_{CONVEX} are meaningless except on nonabstract R's to which these geometric ideas can be applied. The Greek letters φ and ψ will always represent predicates. ψ will usually denote the predicate of main interest, while φ predicates are usually in a large family of easily computed functions; the symbol Φ will refer to that family.

A **predicate** is a function (of subsets of R) that has two possible values. Sometimes we think of these two values as "TRUE" and "FALSE"; other times it is very useful to think of them as "1" and "0." Because there is occasionally some danger of confusing these two kinds of predicate values, we have introduced the notation $\lceil \psi(X) \rceil$ to avoid ambiguity. The *corners* always mean that the "1" and "0" values are to be used. This makes it possible to use the values of predicates as ordinary numbers, and this is important in our theory since, as discussed in Chapter 0, we have to combine evidence obtained from predicates. Any mathematical statement can be used inside the corners: for example, since 3 is less than 5, and 1 is less that 2, we can write

$$\lceil 3 < 5 \rceil = 1,$$
$$\lceil 3 < 5 \rceil + \lceil 1 < 2 \rceil = 2,$$
$$\lceil 3 < 5 \rceil + \lceil 5 < 3 \rceil = 1,$$

or even

$$\lceil 3 < \lceil 5 = 1 \rceil \rceil = 0,$$
$$4 \cdot \lceil 3 < 5 \rceil + 2 \cdot \lceil 6 < 2 \rceil = 4.$$

It will sometimes be convenient to think of the points of R as enumerated in a sequence $x_1, x_2, x_3, \ldots, x_i, \ldots.$ Then many predicates can be expressed in terms of the traditional representations of Boolean algebra. For example the two expressions

$$x_i \vee x_j \qquad\qquad \lceil x_i \in X \quad \text{OR} \quad x_j \in X \rceil$$

have the same meaning, namely, they have value 1 if either or both of x_i and x_j are in X, value 0 if neither is in X. Technically this means that one thinks of a subset X of R as an assignment of values 1 or 0 to the x_i's according to whether the ith point is in X, so "x_i" is used ambiguously both to denote the ith point and to denote the set-function $\lceil x_i \in X \rceil$. We can exploit this by writing predicates in *arithmetic* instead of *logical* forms, that is,

$$\lceil x_1 + x_2 + x_3 > 0 \rceil \quad \text{instead of} \quad x_1 \vee x_2 \vee x_3$$

or even

$$\lceil 2x_1x_2 - x_1 - x_2 > -1 \rceil \quad \text{instead of} \quad x_1 \equiv x_2,$$

where $x_1 \equiv x_2$ is the predicate that is true if both, or neither, but not just one of x_1 and x_2, are in X.

We will need to be able to express the idea that a function may "depend" only on a certain subset of R. We denote by $S(\varphi)$ the subset of R upon which φ "really depends": technically, $S(\varphi)$ is the smallest subset S of R such that, for every subset X of R,

$$\varphi(X) = \varphi(X \cap S),$$

where "$X \cap S$" is the intersection, that is, the set of points that are in both, of X and S. We call $S(\varphi)$ the **support** of φ.

For an infinite space R, some interesting predicates will have $S(\varphi)$ undefined. Consider for example

$$\varphi(X) = \lceil X \text{ contains an infinite set of points} \rceil.$$

One could determine whether $\varphi(X)$ is true by examining the points of X that lie in *any* set S that contains all but a finite number of points of R. And there is no "smallest" such set!

1.2 Functions Linear with respect to a Class of Predicates

Let Φ be a family of predicates defined on R. We say that

ψ is a **linear threshold function** with respect to Φ,

if there exists a number θ and a set of numbers $\alpha(\varphi)$, one for each φ in Φ, such that

$$\psi(X) = \left\lceil \sum_{\varphi \in \Phi} \alpha(\varphi) \cdot \varphi(X) > \theta \right\rceil.$$

That is, $\psi(X)$ is true exactly when the inequality within the $\lceil\ \rceil$'s is true. We often write this less formally as

$$\psi = \lceil \Sigma\, \alpha(\varphi)\varphi > \theta \rceil, \text{ or even as } \psi = \lceil \Sigma\, \alpha_\varphi \varphi > \theta \rceil.$$

For symmetry, we want to include with ψ, its negation

$$\bar{\psi}(X) = \lceil \Sigma\, \alpha(\varphi)\varphi \leq \theta \rceil$$

in the class of linear threshold functions. For a given Φ, we use $L(\Phi)$ to denote the set of all predicates that can be defined in this way—that is, by choosing different numbers for θ and for the α's.

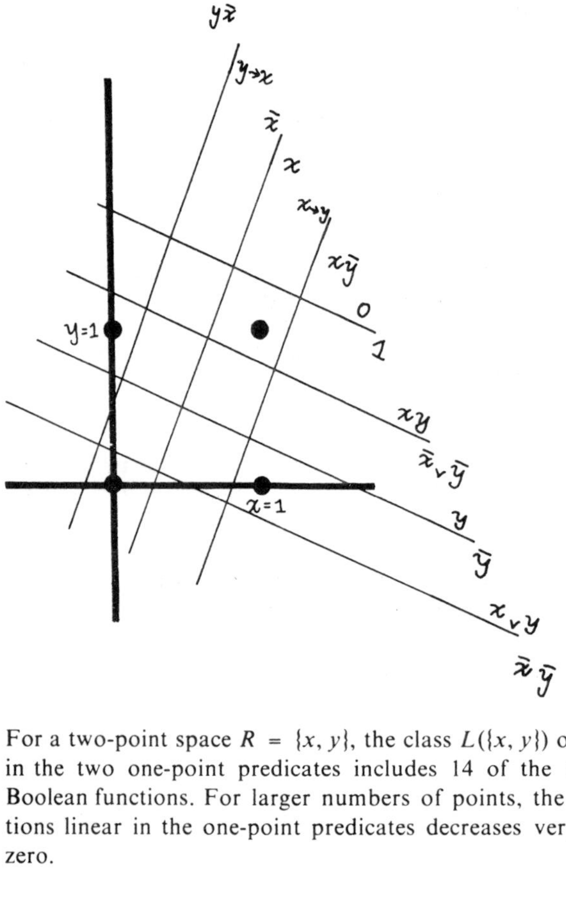

For a two-point space $R = \{x, y\}$, the class $L(\{x, y\})$ of functions linear in the two one-point predicates includes 14 of the $16 = 2^{2^2}$ possible Boolean functions. For larger numbers of points, the fraction of functions linear in the one-point predicates decreases very rapidly toward zero.

1.2.1 Other possible definitions of L(Φ)

Because the definition of $L(\Phi)$ is so central to what follows, it is worth examining it to see which features are essential and which are arbitrary. The following proposition will mention a number of ways the definition could be changed without significantly altering its character. In fact, for finite R, the most important case, all the proposed alternatives lead to strictly equivalent definitions. In the case of infinite R-spaces, some of them lead to different meanings for $L(\Phi)$ but never in a way that will affect any of our subsequent discussions.

Proposition: The following modifications in the formal definition of $L(\Phi)$ result in defining the same classes of predicates.

(1) *If Φ is assumed to contain the constant function, $I(X) \equiv 1$, then θ can be taken to be zero.*

(2) *The inequality sign* "$>$" *can be replaced by* "$<$," "$\geq$," or "$\leq$."

(3) *If R is finite then all the $\alpha(\varphi)$'s, and θ, can be confined to integer values.*

(4) *All the alternatives in* 1–3 *can be chosen independently.*

These assertions are all obviously true; the following proofs are intended mainly to help readers who would like some practice in using our notations.

PROOF OF (1): Define $\alpha'(I) = \alpha(I) - \theta$ and otherwise $\alpha'(\varphi) = \alpha(\varphi)$. Then

$$\lceil \Sigma\, \alpha(\varphi)\varphi(X) > \theta \rceil = \lceil \Sigma\, \alpha'(\varphi)\varphi(X) > 0 \rceil.$$

PROOF OF (2): Let $\alpha'(\varphi) = -\alpha(\varphi)$ and $\theta' = -\theta$. Then

$$\lceil \Sigma\, \alpha(\varphi)\varphi < \theta \rceil = \lceil \Sigma\, \alpha'(\varphi)\varphi > \theta' \rceil.$$

The other replacements follow by exchanging all predicates and their negations.

PROOF OF (3): If R is finite then Φ is finite and we can assume that there is no X for which

$$\Sigma\, \alpha(\varphi)\varphi(X) = \theta.$$

For, if there is such an X we can remedy this by changing θ to $\theta + \delta$, where δ is less than the smallest nonzero value of $|\Sigma \alpha(\varphi)\varphi(X) - \theta|$. Suppose first that all the $\alpha(\varphi)$'s are rational. Let D be the product of all their denominators and define

$$\alpha'(\varphi) = D\alpha(\varphi) \quad \text{and} \quad \theta' = D\theta.$$

Then the $a'(\varphi)$'s are all integers and clearly

$$\lceil \Sigma\, \alpha(\varphi)\varphi(X) > \theta \rceil = \lceil \Sigma\, \alpha'(\varphi)\varphi(X) > \theta' \rceil$$

for all X. Now suppose that some members of $\{\alpha(\varphi)\}$ are irrational. Then replace each $\alpha(\varphi)$ by some rational number $\alpha'(\varphi)$ in the interval

$$\alpha(\varphi) < \alpha'(\varphi) < \alpha(\varphi) + \frac{\delta}{2^{2^{|R|}}},$$

where δ is as defined above. This replacement cannot change the sum $\Sigma\,\alpha(\varphi)\,\varphi(X)$ by as much as δ, so it can never affect the value of $\lceil \Sigma\,\alpha(\varphi)\,\varphi(X) > \theta \rceil$. For there are at most $2^{2^{|R|}}$ different φ's.

1.3 The Concept of Order

Predicates whose supports are very small are too local to be interesting in themselves. Our main interest is in predicates whose support is the whole of R, but which can be represented as linear threshold combinations of predicates with small support. A simple example is

$$\psi(X) = \lceil X \text{ is not empty} \rceil.$$

Clearly $S(\psi) = R$. On the other hand if we let Φ be the set of predicates of the form $\varphi_p(X) = \lceil p \in X \rceil$ we have

$$\begin{cases} |S(\varphi_p)| = 1 \text{ for all } \varphi \text{ in } \Phi, \\ \psi(X) = \lceil \Sigma\, \varphi_p(X) > 0 \rceil. \end{cases}$$

These two statements allow us to say that the *order* of ψ is 1. In general, the **order** of ψ is the smallest number k for which we can find a set Φ of predicates satisfying

$$\begin{cases} |S(\varphi)| \le k \text{ for all } \varphi \text{ in } \Phi, \\ \psi \in L(\Phi). \end{cases}$$

It should be carefully observed that the **order of ψ is a property of ψ alone, and not relative to any particular Φ**. This is what makes it an important "absolute" concept. Those who know the appropriate literature will recognize "order 1" as what are usually called "linear threshold functions."

1.4 Masks and other Examples of Linear Representation

A very special role will be played by predicates of the form

$$\varphi_A(X) = \lceil \text{all members of } A \text{ are in } X \rceil = \lceil A \subset X \rceil.$$

In the conventional Boolean point-function notations, these predicates appear as conjunctions: if $A = \{y_1, \ldots, y_n\}$ then $\varphi_A(X) = y_1 \wedge y_2 \wedge \ldots \wedge y_n$ or, as it is usually written, $\varphi_A(X) = y_1 y_2 \ldots y_n$.

We shall call φ_A the **mask** of the set A. In particular the constant predicate $I(X)$ is the mask of the empty set; and the predicates φ_p in the previous paragraph are the masks of the one-point sets.

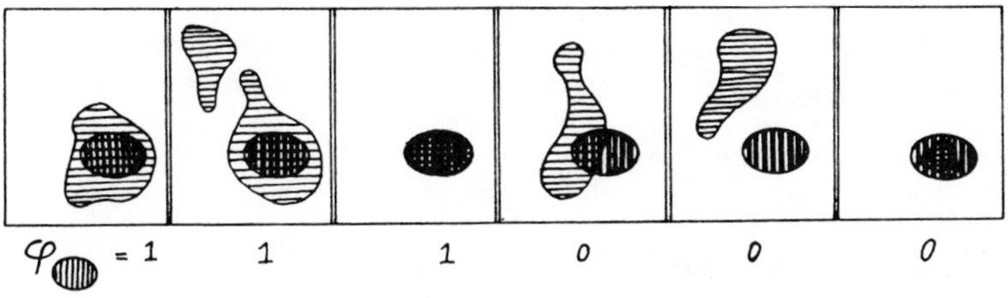

Proposition: All masks are of order 1.

PROOF: Let A be any finite set. It contains $|A|$ points. For each point $x \in A$ define $\varphi_x(X)$ to be $\lceil x \in X \rceil$. Then

$$\varphi_A(X) = \left\lceil \sum_{x \in A} \varphi_x(X) \geq |A| \right\rceil.$$

Example 1: Of the 16 Boolean functions of two variables, all have order 1 except for *exclusive-or*, $x \oplus y$, and its complement *identity*, $x \equiv y$, which are of order 2:

$$x \oplus y = \lceil x\bar{y} + \bar{x}y > 0 \rceil,$$
$$x \equiv y = \lceil xy + \bar{x}\bar{y} > 0 \rceil,$$

where, for example, "$x\bar{y}$" is the predicate of support = 2 which is true only when x is in X and y is not in X. (*Problem: prove* that $x \oplus y$ is not order 1!) Other examples from Boolean algebra are

$$x \supset y = \lceil \bar{x} \vee y \rceil = \lceil y - x > -1 \rceil$$
$$\sim x = \lceil -x > -1 \rceil.$$

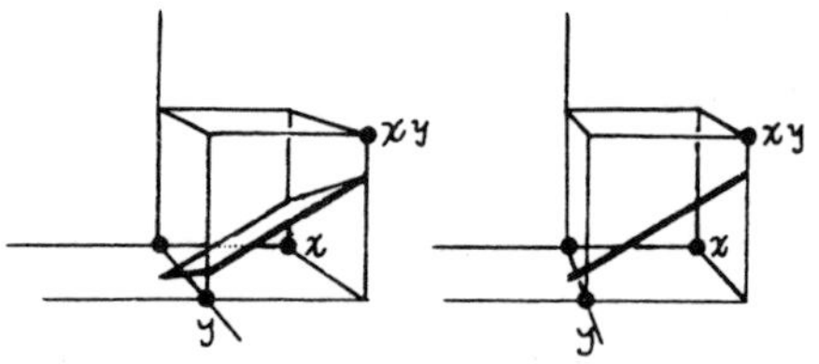

$x \oplus y \in L(\{x, y, xy\})$
(stereoscopic)

One can think of a linear inequality as defining a surface that separates points into two classes, thus defining a predicate. We do not recommend this kind of imagery until Part III.

Any mask has order 1:

$$x \wedge y \wedge z = \lceil x + y + z > 2 \rceil$$

as does any disjunction

$$x \vee y \vee z = \lceil x + y + z > 0 \rceil.$$

Example 2: $x_1 \equiv x_2$ can be represented as a linear combination of masks by

$$x_1x_2 \vee \bar{x}_1\bar{x}_2 = \lceil x_1x_2 + (1 - x_1)(1 - x_2) > 0 \rceil$$
$$= \lceil 2x_1x_2 - x_1 - x_2 > -1 \rceil.$$

A proof that "exclusive-or" and equivalence are not of order 1 will be found in §2.1.

Example 3: Let M be an integer $0 \leq M \leq |R|$. Then the "counting predicate" ψ^M, or $\lceil |X| = M \rceil$, which recognizes that X *contains exactly M points*, is of order 2.

PROOF: Consider the representation

$$\left\lceil (2M - 1) \sum_{\text{all } i} x_i + (-2) \sum_{i<j} x_i x_j \geq M^2 \right\rceil.$$

For any figure X there will be $|X|$ terms x_i with value 1, and $\frac{1}{2}|X| \cdot (|X| - 1)$ terms $x_i x_j$ with value 1. Then the predicate is

$$\lceil (2M - 1) \cdot |X| - |X| \cdot (|X| - 1) - M^2 \geq 0 \rceil = \lceil (|X| - M)^2 \leq 0 \rceil$$

and the only value of $|X|$ for which this is true is $|X| = M$. Observe that, by increasing the threshold we can modify the predicate to accept counts within an arbitrary *interval* instead of a single value.

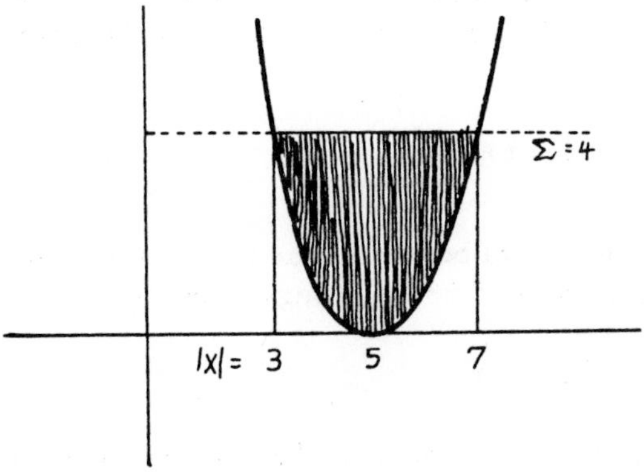

Figure 1.1

We have shown that the order is not greater than 2; Theorem 2.4 will confirm that it is not order 1. Note that the linear form for the counting predicate does not contain $|R|$ explicitly. Hence it works as well as for an infinite space R.

Example 4: The predicates $\lceil |X| \geq M \rceil$ and $\lceil |X| \leq M \rceil$ are of order 1 because they are represented by $\lceil \Sigma x_i \geq M \rceil$ and $\lceil \Sigma x_i \leq M \rceil$.

1.5 The "Positive Normal Form Theorem"

The order of a function can be determined by examining its representation as a linear threshold function with respect to the set of masks (Theorem 1.5.3). To prove this we first show

Theorem 1.5.1: Every ψ is a linear threshold function with respect to the set of all masks, that is, $\psi \in L$(all masks).

PROOF: Any Boolean function $\psi(x_1, \ldots, x_n)$ can be written in the disjunctive normal form

$$C_1(X) \vee C_2(X) \vee \ldots \vee C_p(X),$$

where each $C_j(X)$ has the form of a product (that is, a conjunction)

$$z_1 z_2 \ldots z_n$$

in which each z is either an x_i or an $\bar{x}_i$. Since at most one of the $C_i(X)$ can be true for any X, we can rewrite ψ, using the arithmetic sum

$$C_1(X) + C_2(X) + \ldots + C_p(X).$$

Next, the following formula can be applied to any product containing a barred letter: let \$ and £ be any strings of letters.

$$\$\,\bar{x}_j\,£ = \$(1 - x_j)£ = \$£ - \$x_j£$$

If we continue to apply this, all the bars can be removed, without ever increasing the length of a product.

When all the bars have been eliminated and like terms have been collected together we have

$$\psi(X) = \Sigma \alpha_i \varphi_i(X), \qquad \text{POSITIVE NORMAL FORM}$$

where each φ_i is a mask, and each α_i is an integer. Since $\Sigma \alpha_i \varphi_i(X)$ is 0 or 1, this is the same as

$$\psi(X) = \lceil \Sigma \alpha_i \varphi_i(X) > 0 \rceil.$$

Example: $\lceil x_1 + x_2 + x_3 \text{ is odd} \rceil = x_1 + x_2 + x_3 - 2x_1x_2 - 2x_2x_3 - 2x_3x_1 + 4x_1x_2x_3.$

Theorem 1.5.2: The positive normal form is unique (Optional)

PROOF: To see this let $\{\varphi_i\}$ be a set of masks and $\{\gamma_i\}$ a set of numbers, none equal to zero. Choose a k for which $S(\varphi_k)$ is minimal, that is, there is no $j \neq k$ such that $S(\varphi_j) \subset S(\varphi_k)$. Then

$$\varphi_k(S(\varphi_k)) = 1,$$
$$\varphi_j(S(\varphi_k)) = 0 \qquad j \neq k.$$

It follows that $\Sigma\gamma_i\varphi_i(X)$ is not identically zero since it has the value γ_k for $X = S(\varphi_k)$.

Now if $\Sigma\alpha_i\varphi_i(X) \equiv \Sigma\beta_i\,\varphi_i(X)$ for all X, then $\Sigma(\alpha_i - \beta_i)\varphi_i(X) = 0$ for all X. But

$$\sum_{\text{all } i} (\alpha_i - \beta_i)\varphi_i(X) = \sum_{0 \neq (\alpha_i - \beta_i)} (\alpha_i - \beta_i)\varphi_i(X)$$

It follows that all $\alpha_i = \beta_i$. This proves the uniqueness of the coefficients of the positive normal form of ψ. Note that the positive normal form always has the values 0 and 1 as ordinary arithmetic sums; i.e., without requiring the $\lceil\ \rceil$ device of interpreting the validity of an inequality as a predicate.

Theorem 1.5.3: ψ is of order k if and only if k is the smallest number for which there exists a set Φ of **masks** satisfying

$$\begin{cases} |S(\varphi)| \leq k \text{ for all } \varphi \text{ in } \Phi \\ \psi \in L(\Phi). \end{cases}$$

PROOF: In $\psi = \lceil\Sigma\alpha_i\varphi_i > 0\rceil$, each φ_i can be replaced by its positive normal form. If $|S(\varphi_i)| \leq k$, this will be true also of all the masks that appear in the positive normal form.

Example: A "Boolean form" has order no higher than the degree in its disjunctive normal form. Thus

$$\Sigma\alpha_{ijk}x_ix_j\bar{x}_k = \Sigma\alpha_{ijk}x_ix_j - \Sigma\alpha_{ijk}x_ix_jx_k,$$

illustrating how the negations are removed without raising the order. This particular order-3 form appears later (§6.3) in a perceptron that recognizes convex figures.

It is natural to wonder about the orders of predicates that are Boolean functions of other predicates. Theorem §1.5.4 gives an encouraging result:

Theorem 1.5.4: If ψ_1 has order O_1 and ψ_2 has order O_2, then $\psi_1 \oplus \psi_2$ and $\psi_1 \equiv \psi_2$ have order $\leq O_1 + O_2$.

PROOF: Let $\psi_1 = \lceil \Sigma \alpha_i \varphi_i > 0 \rceil$ and $\psi_2 = \lceil \Sigma \alpha'_j \varphi_j > 0 \rceil$ and assume that the coefficients are chosen so that the inner sums never exactly equal zero.

$$\psi_1 \equiv \psi_2 \quad = \quad \lceil (\Sigma \alpha_i \varphi_i)(\Sigma \alpha'_j \varphi_j) > 0 \rceil \quad = \quad \lceil \Sigma_{i,j} (\alpha_i \alpha'_j) \varphi_i \varphi_j > 0 \rceil$$

But

$$|S(\varphi_i \varphi_j)| \leq |S(\varphi_i)| + |S(\varphi_j)|.$$

The other conclusion follows from $\lceil \psi_1 \oplus \psi_2 \rceil = 1 - \lceil \psi_1 \equiv \psi_2 \rceil$.

Example: Since

$$\psi^M(X) \quad = \quad \lceil \lceil M \geq |X| \rceil \equiv \lceil |X| \geq M \rceil \rceil$$

we conclude that ψ^M has order ≤ 2, which is another way to obtain the result of §1.4, Example 3.

Question: What can be said about the orders of $\lceil \psi_1 \wedge \psi_2 \rceil$ and $\lceil \psi_1 \vee \psi_2 \rceil$? The answer to this question may be surprising, in view of the simple result of Theorem 1.5.4: It is shown in Chapter 4 that for any order n, there exists a pair of predicates ψ_1 and ψ_2, *both of order 1*, for which $(\psi_1 \wedge \psi_2)$ and $(\psi_1 \vee \psi_2)$ have order $> n$. In fact, suppose that $R = A \cup B \cup C$ where A, B, and C are large disjoint subsets of R. Then $\psi_1 = \lceil |X \cap A| > |X \cap C| \rceil$ and $\psi_2 = \lceil |X \cap B| > |X \cap C| \rceil$ each have order 1 because they are represented by

$$\left\lceil \sum_{x_i \in A} x_i > \sum_{x_i \in C} x_i \right\rceil \quad \text{and} \quad \left\lceil \sum_{x_i \in B} x_i > \sum_{x_i \in C} x_i \right\rceil$$

but we shall see in Chapter 4 that $(\psi_1 \wedge \psi_2)$ and $(\psi_1 \vee \psi_2)$ are not even of *finite order* in the sense about to be described in §1.6.

1.6 Predicates of Finite Order

Strictly, a predicate is defined for a particular set R and it makes no formal sense to speak of the *same predicate* for different R's.

But, as noted in §1.0, our real motivation is to learn more about "predicates" defined independently of R—for example, concerning the number of elements in the set X, or other geometric properties of figures in a real Euclidean plane to which X and R provide mere approximations. To be more precise we could use a phrase such as *predicate scheme* to refer to a general construction which defines a predicate for each of a large class of sets R. This would be too pedantic so (except in this section) we shall use "predicate" in this wider sense.

Suppose we are given a predicate scheme ψ which defines a predicate ψ_R for each of a family $\{R\}$ of retinas. We shall say that ψ *is of finite order*, in fact of order $\leq k$, if the orders of the ψ_R are uniformly bounded by k for all R's in the family. Two examples will make this clearer:

1. Let $\{R_i\}$ be a sequence of sets with $|R_i| = i$. For each R_i there is a predicate ψ_i defined by the predicate scheme $\psi_{\text{PARITY}}(X)$ which asserts, for $X \subset R_i$, that "$|X|$ *is an odd number*." As we will see in §3.1, the order of any such ψ_i must be i. Thus ψ_{PARITY} is *not* of finite order.

2. Now let ψ_i be the predicate defined over R_i by the predicate scheme ψ_{TEN}:

$$\psi_i(X) = \lceil |X| = 10 \rceil.$$

We have shown in §1.4, that ψ_i is of order 2 for all R_i with $i > 10$, and it is (trivially) of order zero for $R_1, \ldots, R_9$. Thus the predicate scheme ψ_{TEN} is of finite order; in fact, it has order 2.

In these cases one could obtain the same dichotomy by considering infinite sets R. On an infinite retina the predicate

$$\psi_{\text{TEN}}(X) = \lceil |X| = 10 \rceil$$

is of finite order, in fact of order $= 2$, while

$$\psi_{\text{PARITY}}(X) = \lceil |X| \text{ is odd} \rceil$$

has *no* order. We shall often look at problems in this way, for it is often easier to think about one machine, even of infinite size, than about an infinite family of finite machines. In Chapter 7 we will discuss formalization of the concept of an infinite perceptron. It should be noted, however, that the use of infinite perceptrons does not cover all cases. For example, the predicate

$$\psi(X) = \lceil |X| > \tfrac{1}{2}|R| \rceil$$

is well-defined and of order 1 for any finite R. It is meaningless for infinite R, yet we might like to consider the corresponding predicate scheme to have finite order.

Group Invariance of Boolean Inequalities

2

2.0

In this chapter we consider linear threshold inequalities that are invariant under groups of transformations of the points of the base-space R. The purpose of this, finally achieved in Part II, is to establish a connection between the geometry of R and the realizability of geometric predicates by perceptrons of finite order.

2.1 Example: Coefficients Averaged Over a Symmetry

As an introduction to the methods introduced in this section we first consider a simple, almost trivial, example. Our space R has just two points, x and y. We will prove that the predicate ~~$\psi_\equiv =$~~ $\lceil x = y \rceil$ ~~$[xy \vee \bar{x}\bar{y}]$~~ is not of order 1. ~~(This is the predicate that asserts that X is not a single point.)~~ This predicate asserts that X is all black or all white. One way to prove this is to deduce a contradiction from the hypothesis that numbers α, β, and θ can be found for which

$$\psi_\equiv(x,y) = \lceil x = y \rceil \; \text{~~$xy \vee \bar{x}\bar{y}$~~} = \lceil \alpha x + \beta y > \theta \rceil.$$

We can proceed directly by writing down the conditions on α and β:

$$\psi_\equiv(1,0) = 0 \Rightarrow \alpha \le \theta \qquad (\text{because } \alpha \cdot 1 + \beta \cdot 0 \le \theta)$$
$$\psi_\equiv(0,1) = 0 \Rightarrow \beta \le \theta$$
$$\psi_\equiv(1,1) = 1 \Rightarrow \alpha + \beta > \theta$$
$$\psi_\equiv(0,0) = 1 \Rightarrow 0 > \theta$$

In this simple case it is easy enough to deduce the contradiction, for adding the first two conditions gives us

$$\alpha + \beta \le 2\theta,$$

and this, with the third implies that

$$\theta < 2\theta,$$

and this would make θ positive, contradicting the fourth condition.

But arguments of this sort are hard to generalize to more complex situations involving many variables. On the other hand the following argument, though it may be considered a little more complicated in itself, leads directly to much deeper insights. First we observe that the value of ψ is unchanged when we permute, that is, interchange, x and y. That is,

$$\psi_{\equiv}(x, y) = \psi_{\equiv}(y, x).$$

Thus if one of the following holds, so must the other:

$$\alpha x + \beta y > \theta$$
$$\alpha y + \beta x > \theta;$$

hence

$$\tfrac{1}{2}(\alpha + \beta)\, x + \tfrac{1}{2}(\alpha + \beta)\, y > \theta$$

by adding the inequalities. Similarly, either of

$$\alpha x + \beta y \leq \theta$$
$$\alpha y + \beta x \leq \theta$$

yields

$$\tfrac{1}{2}(\alpha + \beta)\, x + \tfrac{1}{2}(\alpha + \beta)\, y \leq \theta.$$

It follows that if we write γ for $\frac{1}{2}(\alpha + \beta)$, then

$$\psi_{\equiv}(x, y) = \lceil \gamma x + \gamma y > \theta \rceil = \lceil \gamma(x + y) > \theta \rceil.$$

Thus we can construct a new linear representation for ψ in which the coefficients of x and y are equal.

It follows that

$$\psi_{\equiv}(X) = \lceil \gamma\, |X| > \theta \rceil,$$

where $|X|$ is, as usual, the number of points in X.

Now consider the three figures $X_0 = \{\}$, $X_1 = \{x\}$, $X_2 = \{x,y\}$.

$$|X_0| = 0 \quad \text{and} \quad \gamma \cdot 0 > \theta$$
$$|X_1| = 1 \quad \text{and} \quad \gamma \cdot 1 \leq \theta,$$
$$|X_2| = 2 \quad \text{and} \quad \gamma \cdot 2 > \theta.$$

This is clearly impossible. *Thus we learn something about ψ by "averaging" its coefficients after making a permutation that leaves the predicate unchanged.* (In the example γ is the average of α and β.) In §2.3 we shall define precisely the notion of "average" that is involved here.

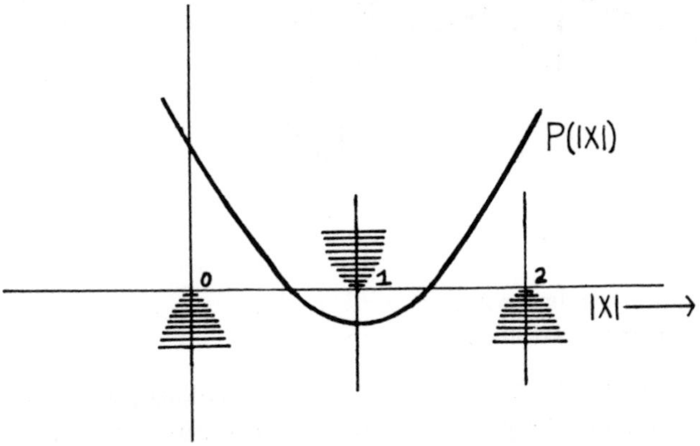

Figure 2.1 The function $P(|X|) = \gamma \cdot |X| - \theta$ has to avoid the shaded regions, but this requires a polynomial of second or higher degree.

2.1.1* Groups and Equivalence-classes of Predicates

The generalization of the procedure of §2.1 involves introducing an arbitrary *group of transformations* on the base space R, and then asking what it means for a predicate ψ to be unaffected by any of these transformations (just as the predicate of §2.1 was unaffected by transposing two points). It is through this idea of "invariance under a group of transformations" that we will be able to attack geometrical problems; in so doing we are adopting the mathematical viewpoint of Felix Klein: every interesting geometrical property is an invariant of some transformation group.

A good example of a group of transformations is *the set of all translations of the plane*: a translation is a transformation that moves every point of the plane into another point, with every point moved the same amount in the same direction; that is, a rigid parallel shift. Figure 2.2 illustrates the effect of two transla-

*This section can be skipped by readers who know the basic definitions of the theory of groups.

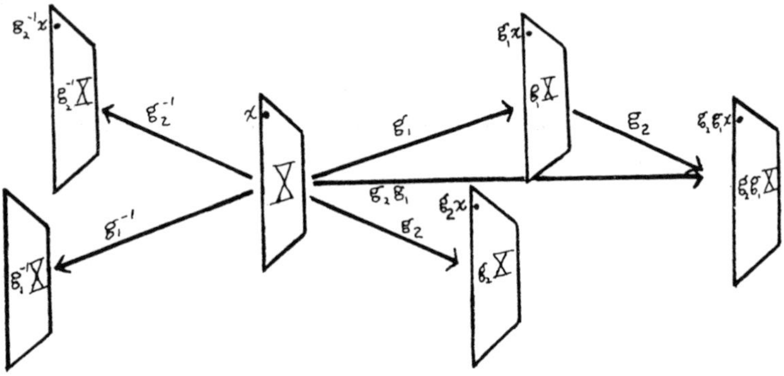

Figure 2.2

tions, g_1 and g_2, on a figure X. The picture illustrates a number of definitions and observations we want to make.

1. We define a translation to operate upon individual points, so that g_1 operating on the point x yields another point g_1x. This "induces" a natural sense in which the g's operate on whole figures; let us define it. If g is one of a group G of transformations—abbreviated "$g \in G$"—and if X is a figure, that is, a subset of R, we define

$$gX = \{gx \mid x \in X\}$$

which is read: gX is (defined to be) the set of all points gx obtained by applying g to points x of X.

2. If we apply to X first one transformation g_1 and then another transformation g_2 we obtain a new figure that could be denoted by "$g_2(g_1X)$." But that same figure could be regarded as obtained by a single transformation—the "composition" of g_2 and g_1—and it is customary to denote this composite by "g_2g_1" and hence the new figure by "g_2g_1X" as shown in the figure. The mathematical definition of group requires that if $g_1 \in G$ and $g_2 \in G$ then their composition g_2g_1 must also be in G.

Incidentally, in the case of the plane-translations, it is always true that $g_1g_2X = g_2g_1X$, as can be seen by completing the parallelogram of X, g_1X, g_2X, and g_2g_1X. This is to be regarded as a coincidence, because it is not always true in other important geometric groups. For example, if G is the group ~~of~~ generated by all rotations about all points in the plane, then for the indicated g_1 and g_2 shown below, the points g_1g_2x and g_2g_1x are quite different.

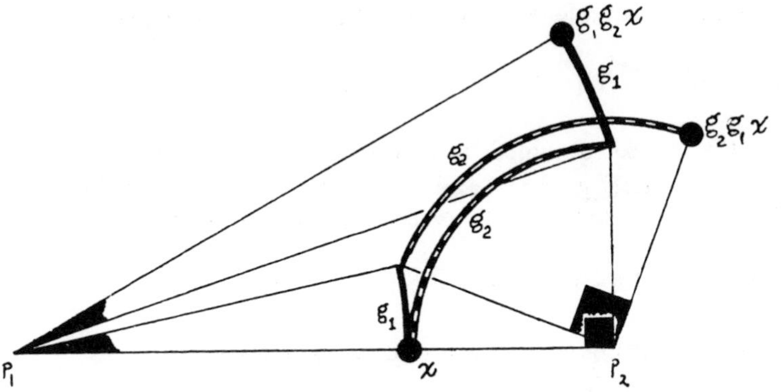

Figure 2.3 Here g_1 is a small rotation about p_1, and g_2 is a 90° rotation about p_2. The figure shows why, for the rotation group, we usually find that $g_1g_2x \neq g_2g_1x$.

3. The final requirement of the technical definition of "group of transformations" is that for each $g \in G$ there must be an inverse transformation called g^{-1}, also in G, with the property that $g^{-1}gx = x$ for every point x. In Figure 2.2 we have indicated the inverses of the translations g_1 and g_2. One can construct the inverse of g_2g_1 by completing the parallelogram to the left. In fact a little thought will show that (in any group!) it is always true that $(g_2g_1)^{-1} = g_1^{-1}g_2^{-1}$.

It is always understood that a group contains the trivial "identity" transformation e, which has the property that for all x, $ex = x$. In fact, since e is the composition of $g^{-1}g$ of any g and its inverse g^{-1}, the presence of e in G already logically follows from the requirements of 2 and 3. It is easy to see also that $gg^{-1} = e$ always.

In algebra books, one finds additional requirements on groups, for example, that

$$(g_1g_2)g_3 = g_1(g_2g_3)$$

for all g_1, g_2, and g_3. For the *groups of transformations* we always use here, this goes without saying, because it is already implicit in the intuitive notion of transformation. The associative law above is seen to hold simply by following what happens to each separate point of R.

4. If h is a particular member of G then the set hG defined by

$$hG = \{hg \mid g \in G\}$$

(that is, the set obtained by composing h with every member of G) is the whole group G and each element is obtained just once. To see this, note first that any element g is obtained:

$$h(h^{-1}g) = (hh^{-1})g = eg = g$$

and $h^{-1}g$ must be in the group. If, say, g_0 happens twice,

$$g_0 = hg_1,$$
$$g_0 = hg_2$$

we would have both of

$$h^{-1}g_0 = h^{-1}hg_1 = g_1$$
$$h^{-1}g_0 = h^{-1}hg_2 = g_2$$

so that g_1 and g_2 could not be different.

5. In most of what follows, and particularly in §2.3, we want to work with groups G that contain only a *finite* number of transformations. But still, we want to capture the spirit of the ordinary Euclidean transformation groups, which are infinite. There are an infinite number of different distances a figure can be translated in the plane: for example, if $g \neq e$ is any nontrivial translation then $g, gg, ggg, \ldots$ are all different. In most cases we will be able to prove the theorems we want by substituting a finite group for the infinite one, if necessary by altering the space R itself! For example, in dealing with *translation* we will often use, instead of the Euclidean plane, a torus, as in Figure 2.4.

The torus is ruled off in squares, as shown. As our substitute for the infinite set of plane-translations, we consider just those torus-transformations that move each point a certain number m of square units around the large equator, and a certain number

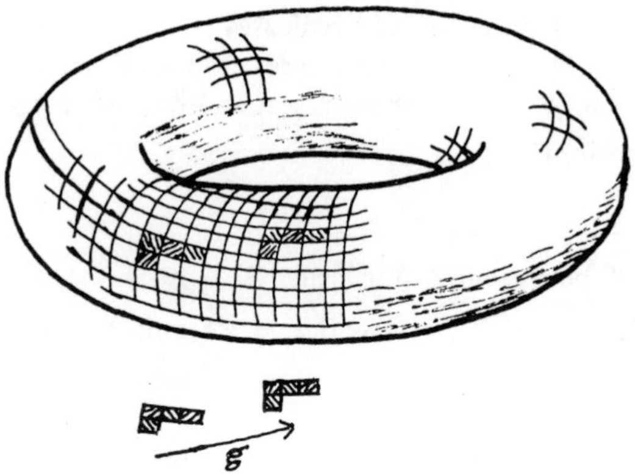

Figure 2.4

n of units around the small equator. There are just a finite number of such "translations." The torus behaves very much like a small part of the plane for most practical purposes, because it can be "cut" and unwrapped (Figure 2.5). Hence for "small" figures and "small" translations there is no important difference between the torus and the plane. This will be discussed further in the introduction to Part II, and in Chapter 7.

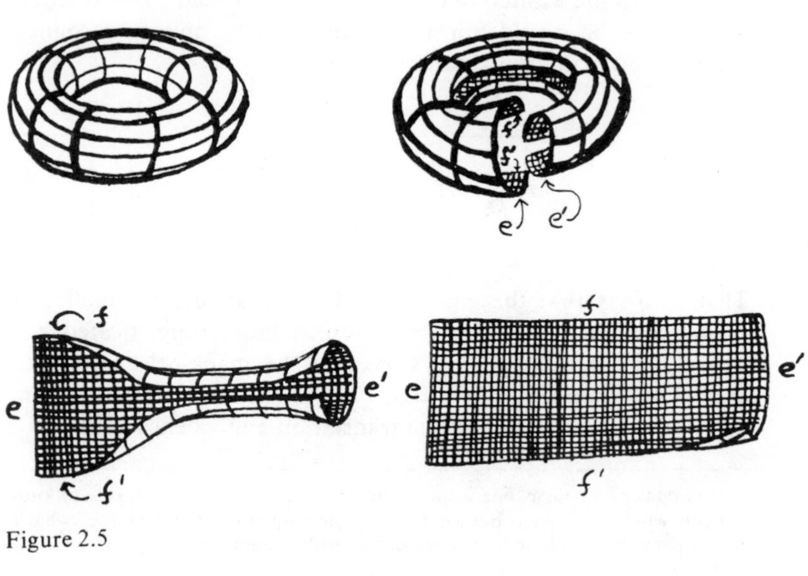

Figure 2.5

2.2 Equivalence-classes of Figures and of Predicates

Given a group G, we will say that two figures X and Y are G-equivalent (and we write $X \underset{G}{\equiv} Y$) if there is a member g of G for for which $X = gY$. Notice that

$X \underset{G}{\equiv} X$ because $X = eX$,

$X \underset{G}{\equiv} Y$ implies $Y \underset{G}{\equiv} X$, because if $X = gY$ then $Y = g^{-1}X$,

$X \underset{G}{\equiv} Y$ and $Y \underset{G}{\equiv} Z$ imply $X \underset{G}{\equiv} Z$, because if $X = gY$ and $Y = hZ$ then $X = ghZ$.

When we choose a group, we thus automatically also set up a classification of figures into equivalence-classes. This is important later, because it will turn out that the "patterns"—or sets of figures—we want to recognize always fall into such classifications when we choose the right groups.

Example: Suppose that G is the set of *all* permutations of a finite set of points R. (A *permutation* is any rearrangement of the points in which no two points are brought together.) Then (theorem!) two figures X and Y are G-equivalent if and only if they both contain the same number of points.

Example: If one wanted to build a machine to read printed letters or numbers, he would normally want it to be able to recognize them whatever their position on the page:

That is to say that this machine's decision should be unaffected by members of the translation group. A more sophisticated way to say the same thing is to state that the machine's perception should be "translation-invariant," that is, it must make the same decision on every member of a translation-equivalence class.*

*In practice, of course, one wants more from the machine: one wants to know not only what is on a page, but where it is. Otherwise, instead of "reading" what is on the page, the machine would present us with anagrams!

In §2.3 we prove an important theorem that tells us a great deal about any perceptron whose behavior is "G-invariant" for some group G, that is, one whose predicate $\psi(X)$ depends only upon the equivalence-class of X. In order to state the theorem, we will have to define what we mean by G-equivalance of *predicates*.

We will say that two predicates φ and φ' are **equivalent**, with respect to a group G

$$\varphi \underset{G}{\equiv} \varphi'$$

if there is a member g of G such that $\varphi(gX)$ *and* $\varphi'(X)$ *are the same for every* X.

It is easy to see that this really is an equivalence relation, that is,

$$\varphi \underset{G}{\equiv} \varphi \text{ for any } \varphi,$$
$$\varphi \underset{G}{\equiv} \varphi' \text{ implies } \varphi' \underset{G}{\equiv} \varphi$$
$$\varphi \underset{G}{\equiv} \varphi' \text{ and } \varphi' \underset{G}{\equiv} \varphi'' \text{ imply } \varphi \equiv \varphi''.$$

Given any predicate φ and group element g, we will define φg to be the predicate that, for each X, has the value $\varphi(gX)$. Thus we always have $\varphi g(X) = \varphi(gX)$. We will say **$\Phi$ is closed under G** if for every φ in Φ and g in G the predicate φg is also in Φ.

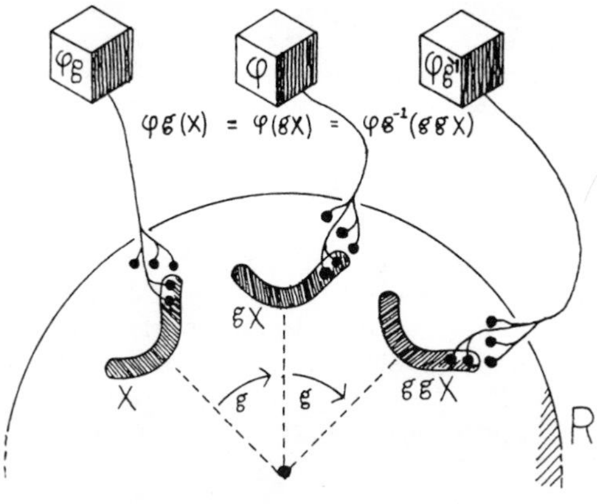

Three φ's Equivalent under a Rotation Group

Now at last we can state and prove our main theorem. It will show that if a perceptron predicate is invariant under a group G, then its coefficients need depend only on the G-equivalence classes of their φ's. This theorem will be our single most powerful tool in all that follows, for it is the generalization of our method of §2.1 and will let us convert complicated problems of geometry into (usually) simple problems of algebra.

2.3 The Group-Invariance Theorem

Suppose that

(1) G is a finite group of transformations of a finite space R;

(2) Φ is a set of predicates on R closed under G;

(3) ψ is in $L(\Phi)$ and invariant under G.

Then there exists a linear representation of ψ,

$$\psi = \left\lceil \sum_{\varphi \in \Phi} \beta_\varphi \varphi > 0 \right\rceil$$

for which the coefficients β_φ depend only on the G-equivalence class of φ, that is,

$$\text{if } \varphi \underset{G}{\equiv} \varphi' \text{ then } \beta_\varphi = \beta_{\varphi'}.$$

These conditions are stronger than they need be. To be sure, the theorem is *not* true in general for infinite groups. A counterexample will be found in §7.10. However, in special cases we can prove the theorem for infinite groups. An example with interesting consequences will be discussed later, in §10.4. It will also be seen that the assumption that G be a group can be relaxed slightly.

We have not investigated relaxing condition (2), and this would be interesting. However, it does not interfere with our methods for showing certain predicates to be *not* of finite order. For when the theorem is applied to show that a particular ψ is *not* in $L(\Phi)$ for a particular Φ, it is done by showing that ψ is not linear even in the G-closure of Φ. Remember that the order of a predicate (§1.3) is defined without reference to any particular set Φ of φ's! And closing a Φ under a group G cannot change the maximum support size of the predicates in the set.

PROOF: Let $\psi(X)$ have a linear representation $\sum_{\varphi \in \Phi} \alpha(\varphi)\, \varphi(X) > 0$.

We use "$\alpha(\varphi)$" instead of α_φ to avoid complicated subscripts. Any element g of G defines a one-to-one correspondence $\varphi \leftrightarrow \varphi g$, that is, a permutation of the φ's. Therefore

$$\sum_{\varphi \in \Phi} \alpha(\varphi)\varphi(X) = \sum_{\varphi \in \Phi} \alpha(\varphi g)\varphi g(X)$$

for all X, simply because the same numbers are added in both sums. Now, *choose an X for which $\psi(X) = 1$.* Since ψ is G-invariant, and g^{-1} is an element of G, we must have

$$\sum \alpha(\varphi g)\varphi g(g^{-1}X) > 0,$$

hence we conclude that for any g in G, if $\psi(X) = 1$,

$$\sum_{\varphi \in \Phi} \alpha(\varphi g)\varphi(X) > 0.$$

Summing these positive quantities for all g's in G, we see that

$$\sum_{g \in G}\left[\sum_{\varphi \in \Phi} \alpha(\varphi g)\varphi(X)\right] > 0.$$

If we collect together the coefficients for each φ, we then obtain

$$\sum_{\varphi \in \Phi}\left[\sum_{g \in G} \alpha(\varphi g)\right]\varphi(X) > 0$$

which is an expression in $L(\varphi)$, that is, can be written as

$$\sum_{\varphi \in \Phi} \beta(\varphi)\varphi(X) > 0.$$

Remember that this depends on assuming that $\psi(X) = 1$. Now choose an X for which $\psi(X) = 0$. Then the same argument will show that

$$\sum_{\varphi \in \Phi} \beta(\varphi)\varphi(X) \le 0.$$

Combining the inequalities for $\psi = 1$ and $\psi = 0$, we conclude that

$$\psi(X) = \left\lceil \sum_{\varphi \in \Phi} \beta(\varphi)\varphi(X) > 0 \right\rceil.$$

It remains only to show, as promised, that

$$\varphi \underset{G}{\equiv} \varphi' \Rightarrow \beta(\varphi) = \beta(\varphi').$$

But $\varphi \equiv \varphi'$ means that there is some h such that $\varphi = \varphi' h$, so

$$\beta(\varphi) = \sum_{g \in G} \alpha(\varphi g) = \sum_{g \in G} \alpha(\varphi' hg) = \sum_{g \in G} \alpha(\varphi' g) = \beta(\varphi')$$

because the one-to-one correspondence $g \leftrightarrow hg$ simply permutes the order of adding the same numbers.

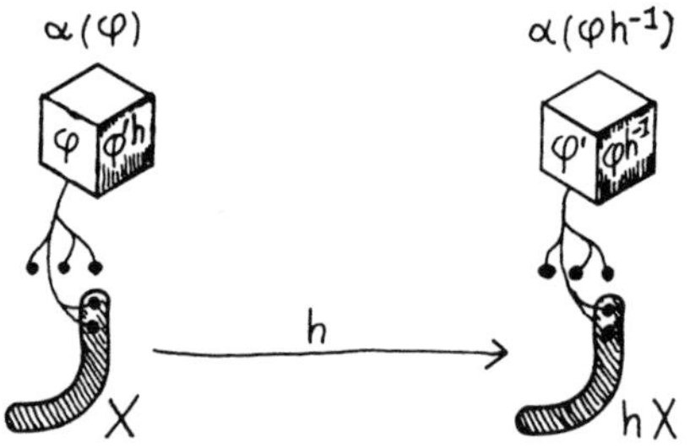

SECOND PROOF: Because of the importance of the theorem, we give another version of the proof, which may seem more intuitive to some readers.

Choose an X for which $\psi(X) = 1$. Then for any $g \in G$ we will have $\psi(gX) = 1$, hence each of the sums

$$\sum \alpha(\varphi)\varphi(gX)$$

will be positive, and so will *their* sum

$$\sum_{\substack{\varphi \in \Phi \\ g \in G}} \alpha(\varphi)\varphi(gX) = \sum_{\substack{\varphi \in \Phi \\ g \in G}} \alpha(\varphi)\varphi g(X).$$

We can think of all the terms of this sum as arranged in a great

$|\Phi| \times |G|$ array

$$\left[\begin{array}{l} \alpha(\varphi_1)\varphi_1 g_1 \ + \alpha(\varphi_2)\varphi_2 g_1 + \cdots + \alpha(\varphi_{|\Phi|})\varphi_{|\Phi|} g_1 \\ + \alpha(\varphi_1)\varphi_1 g_2 \ + \alpha(\varphi_2)\varphi_2 g_2 + \cdots + \alpha(\varphi_{|\Phi|})\varphi_{|\Phi|} g_2 \\ \quad\vdots \qquad\qquad\qquad \vdots \qquad\qquad\qquad\qquad \vdots \\ + \alpha(\varphi_1)\varphi_1 g_{|G|} + \qquad \cdots \qquad + \alpha(\varphi_{|\Phi|})\varphi_{|\Phi|} g_{|G|} \end{array}\right] (X).$$

We want to write this in the form $\beta_1\varphi_1 + \beta_2\varphi_2 + \ldots$ so we have to collect the coefficients of each φ_i. To do so, we have to collect together for each φ_i those terms

$\alpha(\varphi_j)$for which $\varphi_j g_k = \varphi_i$.

The sum of those terms is, of course, β_i. Our real purpose, however, is not to calculate β_i but to show that

$$\varphi_a \equiv \varphi_b \Rightarrow \beta_a = \beta_b.$$

To do this, suppose that in fact $\varphi_a \equiv \varphi_b$, which implies that we can find an element g for which

$$\varphi_a = \varphi_b g.$$

We will use this to establish a one-to-one correspondence between the two sets of elements of the array that add up to form β_a and β_b. Define

"the g_j-entry of φ_k"

to be $\alpha(\varphi_i)\varphi_i g_j$ where i is determined by $\varphi_i g_j = \varphi_k$. Then in the array there is exactly one "g_j-entry of φ_k" for each j and k. (It is irrelevant that there may be *many* different elements h in G that satisfy $\varphi_i h = \varphi_k$. We are concerned here only with each entry's *occurrence* in the array, not with its value.)

Now, if $\alpha(\varphi_i)\varphi_i g_j$ is the g_j-entry of φ_b, then

$$\varphi_i g_j = \varphi_b,$$

and therefore

$$\varphi_i g_j g = \varphi_b g = \varphi_a;$$

hence $\alpha(\varphi_i)\,\varphi_i g_j g$ is the $g_j g$ entry of φ_a.

If we recall that

$$g_j \leftrightarrow g_j g$$

is a one-to-one correspondence within the group elements, as shown in observation 4 of §2.1.1 (see Figure 2.6), we conclude that the corresponding elements in the β_a and β_b sums must have the same coefficients, so the sums β_a and β_b must be equal.

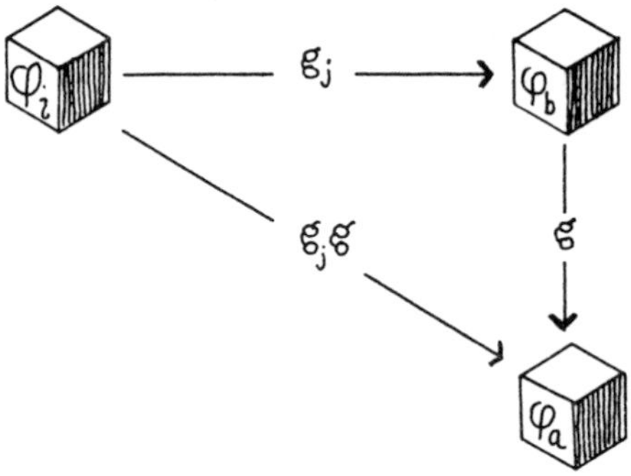

Figure 2.6

Since the same argument holds for the case of $\psi(X) = 0$, the theorem is proved. Extensions of this to certain infinite spaces are discussed in Chapters 7 and 10.

For readers who find these ideas difficult to work with abstractly, some concrete examples of the equivalence classes will be useful; the geometric "spectra" of §5.2 and especially of §6.2 should be helpful.

We shall often use this theorem in the following form:
Corollary 1: Any group-invariant predicate ψ (of order k) that satisfies the conditions of the theorem has a representation

$$\psi = \left[\sum_{\Phi^*} \alpha_\varphi \varphi > 0\right]$$

where Φ^* is the set of **masks** (of degree $\leq k$) and $\alpha_\varphi = \alpha_{\varphi'}$ if $S(\varphi)$ can be transformed into $S(\varphi')$ by an element of G.

PROOF: For masks, $\varphi_A \underset{G}{\equiv} \varphi_B$ if and only if $A = gB$ for some $g \in G$.

Corollary 2: Let $\Phi = \Phi_1 \cup \cdots \cup \Phi_m$ be the decomposition of Φ into equivalence classes by relation $\underset{G}{\equiv}$. Then, under the conditions of the theorem ψ can be written in the form

$$\psi = \lceil \Sigma \alpha_i N_i(X) > 0 \rceil$$

where $N_i(X) = |\{\varphi \mid \varphi \in \Phi_i \text{ AND } \varphi(X)\}|$, that is, the number of φ's of the ith type, equivalent under the group, satisfied by the figure X.

PROOF: ψ can be represented as

$$\left\lceil \sum_{\varphi \in \Phi} \alpha_\varphi \varphi > 0 \right\rceil, \text{ that is,}$$

$$\left\lceil \sum_i \sum_{\varphi \in \Phi_i} \alpha_\varphi \varphi > 0 \right\rceil, \text{ that is,}$$

$$\left\lceil \sum_i \alpha_i \sum_{\varphi \in \Phi_i} \varphi > 0 \right\rceil = \left\lceil \sum_i \alpha_i N_i(X) > 0 \right\rceil.$$

2.4 The Triviality of Invariant Predicates of Order 1: First application of the group-invariance theorem.

Theorem 2.4: Let G be any group of permutations on R that has the property:* for every pair of points (p,q) of R there is at least one g in G such that $gp = q$. Then the only first-order predicates invariant under G are

$$\left.\begin{aligned} \psi(X) &= \lceil |X| > m \rceil \\ \psi(X) &= \lceil |X| \geq m \rceil \\ \psi(X) &= \lceil |X| < m \rceil \\ \psi(X) &= \lceil |X| \leq m \rceil \end{aligned}\right\} \text{ for some } m.$$

*This property, shared by most of the interesting geometric groups, is usually called "transitivity." Pure rotations about a fixed center constitute an exception, as does the group of all translations parallel to a fixed direction in the plane. But the groups of all rotations about all centers, or all translations, etc., are transitive.

PROOF: Since all the one-point predicates φ_p are equivalent, we can assume that

$$\psi(X) = \left\lceil \sum_{p \epsilon X} \alpha \varphi_p > \theta \right\rceil,$$

that is, the coefficients are independent of p. But $\Sigma \alpha \; \varphi_p > \theta$ is the same as $\Sigma \varphi_p > \theta/\alpha$ for $\alpha > 0$. (For negative α we have to use "$<$" instead.) And

$$\sum_{p \epsilon X} \varphi_p = |X| .$$

Thus order-1 predicates invariant under the usual geometric groups can do nothing more than define simple "$\geq m$"-type inequalities on the size or "area" of the figures. In particular, taking the translation group G we see that no first-order perceptron can distinguish the A's in the figure on p. 46 from some other translation-invariant set of figures of the same area.

2.4.1 Noninvariant Predicates of Order 1

If one gives up geometric group invariance there are still some simple but useful predicates of order 1, for we can represent inequalities related to the ordinary integrals. For example, the following predicates of plane figures can be realized: let x_p and y_p be the x and y coordinates of the point p:

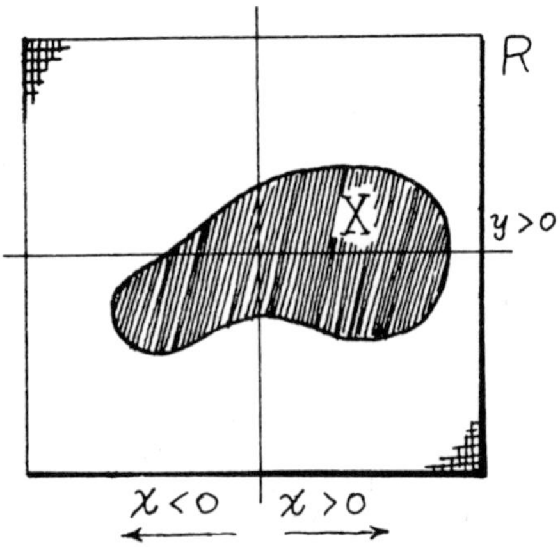

Figure 2.7

[X has more area in the right half-plane than in the left]

$$= \left\lceil \sum_{\substack{\text{right}\\\text{half}}} \varphi_p - \sum_{\substack{\text{left}\\\text{half}}} \varphi_p > 0 \right\rceil,$$

⌈The center of gravity of X is right of center⌉
$= \lceil \Sigma\, x_p \varphi_p > 0 \rceil$ (see Figure 0.3, p. 11),

⌈The nth central moment of X about the origin is greater than θ⌉
$= \lceil \Sigma\, \varphi_p \left(\sqrt{x_p^2 + y_p^2}\right)^n > \theta \rceil$,

and so on. But these "moment-type" predicates are restricted to having their reference coordinates in the absolute plane, and not in the figure X. For example one *cannot* realize, with order 1,

⌈The second moment of X about
its own center of gravity is greater than θ⌉

because that predicate *is* invariant under the (transitive) translation group.

MATHEMATICAL REMARK:
There is a relation between these observations and Haar's theorem on the uniqueness up to a constant factor of invariant measures. For finite sets and transitive groups the unique Haar measure is, in fact, the counting-function $\mu(X) = |X|$.

The set function defined by

$$\mu(X) = \sum \alpha_i x_i = \sum_{x_i \in X} \alpha_i$$

satisfies $\mu(X) + \mu(Y) = \mu(X \cup Y) + \mu(X \cap Y)$. If we defined invariance by $\mu(X) = \mu(gX)$ it would follow immediately from Haar's theorem that $\mu(X) = c\,|X|$, where c is a constant. Our hypothesis on μ is slightly weaker since we merely assume

$$\mu(X) > \theta \Longleftrightarrow \mu(gX) > \theta,$$

and deduce a correspondingly weaker conclusion, that is,

$$(\mu(X) > \theta) \Longleftrightarrow (c\,|X| > \theta).$$

In the general case the relation between an invariance theorem and the theory of Haar measure is less clear since the set function $\Sigma\, \alpha_\varphi \varphi(X)$ is not in general a measure. This seems to suggest some generalization of measure but we have not tried to pursue this. Readers interested in the history of ideas might find it interesting to pursue the relation of these results to those of Pitts and McCulloch [1947].

3

3.0

In this chapter we study the orders of two particularly interesting predicates. Neither of them is "geometric," because their invariance groups have too little structure. But in §5, we will apply them to geometric problems by picking out appropriate "subgroups" which have the right invariance properties.

3.1 The Parity Function

In this section we develop in some detail the analysis of the very simple predicate defined by

$$\psi_{\text{PARITY}}(X) = \lceil |X| \text{ is an odd number} \rceil.$$

Our interest in ψ_{PARITY} is threefold: it is interesting in itself; it will be used for the analysis of other more important functions; and, especially, it illustrates our mathematical methods and the kind of questions they enable us to discuss.

Theorem 3.1.1: ψ_{PARITY} is of order $|R|$. That is, to compute it requires at least one partial predicate whose support is the *whole space R*.

PROOF: Let G be the group of all permutations of R. Clearly ψ_{PARITY} is invariant under G. (Because moving points around can't change their number!)

Now suppose that $\psi_{\text{PARITY}} = \lceil \Sigma \alpha_i \varphi_i > 0 \rceil$ where the φ_i are the masks with $|S(\varphi_i)| \leq K$. The group invariance theorem tells us that we can choose the coefficients so that they depend only on the equivalence classes defined by $\underset{G}{\equiv}$.

But then α_i depends *only* on $|S(\varphi_i)|$. To see this observe (1) all masks with the same support are identical, and (2) all sets of the same size can be transformed into one another by elements of G,

$$\varphi_i \underset{G}{\equiv} \varphi_j \Longleftrightarrow |S(\varphi_i)| = |S(\varphi_j)|.$$

Thus ψ_{PARITY} can be written, using Corollary 2 of §2.3, as

$$\left\lceil \sum_{j=0}^{K} \alpha_j \left[\sum_{\Phi_j} \varphi(X) \right] > 0 \right\rceil = \left\lceil \sum_{j}^{K} \alpha_j N_j(X) > 0 \right\rceil,$$

where $\{\Phi_j\}$ is the set of masks whose supports contain exactly j elements. We now calculate for an arbitrary subset X of R,

$$N_j(X) = \sum_{\varphi \in \Phi_j} \varphi(X).$$

Since $\varphi(X)$ is 1 if $S(\varphi) \subset X$ and 0 otherwise, $N_j(X)$ is the number of subsets of X with j elements, that is,

$$N_j(X) = \binom{|X|}{j} = \frac{|X|(|X| - 1) \ldots (|X| - j + 1)}{j!}$$

which is a polynomial of degree j in $|X|$. It follows that

$$\sum_{j=0}^{K} \alpha_j N_j(X)$$

is a polynomial of degree $\leq K$ in $|X|$, say $P(|X|)$.

Now consider any sequence of sets $X_0, X_1, \ldots, X_{|R|}$ such that $|X_i| = i$. Since $P(|X|) > 0$ if and only if $|X|$ is odd,

$$P(|X_0|) \leq 0, \quad P(|X_1|) > 0, \quad P(|X_2| \leq 0, \ldots,$$

that is $P(|X|)$ crosses the x-axis $|R|$ times as $|X|$ increases from 0 to $|R|$. But P is a polynomial of degree K. It follows (see Figure 3.1) that $K \geq |R|$. Q.E.D.

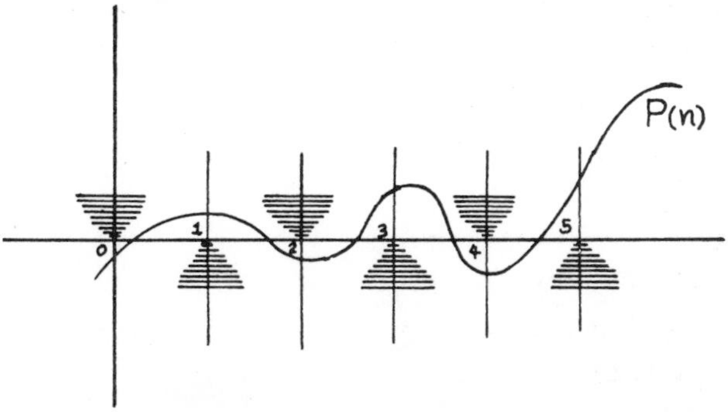

Figure 3.1 A polynomial that changes direction $K - 1$ times must have degree at least K.

From this we obtain the

Theorem 3.1.2: If $\psi_{\text{PARITY}} \in L(\Phi)$ and if Φ contains only masks, then Φ contains every mask.

PROOF: Imagine that, even if Φ contains only masks, and the mask whose support is A does not belong to Φ, it were possible to write

$$\psi_{\text{PARITY}} = \left\lceil \sum_{\varphi \in \Phi} \alpha_\varphi \varphi > 0 \right\rceil.$$

Now define, for any ψ, the predicate $\psi^A(X)$ to be $\psi(X \cap A)$. Then ψ^A_{PARITY} is the parity function for subsets of A, and has order $|A|$ by the previous theorem. To study its representation as a linear combination of masks of subsets of A we consider φ^A for $\varphi \in \Phi$. If $S(\varphi) \subset A$, clearly $\varphi^A = \varphi$; otherwise φ^A is identically zero since

$$\begin{aligned} S(\varphi) \not\subset A \quad \Rightarrow \quad S(\varphi) \not\subset X \cap A \quad &\Rightarrow \quad \varphi(X \cap A) = 0 \\ &\Rightarrow \quad \varphi^A(X) = 0. \end{aligned}$$

Thus, *either* $S(\varphi^A)$ is a *proper* subset of A, or φ^A is identically zero. Now let Φ^A be the set of masks in Φ whose supports are subsets of A. Then

$$\psi^A_{\text{PARITY}} = \left\lceil \sum_{\varphi \in \Phi^A} \alpha_\varphi \varphi > 0 \right\rceil.$$

And for all $\varphi \in \Phi^A$, $|S(\varphi)| < |A|$. But this is in contradiction with Theorem 3.1.1 since it implies that the order of ψ^A_{PARITY} is less than $|A|$. Thus the hypothesis is impossible and the theorem proven.

Corollary 1: If $\psi_{\text{PARITY}} \in L(\Phi)$ then Φ must contain at least one φ for which $|S(\varphi)| = |R|$.

The following theorem, also immediate from the above, is of interest to students of threshold logic:

Corollary 2: Let Φ be the set of all ψ^A_{PARITY} for *proper* subsets A of R. Then $\psi_{\text{PARITY}} \notin L(\Phi)$.

The further analysis of ψ_{PARITY} in Chapter 10 shows that functions which might be recognizable, in principle, by a very large percep-

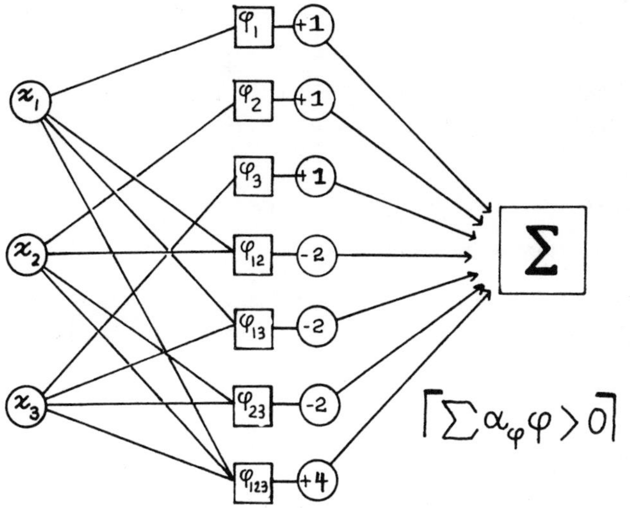

Group-invariant coefficients for the $|R| = 3$ parity predicate.

tron, might not actually be realizable in practice because of impossibly huge coefficients. For example, it will be shown that in any representation of ψ_{PARITY} as linear in the set of masks the ratio of the largest to the smallest coefficients must be $2^{|R|-1}$.

3.2* The "One-in-a-box" Theorem

Another predicate of great interest is associated with the geometric property of "connectedness." Its application and interpretation is deferred to Chapter 5; the basic theorem is proved now.

Theorem 3.2: Let $A_1, \ldots, A_m$ be disjoint subsets of R and define the predicate

$$\psi(X) = \lceil |X \cap A_i| > 0, \text{ for every } A_i \rceil,$$

that is, there is at least one point of X in each A_i. If for all i, $|A_i| = 4m^2$, then the order of ψ is $\geq m$.

*This theorem is used to prove the theorem in §5.1. Because §5.7 gives an independent proof (using Theorem 3.1.1), this section can be skipped on first reading.

Corollary: If $R = A_1 \cup A_2 \cup \ldots \cup A_m$, the order of ψ is at least $\frac{1}{4}|R|^{1/3}$.

PROOF: For each $i = 1, \ldots, m$ let G_i be the group of permutations of R which permute the elements of A_i but do not affect the elements of the complement of A_i.

Let G be the group generated by all elements of the G_i.

Clearly ψ is invariant with respect to G.

Let Φ be the set of masks of degree k or less. To determine the equivalence class of any $\varphi \in \Phi$ consider the "occupancy numbers":

$$|S(\varphi) \cap A_i|.$$

Note that $\varphi_1 \underset{G}{\equiv} \varphi_2$ if and only if $|S(\varphi_1) \cap A_i| = |S(\varphi_2) \cap A_i|$ for each i. Let $\Phi_1, \Phi_2, \ldots$ be the equivalence classes.

Now consider an arbitrary set X and an equivalence class Φ_j. We wish to calculate the number $N_j(X)$ of members of Φ_j satisfied by X, that is,

$$N_j(X) = |\{\varphi | \varphi \in \Phi_j \text{ AND } S(\varphi) \subset X\}|.$$

A simple combinatorial argument shows that

$$N_j(X) = \binom{|X \cap A_1|}{|S(\varphi) \cap A_1|}\binom{|X \cap A_2|}{|S(\varphi) \cap A_2|}\cdots\binom{|X \cap A_m|}{|S(\varphi) \cap A_m|},$$

where

$$\binom{y}{n} = \frac{y(y-1)\ldots(y-n+1)}{n!}$$

and φ is an arbitrary member of Φ_j. Since the numbers $|S(\varphi) \cap A_i|$ depend only on the classes Φ_j and add up to not more than k, it follows that $N_j(X)$ can be written as a polynomial of degree k or less in the numbers $\mathbf{x}_i = |X \cap A_i|$:

$$N_j(X) = P_j(x_1, \ldots, x_m).$$

Now let $\lceil \Sigma \alpha_\varphi \varphi > 0 \rceil$ be a representation of ψ as a linear threshold function in the set of masks of degree less than or equal to k. By the argument which we have already used several times we can assume that α_φ depends only on the equivalence class of φ and write

$$\Sigma \alpha_\varphi \varphi(X) = \Sigma \beta_j \left[\sum_{\varphi \in \Phi_j} \varphi(X) \right] = \Sigma \beta_j N_j(X) = \Sigma \beta_j P_j(x_1, \ldots, x_m)$$

which, as a sum of polynomials of degree at most k, is itself such a polynomial. Thus we can conclude that there exists a polynomial of degree at most k, $Q(x_1, \ldots, x_m)$ with the property that

$$\psi(X) = \lceil Q(x_1, \ldots, x_m) > 0 \rceil \qquad (x_i =_{df} |X \cap A_i|),$$

that is, that if all x_i lie in the range

$$0 \leq x_i \leq 4m^2,$$

then

$$Q(x_1, \ldots, x_m) > 0 \iff x_i > 0 \text{ for all } i.$$

In $Q(x_1, \ldots, x_m)$ make the formal substitution,

$$x_i = [t - (2i - 1)]^2.$$

Then $Q(x_1, \ldots, x_m)$ becomes a polynomial of degree at most $2k$ in t. Now let t take on the values $t = 0, 1, \ldots, 2m$. Then

$$x_i = 0 \text{ for some } i, \text{ if } t \text{ is odd; in fact, for } i = \tfrac{1}{2}(t + 1);$$

but

$$x_i > 0 \text{ for all } i, \text{ if } t \text{ is even.}$$

Hence, by the definition of the ψ predicate, Q must be positive for even t and negative or zero for odd t. By counting the number of changes of sign it is clear that $2k \geq 2m$, that is, $k \geq m$. This completes the proof.

4.0

In this chapter we prove the "And/Or" theorem stated in §1.5.

Theorem 4.0: There exist predicates ψ_1 and ψ_2 of order 1 such that $\psi_1 \wedge \psi_2$ and $\psi_1 \vee \psi_2$ are not of finite order.

We prove the assertion for $\psi_1 \wedge \psi_2$. The other half can be proved in exactly the same way. The techniques used in proving this theorem will not be used in the sequel and so the rest of the chapter can be omitted by readers who don't know, or who dislike, the following kind of algebra.

4.1 Lemmas

We have already remarked in §1.5 that if $R = A \cup B \cup C$ the predicate $\lceil |X \cap A| > |X \cap C| \rceil$ is of order 1, and stated without proof that if A, B, and C are disjoint (see Figure 4.1), then

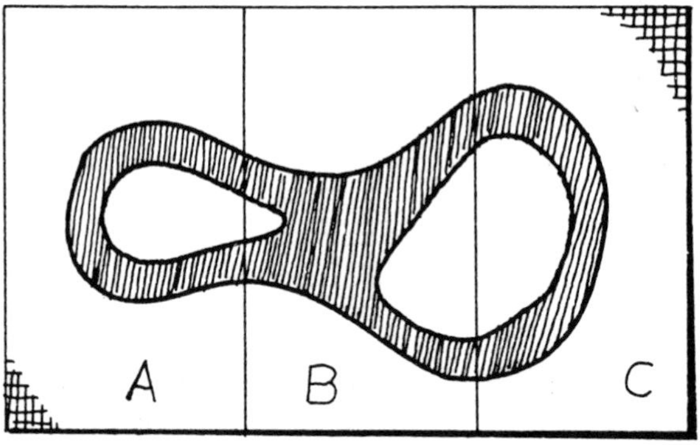

Figure 4.1

$$\lceil (|X \cap A| > |X \cap C|) \wedge (|X \cap B| > |X \cap C|) \rceil$$

is not of bounded order as $|R|$ becomes large. We shall now prove this assertion. We can assume without any loss of generality that the three parts of R have the same size $M = |A| = |B| = |C|$, and that $|R| = 3M$. We will consider predicates of the stated form for different-size retinas. We will prove that

If $\psi_M(X)$ is the predicate of the stated form for $|R| = 3M$, then the order of ψ_M increases without bound as $M \to \infty$.

The proof follows the pattern of proofs in Chapter 3. We shall assume that the order of $\{\psi_M\}$ is bounded by a fixed integer N

for all M, and derive a contradiction by showing that the associated polynomials would have to satisfy inconsistent conditions. The first step is to set up the associated polynomials for a fixed M. We do this by choosing the group of permutations that leaves the sets A, B, and C fixed but allows arbitrary permutations within the sets. The equivalence class of a mask φ is then characterized by the three numbers, $|A \cap S(\varphi)|$, $|B \cap S(\varphi)|$, and $|C \cap S(\varphi)|$. For any given mask φ and set X the number of masks equivalent to φ and satisfied by X is

$$N_\varphi(X) = \binom{|A \cap X|}{|A \cap S(\varphi)|} \times \binom{|B \cap X|}{|B \cap S(\varphi)|} \times \binom{|C \cap X|}{|C \cap S(\varphi)|}.$$

Since we are assuming $|S(\varphi)| \leq N$, we can be sure that $N_\varphi(X)$ is a polynomial of degree at most N in the three numbers

$$x = |A \cap X|, \qquad y = |B \cap X|, \qquad z = |C \cap X|.$$

Let Φ be the set of masks with $|\text{support}| \leq N$. Enumerate the equivalence classes of Φ and let $N_i(X)$ be the number of masks of the ith class satisfied by X. The group invariance theorem allows us to write

$$\psi_M(X) = \lceil \Sigma \beta_i N_i(X) > 0 \rceil.$$

The sum $\Sigma \beta_i N_i(X)$ is a polynomial of degree at most N in x, y, z. Call it $P_M(x, y, z)$.

Now, by definition, for those values of x, y, z which are possible occupancy numbers, that is, nonnegative integers $\leq M$,

$$P_M(x, y, z) > 0 \text{ if and only if } x > z \text{ AND } y > z.$$

We shall show, through a series of lemmas, that this cannot be true for all M.

Lemma 1: Let $P_1(x, y, z)$, $P_2(x, y, z), \ldots,$ be an infinite sequence of nonzero polynomials of degree at most N, with the property that for all *positive integers* x, y, z less than M

$$x > z \text{ AND } y > z \quad \text{implies} \quad P_M(x, y, z) \geq 0$$

SEPARATION CONDITIONS

$$x \leq z \text{ OR } y \leq z \quad \text{implies} \quad P_M(x, y, z) \leq 0.$$

Then there exists a single nonzero polynomial $P(x,y,z)$ of degree at most N with the property that the separation conditions, with P in the place of P_M, hold for ALL positive integral values of x, y, z. It should be observed that we have had to weaken the separation conditions by allowing equality in both conditions since inequality would not be preserved in the limit. Consequences of this will make themselves felt in the proof of Lemma 2.

PROOF: Write

$$P_M(x, y, z) = \sum_{i=1}^{T} C_{M,i} m_i(x, y, z),$$

where $m_1, m_2, \ldots, m_T$ is an enumeration of the monomials of degrees $\leq N$ in x, y, z.

Since the conditions on P_M are preserved under multiplication by a positive scaling factor, we can assume that

$$\Sigma C^2_{M,i} = 1.$$

Now consider the set of points in T-dimensional space

$$C_M = (c_{M,1}, c_{M,2}, \ldots, c_{M,T}), \qquad M = 1, 2, \ldots .$$

These all lie in a compact* set—the surface of the unit T-dimensional sphere. There is, therefore, a subsequence C_{M_j} which converges to a limit

$$C_{M_j} \rightarrow C = (c_1, c_2, \ldots, c_T)$$

in the sense that, for each i,

$$\lim_{j\to\infty} c_{M_j,i} \rightarrow c_i.$$

The polynomial

$$P(x, y, z) = \sum_{i=1}^{T} c_i m_i(x, y, z)$$

---

*See index.

inherits the separation conditions for all positive integral values of x, y, z. That it is not identically zero follows from the fact that the c_i inherit the condition $\Sigma c_i^2 = 1$.

In order to prove our main theorem, we first establish a corresponding result for polynomials in two variables, and later (Lemma 3) adapt it to $P(x, y, z)$.

Lemma 2: *If a polynomial $f(\alpha, \beta)$ satisfies the following conditions for all integral values of α and β, then it is identically zero:*

$$\alpha > 0 \text{ AND } \beta > 0 \quad \text{implies} \quad f(\alpha, \beta) \geq 0,$$

$$\alpha \leq 0 \text{ OR } \beta \leq 0 \quad \text{implies} \quad f(\alpha, \beta) \leq 0.$$

PROOF: Suppose that $f(\alpha, \beta)$ could satisfy these conditions yet not be identically zero. Then we could write it in the form

$$f(\alpha, \beta) = \beta^N g(\alpha) + r(\alpha, \beta)$$

with $g(\alpha)$ not identically zero and with $r(\alpha, \beta)$ of degree lower than N in β. We can then find a number $\alpha_0 > 0$ such that neither of $g(\pm\alpha_0)$ is zero, and then we can choose a number β_0 so large that all four of the inequalities

$$|\beta_0^N g(\pm\alpha_0)| > |r(\pm\alpha_0, \pm\beta_0)|$$

are satisfied so that $r(\pm\alpha_0, \pm\beta_0)$ cannot affect the sign of $f(\pm\alpha_0, \pm\beta_0)$. Then, since

$$f(-\alpha_0, \beta_0) < 0$$

we have

$$g(-\alpha_0) < 0;$$

hence

$$(-\beta_0)^N g(-\alpha_0) > 0;$$

hence

$$f(-\alpha_0, -\beta_0) > 0;$$

which contradicts the conditions, and hence proves the lemma.

4.2 A Digression on Bézout's Theorem

Readers familiar with elementary algebraic geometry will observe that the lemma would follow immediately from Bézout's theorem if the conditions could be stated for all real values of α and β. We would then merely have to prove that the doubly infinite L of the Figure 4.2 is not an algebraic curve.

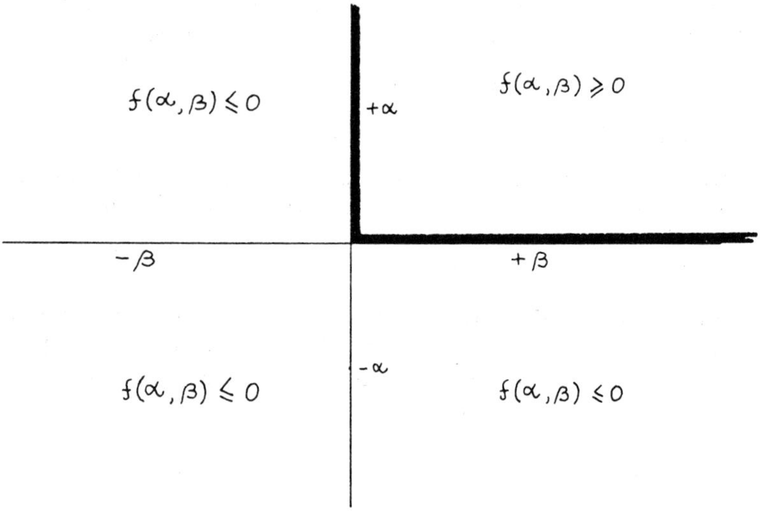

Figure 4.2

Bézout's theorem tells us that if the intersection of an algebraic curve L with an irreducible algebraic curve Y contains an infinite number of points, it must contain the whole of Y. But the L contains the positive half of the y axis. Straight lines are irreducible, so L would have to contain the entire y axis if it were algebraic.

Unfortunately, because our conditions hold only on integer lattice-points, we must allow for the possibility that $f(\alpha, \beta) = 0$ takes a more contorted form as, for example, in Figure 4.3. Part of the pathological behavior of this curve is irrelevant. Since a polynomial of degree N can cut a straight line only N times, the incursions into the interiors of the quadrants can be confined to a bounded region. This means that the curve $f(\alpha, \beta) = 0$ must "asymptotically occupy" the parts of the "channel" illustrated in Figure 4.4.

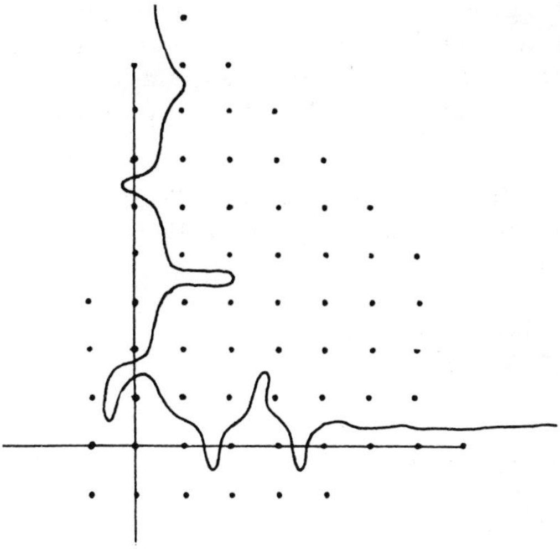

Figure 4.3

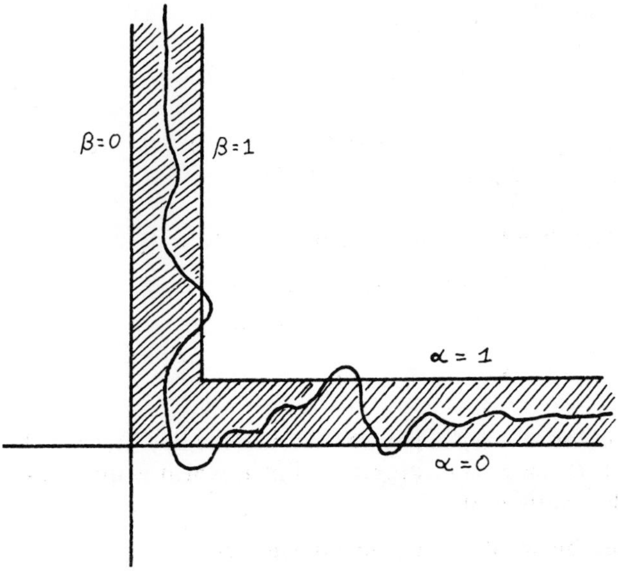

Figure 4.4

It seems plausible that a generalization of Bézout's theorem could be formulated to deduce from this that the curve must enter the negative halves in a sense that would furnish an immediate and more illuminating proof of our lemma. We have not pursued this conjecture.

Lemma 3: If a polynomial $P(x,y,z)$ satisfies the following conditions for all positive integral values of x, y, and z, then it is identically zero:

$$x > z \text{ AND } y > z \quad \text{implies} \quad P(x,y,z) \geq 0,$$
$$x \leq z \text{ OR } \; y \leq z \quad \text{implies} \quad P(x,y,z) \leq 0.$$

PROOF: Suppose that $P(x,y,z)$ had these properties, but were not identically zero. Define $Q(\alpha,\beta,z) \equiv P(z+\alpha, z+\beta, z)$ and write

$$Q(\alpha,\beta,z) = z^M f(\alpha,\beta) + r(\alpha,\beta,z),$$

where r is of degree less than M in z, and $f(\alpha,\beta)$ is not identically zero. Then we can show that f must satisfy the conditions in Lemma 2: Choose any α_0 and β_0 for which $f(\alpha_0,\beta_0) \neq 0$. Choose a z_0 so large that

$$z_0 + \alpha_0 > 0, \quad z_0 + \beta_0 > 0, \quad \text{and} \quad |z_0^M f(\alpha_0,\beta_0)| > |r(\alpha_0,\beta_0,z_0)|.$$

It follows that $f(\alpha_0,\beta_0) \geq 0 \Leftrightarrow Q(\alpha_0,\beta_0,z_0) \geq 0$, that is, if and only if $P(z_0+\alpha_0, z_0+\beta_0, z_0) \geq 0$. Thus

$$\begin{aligned}
\alpha_0 > 0 \text{ AND } \beta_0 > 0 &\Rightarrow z_0 + \alpha_0 > z_0 \text{ and } z_0 + \beta_0 > z_0 \\
&\Rightarrow P(z_0+\alpha_0, z_0+\beta_0, z_0) \geq 0 \\
&\Rightarrow f(\alpha_0,\beta_0) \geq 0, \text{ and similarly,} \\
\alpha_0 < 0 \text{ OR } \; \beta_0 < 0 &\Rightarrow f(\alpha_0,\beta_0) \leq 0.
\end{aligned}$$

But this is true for all α_0, β_0. Thus by the Lemma 2, $f(\alpha,\beta) \equiv 0$. It follows that $Q(x,y,z)$ is of degree zero in z, which is only possible if P is identically zero.

This concludes the proof of the And/Or Theorem.

GEOMETRIC THEORY OF LINEAR INEQUALITIES

II

Introduction to Part II

The analysis of geometric properties of perceptrons begins, in Chapter 5, with the study of the predicate $\psi_{\text{CONNECTED}}$: Is the figure X all connected together in the sense that between any two points of figure there is a continuous path that lies entirely within the figure (see §0.5)? We chose to investigate *connectedness* because of a belief that this predicate is nonlocal in some very deep sense; therefore it should present a serious challenge to any basically local, parallel type of computation. Originally, we tried to prove that $\psi_{\text{CONNECTED}}$ is not of finite order by exploiting its sensitivity to small changes in X—any connected figure is easily converted to a disconnected figure by making a thin cut or by adding an isolated point—but we were unable to convert this to a real proof.

The successful methods were based on using the group-invariance theorem, but indirectly. We recall that in dealing with ψ_{PARITY} we began by identifying the largest possible group of transformations of R that leaves ψ invariant—in the case of ψ_{PARITY} the group of all permutations. We then used this group to coalesce the φ's into equivalence classes, and eventually reduced the problem about representing ψ in $L(\Phi)$ to a problem about polynomials in enumeration functions.

But in the case of $\psi_{\text{CONNECTED}}$, we find that any attempt to apply this technique *directly* leads to severe problems associated with the representation of a general topological transformation on a discrete retina. Fortunately, it was possible to "reduce" the problem to a simple one involving more tractable groups. In fact, we see in §5.1 that if a perceptron could discriminate between just certain restricted instances of connectedness, then it could be made to simulate the "one-in-a-box" predicate of §3.2. If this were possible, we would have, logically:

$$\begin{aligned}\psi_{\text{CONNECTED}} \text{ is finite order } &\Rightarrow \psi_{\text{CONNECTED}\,|\,\text{RESTRICTED}} \text{ is finite order}\\ &\Rightarrow \psi_{\text{ONE-IN-A-BOX}} \text{ is finite order,}\end{aligned}$$

and since the last is false, so is the first.

Toward the end of Chapter 5, this firmly negative result—that $\psi_{\text{CONNECTED}}$ is not of finite order—is generalized to show that the same is true of all *topological* predicates, with one single type of exception. Only the *Euler number*, the lowest and simplest of all

For those readers interested in theories of perception, and those concerned with practical applications, the (negative) results in §6.6 deserve much more emphasis.

the topological invariants, can be recognized by the finite-order predicate-scheme.

In Chapter 6 we obtain a series of positive results. There are a variety of geometric properties, in addition to ψ_{CONVEX} and ψ_{CIRCLE} mentioned in §0.5, that are quite clearly of finite (and in fact of rather low) order. These include particular forms like *triangles* or *squares* or letters of the alphabet. From some of these a type of description emerges that we call "geometric spectra." These can be regarded either as local geometric properties or as simple statistical qualities of the patterns. The fact that perceptrons can recognize certain patterns related to these spectra is probably responsible for some of the false optimism about the capabilities of perceptrons in general. At the end of Chapter 6 we see that while these patterns can be identified in isolation, the perceptron cannot detect them in more complicated contexts.

Chapter 7 is a curious detour. It turns out that certain predicates that do not seem at first to have finite order—such as *symmetries*, or *similarities between pairs of figures*—can in fact be realized by finite-order predicate-schemes. But the realizations have a peculiar unreality, for their coefficients grow at such astronomical rates as to be physically meaningless. The incident seems to have an important moral; even within a simple combinatorial subject such as this, one must be on guard for nonobvious codes or representations of things. The linear forms obtained by the "stratification" method of Chapter 7 have a quality somewhat like the Gödel numbers of logic, or the "nonstandard models" of mathematical analysis. Our intuition is still weak in the field of computation, and there are surely many more surprises to come.

We study the diameter-limited perceptron in Chapter 8. Here the situation is much simpler, and one does not even need the algebraic theory to obtain generally negative results. For the most part, it turns out that the diameter-limited machines are subject to limitations similar to those of the order-1 machines. In certain respects they seem different: for example, in their ability to approximate certain integral-like computations. This makes it possible for them to recognize ψ_{CIRCLE} within some accuracy limitations. And, they can compute a narrowly limited class of predicates related to the Euler number.

The predicate $\psi_{\text{CONNECTED}}$ seemed so important in this study that we felt it appropriate to try to relate the perceptron's performance to that of some other, fundamentally different, computation schemes. In Chapter 9 we study it in the context of a wide variety of models for geometric computation. We were surprised to find that, for serial computers, only a very small amount of memory was required. One might have supposed that something like a "push-down list" would be needed so that the machine could retrace its steps in the course of exploring the maze of possible paths through a figure.

Representing Geometrical Patterns

We are about to study a number of interesting geometrical predicates. But as a first step, we have to provide the underlying space R with the topological and metric properties necessary for defining geometrical figures; this was not necessary in the case of predicates like parity and others related to counting, for these were not really geometric in character.

The simplest procedure that is rigorous enough yet not too mathematically fussy seems to be to divide the Euclidean plane, E^2, into squares, as an infinite chess board. The set R is then taken as *the set of squares*. A figure X_E of E^2 is then identified with the squares that contain at least one point of X_E. Thus to any subset X_E of E^2 corresponds the subset X of R defined by

$x \in X$ *if at least one point of* X_E *lies in the square* x.

Now, although X and X_E are logically distinct no serious confusion can arise if we identify them, and we shall do so from now on. Thus we refer to certain subsets of R as "circles," "triangles," etc., meaning that they can be obtained from real circles and triangles by the map $X_E \rightarrow X$. Of course, this means that near the "limits of resolution" one begins to obtain apparent errors of classification because of the finite "mesh" of R. Thus a small circle will not look very round.

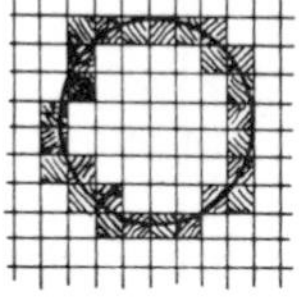

If it were necessary to distinguish between E^2 and R we would say that two figures X_E, X'_E of E^2 are in the same *R-tolerance* class if $X = X'$. There is no problem with the *translation* groups that play the main roles in Chapters 6, 7, and 8. There is a serious problem of handling the tolerances when discussing, as in §7.6, *dilations* or *rotations*. Curiously, the problem does not seem to arise in discussing general topological equivalence, in Chapter 5, because we can prove all the theorems we know by using less than the full group of topological transformations.

$\psi_{\text{CONNECTED}}$: A Geometric Property with Unbounded Order

5

5.0 Introduction

In this chapter we begin the study of *connectedness*. A figure X is *connected* if it is not composed of two or more separate, non-touching, parts. While it is interesting in itself, we chose to study the connectedness property especially because we hoped it would shed light on the more basic, though ill-defined, question of *local* vs. *global* property. For connectedness is surely global. One can never conclude that a figure is connected from isolated local experiments. To be sure, in the case of a figure like

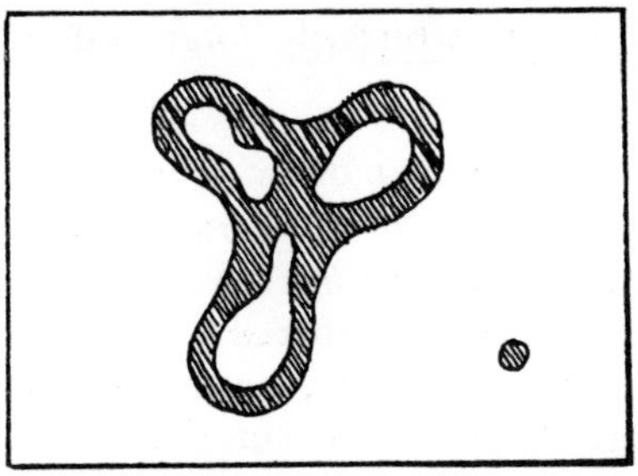

one would discover, by looking locally at the neighborhood of the isolated point in the lower right corner, that the figure is *not* connected. But one could not conclude that a figure *is* connected, from the absence of any such local evidence of disconnectivity. If we ask which one of these two figures is connected

Figure 5.1

it is difficult to imagine any local event that could bias a decision toward one conclusion or the other. Now, this is easy to *prove*, for example, in the narrow framework of the *diameter-limited* concept of *local* (see §0.3 and Chapter 8). It is harder to establish for the order-limited framework. But the diameter-limited case gives us a hint: by considering a particular subclass of figures we might be able to show that the problem is equivalent to that of recognizing a *parity*, or something like it, and this is what we in fact shall do.

5.1* The Connectedness Theorem

Two points of R are *adjacent* if they are squares with a common edge.† A figure is **connected** if, given any two points (that is, "squares") p_1, p_2 of the figure, we can find a path in the figure through adjacent points from p_1 to p_2.

Theorem 5.1: The predicate $\psi_{\text{CONNECTED}}(X) = \lceil X \text{ is connected}\rceil$ is not of finite order (§1.6), that is, it has arbitrarily large orders as $|R|$ grows in size.

PROOF: Suppose that $\psi_{\text{CONNECTED}}(X)$ could have order $< m$. Consider an array of squares of R arranged in $2m + 1$ rows of $4m^2$ squares each (Figure 5.2). Let Y_0 be the set of points shaded in the diagram, that is, the array of points in odd-numbered rows, and let Y_1 be the remaining squares of the array. Let **F** be the family of figures obtained from the figure Y_0 by adding subsets of Y_1,

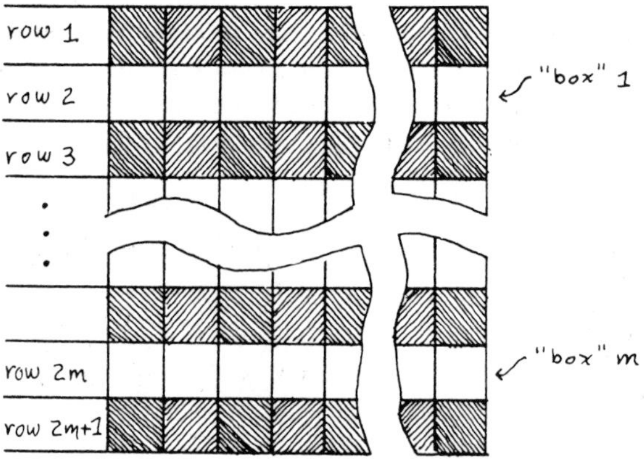

Figure 5.2

*We will give two other proofs from different points of view. The proof in §5.5 is probably the easiest to understand by itself, but the proof in §5.7 gives more information about the way the order grows with the size of R.

†We can't allow corner contact, as in , to be considered as connection. For this would allow two "curves" to cross without "intersecting"—and not even the Jordan curve theorem would be true. The problem could be avoided by dividing E^2 into hexagons instead of squares!

that is, $X \in \mathbf{F}$ if it is of the form $Y_0 \cup X_1$, where $X_1 \subset Y_1$. Now X will be connected if and only if X_1 contains at least one square from each even row; that is, if the set X_1 satisfies the "one-in-a-box" condition of §3.2.

To see the details of how the one-in-a-box theorem is applied, if it is not already clear, consider the figures of family **F** as a subset of all possible figures on R. Clearly, if we had an order-k predicate $\psi^k_{\text{CONNECTED}}$ that could recognize connectivity on R, we could have one that works on **F**; namely the same predicate with constant zero values to all variables not in $Y_0 \cup Y_1$. And since all points of the odd rows have always value 1 for figures in **F**, this in turn means that we could have an order-k predicate to decide the one-in-a-box property on set Y_1; namely the same predicate further restricted to having constant unity values to the points in Y_0. Thus each Boolean function of the original predicate $\psi^k_{\text{CONNECTED}}$ is replaced by the function obtained by fixing certain of its variables to zero and to one; this operation can never increase the order of a function. But since this last predicate cannot exist, neither can the original $\psi^k_{\text{CONNECTED}}$. This proof shows that $\psi_{\text{CONNECTED}}$ has order at least $C\,|R|^{1/3}$. In §5.7 we show it is at least $C\,|R|^{1/2}$.

5.2 An Example

Consider the special case for $k = 2$, and the equivalent one-in-a-box problem for a space of the form

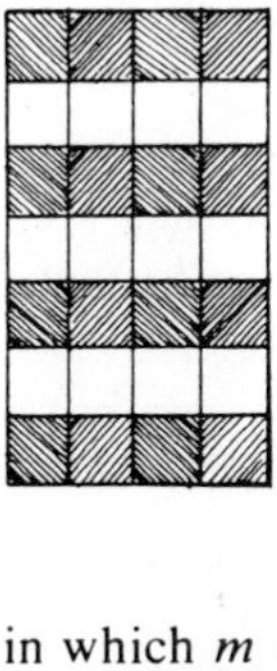

in which $m = 3$ and there are just 4 squares in each box. Now consider a ψ of degree 2; we will show that it cannot characterize the connectedness of pictures of this kind. Suppose that $\psi = \lceil \Sigma \alpha_i \varphi_i > \theta \rceil$ and consider the equivalent form, symmetrized under the full group of permutations that interchange the rows *and* permute within rows.* Then there are just three equivalence-classes of masks of degree ≤ 2, namely:

Single points: $\varphi_i^1 = x_i$,
Point-pairs: $\varphi_{ij}^{11} = x_i x_j$ (x_i and x_j in same row),
Point-pairs: $\varphi_{ij}^{12} = x_i x_j$ (x_i and x_j in different rows).

Hence any order-2 predicate must have the form

$$\psi = \lceil \alpha_1 N_1(X) + \alpha_{11} N_{11}(X) + \alpha_{12} N_{12}(X) > \theta \rceil$$

where N_1, N_{11}, and N_{12} are the numbers of point sets of the respective types in the figure X. Now consider the two figures:

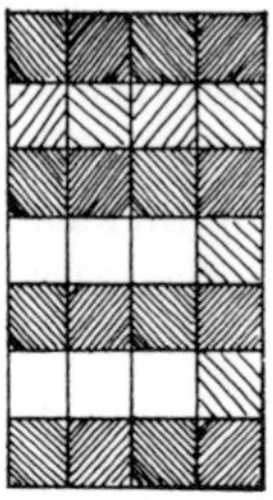

$\psi_{\text{CONNECTED}}(X_1) = 1$

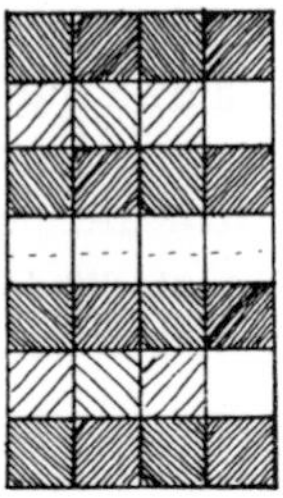

$\psi_{\text{CONNECTED}}(X_2) = 0$

In each case one counts

$$N_1 = 6, \qquad N_{11} = 6, \qquad N_{12} = 9;$$

hence ψ has the same value for both figures. But X_1 is connected while X_2 is not! Note that here $m = 3$ so that we obtain a contradiction with $|A_i| = 4$, while the general proof required $|A_i| = 4m^2 = 36$. The same is true with $|A_i| = 3$, $m = 4$, because $(3, 1, 1, 1) \cong (2, 2, 2, 0)$. It is also known that if $m = 6$, we can get a similar result with $|A_i| = 16$. This was shown by Dona Strauss.

The case of $m = 3$, $|A_i| = 3$ *is* of order 2, since one can write

$$\psi_{\text{CONNECTED}} = \lceil 3N_1(X) - 2N_{11}(X) > 8 \rceil.$$

*Note that this is not the same group used in proving Theorem §3.2. There we did not use the row-interchange part of the group.

The proof method used in these examples is an instance of the use of what we call the "geometric n-tuple spectrum," and the general principle is further developed in Chapter 6.

5.3 Slice-wise Connectivity

It should be observed that the proof in §5.1 applies not only to the property of connectivity in its classical sense but to the stronger predicate defined by:

⌈*There is a straight line L such that X does not intersect L and does not lie entirely to one side of L*⌉.

The general definition of connectedness would have "curve" for L instead of "straight line," and one would expect that this would require a higher order for its realization.

5.4 Reduction of One Perceptron to Another

In proving that $\psi_{\text{CONNECTED}}$ is not of finite order, our approach was first to prove this about a different (and simpler) predicate $\psi_{\text{ONE-IN-A-BOX}}$. Then we showed that $\psi_{\text{CONNECTED}}$ could be used, *on a certain subset of figures*, to compute $\psi_{\text{ONE-IN-A-BOX}}$: therefore its order must be at least as high. There are, of course, many other figures that $\psi_{\text{CONNECTED}}$ will have to classify (in addition to those that contain all points of Y_0 in §5.1), but it was sufficient to study the predicates' behavior just on this subclass of figures.

We will use this idea again, many times, but the situation will be slightly more complicated. In the case just discussed, both predicates were defined on figures in the *same* retina, but in the sequel, we will often want to establish a relation between two predicates defined on different spaces. The flexibility to do this is established by the following simple theorem.

5.4.1 The Collapsing Theorem

This theorem will enable us to deduce limits on the order of a predicate ψ on a set R from information about the order of a related predicate $\hat{\psi}$ on a set $\hat{R}$.

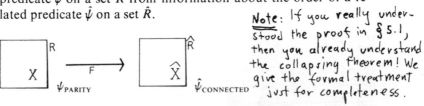

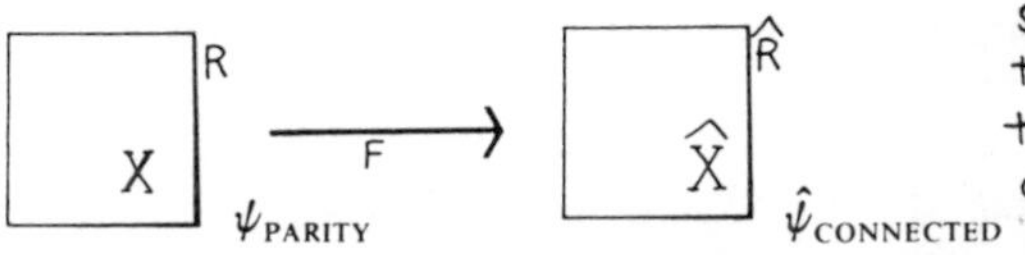

Note: If you really understood the proof in §5.1, then you already understand the collapsing theorem! We give the formal treatment just for completeness.

Let F be a function that associates with any figure X in R, a figure $\hat{X} = F(X)$ in $\hat{R}$. Now let $\hat{\psi}$ be any predicate on $\hat{R}$. This predicate *defines* a predicate ψ on R by the computation

$$\psi(X) = \hat{\psi}(F(X)) = \hat{\psi}(\hat{X}).$$

Theorem 5.4.1: *The order of $\hat{\psi}$ is $\geq$ the order of ψ, provided that each point of $\hat{R}$ depends upon at most one point of R*, in the sense that for each point $\hat{x}$ of $\hat{R}$, either it has a constant value

$\hat{x} \in \hat{X}$ for all X, or

$\hat{x} \notin \hat{X}$ for all X,

or else there is a point x such that either

$\lceil x \in X \rceil \equiv \lceil \hat{x} \in \hat{X} \rceil$ for all X, or

$\lceil x \in X \rceil \equiv \lceil \hat{x} \notin \hat{X} \rceil$ for all X

PROOF: Suppose that $\hat{\psi}$ has a realization of order K:

$$\lceil \Sigma \alpha_i \hat{\varphi}_i > \theta \rceil.$$

Then ψ has a realization

$$\lceil \Sigma \alpha_i \varphi_i > \theta \rceil$$

where $\varphi_i(X)$ is $\hat{\varphi}_i(F(X))$. To see that $|S(\varphi_i)| \leq K$, recall that $\hat{\varphi}_i$ depends on at most K points of $\hat{R}$, and these in turn depend on at most K points of R. So $\varphi_i(X) = \hat{\varphi}_i(F(X))$ depends on at most K points of R.

Example: A typical application of this construction is illustrated as follows (see Figure 5.3). The set R has three points (x_1, x_2, x_3).

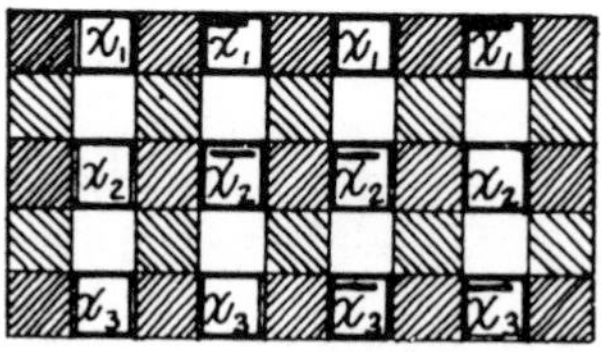

Figure 5.3

The set $\hat{R}$ has 45 points. In the diagram, these fall into three classes: 8 points shown as white, 25 points shown as black, and 12 points labeled x_i or $\bar{x}_i$. F is defined in the following way: Given a set X, in R, $F(X)$ must contain *all* the black squares, *no* white squares, the squares labeled x_i only if $x_i \in X$, and the squares labeled $\bar{x}_i$ only if $x_i \notin X$.

5.5 Huffman's Construction for $\psi_{\text{CONNECTED}}$

We shall illustrate the application of the preceding concept by giving an alternative proof that $\psi_{\text{CONNECTED}}$ has no finite order, based on a construction suggested to us by D. Huffman.

The intuitive idea is to construct a switching network that will be connected if an odd number of its n switches are in the "on" position. Thus the connectedness problem is reduced to the parity problem. Such a network is shown in Figure 5.3 for $n = 3$. The interpretation of the symbols x_i and $\bar{x}_i$ is as follows: when x_i is in the "on" position contact is made wherever x_i appears, and broken wherever $\bar{x}_i$ appears; when x_i is in the "off" position contact is made where $\bar{x}_i$ appears and broken where x_i appears. It is easy to see that the whole net is connected in the electrical and topological sense if the number of switches in the "on" position is 1 or 3. The generalization to n is obvious:

1. List the terms in the conjunctive normal form for ψ_{PARITY} considered as a point function, which in the present case can be written

$$(x_1 \vee x_2 \vee x_3) \wedge (\bar{x}_1 \vee \bar{x}_2 \vee x_3) \wedge (x_1 \vee \bar{x}_2 \vee \bar{x}_3) \wedge (\bar{x}_1 \vee x_2 \vee \bar{x}_3)$$

2. Translate this Boolean expression into a switching net by interpreting conjunction as series coupling and disjunction as parallel coupling.

3. Construct a perceptron which "looks at" the position of the switches.

The reduction argument in intuitive form is as follows: the Huffman switching net can be regarded as defining a class **F** of geometric figures which are connected or not depending on the parity of a certain set, the set of switches that are in "on" position. We thus see how a perceptron for $\psi_{\text{CONNECTED}}$ on one set $\hat{R}$ can be used as a perceptron for ψ_{PARITY} on a second set R. As a perceptron for ψ_{PARITY}, it must be of order at least

$|R|$. Thus the order of $\psi_{\text{CONNECTED}}$ must be of order $|R|$. We can use the collapsing theorem §5.4.1 to formalize this argument. But before doing so note that a certain price will be paid for its intuitive simplicity: the set $\hat{R}$ is much bigger than the set R; in fact $|\hat{R}|$ must be of the order of magnitude of $2^{|R|}$, so that the best result to be obtained from the construction is that the order of $\psi_{\text{CONNECTED}}$ must increase as $\log |\hat{R}|$. This gives a weaker lower bound than was found in §5.1: $\log |\hat{R}|$ compared with $|\hat{R}|^{1/3}$.

To apply the collapsing theorem we simply define the space R to be the three-point space R described at the end of §5.4. Then ψ_{PARITY} on R is equal to $\psi_{\text{CONNECTED}}$ on $\hat{R}$ for those figures obtained by applying F to figures on R. The collapsing theorem states that the order of ψ_{PARITY} is $\leq$ the order of $\psi_{\text{CONNECTED}}$.

5.6 Connectivity on a Toroidal Space $|R|$

Our earliest attempts to prove that connectedness has unbounded order led to the following curious result:

Theorem 5.6: The predicate $\psi_{\text{CONNECTED}}$ on a $2n \times 6$ toroidally connected space has order $\geq n$.

The proof is by construction: consider the space

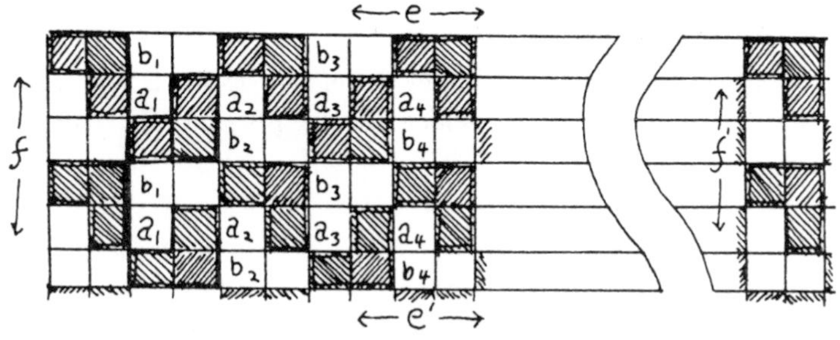

in which the edges e, e' and f, f' are considered to be identical (see also Figure 2.5). Now consider the family **F** of subsets of R that satisfy the conditions

1. All the shaded points belong to each $X \in$ **F**,

2. For each $X \in$ **F** and each i, either both points marked a_i or both points b_i are in **F**, but no other combinations are allowed.

Then it can be seen, for each $X \in$ **F**, that X has either one connected component or X divides into two separate connected figures. Which case actually occurs depends only on the parity of the number of a_i's in X. Then using the collapsing theorem and Theorem §3.1.1, we find that $\psi_{\text{CONNECTED}}$ has order $\geq \frac{1}{12}|R|$.

The idea for Theorem 5.6 came from the attempt to reduce *connectivity* to *parity* directly by representing the switching diagram shown in Figure 5.4. If an even number of switches are in the "down" position then x is connected to x' and y to y'. If the number of down switches is odd, x is connected to y' and x' to y. This diagram can be drawn in the plane by bringing the vertical connections around the end (see Figure 5.11); then one finds that the predicate $\lceil x$ is connected to $x'\rceil$ has for order some

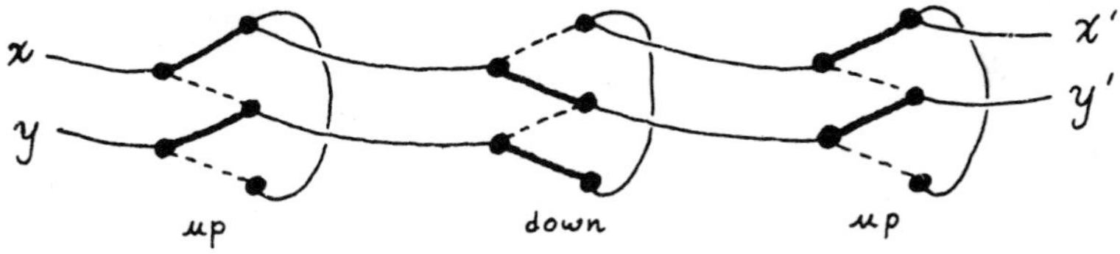

Figure 5.4

constant multiple of $|R|^{1/2}$. If we put the toroidal topology on R, the order is known (§5.6) to be greater than a constant fraction of $|R|$; this is also true for a 3-dimensional Euclidean R. These facts strongly suggest that our bound for the order of $\psi_{\text{CONNECTED}}$ is too low for the plane case.

5.7 A Better Bound for $\psi_{\text{CONNECTED}}$ in the Plane

The following construction shows that the order of $\psi_{\text{CONNECTED}}$ is $\geq$ CONST $\cdot\,(|R|^{1/2})$ for two-dimensional figures. It results from modifying Figure 5.4 so as to connect x to x'. This is easy for the torus, but for a long time we thought it was impossible in the plane.

We first define a "4-switch" to be the pair of figures

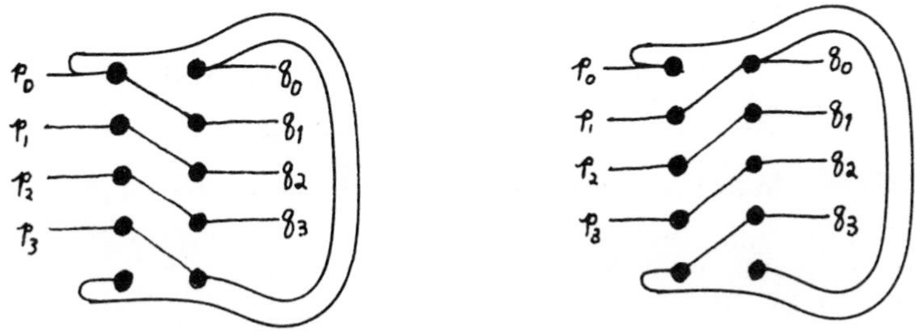

Figure 5.5

In the *down* state, one can see that

p_i is connected to $q_{(i+1)_4}$,

where $(j)_4$ is the remainder when j is divided by 4. In the *up* state, we have

p_i is connected to $q_{(i-1)_4}$.

Now consider the effect of cascading n such switches, as shown in Figure 5.6.

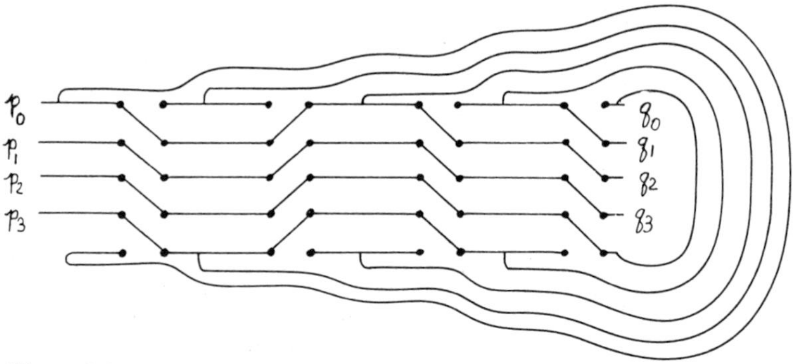

Figure 5.6

This simply iterates the effect: in fact, if d switches are *down* and u switches are *up*, we have

p_i is connected to $q_{(i+d-u)_4}$

for all i. Now, since every switch is either *up* or *down*,

$d + u = n$, hence

$q_{(i+d-u)_4} = q_{(i+2d-n)_4}$,

and we notice that this depends only upon the parity of d. ~~For $(x + 2(d + 2))_4 = (x + 2d + 4)_4 = (x + 2d)_4$.~~

Next, we add fixed connections that tie together the terminals

$q_{(1-n)_4}$, $q_{(2-n)_4}$, and $q_{(3-n)_4}$.

Then if d is even, p_1, p_2, p_3 are tied together

while if d is odd, p_3, p_0, p_1 are tied together.

In each case p_1 and p_3 are connected, so we can ignore, say, p_3. So the connectivity of the system has just two states, depending on the parity of the number of switches in *down* position, and these states can be represented as shown below.

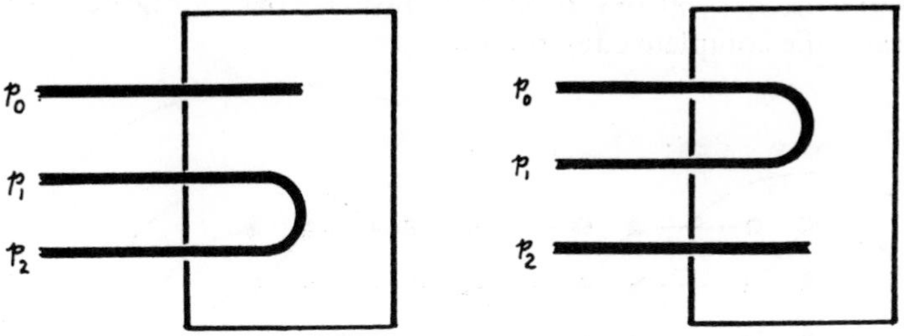

Figure 5.7

To prove our theorem we simply tie p_1 and p_2 together.

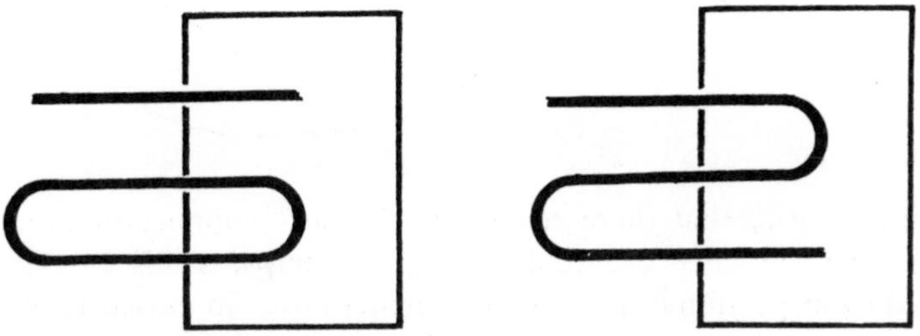

Figure 5.8

It remains only to realize the details of the "4-switches." Figure 5.9 illustrates the two configurations.

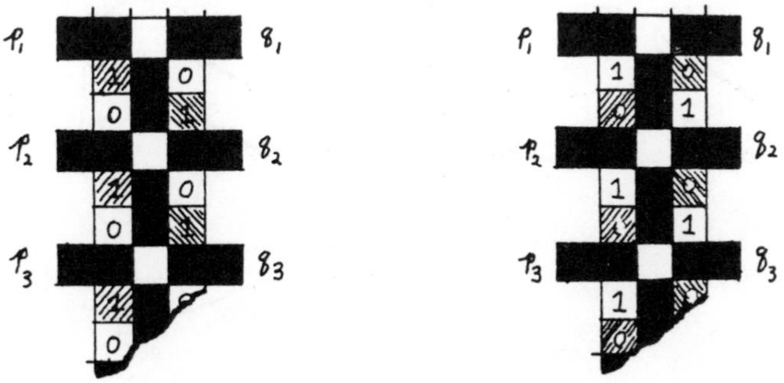

Figure 5.9

Remember that  is not a connection. When the entire construction is completed for n switches, the network will be about $5n$ squares long and about $2n + 12$ squares high, so that the number of switches can grow proportionally to $|R|^{1/2}$. It follows that the order of $\psi_{\text{CONNECTED}}$ grows at least as fast as $|R|^{1/2}$. Figure 5.10 illustrates the complete construction.

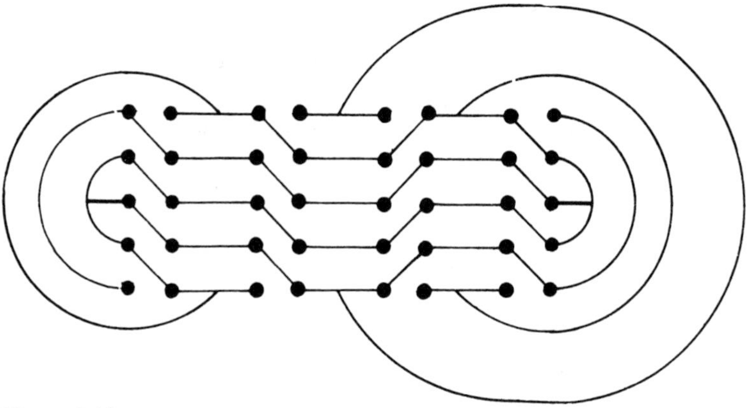

Figure 5.10

One must verify that there remain no "stray" connection lines that are not attached eventually to p_0, p_1, or p_2. This can be verified by inspection of Figure 5.6. Furthermore, no closed loops are formed, other than the one indicated in left-hand part of Figure 5.8.

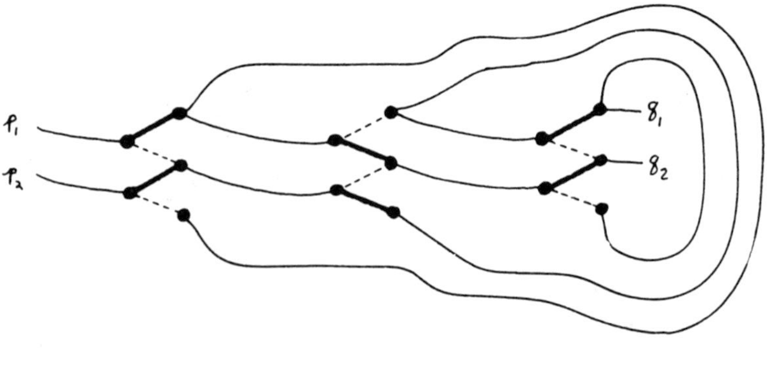

Figure 5.11

The idea for Theorem 5.7 comes from observing that in the planar version of Figure 5.4 (see Figure 5.11) we have $p_1 \leftrightarrow q_1$ and $p_2 \leftrightarrow q_2$ for one parity and $p_1 \leftrightarrow q_2$ and $p_2 \leftrightarrow q_1$ for the other. If we could make a permanent additional direct connection from p_1 to q_1 then the whole net would be connected or disconnected according to the parity. But this is topologically impossible, and because the construction appeared incompleteable we took the long route through proving and applying the one-in-a-box theorem. Only later did we realize that the $p_1 \leftrightarrow q_1$ connection could be made "dynamically," if not directly, by the construction in Figure 5.10.

5.7.2 The Order of $\psi_{\text{CONNECTED}}$ as a Function of $|R|$

What is the true order? Let us recall that at the root of the proof methods we used was the device (§5.0) of considering not all the figures but only special subclasses with special combinatorial features. Thus even the order $\frac{1}{12}|R|$ of §5.6 is only a lower bound. Our suspicion is that the order cannot be less than $\frac{1}{2}|R|$. As for the number of φ's required, Theorem 3.1.2 and the toroidal results give us $\geq 2^{|R|/12}$, but this too, is only a lower bound, and one suspects that nearly all the masks are needed. Another line of thought suggests that one might get by with an order like the logarithm of the number of connected figures, but that has probably not much smaller an exponent.

Examination of the toroidal construction in §5.6 might make one suspect that the result, $\psi_{\text{CONNECTED}} \geq \frac{1}{12}|R|$ is an artifact resulting from the use of a long, thin torus. Indeed, for a "square" torus we could not get this result because of the area that would be covered by the connecting bridge lines. This clouds the conclusion a little. On the other hand, if we consider a *three*-dimensional R, then there is absolutely no difficulty in showing that $\psi_{\text{CONNECTED}} \geq (1/K)\ |R|$, for some moderate value of K. It is hard to believe that the difference in dimension could matter very much.

5.8 Topological Predicates

We have seen that $\lceil X$ is connected$\rceil$ is not of finite order and we shall see soon that $\lceil X$ contains a hole$\rceil$ is also not of finite order. ~~Curiously enough the predicate~~

~~$\lceil X$ is connected OR X contains a hole$\rceil$~~

Not quite true, but see p. 89.

~~has finite order, even though neither disjunct does—an instance of the opposite of the And/Or phenomenon.~~ This will be shown by a construction involving the Euler relation for orientable geometric figures.

5.8.1 The Euler Polygon Formula

Two-dimensional figures have a topological invariant* that in polygonal cases is given by

$$B(X) = |\text{faces}(X)| - |\text{edges}(X)| + |\text{vertices}(X)|.$$

The sums under the examples in Figure 5.12 illustrate this formula by counting the number of faces, edges, and vertices, respectively. Use of the formula presupposes that a figure is cut into sufficiently small pieces that each "face" be *simple*—that is, contain no holes. It is a remarkable fact that $B(X)$ will have the same value for any dissection of X that meets this condition.

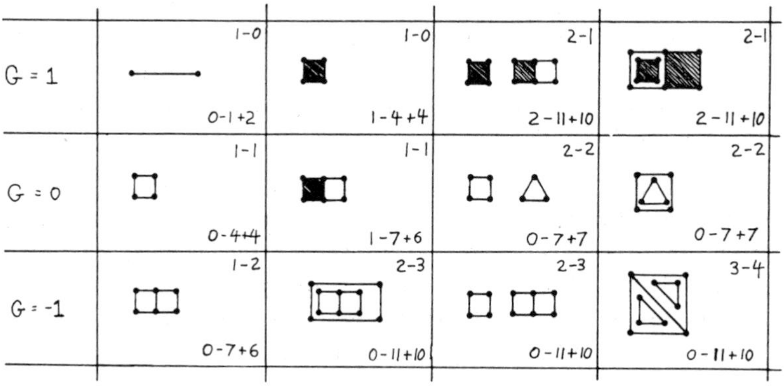

Figure 5.12

In our context of figures made up of checkerboard squares, $B(X)$ can be computed by a low-order linear sum $G(X)$ defined as follows:

$$G(X) = \Sigma\alpha_i x_i + \Sigma\alpha_{ij} x_i x_j + \Sigma\alpha_{ijkl} x_i x_j x_k x_l, \text{ where}$$

*For our purposes here, a "topological invariant" is nothing more than a predicate that is unchanged when the figure is distorted without changing connectedness or inside-outside relations of its parts.

$\alpha_i = 1$ for each point  of R, **vertices**

$\alpha_{ij} = -1$ for each adjacent pair  or , **edges**

$\alpha_{ijkl} = 1$ for each square 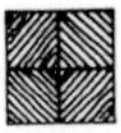, **faces**

$G(X)$ and $B(X)$ exactly agree on checkerboard figures without corner contacts like  . When they disagree in such cases, our definition of connectedness requires the value of $G(X)$.

The importance of $G(X)$ in our theory lies in the fact that although it is highly *local*—in fact, diameter limited and finite order—it is equivalent to the global formula

$$E(X) = |components\,(X)| - |holes\,(X)|.$$

A **component** of a figure is the set of all points connected to a given point.
A **hole** of a figure is a component of the complement of a figure. We assume that a figure is surrounded by an "outside" that does not count as a hole. Also, we have to define "corner contact" to be a connection, when dealing with a figure's complement.

Now we will prove that the local formula $G(X)$ and the global formula $E(X)$ are equivalent. First we will give a rather direct demonstration. Then in §5.8.2 we will give another kind of proof, based on deforming one figure into another, that will give a better insight into the proof of the main theorem of §5.9.

Any figure X can be obtained by beginning with a one-square figure and adding squares one at a time. For a single square we have

$$G(X) = E(X) = 1.$$

Adding a square that is not adjacent to any square already in X adds 1 to $G(X)$, and (since it is a new component!) adds 1 to $E(X)$.

Adding a square adjacent to exactly one other square cannot change $E(X)$, and adds exactly $0 - 1 + 1 = 0$ to $G(X)$.

Three kinds of things can happen when one adds a square adjacent to *two* others. When the new square fills in a corner, as in

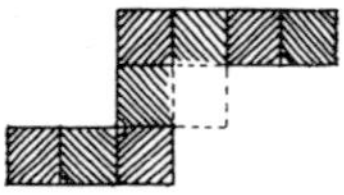

then $1 - 2 + 1 = 0$ is added to G, leaving it unchanged, and neither is $E(X)$ changed in this case. But when the new square connects two others that were *not* already connected together, as in

or

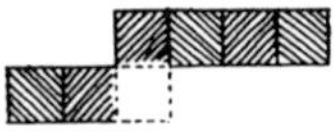

then there is a net decrease of $1 - 2 + 0 = -1$ in G together with a decrease in $E(X)$, because we have joined two previously separated parts. Finally, if the added square connects two squares that are already connected by some remote path, as in,

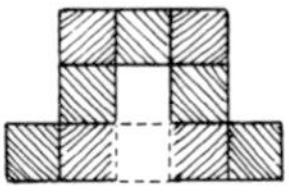

or

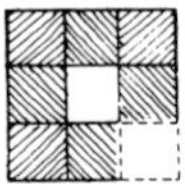

then a region of space is cut off—a hole is formed, decreasing E by 1 and again the change in G is $1 - 2 + 0 = -1$. Case analyses of the 3-neighbor and 4-neighbor situations complete the proof: these include partial fills like

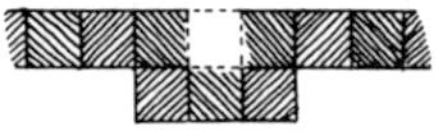

or

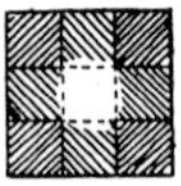

which add $1 - 3 + 2 = 0$ and $1 - 4 + 4 = 1$. Notice that in the latter case, G is increased by one unit, as the hole is finally filled-in. *In each case either G was unchanged, or the topology of the figure X was changed.* (All this corresponds to an argument in algebraic topology concerning addition of edges and cells to chain-complexes.) This proves

Theorem 5.8.1: $E(X) = G(X)$. It follows immediately that the predicate $\lceil G(X) < n \rceil$ is realized with order ≤ 4. This leads to some curious observations: If we are *given* that the figures X are restricted to the connected (= one-component) figures then an order-4 machine can recognize

$$\lceil X \text{ has no holes} \rceil = \lceil G(X) > 0 \rceil$$

or

$$\lceil X \text{ has less than 3 holes} \rceil = \lceil G(X) > -2 \rceil.$$

Similarly, given that there are no holes, we can recognize $\psi_{\text{CONNECTED}}$!

But of course we cannot conclude that these can be recognized *unconditionally* by a finite-order perceptron.

Note that this topological invariant is thus seen to be highly "local" in nature—indeed all the φ's satisfy a very tight diameter-limitation! Now returning to our initial claim we note that

$$\lceil G(X) = n \rceil \equiv (\lceil G(X) \leq n \rceil \equiv \lceil G(X) \geq n \rceil).$$

By Theorem 1.5.4 we can conclude that $\lceil G(X) = N \rceil$ has order $\leq$ 8. But the proof of that theorem involves constructing product-φ's that are *not* diameter-limited, and we show §8.4 that this predicate cannot be realized by diameter-limited perceptrons.

5.8.2 Deformation of Figures into Standard Forms

The proof of Theorem §5.8.1 shows that $G(X)$ will take the same values on any two figures X and Y that have the same value of $E = |\text{components}| - |\text{holes}|$. Now we will show that one can make a sequence of figures $X, \ldots, X_i, \ldots, Y$, each differing from its predecessor in one locality, and all having the same values for $G = E$. It is easy to see how to deform figures "smoothly" without changing G or E, in fact, without changing holes or components. For example, the sequence

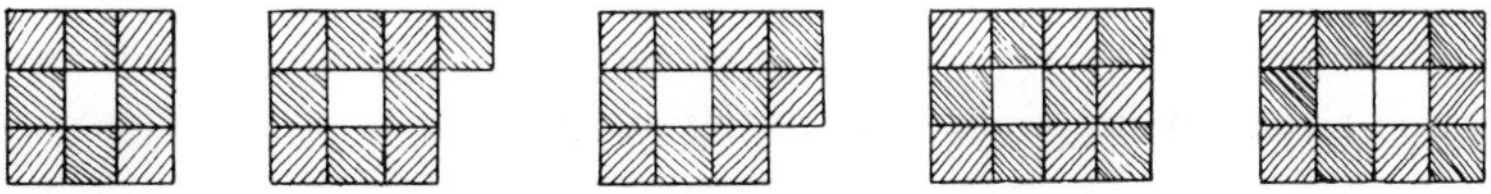

can be used to enlarge a hole. Now we observe that if a component C_0 lies within a hole H_1 of another component C_1, then C_0 can be moved to the outside without changing $E(X)$ or $G(X)$. Suppose, for simplicity, that C_1 touches the "outside" and that C_0 is "simply" in H_1; that is, there is no component C' also enclosing C_0

Then C_0 can be removed from H_1 by a series of deformations in which, first, H_1 is drawn to the periphery

and then C_0 is temporarily attached:

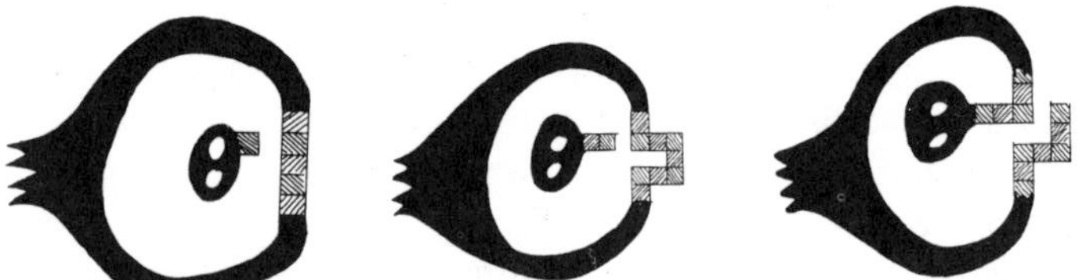

Notice that this does not change the value of $G(X)$. Also, since it reduces both C and H by unity, it does not change $E(X) = C(X) - H(X)$.

We can then swing C_1 around to the outside

and reconnect to obtain

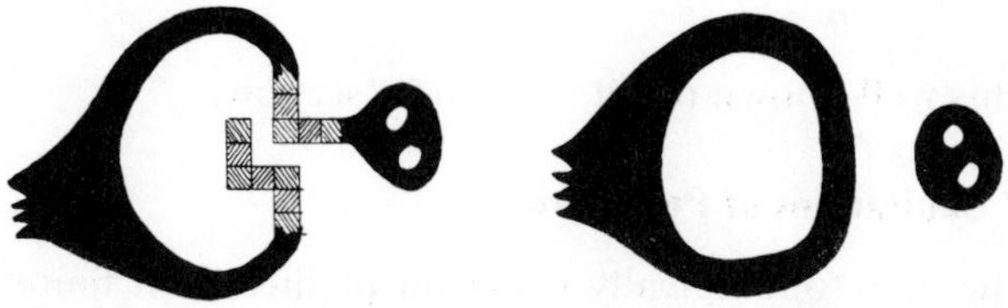

again without changing $G(X)$ or $E(X)$. Clearly, we can eventually clear out *all* holes, by repeating this on each component as it comes to the outside. When this is done, we will have some number of components, each of which may have some empty holes, and they can be all deformed into standard types of figures like

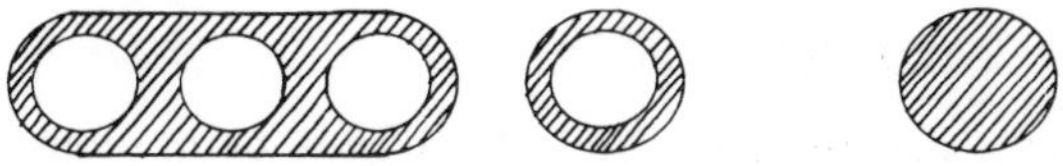

Now by reversing the previous operation that took us from step 6 to 7, we can fuse any component that has a hole with any other component, for example,

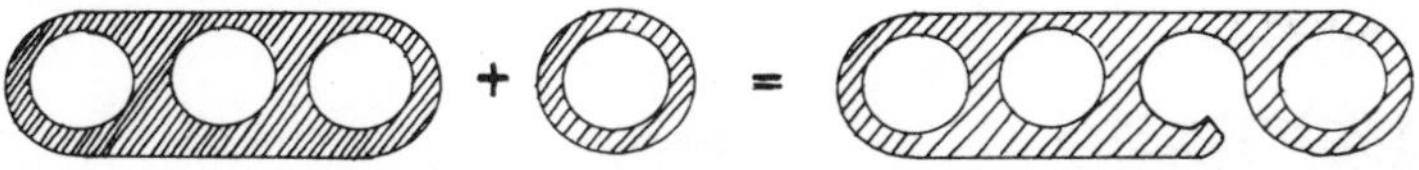

and thus one can reduce simultaneously both C and H until H is zero or C is unity. At this point one has either

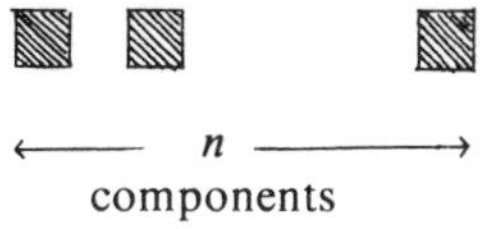

or

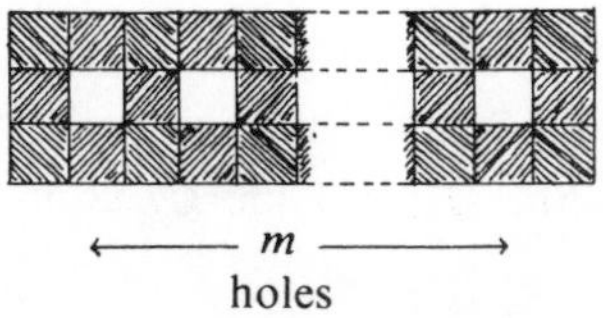

In each case one can verify that

$$G(X) = E(X) = n$$

or

$$G(X) = E(X) = 1 - m.$$

We will apply this well-known result in the next section.

5.9 Topological Limitations of Perceptrons

Theorem 5.9: The only topologically invariant predicates of finite order are functions of the Euler number $E(X)$.

The authors had proved the corresponding theorem for the diameter-limited perceptron, and conjectured that it held also for the order-limited case but were unable to prove it. It was finally established by Michael Paterson, and §5.9.1 is based upon his idea.

5.9.1 Filling Holes

Suppose that $C(X) \geq 2$ and $H(X) \geq 1$.

Choose a hole H_0 in a component C_0. Let C_1 be a component "accessible" to C_0, that is, there is a path P_{01} from a boundary point of C_0 to a boundary point of C_1 that does not touch X. Let P_{00} be a path *within* C_0 from a point on the boundary of hole H_0 to a point on another boundary of C_0, such that p_{00} and p_{01} are connected.

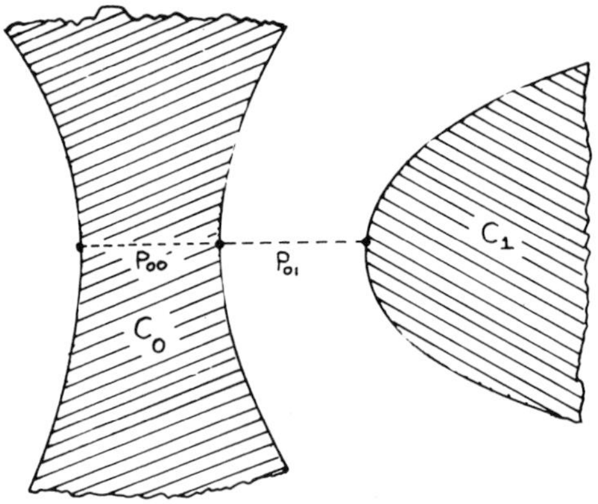

This is always possible even if C_1 is within H_0, outside C_0 completely, or within some other hole in C_0.

Now, if $\psi(X)$ is a topologically invariant predicate, its value will not be changed when we deform the configuration in the following way:

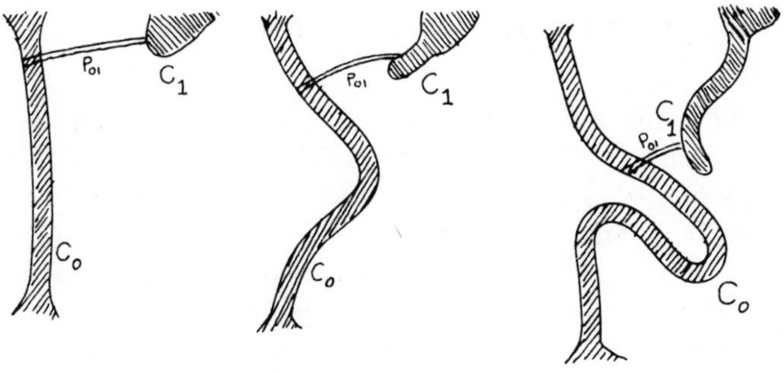

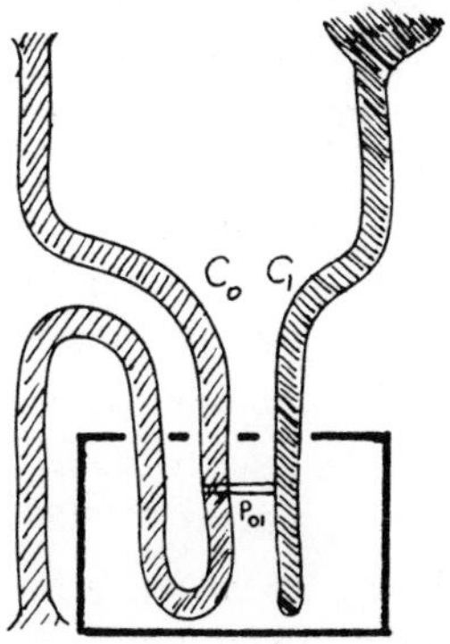

Finally suppose that we were permitted to change the connections in the box, to

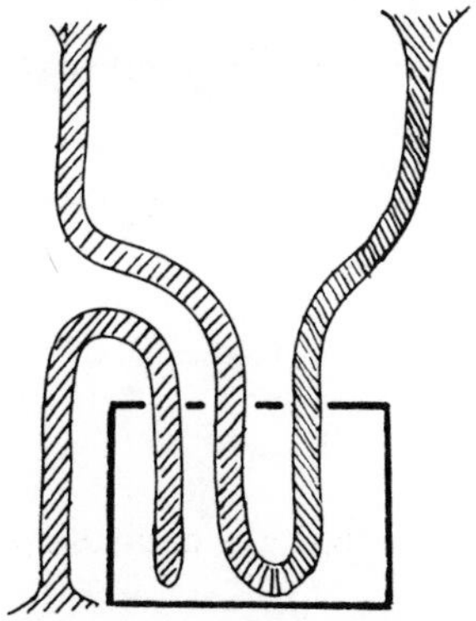

In effect, this would cut along P_{00}, removing a hole, and connect across one side of P_{01}, reducing by unity the number of components. Thus it would leave $E(X)$ unchanged.

Now we will show that making this change cannot affect the value of ψ!

Suppose that ψ has order k. Deform the figure (X) until the box contains a cascade of $k + 1$ "4-switches." (See Figure 5.6.) This does not change the topology, so it leaves ψ unchanged. Now consider the 2^{k+1} variants of X obtained by the 2^{k+1} states of the cascade switch. If ψ has the same value for all of these, then we obviously can make the change, trivially, without affecting ψ. If two of these give *different* values, say $\psi(X') \neq \psi(X'')$, then these must correspond to different parities of the switches, because ψ is a topological invariant. But if this is so, then ψ must be able to tell the parity of the switch, since all X's of a given parity class are topological equivalents (see details in §5.7). But because of the collapsing theorem, we know that this cannot be: ψ must become "confused" on a parity problem of order $> k$. Therefore all figures obtained by changing the switches give the same value for ψ, so we can apply the transformations described in §5.8.2 without changing the values of ψ.

5.9.2 The Canonical Form

We can use the method of §5.9.1 and §5.8.2 to convert an arbitrary figure X to a canonical form that depends only upon $E(X)$ as follows: we simply repeat it until we run out of holes or components. At this point there must remain either

1. A single component with one or more holes, or

2. One or more simple solid components according to whether or not $E(X) \leq 0$.

In case 1 the final figure is topologically equivalent to a figure like

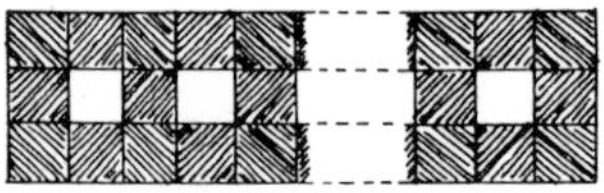

← m →
holes

with $1 - E(X)$ holes, while in case 2 the final figure is equivalent to one like

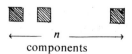

← n →
components

with $E(X)$ solid squares. Clearly, then, any two figures X and X' that have $E(X) = E(X')$ must also have $\psi(X) = \psi(X')$. This completes the proof of Theorem 5.9 which says that $\psi(X)$ must depend only upon $E(X)$.

REMARK: There is one exception to Theorem 5.9 because the canonical form does not include the case of the all-blank picture! For the predicate

$\lceil X$ is nonempty$\rceil$

is a topological invariant but is not a function of $E(X)$! See §8.1.1 and §8.4.

There are many other *topological* invariants besides the number of components of X, and $G(X)$, for example,

$\lceil$a component of X lies within a hole within another component of $X\rceil$.

The theorem thus includes the corollary that no finite-order predicate can distinguish between figures that *contain* others (left below) and those (right below) that don't.

Problem: What are the extensions of this analysis to topological predicates in higher dimensions? Is there an interpretation of $\Sigma\alpha_i\varphi_i$ as a cochain on a simplicial complex, in which the threshold operation has some respectably useful meaning?

That $\lceil X$ is composed only of Simple Closed Curves$\rceil$ is conjunctively local, diameter-limited is interesting in view of the ability of young children to deal reasonably well with such "topological" concepts. For this shows that no "topological process" is required; one need only note the non-occurance of ends or breaks.

$G(X) = \Sigma\,\varphi_{\blacksquare} - \varphi_{\boxplus}$! (Steve Gray)

Geometric Patterns of Small Order: Spectra and Context

6

6.0 Introduction to Chapters 6 and 7

In Chapters 6 and 7 we study predicates that are more strictly geometric than is connectedness. An example typical of the problems discussed is to recognize all *translations* of a particular figure or class of figures. In one sense the results are more positive than those of the previous chapter. Many such problems can be solved using low-order perceptrons, and the two chapters will be organized around two techniques for constructing geometrical predicates whose orders are often surprisingly small.

The technical content of this introduction will be partly incomprehensible until after Chapter 7 is read. It is intended, if read in the proper spirit, to provide an atmosphere enveloping this series of results and observations with a certain coherence.

Whenever we can apply the group invariance theorem, the study of invariant predicates of small order reduces to the study of a few kinds of elementary local predicates. The bigger the group, the smaller and simpler becomes this set of elementary predicates. Because ψ_{PARITY} is invariant under the biggest possible group (namely, all permutations) we were able to use for the elementary predicates the simple masks, classified merely according to the sizes of their support sets. Interesting geometric predicates will not survive such drastic transformations. Groups such as *translations* or *general rigid motions*, lead to more numerous equivalence-types of partial predicates. Figures satisfying invariant predicates will nevertheless be characterized entirely by the sets of numbers which tell us how many of each type of partial predicate they satisfy. We shall call these sets *spectra* and show in Chapter 6 how to use them.

Chapter 7 will center around a very different technique for constructing geometric predicates. Whenever the group can be ordered in an appropriate way we can *stratify* the set of figures equivalent, under the group, to a given one, by the rank order of the group element necessary to effect the transformation. We can thus (in many interesting cases) split the recognition problem into two parts: recognize the stratum to which the figure belongs and then apply a simple test appropriate to the stratum. This description has an air of serial rather than parallel computation and, indeed, part of its interest is that it shows at least one way of simulating a serial, or *conditional*, operation using a parallel procedure.

Naturally a price has to be paid for this simulation. Our method of achieving it leads to extremely large coefficients in the linear representations obtained. Taken in itself this does not exclude the possibility of some other procedure achieving the same result more cheaply. We are therefore led (in Chapter 10) to a new area of study—the bounds on coefficient sizes—and to some intriguing, though as yet only partially understood, results.

We recall that our proof of the group-invariance theorem assumed that the group was finite. The ordering we use in stratification assumes that the group is infinite: for example, the translations on the infinite plane are ordered in the obvious way, but this becomes impossible if the group is made finitely cyclic by the toroidal construction described in §5.6. When we first ran into this conflict, the techniques of stratification and those related to group invariance (spectra, etc.) seemed to be strictly disjoint areas of research. But further study brought them together in a possibly deep way. We can in fact rescue the group-invariance theorem in some infinite cases by assuming that the coefficients are bounded. For example, suppose that $\psi(X)$ is a predicate defined for *finite figures*, X, on the infinite plane and is invariant under the group of translations. Then it can be expressed as an infinite linear form, for example,

$$\psi(X) = \left\lceil \sum_{\Phi} \alpha_{\varphi} \varphi(X) > \theta \right\rceil,$$

where Φ is an infinite set (for example, the masks) chosen so that for any finite X all but a finite number of terms in the sum will vanish. Now, if we know that the α_{φ} are bounded we can use (by Theorem 10.4.1) the group-invariance theorem. In some particular cases this yields an order *greater* than that obtained by stratification. The contradiction can be dissipated only by concluding that the coefficients α_{φ} *cannot* be bounded for *any* low-order representative. It follows that the largeness of the coefficients produced by our stratification procedure is not merely an accidental result of an inept algorithm (though, of course, the actual values might be; we have not shown that they are minimal).

We were, of course, delighted to find that what seemed at first to be a limitation of our favorite theorem could be used to yield a valuable result. But our feeling that the situation is deeply interesting goes beyond this immediate (and practical) problem of sizes of coefficients. It really comes from the intrusion of the *global structure* of the transformation group. For a long time we believed that the recognition of all translations of a *given* figure was a high-order problem. Stratification showed we were wrong. But we have not been able to find low-order predicates for the corresponding problem when the group contains large finite cyclic subgroups such as rotations or translations on the torus, and we continue to entertain the conjecture that these are not finite-order problems.

Complementing the positive results of Chapter 6 will be found one negative theorem of considerable practical interest. This concerns the recognition of figures *in context*. It is easy to decide, using a low-order predicate, whether a given figure *is*, say, a rectangle. The new kind of problem is to decide whether the figure *contains* a rectangle and, perhaps, something else as well (see Figure 6.1).

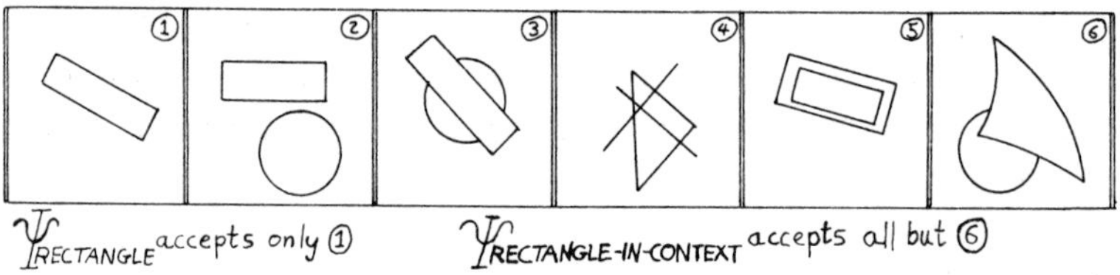

Figure 6.1

It seems obvious that recognition-in-context should be somewhat harder, perhaps requiring a somewhat higher order. We shall show (§6.6) that it is worse than that: it is not even of finite order!

Finally it should be noted that we manage, once more, to avoid the need to use a tolerance theory to escape from the limitations of our square-grid arrays. The translation group does not raise this problem. The rotation group does; but we say all we have to say in the context of 90° rotations. The similarity group suggests the most serious difficulties: one can dilate a figure easily enough, but how can one contract a small one? As it happens we have nothing interesting to say about this group. We urge future workers to be less cowardly.

In §6.1–§6.4 we begin by showing that certain patterns have orders $= 1$, $= 2$, ≤ 3, ≤ 4, respectively. In most cases we usually have not established the *lower* bound on the orders and have no systematic methods for doing so.

6.1 Geometric Patterns of Order 1

When we say "geometric property" we mean something invariant under translation, usually also invariant under rotation, and often invariant under dilation. The first two invariances combine to define the "congruence" group of transformations, and all three treat alike the figures that are "similar" in Euclidean geometry. For order 1 we know that coefficients can be assumed to be equal.* Therefore, the only patterns that can be of order 1 are those defined by a single *cut* in the cardinality or area of the set:

$$\psi = \lceil |X| > A \rceil \quad \text{or} \quad \psi = \lceil |X| < A \rceil.$$

Note: If translation invariance is *not* required, then perceptrons of order 1 can, of course, compute other properties, for example, concerning *moments* about *particular* points or axes. (See §2.4.1.) However, these are not "geometric" in the sense of being suitably invariant. So while they may be of considerable practical importance, we will not discuss them further.†

6.2 Patterns of Order 2, Distance Spectra

For $k = 2$ things are more complicated. As shown in §1.4, Example 3, it is possible to define a double cut or segment $\lceil A_1 < A < A_2 \rceil$, in the area of the set and recognize the figures whose areas satisfy

$$\psi = \lceil A_1 < |X| < A_2 \rceil.$$

In fact, in general we can always find a function of order $2k$ that recognizes the sets whose areas lie in any of k intervals. But let us

*All the theorems of this chapter assume that the group invariance theorem can be applied, even though the translation group is not finite. This can be shown to be true if (Theorem 10.4) the coefficients are bounded; it can be shown in any case for order 1, and there are all sorts of other conditions that can be sufficient. In §7.10 we see that the group-invariance theorem is not always available. We do not have a good general test for its applicability. Of course, the coefficients will be bounded in any physical machine!

†See, for example, Pitts and McCulloch [1947] for an eye-centering servomechanism—using an essentially order-1 predicate.

return to patterns with geometric significance. First, consider only the group of translations, and masks of order 2. Then two masks x_1x_2 and $x_1'\,x_2'$ are equivalent if and only if the difference *vectors*

$$\overrightarrow{x_1 - x_2} \quad \text{and} \quad \overrightarrow{x_1' - x_2'}$$

are equal, with same or opposite sign. Thus, with respect to the translation group, any order-2 predicate can depend only on a figure's "difference-vector spectrum," defined as the sequence of ~~the numbers of pairs of points separated by each angle and distance pair.~~ The two figures

the numbers of such pairs in each difference-direction class.

 and 

have the same difference-vector spectra, that is,

"vector"	number of pairs
	4
	1
	2
	1
	1
	1

Hence no order-2 predicate can make a classification which is both translation invariant and separates these two figures. In fact, an immediate consequence of the group-invariance theorem is:

Theorem 6.2: Let $\psi(X)$ be a translation-invariant predicate of order 2. Define $n_v(X)$ to be the number of pairs of points in X that are separated by the vector v. Then $\psi(X)$ can be written

$$\psi(X) = \left\lceil \sum_{\nu} \alpha_\nu n_\nu(X) > \theta \right\rceil.$$

PROOF: n_ν predicates in the class Φ_ν are satisfied by any translation of X. By Theorem 2.3 they can all be assigned the same coefficient.

Corollary: Two figures with the same translation spectrum $n(\nu)$ cannot be distinguished by a translation-invariant order-2 perceptron. (But see footnote to §6.1.)

Conversely if the spectra are different, for example $n_{\nu_1}(A) < n_{\nu_1}(B)$, then the translations of two figures can be separated by $\lceil n_{\nu_1}(X) < n_{\nu_1}(B) \rceil$. But *classes* made of different figures may not be so separable.

Example: the figures

 and 

are indistinguishable by order-2 predicates, while

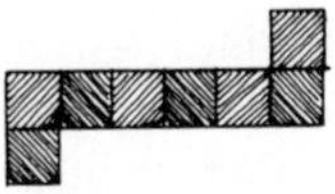 and 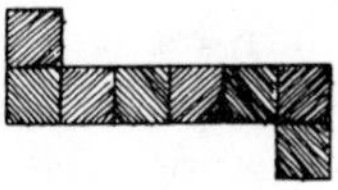

have different difference-vector spectra and can be separated. If we add the requirement of invariance under rotations, the latter pair above becomes indistinguishable, because the equivalence-classes now group together all differences of the same length, whatever their orientation.

Note that we did *not* allow reflections, yet these reflectionally opposite figures are now confused! One should be cautious about using "intuition" here. The theory of general rotational invariance requires careful attention to the effect of the discrete retinal approximation, but could presumably be made consistent by a suitable tolerance theory; for the dilation "group," there are serious difficulties. (For the group generated by the 90° rotations, the example above fails but the following example works.)

An interesting pair of figures rotationally distinct, but nevertheless indistinguishable for $k = 2$, is the pair

  and

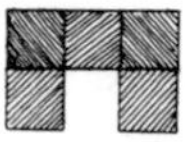

which have the same (direction-independent) distance-between-point-pair spectra through order 2, namely,

$|x_i - x_j| = 1$ from 4 pairs

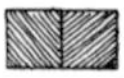

$|x_i - x_j| = \sqrt{2}$ from 2 pairs

$|x_i - x_j| = 2$ from 2 pairs

$|x_i - x_j| = \sqrt{5}$ from 2 pairs

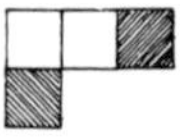

and each has 5 points (the order-1 spectrum).

The group-invariance theorem, §2.3, tells us that any group-invariant perceptron must depend only on a pattern's "occupancy numbers," that is, exactly the "geometric spectra" discussed here. Many other proposals for "pattern-recognition machines"—not perceptrons, and accordingly not representable simply as linear forms—might also be better understood after exploration of their relation to the theory of these geometric spectra. But it seems unlikely that this kind of analysis would bring a great deal to the study of the more "descriptive" or, as they are sometimes called, "syntactic" scene-analysis systems that the authors secretly advocate.

Another example of an order-2 predicate is

[X lies within a row or column and has $\leq n$ segments]

which can be defined by

[$\Sigma \, \alpha_{\blacksquare\square} + \Sigma \, \alpha_{\blacksquare\atop\square} - \Sigma \, \alpha_{\blacksquare} + n\Sigma$ (all non-collinear pairs) $\leq n$].

6.3 Patterns of Order 3

6.3.1 Convexity

A particularly interesting predicate is

$\psi_{\text{CONVEX}}(X) = \lceil X \text{ is a single, solid convex figure} \rceil.$

That this is of order ≤ 3 can be seen from the definition of "convex": X is convex if and only if every line-segment whose end points are in X lies entirely within X. It follows that X is convex if and only if

$$a \in X \text{ AND } b \in X \Rightarrow \text{midpoint}([a,b]) \in X;$$

hence

$$\psi_{\text{CONVEX}}(X) = \left\lceil \sum_{\text{all } a,b \text{ in } X} \lceil \text{midpoint } [a,b] \text{ not in } X \rceil < 1 \right\rceil$$

has order ≤ 3 and presumably order $= 3$. This is a "conjunctively local" condition of the kind discussed in §0.2.

Note that if a *connected* figure is not convex one can further conclude that it has at least one "local" concavity, as in

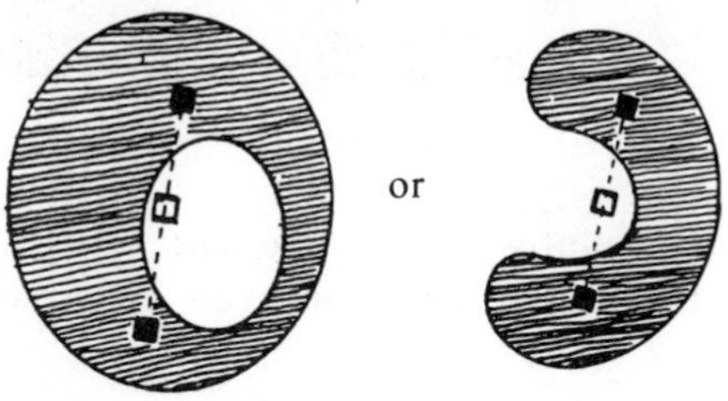

with the three points arbitrarily close together. Thus, if we are given that X is connected, then convexity can be realized as *diameter-limited* and order 3. If we are not sure X is connected, then the preceding argument fails in the diameter-limited case because a *pair* of convex figures, widely separated, will be accepted:

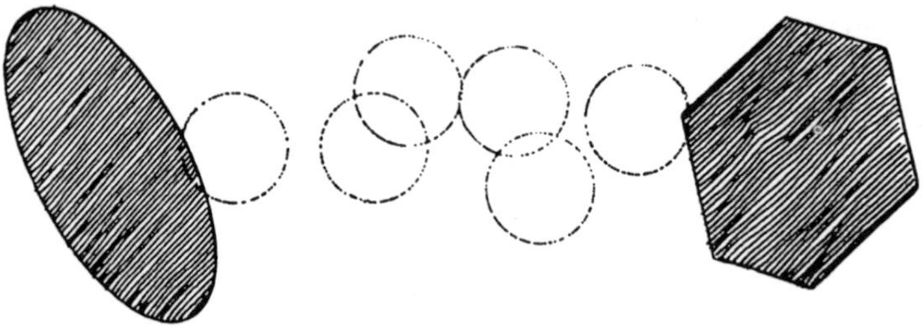

Indeed, convexity is probably not order 3 under the additional restriction of diameter limitation, but one should not jump to the conclusion that it is not diameter-limited of any order, because of the following "practical" consideration:

Even given that a figure is connected, its "convexity" can be defined only relative to a precision of tolerance. In addition figures must be uniformly bounded in size, or else the small local tolerance becomes globally disastrous. But within this constraint, one can *approximate* an estimate of curvature, and define "convex" to be $\int(\text{curvature}) \leq 4\pi$. We will discuss this further in §8.3 and §9.9.

6.3.2 Rectangles

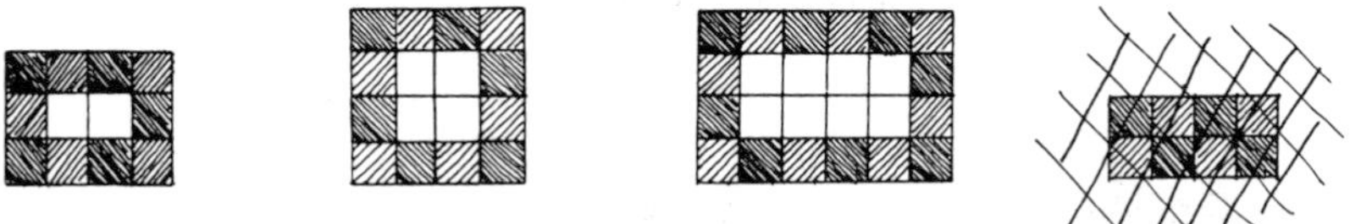

Figure 6.2 Some "hollow" rectangles.

Within our square-array formulation, we can define with order 3 the set of solid axis-parallel rectangles. This can even be done with diameter-limited φ's, by

$[\Sigma\ \varphi$  $+\ \Sigma\ \varphi$  $\leq 4]$

where all φ's equivalent under 90° rotation are included. The hollow rectangles are caught by

[~~2~~ 5 $\Sigma\ \varphi$  $+\ \Sigma\ \varphi$  $\leq$ ~~12~~ 24] where the coefficients are chosen to exclude the case of two or more separate points. These examples are admittedly weakened by their dependence on the chosen square lattice, but they have an underlying validity in that the figures in question are definable in terms of being rectilinear with not more than four corners, and we will discuss this slightly more than "conjunctively local" kind of definition in Chapter 8.

One would suppose that the sets of hollow and solid *squares* would have to be of order 4 or higher, because the comparison of side-lengths should require at least that. It is surprising, therefore, to find they have order 3. The construction is distinctly not conjunctively local, and we will postpone it to Chapter 7.

6.3.3 Higher-order Translation Spectra

If we define the 3-vector spectrum of a figure to be the set of numbers of 3-point masks satisfied in each translation-equivalence class, it is interesting to note the following fact (which is about geometry, and not about linear separation).

Theorem 6.3.3: Figures are uniquely characterized (up to translation) by their 3-vector spectra, even in higher dimensions.

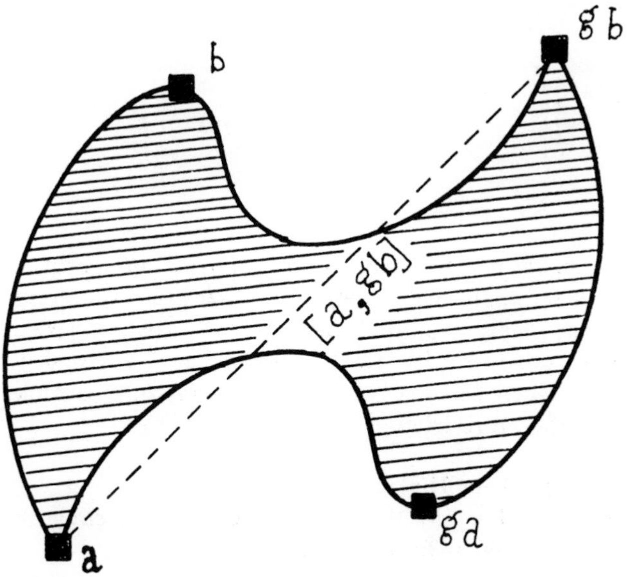

Figure 6.3

The proof shows that the longest vectors that can be inscribed in a figure are unique in each direction: no other vector can be parallel, and equal in length, to a longest vector.

PROOF: Let X be a particular figure. The figure X has a maximal distance D between two of its points. Choose a pair (a,b) of points of X with this distance and consider the set $\Phi_{ab} = \{\varphi_{a,b,x}\}$ of masks of support 3 that contain a,b and any other point x of X. Each such mask must have coefficient equal to unity in the translation spectrum of X, for if X contained two translation-equivalent masks

$x_a x_b$ and $x_{ga} x_{gb}$

~~$\varphi_{a,b,x}$ and $\varphi_{ga,gb,gx}$~~

then one of the distances $[a,gb]$ or $[ga,b]$ would exceed D, for they are diagonals of a parallelogram with one side equal to D (see Figure 6.3).

Thus any translation of X must contain a *unique* translation of (a,b) and the part of its spectrum corresponding to $\Phi_{a,b}$ allows one to reconstruct X completely (see Figure 6.4).

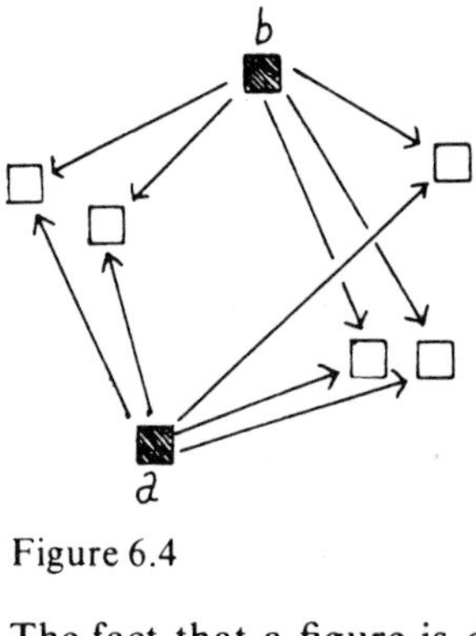

Figure 6.4

The fact that a figure is *determined* by its 3-translation spectrum does not, of course, imply that recognition of classes of figures is order 3. (It does imply that the translations of two different figures can be so separated. In fact, the method of §7.3, Application 7, shows this can be done with order 2, but only outside the bounded-coefficient restriction.)

6.4 Patterns of Order 4 and Higher

We can use the fact that any three points determine a circle to make an order-4 perceptron for the predicate

$\lceil X$ is the perimeter of a complete circle$\rceil$

by using the form

$$\left\lceil \sum_{d \notin C_{abc}} x_a x_b x_c x_d + \sum_{d \in C_{abc}} x_a x_b x_c \bar{x}_d < 1 \right\rceil,$$

where C_{abc} is the circle* through x_a, x_b, and x_c. Many other curious and interesting predicates can be shown by similar arguments to have small orders. One should be careful not to conclude that there are practical consequences of this, unless one is prepared to face the facts that

1. Large numbers of φ's may be required, of the order of $|R|^{k-1}$ for the examples given above.

2. The threshold conditions are sharp, so that engineering considerations may cause difficulties in realizing the linear summation, especially if there is any problem of noise. Even with simple square-root noise, for $k = 3$ or larger the noise grows faster than the retinal size. The coefficient sizes are often fatally large, as shown in Chapter 10.

3. A very slight change in the pattern definition† often destroys its order of recognizability. With low orders, it may not be possible to define tolerances for reasonable performance.

6.5 Spectral Recognition Theorems

A number of the preceding examples are special cases of the following theorems. (The ideas introduced here are not used later.) The group-invariance theorem (§2.3) shows that if a predicate ψ is invariant with respect to a group G, then if $\psi \in L(\Phi)$ for some Φ it can be realized by a form

$$\psi = \left\lceil \sum_i \beta_i N_i(X) > 0 \right\rceil$$

where N_i is the number of φ's satisfied by X in the ith equivalence class. In §5.2 we touched on the "difference vector spectrum" for geometric figures under the group of translations of the plane.

---

*Again there is a tolerance problem: what *is* a circle in the discrete retina? See §8.3.

†Our formula accepts (appropriately) zero- and one-dimensional "circles." This phenomenon cannot be avoided, in any dimension, by a conjunctively local predicate.

Those spectra are in fact the numbers $N_i(X)$ for order 0, 1, and 2. If a G-invariant ψ cannot be described for *any* condition on the N_i's for a given Φ, then obviously ψ is not in $L(\Phi)$. The following results show some conditions on the N_i that imply that ψ is of finite order.

Suppose that ψ is defined by m simultaneous equalities:

$$\psi(X) \equiv \lceil N_1(X) = n_1 \text{ AND } N_2(X) = n_2 \text{ AND } \cdots \; N_m(X) = n_m \rceil,$$

where $n_1, \ldots, n_m$ is a finite sequence of integers. The order of ψ is not more than twice the maximum of the orders of the φ's associated with the N_i's. We will state this more precisely as

Theorem 6.5: Let

$$\Phi = \Phi_1 \cup \Phi_2 \cup \cdots \cup \Phi_m,$$

and

$$N_i(X) = |\{\varphi \mid \varphi \in \Phi_i \text{ AND } \varphi(X) = 1\}| = \sum_{\varphi \in \Phi_i} \varphi(X).$$

Then the order of

$$\psi(X) = \lceil N_i(X) = n_i, \text{ for } 1 \leq i \leq m \rceil$$

is at most twice

$$\max \{|S(\varphi)|; \varphi \in \Phi\}.$$

The goal of the proof is to show that the definition of ψ can be put in the form of a linear threshold expression, namely,

$$\psi(X) = \lceil \Sigma (N_i(X) - n_i)^2 < 1 \rceil.$$

As it stands this is *not* a linear threshold combination of predicates. To recast it into the desired shape we introduce an *ad hoc* convention that will not be used elsewhere. Given any set Φ of predicates we construct a new set of predicates Φ^2 by listing all pairs of (φ_i, φ_j) of predicates in Φ and defining

$$\varphi_{ij}(X) = \varphi_i(X) \wedge \varphi_j(X).$$

Many of the predicates so constructed will be logically equivalent, for example, $\varphi_{ij} = \varphi_{ji}$, but we make the convention that these are to be counted as distinct members of Φ^2. (This means that in a very strict sense Φ^2 is a set of "predicate forms" rather than of predicates.)

The effect of the convention is to simplify the arithmetic and logic of the counting argument we are about to use. Let X be a figure for which exactly N predicates in Φ are satisfied. Obviously N^2 predicates of Φ^2 will be satisfied by X, that is,

$$\sum_{\Phi^2} \varphi(X) = N^2.$$

Now let $\Phi_1, \Phi_2, \ldots,$ be an enumeration of the equivalence classes of Φ. Since the number of predicates of Φ_i satisfied by X is

$$N_i(X) = \sum_{\Phi_i} \varphi(X);$$

then, as we have seen,

$$\sum_{\Phi_i^2} \varphi(X) = N_i^2(X).$$

Thus

$$\sum_i \left\{ \sum_{\Phi_i^2} \varphi(X) - 2n_i \sum_{\Phi_i} \varphi(X) + n_i^2 \right\} = \sum_i \{(N_i(X) - n_i)^2\}.$$

To represent the left-hand side of this equation in the standard linear threshold predicate form we define $\Phi' = \Phi^2 \cup \Phi \cup$ {the constant predicate}, and write

$$\psi(X) = \left\lceil \sum_{\Phi'} \alpha(\varphi)\,\varphi(X) < 1 \right\rceil$$

where

$$\alpha(\varphi) = 1 \text{ for } \varphi \in \Phi^2$$
$$\alpha(\varphi) = -2n_i \text{ for } \varphi \in \Phi_i$$
$$\alpha(\text{constant}) = \Sigma n_i^2.$$

To complete the proof of the theorem we have only to observe that

$$\begin{aligned} |S(\varphi_{i,j})| &= |S(\varphi_i) \cup S(\varphi_j)| \\ &\leq |S(\varphi_i)| + |S(\varphi_j)| \\ &\leq 2\,(\max |S(\varphi)|) \end{aligned} \qquad \text{Q.E.D.}$$

6.5.1 Extended Exact Matching

An obvious generalization of Theorem 6.5 is this: Suppose that ψ is defined by

$$\psi(X) \equiv \bigvee_{i=1}^{n} \bigwedge_{j=1}^{m} (N_j(X) = n_{ij}),$$

that is, ψ satisfies any one of a number of exact conditions on the N_i. Then ψ is of finite order, for we can realize the polynomial form

$$\prod_{i=1}^{n} \sum_{j=1}^{m} (N_j(X) - n_{ij})^2$$

by methods like those in the previous paragraph. However, the extension now requires Boolean products of predicates of different equivalence classes, and the maximal order required will be $\leq 2n \cdot \max |S(\varphi)|$.

Note that if one were not aware of the And/Or phenomenon, one might be tempted to try to obtain §6.5.1 from §6.5 via the false conjecture

$$\bigvee^{n} \text{(predicates of order } k\text{) is order} \leq nk.$$

6.5.2 Mean-Square Variation

In the expressions for the predicates discussed in §6.5.1, we could increase θ to higher values:

$$\lceil \Sigma(N_i - n_i)^2 < \theta \rceil.$$

Then the system will accept exactly those figures for which the *sum of the squares* of the differences of the N_i's and the n_i's are bounded by θ. Any pattern-classification machine will be sensitive to certain kinds of distortion, and this observation hints that it might be useful to study such machines, and perceptrons in particular, in terms of their spectrum-distortion characteristics. Unfortunately, we don't have any good ideas concerning the geometric meaning of such distortions. The geometric nature of this sort of "invariant noise" is an interesting subject for speculation, but we have not investigated it.

6.6 Figures in Context

For practical and theoretical reasons it is interesting to study the recognition of figures "in context": like,

$\psi(X)$ = [a *subset* of X is a square],

$\psi(X)$ = [a *connected component of* X is a square],

or, to begin to consider three-dimensional projection problems,

$\psi(X)$ = [X contains a significant portion of the outline of a partially obscured square].

The examples show that there is more than one natural meaning one could give to the intuitive project of recognizing instances of patterns embedded in contexts. We do not know any general definition that might cover all natural senses, and are therefore unable to state general theorems. We do, nevertheless, claim that *the general rule is for low-order predicates to lose their property of finite order when embedded in context in any natural way.* To illustrate the thesis we shall pick a particularly common and apparently harmless interpretation: For any predicate $\psi(X)$ define a new one by

$$\psi_{\text{IN CONTEXT}}(X) = [\psi(Y) \text{ for some connected component of } X].$$

It will be obvious that the techniques we use can be adapted trivially to many other definitions.

Intuitively, we would expect $\psi_{\text{IN CONTEXT}}$ to be much harder for a perceptron since the context of each component acts as noise and the parallel operation of the device allows little chance for this to be separated and ignored. The point appears particularly clearly in the cases where ψ uses rejection rules. These cannot be transferred over to $\psi_{\text{IN CONTEXT}}$ for very obvious reasons. Similarly, we will lose the stratification methods of Chapter 7 and, indeed, most of our technical tricks used to obtain low-order representations of predicates. The next two theorems show how this intuitive idea can be given a rigorous form. It should, however, be observed that no simple generalization is possible about the relation of ψ to $\psi_{\text{IN CONTEXT}}$ since some ψ's become degenerate in context. For example, $\psi_{\text{CONNECTED}}$ becomes degenerate in context because *every* set has a connected component!

Theorem 6.6.1: Let R be a finite square retina and let $\psi(X)$ be

$$\psi(X) = \lceil X \text{ is exactly one horizontal line across the retina} \rceil.$$

Then ψ is of order 2 but $\psi_{\text{IN CONTEXT}}$ is not of finite order.

PROOF: We leave as an exercise the proof that ψ as defined has order 2. To show that $\psi_{\text{IN CONTEXT}}$ is not of finite order we merely observe that it is the negation of the negative of the one-in-a-box predicate, ψ_1, namely the predicate that asserts there is no horizontal white line across the retina. Its negative (in the photographic sense) asserts that there is no horizontal black line. Now ψ_1 is not of finite order, and one can show in general that the same is true of any such predicate's negative. Finally, by reversing the predicate's inequality we find the same is true for the desired

$$\psi_{\text{IN CONTEXT}} = \lceil X \text{ contains a horizontal line across the retina} \rceil.$$

Theorem 6.6.2: Let $\psi(X)$ be

$$\lceil X \text{ is a hollow square} \rceil.$$

Then $\psi_{\text{IN CONTEXT}}$ is not of finite order:

[One component of X is a hollow square].

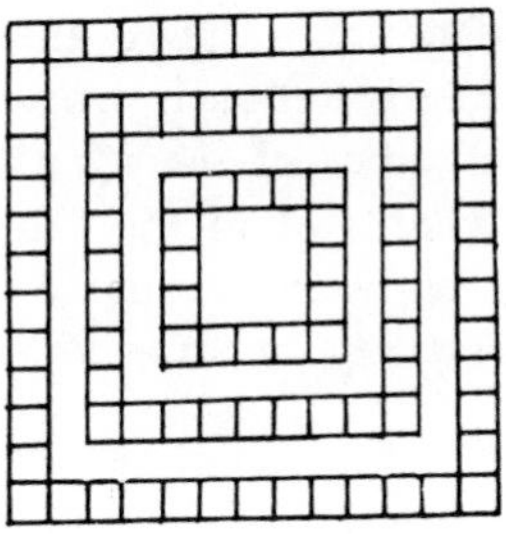

PROOF: The proof is exactly the same as the previous except that the "boxes" or horizontal lines are folded into squares and mapped without overlap into a larger retina. Again, it can be shown that ψ itself is of finite order; in this case, order 3.

Note: An alternative proof method is to fold the lines of switching elements used in the Huffman construction for connectivity (§5.5).

It is our conviction that the deterioration of the perceptron's ability to recognize patterns embedded in other contexts is a serious deterrent to using it in real, practical situations. Of course this deficiency can be mitigated by embedding the perceptron in a more serial process—one in which the figure of interest is isolated and separated from its context in an earlier phase. But this presupposes enough recognition ability, in the "preprocessing" phase, to discern and remove the most commonly encountered contextual disturbances, and this may be much harder than the "processing" phase. We treat this further in Chapter 13.

7

7.1 Equivalence of Figures

In previous chapters we discussed the recognition of patterns—classes of figures closed under the transformations of some group. We now turn to the related question of recognizing the *equivalence*, under a group, of an arbitrary *pair* of figures. The results below were surprising to us, for we had supposed that such problems were not generally of finite order. A number of questions remain open, and the superficially positive character of the following constructions is clouded by the apparently enormous coefficients they require, and the manner in which they increase with the size of the retina.

A typical problem has this form: The retina*

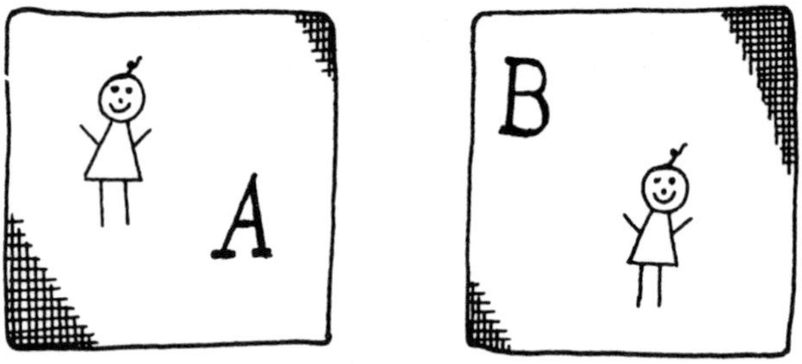

is presented as two equal parts A and B and we ask: is the figure in part B a rigid translation of the figure in part A? More generally, is there an element g from some given group G of transformations for which the figure in B is the result of g operating on the figure in A? What order predicates are required to make such distinctions? The results of this chapter all derive from use of a technique we call *stratification*. Stratification makes it possible, under certain conditions, to simulate a sequential process by a parallel process, in which the results are so weighted that, if certain conditions are satisfied, some computations will numerically outweigh effects of others. The technique derives from the following theorem:

*All the theorems of this chapter apply *directly* to perceptrons on infinite retinas; that is, without having to consider limiting processes on sequences of finite retinas as proposed in §1.6. The transformation groups, too, are infinite, and the group-invariance theorem is not used. Because this material is somewhat more specialized than the rest, we will regress a little toward the conventional and hideous style of mathematical exposition, in which theorems are stated and proved before explaining what they are for.

The compromise noted in the preceding footnote has proved disastrous for most readers, which is a shame because the basic idea is so simple. We have therefore added, on page 128, a numerical example to illustrate the technique, and if you understand how it works you should have no trouble after skipping to §7.3.

7.2 The Stratification Theorem

Let $\Pi = \{\pi_1, \pi_2, \ldots, \pi_j, \ldots\}$ be a sequence of different masks and define a sequence $C_1, \ldots, C_j, \ldots$, of classes by

$$X \in C_j \iff [\pi_j(X) \quad \text{AND} \quad (k > j \Rightarrow \sim\pi_k(X))].$$

Thus X is in C_j if j is the highest index for which $\pi_i(X)$ is true, as is illustrated below.

$\pi_1 = 1$	$\pi_1 = ?$	$\pi_1 = ?$	...
$\pi_2 = 0$	$\pi_2 = 1$	$\pi_2 = ?$	...
$\pi_3 = 0$	$\pi_3 = 0$	$\pi_3 = 1$	...
$\pi_4 = 0$	$\pi_4 = 0$	$\pi_4 = 0$	...
...	...	...	...
C_1	C_2	C_3	...

Figure 7.1 The partition into $C_j(x)$.

Let $\Phi = \{\varphi_i\}$ be a family of predicates and let $\psi_1, \ldots, \psi_j, \ldots$, be an ordered sequence of predicates in $L(\Phi)$ that are each *bounded* in the sense that for each ψ_j there is a linear form Σ_j with integer coefficients such that

$$\Sigma_j = \sum_i \alpha_{ij}\varphi_i - \theta_j \quad \text{AND} \quad \psi_j = \lceil \Sigma_j > 0 \rceil$$

and a bound B_j such that

$$|\Sigma_j(X)| < B_j$$

for all finite $|X|$. (The proof actually requires only that each $|\Sigma_j(X)|$ be bounded on each C_k.)

Theorem 7.2: The predicate $\psi(X) = \lceil X \in C_j \Rightarrow \psi_j(X) \rceil$ obtained by taking on each C_j the values of the corresponding ψ_j, lies in $L(\Phi \cdot \Pi)$; that is, it can be written as a form

$$\psi(X) = \lceil \Sigma \alpha_{jk}(\pi_j \wedge \varphi_k) > \theta \rceil.$$

PROOF: It is easy to see that every finite X will lie in one of the C_j. Define

$$S_1 = \pi_1 \cdot \Sigma_1,$$

and for $j > 1$ define inductively

$$\begin{cases} M_j = \max\limits_{C_j} |S_{j-1}|, \\ S_j = S_{j-1} - \pi_j M_j + (2M_j + 1) \cdot \pi_j \cdot \Sigma_j. \end{cases}$$

The bounds B_j assure the existence of the M_j's. Now write the formal sum generated by this infinite process as

$$S = \Sigma \alpha_{jk}(\pi_j \wedge \varphi_k),$$

and we will show that $\psi(X) = \lceil S(X) > 0 \rceil$. The infinite sum is well-defined because for any finite X in any C_j there will be only a finite number of nonzero $\pi_j \wedge \varphi_k$ terms. *Base:* It is clear that if X is in C_1 then $S_1 = \Sigma_1$ so $\psi(X) = \lceil S_1(X) > 0 \rceil$. *Induction:* Assume that if X is in C_{j-1} then $\psi(X) = \lceil S_{j-1}(X) > 0 \rceil$. Now the coefficients are integers, so if $X \epsilon C_j$, $\pi_j = 1$ and

$$\begin{cases} \text{if } \psi(X) \text{ then } \Sigma_j \geq 1 \text{ so } S_j \geq [-M_j - M_j + 2M_j + 1] = 1, \\ \text{if } \sim\psi(X) \text{ then } \Sigma_j \leq 0 \text{ so } S_j \leq [M_j - M_j] = 0. \end{cases}$$

Q.E.D.

Corollary 7.2: The order of $\psi(X)$ is no larger than the sum of the maximum |support| in Φ and the maximum |support| in Π. This follows because the predicates in Φ occur only as conjuncts with predicates in Π.

The idea is that the domain of $\psi(X)$ is divided into the disjoint classes or "strata," C_j. Within each stratum the $-\pi_j M_j$ term is so large that it negates all decisions made on lower strata, unless the ψ_j test is passed. In all the applications below, the strata represent, more or less, the different possible deviations of a figure from a "normal" position. Hence there is a close connection between the possibility of constructing "stratified" predicates, and the conventional "pattern recognition" concept of identifying a figure first by *normalizing* it and then by comparing the normalized image with a prototype. This, of course, is usually a serial process.

It should be noted that predicates obtained by the use of this theorem will have enormous coefficients, growing exponentially or faster with the stratification index j. Thus the results of this chapter should not be considered of practical interest. They are more of theoretical interest in showing something about the relation of the structure of the transformation groups to the orders of certain predicates invariant under those groups.

7.3 Application 1: Symmetry along a Line

Let $R = \ldots, x_s, \ldots,$ be the points of an infinite linear retina, that is, $-\infty < s < \infty$; it is convenient to choose an arbitrary origin x_0 and number the squares as shown:

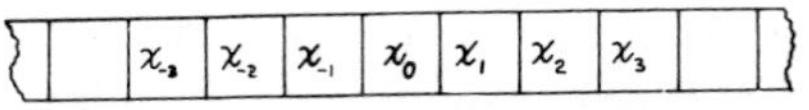

Suppose that X is a figure in R with finite $|X|$. We ask whether

$$\psi_{\text{SYMMETRICAL}}(X) = \lceil X \text{ has a symmetry under reflection} \rceil$$

is of finite order.

It should be observed that the predicate would be trivially of order 2 if the center of symmetry were fixed in advance. But $\psi_{\text{SYMMETRICAL}}$ allows it to be anywhere along the infinite line.

We will "stratify" $\psi_{\text{SYMMETRICAL}}$ by finding sequences $\pi_1, \ldots,$ and $\psi_1, \ldots,$ that allow us to test for symmetry, using the following trick: the π_i's will "find" the two "end points" of X and the corresponding ψ_i's will test the symmetry of a figure, assuming that it has exactly these end points. Our goal, then, is to define the π_i's so that each C_j will be the class of figures with a certain pair of end points. To do this we need $\pi_1, \ldots,$ to be an enumeration of all segments (x_s, x_{s+d}) for every s and for every $d \geq 0$, with the property that any term (x_s, x_{s+d}) must follow any term (x_{s+a}, x_{s+b}) with $0 \leq a \leq b \leq d$. There do indeed exist such sequences, for example:

$\pi_1 = x_0 x_0$

$\pi_2 = x_1 x_1$

$\pi_3 = x_0 x_1$

$\pi_4 = x_{-1} x_{-1}$

$\pi_5 = x_{-1} x_0$

$\pi_6 = x_{-1} x_1$

$\pi_7 = x_2 x_2$

$\pi_8 = x_1 x_2$

$\vdots$

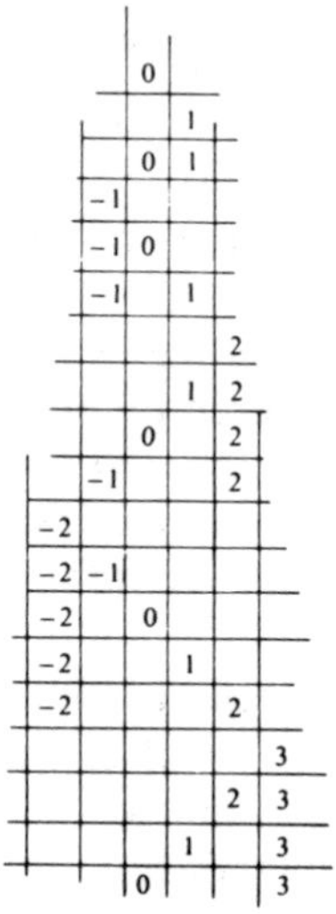

It can be seen that (1) each segment occurs eventually, and (2) no segment is ever followed by another that lies within it. Therefore, if x_s, x_{s+d} *are* the extreme left and right points of X, then X will lie in precisely the C_j for that (x_s, x_{s+d}). Now define ψ_j to be

$$\psi_j = \lceil x_{s+i} = x_{s+d-i},\ i = 0, \ldots, d \rceil$$

or, equivalently,

$$\psi_j = \left\lceil \sum_{i=0}^{d} (x_{s+i})(1 - x_{s+d-i}) \leq 0 \right\rceil$$

showing that it is a predicate of order 2 bounded by $B_j = d + 1$.

So, finally, application of the stratification theorem shows that $\psi_{\text{SYMMETRICAL}}$ has order ≤ 4, since the ψ's have order ≤ 2 and the π's have support ≤ 2.

7.4 Application 2: Translation-Congruence along a Line

Let $\ldots, x_s, \ldots$, and $\ldots, y_t, \ldots$, be the points of two infinite linear retinas, that is, $-\infty < x_s < \infty$ and $-\infty < y_t < \infty$:

Let X be a figure composed of a part X_A in the left retina and a part X_B in the right retina. We want to construct

$\psi_{\text{TRANSLATE}}(X) = \lceil$the (finite) pattern in A is a translate of the pattern in $B\rceil$.

To "stratify" $\psi_{\text{TRANSLATE}}$ we have to find a sequence π_i that allows us to test, with appropriate ψ_i's, whether the A and B parts of X are congruent. We will do this by a method like that used in §7.2.1, but we now have to handle two segments simultaneously. That is, we need a sequence of π_j's that enumerates all quadruples in such a way that a figure lies in C_j if and only if the end points of its A and B parts are precisely the corresponding values of x_s, x_{s+d_x}, y_t, and y_{t+d_y}. There does indeed exist such a sequence (!), and one can be obtained from the π_i's of §7.2.1 as follows (the reader might first try to find one himself).

Define π_{jk} to be the four-point mask obtained by

$$\pi_{jk}(X) = \pi_j(X_A) \cdot \pi_k(X_B),$$

that is, by choosing according to i two points of A and according to j two points of B. The master sequence requires us to enumerate all π_{ij}'s under the condition that no π_{ab} can precede any π_{cd} if both $a \geq c$ and $b \geq d$.

A solution is

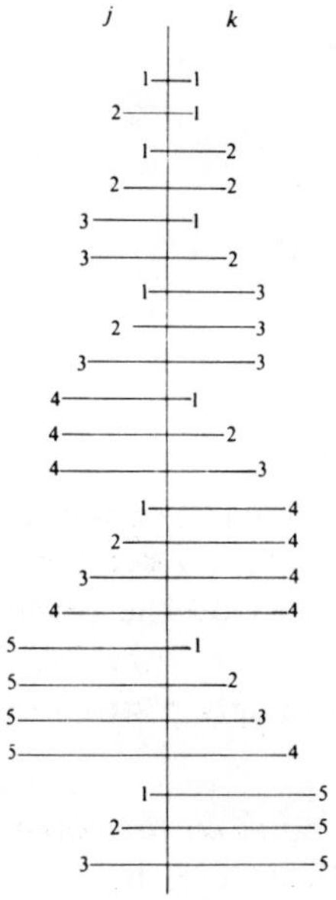

$\pi_{11}; \pi_{21}, \pi_{12}, \pi_{22}; \pi_{31}, \pi_{32}, \pi_{13}, \pi_{23}, \pi_{33}; \ \pi_{41}, \pi_{42}, \pi_{43}, \pi_{14}, \pi_{24}, \ldots,$ and for the π_{jk} term in this sequence, an appropriate predicate $\psi_{(jk)}$ is

$\psi_{(jk)}$ = ⌈the segments defined by π_j and π_k have the same lengths, and the x's and y's in those intervals have the same values at corresponding points⌉.

This is an order-2 predicate, and bounded (by the segment lengths). The π_j's now have support 4, so $\psi_{\text{TRANSLATE}}(X)$ has finite order ≤ 6. Actually, having found both extrema of X_A, it is necessary only to find *one* end of X_B, so a slightly different construction using the method of §7.9 would show that the order of $\psi_{\text{TRANSLATE}}$ is ≤ 5.

7.5 Application 3: Translation on the Plane

The method of application 2 can be applied to the problem of the two-dimensional translations of a bounded portion of the plane by using the following trick. Let each copy of the retina be an $(m \times m)$ array. Arrange the squares into a sequence $\{x_i\}$ with the square at (a, b) having index $ma + b$. In effect, we treat the retina as a cylinder and index its squares so:

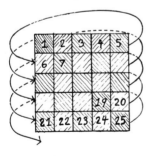

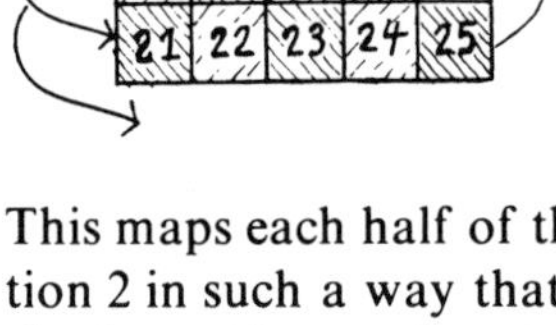

This maps each half of the retina onto a line like that of application 2 in such a way that *for limited translations that do not carry the figure X over the edge of the retina*, translations on the plane are equivalent to translations on the line, and an order-5 predicate can be constructed. In §7.6 we will show how the ugly restriction just imposed can be eliminated!

Application 4. 180° rotation about undetermined point on the plane. With the same kind of restriction, this predicate can be constructed (with order 4) from application 1 by the same route that derived application 3 from application 2. Similarly, we can detect reflections about undetermined vertical axes.

7.6 Repeated Stratification

In the conditions of the stratification theorem, the only restriction on the ψ_j's is that they be suitably bounded. In certain applications the ψ_j's themselves can be obtained by stratification. This is particularly easy to do when the support of ψ_j is finite, for then boundedness is immediate. To illustrate this repeated stratification we will proceed to remove the finite restriction in application 3 of §7.5.

First enumerate all the points of each of two infinite plane retinas A and B according to the more or less arbitrary pattern:

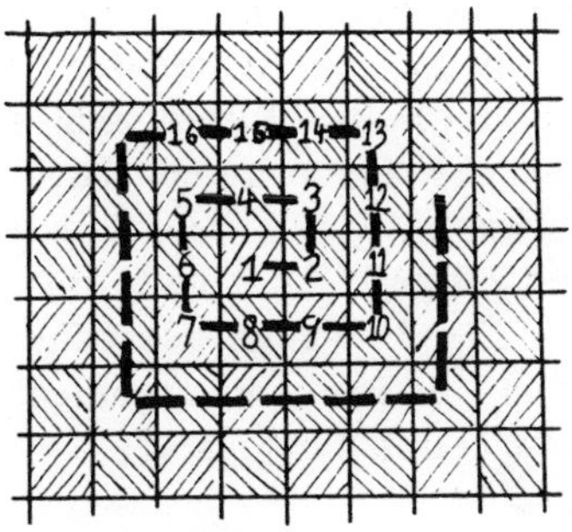

Figure 7.2

to obtain two sequences $x_1, \ldots, x_s, \ldots$, and $y_1, \ldots, y_t, \ldots$.

Now we will invoke precisely the same enumeration as in §7.4, but with the definition

$$\pi_{jk}(X) = (x_j \in X_A \quad \text{AND} \quad y_k \in X_B) = x_j \cdot y_k.$$

Then $C_{(jk)}$ is the class of pairs (X_A, X_B) for which

$$\begin{cases} j = \max \{s | x_s \in X_A\} \\ k = \max \{t | y_t \in X_B\}. \end{cases}$$

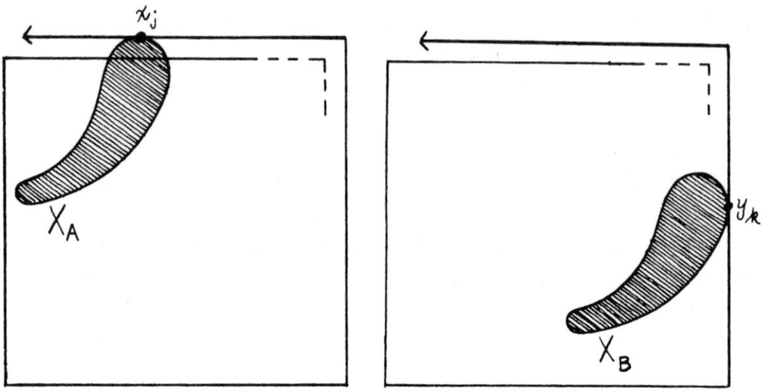

Figure 7.3

We need only a (bounded) $\psi_{(jk)}$ that decides whether X_A is a translate of X_B for figures in C_{jk}. But the figures in C_{jk} all lie within bounded portions of the planes, in fact within squares of about $[\max(j,k)]^{1/2}$ on a side around the origins. Within such a square—or better, within one of twice the size to avoid "edge-effects"—we can use the result of application 3, §7.5, to obtain a predicate $\psi_{(jk)}$ with exactly the desired property, and with finite support! The resulting order is $\leq 5 + 2 = 7$. We have another construction for this predicate of order ≤ 5. The same argument can be used to lift the restrictions in application 4 of §7.5.

7.7 Application 5: The Axis-parallel Squares in the Plane

We digress a moment to apply the method of the last section to show that the predicate

$\psi_{\blacksquare}(X) = \lceil X$ is a solid (hollow) axis-parallel square$\rceil$,

where the form may lie anywhere in the infinite plane, has order ≤ 3.

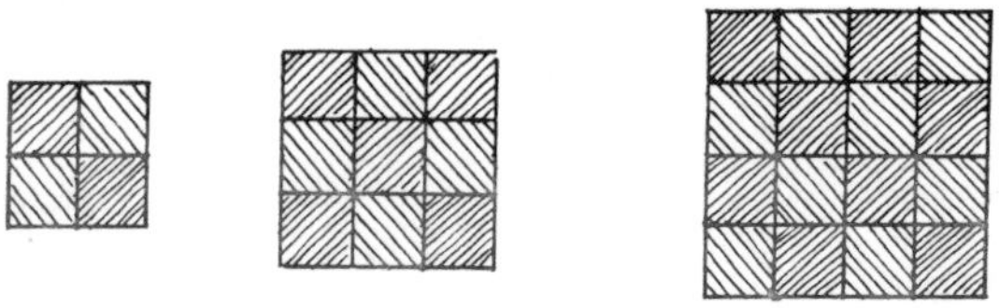

(We consider this remarkable because informal arguments, to the effect that two sides must be compared in length while the interior is also tested, suggest orders of at least 4. The result was discovered, and proven by another method, by our student, John White.)

We enumerate the points $x_1, \ldots,$ of a single plane, just as in §7.6 and simply set $\pi_j = x_j$. Then C_j is the set of figures whose "largest" point is x_j. If X is a square, the situation is like one of the cases shown in Figure 7.4. We then construct ψ_j by stratifying

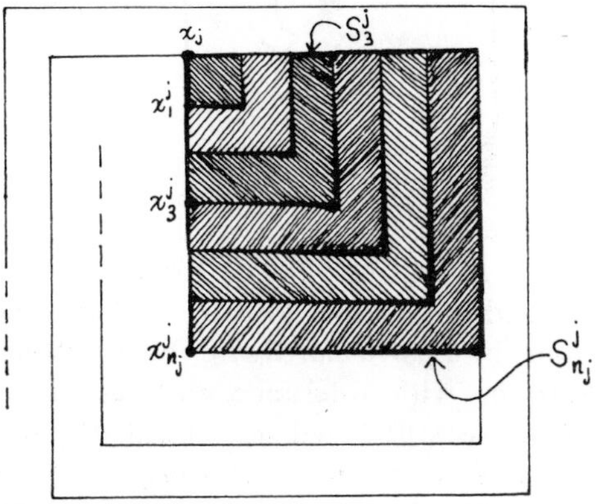

Figure 7.4

as follows: Let $x_1^j, x_2^j, \ldots, x_{nj}^j$ be the finite sequence obtained by stepping into the spiral figure orthogonally from x_j. Define $\pi_i^j = x_i^j$ so that C_i^j will contain all the squares of length i on a side that are "stopped" by x_j. But there is only one such square, call it S_i^j. So to complete the double stratification we need only provide predicates ψ_i^j to recognize the squares S_i^j. But this can be done by

$$\psi_i^j = \lceil \Sigma \alpha_k x_k \geq i^2 \rceil$$

where

$$\alpha_k = \begin{cases} 1 & \text{if } x_k \in S_i^j \\ -1 & \text{if } x_k \notin S_i^j \wedge k < j \\ =0 & \text{otherwise} \end{cases}$$

Then ψ_i^j is of order 1. So $\psi_{\square}$ has order ≤ 3! Q.E.D.

7.8 Application 6: Figures Equivalent under Translation and Dilation

Can a system of finite order recognize equivalence of two arbitrary figures under translation *and* size change?

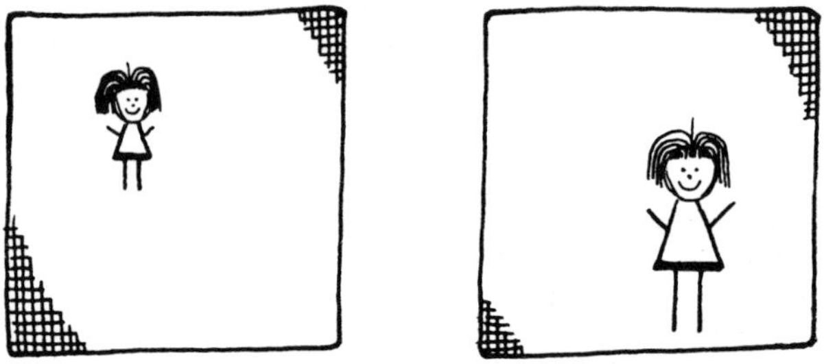

Some reflection about the result and methods used in §7.6 and §7.7 will suggest that we have all the ingredients, for §7.6 shows how to handle translation, and §7.7 shows how to recognize all the translations and dilations of a *particular* figure. Now *dilation* involves serious complications with tolerance and resolution limits, in so far as our theory is still based on a fixed, discrete retina, and we do not want to face this problem squarely. None the less, it is interesting that the desired property can at least be approximated with finite order, in an intuitively suggestive fashion. (We do not think that a similar approximation can be made in the case of rotation invariance, because the problem there is of a different kind, one that cannot be blamed on the discrete retina. Rather, it is because the transformations of a rotation group cannot be simply ordered, and this "blocks" stratification methods.)

Our method begins with the technique used in §7.6 to find predicates $\pi_{(jk)}$ that "catch" the two figures in boxes. Then, just as in §7.6, the problem is reduced to finding predicates $\psi_{(jk)}$ that need only operate within the boxes of Figure 7.2. We construct the $\psi_{(jk)}$'s by a brutal method: within each box we use the simple enumeration of points described in §7.5. Then we stratify four times (!) in succession with respect to

x = highest and leftmost point of A,

y = highest and leftmost point of B,

x' = lowest and rightmost point of A,

y' = lowest and rightmost point of B.

We will need to define predicates $\psi^{(jk)}_{x,y,x',y'}$ for this. If the two vectors $x - x'$ and $y - y'$ do not have the same direction we set $\psi = 0$; otherwise we need a ψ to test whether or not for every vector displacement v

$$y + v \equiv x + \frac{|x - x'|}{|y - y'|} \cdot v,$$

and this is an order-2 predicate, leading finally to total order $\leq 2 + 4 + 2 = 8$. Of course, on the discrete retina the indicated operations on vectors will be ill-defined, but it seems clear that the result is not vacuous: for example, we could ask for recognition of the case where X_B is a translate *and* an integer multiple of X_A in size, with each black square of X_A mapping into a correspondingly larger square in X_B. We have another construction for this predicate of order ≤ 6.

7.9 Application 7: Equivalents of a Particular Figure

In constructing ψ for application 5, we noted that one can always construct an order-1 predicate to detect precisely one particular figure X_0 by using $\lceil \Sigma_{x \in X_0} \bar{x} + \Sigma_{x \notin X_0} x \geq 1 \rceil$. It follows that if we can construct a stratification $\{\pi_i\}$ for a group G such that

$$X \in C_i \text{ AND } gX \in C_i \implies (gX = X),$$

then we can recognize exactly the G-equivalents of a given figure X_0 (with one order higher than the order used by the stratification π's). This is suggestive of a machine that brings figures into a normal form in the first stage of a recognition process. For this case our general construction method takes a very simple form: Consider a particular figure X_0 consisting of the ordered sequence of points $\{x_{i_1}, \ldots, x_{i_p}\}$ on the half-line

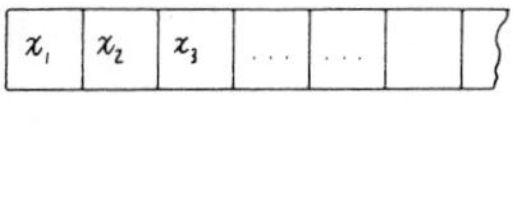

Let $\pi_j(X) = \lceil x_j \in X \rceil$ and define $\psi_j(X)$ as

$$\left\lceil \sum \lceil x_{k-j+i_p} \in X_0 \rceil \bar{x}_k + \sum \lceil x_{k-j+i_p} \in X_0 \text{ AND } k < j \rceil x_k < 1 \right\rceil$$

ignoring for the moment points with negative indices. Then, except for "edge effects" we obtain a predicate of order 2 that recognizes precisely the translates of X_0. Next we observe that there is really no difficulty in extending this to the two-way infinite line, for we can enumerate the π_i's in the order

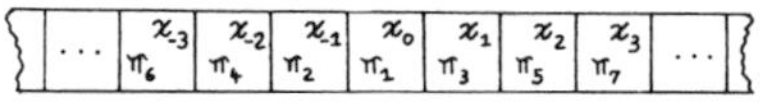

so that if a figure ends up in class C_{2j} we will have found its leftmost point X_{-j}, and if it is in a C_{2j+1} we will have found its rightmost point X_j. In either case we can construct an appropriate ψ. Hence, finally, we see that there exists for any given figure X_0 a predicate of order 2 that recognizes precisely the linear translations of X_0, and there is no problem about boundedness because all ψ supports are finite.

7.10 Apparent Paradox

Consider the case of $X_0 =$  .

We have just shown that there exists a ψ of order 2 that accepts just the translates of this figure. Hence ψ must reject the non-equivalent figure, . But both of these figures have exactly the same n-tuple distribution spectrum (see §6.2 and §6.5) up to order 2! Each has 3 points, and each has 1 adjacent pair, 1 pair two units apart, and 1 pair 3 units apart. Therefore, if all group-equivalent φ's had the same weights, a perceptron of order ≥ 3 would be needed to distinguish them. Thus if we could apply the group-invariance theorem we would in fact obtain a proof that *no* perceptron of order 2 can distinguish between these. This would be a contradiction! What is wrong? The answer is that the group-invariance theorem does not in general apply to predicates invariant under infinite groups. When a group is finite, for example, the cyclic translation group of the toroidal spaces we have considered from time to time, one can always use the group-invariance theorem to make equal the coefficients of equivalent φ's. But we cannot use it together with stratification to construct the predicate on infinite groups.

With infinite groups we can use stratification for normalizing, but then we must face the possibility of getting unbounded coefficients within equivalent φ's; and then the group-averaging operations do not, in general, converge. This will be shown as a theorem in §10.4.

We conjecture that predicates like the "twins" of §7.5 are not of finite order with bounded coefficients. In any case, it would be interesting to know whether there are such predicates.

7.11 Problems

A number of lines of investigation are intriguing: what is the relation between the possible stratifications, including repeated ones, and algebraic decompositions of the group into different kinds of subgroups? For what kinds of predicates can the group-invariance theorem be extended to infinite groups? What predicates have bounded coefficients in each equivalence class, or in each degree? Under what conditions do the "normal-form stratifications" of application 7 exist? For example, *we conjecture that on circles or toroids, there is no bound on the order of predicates ψ that select unique "normal form" figures under rotation groups:*

$$\psi(X) \quad \text{AND} \quad \psi(gX) \quad \Rightarrow \quad X = gX.$$

We suspect that this may be the reason we were unable to extend the method of application 6 to the full Euclidean similarity group, including rotation.

We note that the condition in Theorem 7.2 that the predicates $\{\pi_j\}$ be masks is probably stronger than necessary. We have not looked for a better theorem.

Stratified predicates probably are physically unrealizable because of huge coefficients. It would be valuable to have a form of Theorem 7.2 that could help establish lower bounds on the coefficients.

A stratification seems to correspond to a serial machine that operates sequentially upon the figure, with a sequence of group transformation elements, until some special event occurs, establishing its membership in C_j, and then applies a "matching test" corresponding to ψ_j. The set of ψ_j's must contain information about the figures in all transformed positions, so the possibility of a perceptron accomplishing such a recognition should not suggest that the machine has any special generalization ability with respect to the group in question; rather, it suggests the opposite! The apparent enormity of the coefficient hierarchies casts a gloomy shadow on the practicality of learning stratified coefficients by reinforcement, since reinforcing a figure in C_j cannot work until it has depressed all discriminations in all preceding classes. This is discussed further in Chapter 10 and 11.

EXAMPLE: to recognize the translates of the pattern  $= X_0$.
Let R be the half-line x_1 x_2 x_3 . . . and let Ψ be the desired predicate: $\lceil X$ has exactly 3 black squares, in the pattern $X_0 \rceil$
We will show that Ψ has order 2. First we define a special predicate ψ_j for each instance of Ψ as follows:

$\psi_j(X) = \lceil$The leftmost j squares of X is exactly  $\rceil$
←j-4 squares→

$$= \lceil \Sigma_j > 0 \rceil \text{ where } \Sigma_j = (\bar{x}_1 + \bar{x}_2 + \ldots + x_{j-3} + \bar{x}_{j-2} + x_{j-1} + x_j + j - \tfrac{1}{2})$$

Note that each Σ_j has order 1. Make $\Sigma_1 = \Sigma_2 = \Sigma_3 = 0$.
Now we can express $\Psi(X)$ as something like

$$\Psi(X) = \lceil \psi_j(X) \text{ AND } x_j \text{ is the rightmost black square of } X \rceil$$

but can we express the implied selection of the correct ψ_j within the linear threshold framework? Yes, by using a trick! Let $\{M_j\}$ be a sequence of numbers that grows large very quickly, e.g., $M_1 = 10$ $M_2 = 10^{10}$ . . . $M_{j+1} = 10^{M_j}$. Then

$$\Psi = \lceil M_4 x_4 \Sigma_4 + M_5 x_5 \Sigma_5 + \ldots + M_j x_j \Sigma_j + \ldots > 0 \rceil$$

~~because the term with the right-most black~~ x_j will outweigh all earlier terms and so determine the sign of the whole sum. The entire chapter is based on various ways to exploit this simple yet bizarre concept. The simple x_j terms of this example correspond to the π_j masks of the text.

8

8.0

In this chapter we discuss the power and limitations of the "diameter-limited" perceptrons: those in which φ can see only a circumscribed portion of the retina R.

We consider a machine that sums the weighted evidence about a picture obtained by experiments φ_i, each of which report on the state of affairs within a circumscribed region of *diameter less than or equal to some length* D, that is, Diameter $(S(\varphi)) \leq D$.

One gets two different theories when, in considering diameter-limited predicate-schemes, one takes D as

(1) an absolute length, or

(2) a fixed fraction of the size of R.

Generally, it is more interesting to choose (1) for positive results. For negative results, (1) is usually a special case of an order-limited theory, and (2) gives different and sometimes stronger results. The theory did not seem deep enough to justify trying to determine in each case the best possible result. From a practical point of view one merely wants D to be small enough that none of the φ's see the whole figure (for otherwise we would have no theory at all) and large enough to see interesting features.

8.1 Positive Results

We will first consider some things that a diameter-limited perceptron can recognize, and then some of the things it cannot.

8.1.1 Uniform Picture

A diameter-limited perceptron can tell when a picture is entirely black, or entirely white: choose φ_i's that *cover* the retina in regions (that may overlap) and define φ_i to be zero if and only if all the points it can see are white. Then

$$\Sigma\varphi_i > 0$$

if the picture has one or more black points, and ≤ 0 if the picture is blank. Similarly, we could define the φ_i's to distinguish the all-black picture from all others.

These patterns are recognizable because of their "conjunctively local" character (see §0.6): no φ-unit can really say that there is strong evidence that the figure is all white (for there is only the faintest correlation with this), but any φ can definitely say that it has conclusive evidence that the picture is *not* all white. Some interesting patterns have this character, that one can *reject* all pictures not in the class because each must have, somewhere or other, a local feature that is definitive and can be detected by what happens within a region of diameter D.

8.1.2 Area Cuts

We can distinguish, for any number S, the class of figures whose area is greater than S. To do this we define a φ_p for each point to be 1 if p is black, 0 otherwise. Then

$$\Sigma \varphi_p > S$$

is a recognizer for the class in question.

8.1.3 Triangles and Rectangles

We can make a diameter-limited perceptron recognize the figures consisting of exactly one triangle (either solid or outline) by the following trick: We use two kinds of φ's: the first has value $+1$ if its field contains a vertex (two line segments meeting at an angle), otherwise its value is zero. The second kind, $\hat{\varphi}_i$, has value zero if its field is blank, or contains a line segment, solid black area, or a vertex, but has value $+1$ if the field contains anything else, including the end of a line segment. Provide enough of these φ's so that the entire retina is covered, in nonoverlapping fashion, by both types. Of course, this won't work when a vertex occurs at the edge of a φ-support. By suitable overlapping, and assignment of weights, the system can be improved, but it will always be an approximation of some sort. This applies to the definition of "line segment," etc., as well as to that of "vertex." See §8.3. Finally assign weight 1 to the first type and a very large positive weight W to those of the second type. Then

$$\Sigma \varphi_i + W \Sigma \hat{\varphi}_i < 4$$

will be a specific recognizer for triangles. (It will, however, accept the blank picture, as well). Similarly, by setting φ's to recognize only right angles, we can discern the class of rectangles with

$$\Sigma \varphi_i + W \Sigma \hat{\varphi}_i < 5.$$

A few other geometric classes can be captured by such tricks, but they depend on curious accidents. A rectangle is characterized by having four right angles, and none of the exceptions detected by the $\hat{\varphi}_i$'s. In §6.3.2 we did this for axis-parallel rectangles: for others there are obviously more serious resolution and tolerance problems. But there is no way to recognize the squares, even axis-parallel, with diameter-limited φ's; the method of §7.2.5 can't be so modified.

8.1.4 Absolute Template-matching

Suppose that one wants the machine to recognize exactly a certain figure X_0 and no other. Then the diameter-limited machine can be made to do this by partitioning the retina into regions, and in each region a φ function has a value 0 if that part of the retina is exactly matched to the corresponding part of X_0, otherwise the value is 1. Then

$$\Sigma \varphi < 1$$

if and only if the picture is exactly X_0.

Note, however, that this scheme works just on a particular object in a particular position. It cannot be generalized to recognize a particular object in *any* position. In fact we show in the next section that even the simplest figure, that consists of just one point, cannot be recognized independently of position!

8.2 Negative Results

8.2.1 The Figure Containing One Single Black Point

This is the fundamental counterexample. We want a machine

$$\Sigma \alpha_\varphi \varphi \geq \theta$$

to accept figures with area 1, but reject figures with area 0 or area greater than 1. To see that this cannot be done with diameter-limited perceptrons, suppose that $\{\varphi\}$, $\{\alpha\}$, and θ have been selected. Present first the blank picture X Then if $f(X)$ $\Sigma \alpha_i \varphi_i(X)$, we have $f(X_0) < \theta$. Now present a figure X_1 containing only one point x_1. We must then have

$$f(X_1) \geq \theta.$$

The change in the sum must be due to a change in the values of some of the φ's. In fact, it must be due to changes only in φ's for which $x_1 \epsilon S(\varphi)$, since nothing else in the picture has changed. In any case,

$$f(X_1) - f(X_0) > 0.$$

Now choose another point x_2 which is further than D away from x_1. Then no $S(\varphi)$ can contain both x_1 and x_2. For the figure X_2 containing only x_2 we must also have

$$f(X_2) = \Sigma \alpha_i \varphi_i \geq \theta.$$

Now consider the figure X_{12} containing both x_1 and x_2. The addition of the point x_1 to X_2 can affect only φ's for which $x_1 \epsilon S(\varphi)$, and these are changed exactly as they are changed when the all-blank picture X_0 is changed to the picture X_1. Therefore

$$f(X_{12}) = f(X_2) + [f(X_1) - f(X_0)].$$

But then the two previous inequalities yield

$$f(X_{12}) > \theta$$

which contradicts the requirement that

$$f(X_{12}) < \theta.$$

Of course, this is the same phenomenon noted in §0.3 and §2.1. And it gives the method for proof of the last statement in §8.1.3.

8.2.2 Area Segments

The diameter-limited perceptron cannot recognize the class of figures whose areas A lie between two bounds $A_1 \leq A \leq A_2$.

PROOF: this follows from the method of §8.2.1, which is a special case of this, with $A_1 = 1$ and $A_2 = 1$. We recall that this recognition is possible with order 2 if the diameter limitation is relaxed using the method of §1.4, example 7.

8.2.3 Connectedness

The diameter-limited perceptron cannot decide when the picture is a single, connected whole, as distinguished from two or more disconnected pieces. At this point the reader will have no difficulty in seeing the formal correctness of the proof we gave of this in §0.8.

8.3 Diameter-limited Integral Invariants

We observed in §6.3.1 that convexity has order 3, but that the construction used there would not carry over to the diameter-limited case, because it would not reject a figure with two widely separated convex components. On the other hand, §8.1.3 shows how a diameter-limited predicate can capture some particular convex figures. The latter construction generalizes, but leads into serious problems about tolerance and into questions about differentials.

Suppose that we define a diameter-limited family of predicates Φ_c using the following idea: Choose an $\epsilon > 0$. Cover R with a partition of small cells C_j. For each integer k define φ_{jk} to be 1 if $C_j \cap X$ contains an "edge" with change-in-direction greater than $k\epsilon$ and otherwise $\varphi_{jk} = 0$.

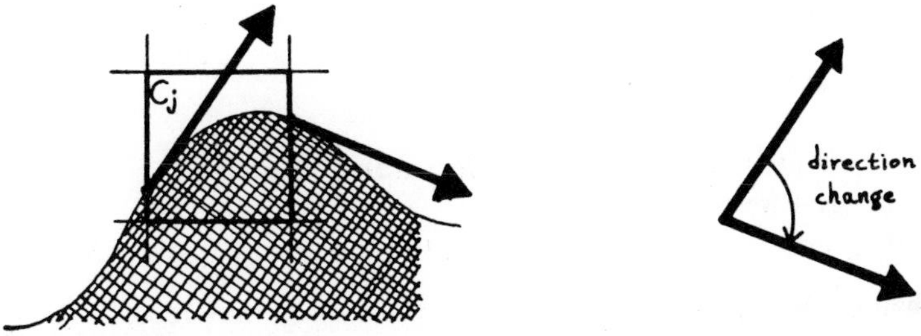

Now consider the "integral"

$$\sum_{jk} \epsilon\,\varphi_{jk}.$$

The contribution to the sum of each segment of curve will be $\epsilon \cdot c/\epsilon = c$, where c is the magnitude of the change in direction of the segment; hence the total sum is the "total curvature." Finally we claim that we can "realize" ψ_{CONVEX} as

$$\left\lceil \sum_{jk} \epsilon\,\varphi_{jk} \le 2\pi \right\rceil,$$

because the total curvature of *any* figure must be $\ge 2\pi$ and only (and all) convex figures achieve the equality. We ignore figures that reach the edge of the retina and such matters.

A similar argument can be used to construct a predicate that uses the *signed* curvature to realize functions of the Euler characteristic of the form $G(X) < n$, since that invariant is just the total signed curvature divided by 2π. Of course on the *quantized* plane the diameter-limited predicate of §5.8.1 does this more simply.

One could go on to describe more sophisticated predicates that classify figures by properties of their "differential spectra."

However, we do not pursue this because these observations already raise a number of serious questions about tolerances and approximations. There are problems about the uniformity of the coverings, the sizes of ϵ and the diameter-limited cells C_j, and problems about the cumulative errors in summing small approximate quantities. Certainly within the $E^2 \rightarrow R$ square map described in Chapter 5, or anything like it, all such predicates will give peculiar results whenever the diameter cells are not large compared to the underlying mesh, or small compared to the relevant features of the X's. The analysis, in §9.3, of ψ_{CONVEX} attempts to face this problem.

For example, we can regard the recognition of rectangles, as done in §6.3.2, as a pure artifact in this context, because it so depends on the mesh. The description in §8.1.3 of another form of the same predicate is worded in such a way that one *could* make reasonable approximations, within reasonable size ranges.

8.4 Proof of Uniqueness of the Eulerian Invariants for Diameter-Limited Perceptrons

In this section we show, as promised at the end of Chapter 5, that

Theorem 8.4: Diameter-limited perceptrons cannot recognize any nontrivial topological properties except the Eulerian predicates

$$\lceil E(X) > n \rceil \qquad \text{and} \qquad \lceil E(X) < n \rceil.$$

PROOF: The argument of §5.8 shows that $\psi(X)$ must be a function of $E(X)$. This is immediate for the absolute diameter-limit, which is a special case of order-limit. The argument, with suitable modifications, carries over to relative diameter-limits. Now consider two figures A and B that differ only in a single interior square:

A

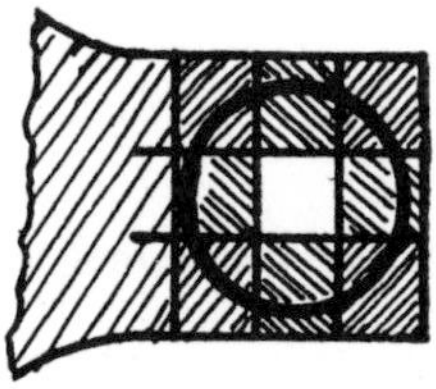

B

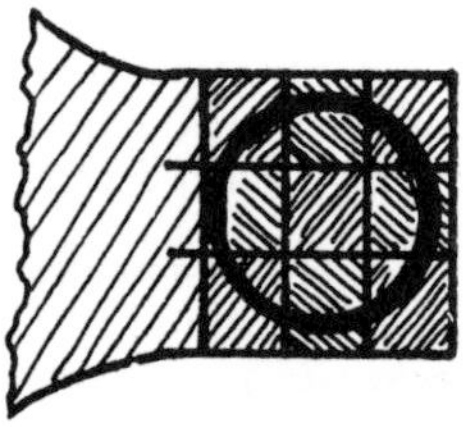

NOTE: Another sense of "local", that fuses the ideas of diameter-limit and order-limit, permits each φ to depend on up to n separate regions of small diameter. We say that such a perceptron has "DIFFERENTIAL ORDER n". The predicate ⌈X is a solid square⌉ has differential order 2! We now feel that this is the most interesting "restriction" (see p. 12) for further research on computational geometry, for many practical, mathematical and physiological reasons. (continued below)

---

where the circle shows the range of the diameter limit. Then suppose that $\psi(X) = \lceil \Sigma\, \alpha_\varphi\, \varphi(X) > \theta \rceil$ and consider the difference

$$\Delta = \Sigma \alpha_\varphi \varphi(B) - \Sigma \alpha_\varphi \varphi(A).$$

Now if it happens that $\Delta \geq 0$ then

$$\psi(B) \geq \psi(A),$$

hence removing a hole cannot decrease ψ. By topological equivalence, adding a component has the same effect upon $E(X)$ and hence upon $\psi(X)$. Thus, if $\Delta \geq 0$, then

$$E(B) > E(A) \Rightarrow \psi(B) \geq \psi(A),$$

and similarly, if $\Delta \leq 0$ then

$$E(B) > E(A) \Rightarrow \psi(B) \leq \psi(A).$$

It follows that in each case there must be an n such that (if $\Delta \geq 0$)

$$\psi(X) = \lceil E(X) > n \rceil$$

or (if $\Delta \leq 0$)

$$\psi(X) = \lceil E(X) < n \rceil$$

or else ψ is a constant.

The trivial exceptions are the constant predicates and the uniform predicates of §8.1.1, which are exceptions to the canonical form of §5.8.

The differential-order idea suggests ways to free the theory from annoying artefacts of the discrete partition of the "retina" (now we can talk about any square without reference to the artificial checkerboard); we can more clearly face problems about approximation errors and tolerances, and deal directly with ordinary concepts like continuity, curvature, or convexity, replacing opportunistic but unnatural combinational proofs by more appropriate methods of metrical and integration theories.

9

9.0 Connectedness and Serial Computation

It seems intuitively clear that the abstract quality of connectedness cannot be captured by a perceptron of finite order because of its inherently serial character: one cannot conclude that a figure is connected by any simple order-independent combination of simple tests. The same is true for the much simpler property of *parity*. In the case of parity, there is a stark contrast between our "worst possible" result for finite-order machines (§3.1, §10.1) and the following "best possible" result for the *serial* computation of parity. Let $x_1, x_2, \ldots, x_n$ be any enumeration of the points of R and consider the following algorithm for determining the parity of $|X|$:

START: Set i to 0.

EVEN: Add 1 to i.
If $i = |R|$ then STOP; $\psi_{\text{PARITY}} = 0$.
If $x_i = 0$, go to EVEN; otherwise go to ODD.

ODD: Add 1 to i.
If $i = |R|$ then STOP; $\psi_{\text{PARITY}} = 1$.
If $x_i = 0$, go to ODD; otherwise go to EVEN.

Now this program is "minimal" in two respects: first in the number of computation-steps per point, but more significant, in the fact that the program requires no temporary storage place for partial information accumulated during the computation, other than that required for the enumeration variable i. [In a sense, the process requires one binary digit of current information, but this can be absorbed (as above) into the algorithm structure.]

This suggests that it might be illuminating to ask for connectedness: how much memory is required by the best serial algorithm? The answer, as shown below, is that it requires no more than about 2 times that for storing the enumeration variable alone! To study this problem it seems that the Turing-machine framework is the simplest and most natural because of its uniform way of handling information storage.

9.1 A Serial Algorithm for Connectedness

Connectedness of a geometric figure X is characterized by the fact that between any path (p,q) of points of X there is a path that lies entirely in X. An equivalent definition, using any enumeration $x_1, \ldots, x_{|R|}$ of the points of R is: *X is connected when each point x_i in X, except the first point in X, has a path to some x_j in X for which $i > j$.* (Proof: By recursion, then, each point of X is connected to the *first* point in X.) Using this definition of connectedness we can describe a beautiful algorithm to test whether X is connected. We will consider only figures that are "reasonably regular"—to be precise, we suppose that for each point x_i on a boundary there is defined a unique "next point" x_{i^*} on that boundary. We choose x_{i^*} to be the boundary point to one's right when standing on x_i and facing the complement of X. We will also assume that points x_i and x_{i+1} that are *consecutive* in the enumeration are *adjacent* except at the edges of R. Finally, we will assume that X does not touch the edges of the space R.

Assume also that X never becomes just one square "thin", as misleadingly shown in the next figure.

START: Set i to 0 and go to SEARCH.

SEARCH: Add 1 to i. If $i = |R|$, stop and print "*X is NULL.*"
If $x_i \in X$ then go to SCAN, otherwise go to SEARCH.

SCAN: Add 1 to i. If $i = |R|$, stop and print "*X is connected.*"
If $x_{i-1} \notin X$ AND $x_i \in X$ then set j to i and go to TRACE, otherwise go to SCAN.

TRACE: Set j to j^*.
If $j = i$, stop and print "*X is disconnected.*"
If $j > i$, go to TRACE.
If $j < i$, go to SCAN.

Notice that at any point in the computation, it is sufficient to keep track of the two integers i and j; we will see that no extra memory space is needed for $|R|$.

Analysis: SEARCH simply finds the first point of X in the enumeration of R. Once such a point of X is found, SCAN searches through all of R, eventually testing every point of X. The current point, x_i, of SCAN is tested as follows: If x_i is not in X, then no test is necessary and SCAN goes on to x_{i+1}. If the previous point x_{i-1} was in X (and, by induction, is presumed to have passed the test) then x_i, if in X, is connected to x_{i-1} by adjacency. Finally, if $x_i \in X$ and

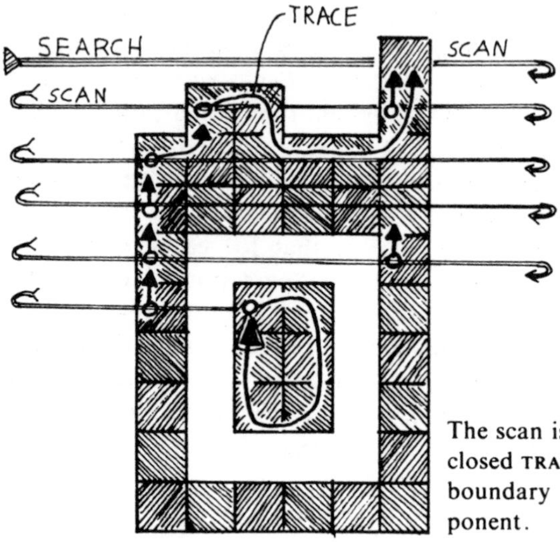

The scan is terminated by the closed TRACE loop around the boundary of the inner component.

$x_{i-1} \notin X$, then x_i is on a boundary curve B. TRACE circumnavigates this boundary curve. Now if B is a boundary curve it is either (1) an exterior boundary of a previously encountered component of X, in which case some point of B must have been encountered

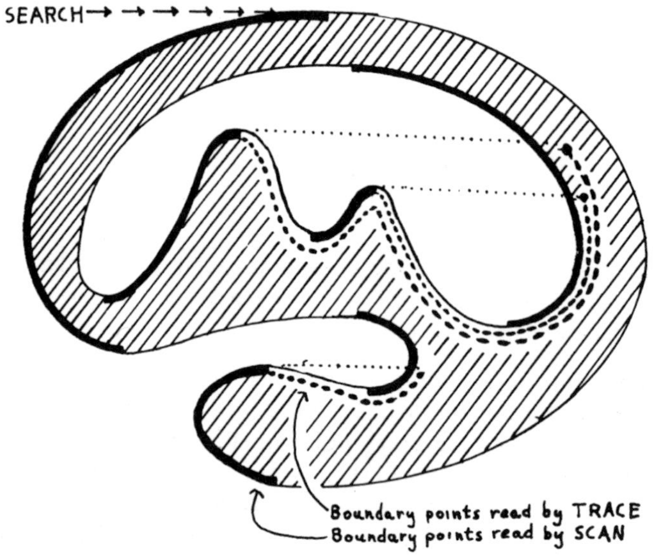

Figure 9.1

before, or (2) B is an interior boundary curve, in which case a point of B must have been encountered before reaching x_{i-1} which is *inside* B, or (3) B is the exterior boundary curve of a never-before-encountered component of X, the only case in which TRACE will return to x_i without meeting an x_j for which $j < i$. Thus SCAN will run up to $i = |R|$ if and only if X has a single nonempty connected component (see Figure 9.1).

9.2 The Turing-Machine Version of the Connectedness Algorithm

It is convenient to assume that R is a $2^n \times 2^n$ square array. Let $x_1, \ldots, x_{|R|}$ be an enumeration of the points of R in the order

1,	$2^n + 1$,	...	$(2^n - 1)2^n + 1$,
2,	$2^n + 2$,	...	$(2^n - 1)2^n + 2$,
.	.	...	.
.	.	...	.
.	.	...	.
2^n,	$2^n + 2^n$,	...	$(2^n - 1)2^n + 2^n$.

This choice of dimension and enumeration makes available a simple way to represent the situation to a Turing machine. The Turing machine must be able to specify a point x_i of R, find whether $x_i \in X$, and in case x_i is a boundary point of X, find the index i^* of the "right neighbor" of x_i. The Turing-machine tape will have the form

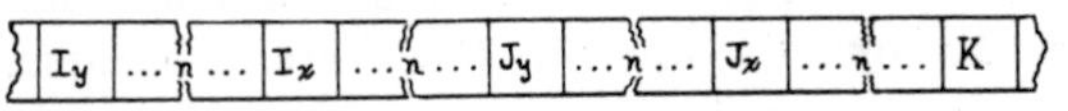

where "..n.." denotes an interval of n blank squares. Then the intervals to the right of I_x and I_y can hold the x and y coordinates of a point of R.

We will suppose that the Turing machine is coupled with the outside world, that is, the figure X, through an "oracle" that works as follows: certain internal states of the machine have the property that when entered, the resulting next state depends on whether the coordinates in the I(or J) intervals designate a point in X. It can be verified, though the details are tedious, that all the operations described in the algorithm can be performed by a fixed Turing machine that uses no tape squares other than those in the ". .*n*. ." intervals. For example, "$i = |R|$" if and only if there are all zeros in the ". .*n*. ."'s following I_x and I_y. "Add 1 to i" is equivalent to "start at J_y and move left, changing 1's to 0's until a 0 is encountered (and changed to 1) or until I_y is met. The only nontrivial operation is computing j^* given j. But this requires only examining the neighbors of x_j, and that is done by adding ± 1 to the J_x and J_y coordinates, and consulting the oracle.

Since the Turing machine can keep track of which ". .*n*. ." interval it is in, we really need only one symbol for punctuation, so the Turing machine can be a 3-symbol machine. By using a block encoding, one can use a 2-symbol machine, and, omitting details, we obtain the result:

Theorem 9.2: For any ϵ there is a 2-symbol Turing machine that can verify the connectedness of a figure X on any rectangular array R, using less than $(2 + \epsilon) \log_2 |R|$ squares of tape.

We are fairly sure that the connectedness algorithm is minimal in its use of tape, but we have no proof. (In fact, we are very weak in methods to show that an algorithm is minimal in storage; this is discussed in Chapter 12.) Incidentally, it is not hard to show that $\lceil |X| \text{ is prime} \rceil$ requires no more than $(2 + \epsilon) \log_2 |R|$ squares (and presumably needs more than $(2 - \epsilon) \log_2 |R|$).

We have little definite knowledge about geometric predicates that require higher orders of storage, but we suspect that, in an appropriate sense, recognizing the topological equivalence of two figures (for example, two components of X) requires something more like $|R|$ than like $\log |R|$ squares. There are, of course, recursive function-theoretic predicates that require arbitrarily large amounts of storage, but none of these are known to have straightforward geometric interpretations.

9.2.1 Pebble Automata

A variant of this computation model has been studied by M. Blum and C. Hewitt. The Turing machine is replaced by a finite-state automation which moves about on the retina, reading the color of the cell on which it is currently located. As a function of this input and its current state, the automaton determines its next state and one of four possible moves: north, east, south, west. A properly designed automaton should operate on any retina, however large, provided that it is given a way to detect the edge of the array. This is a convenient way to realize the idea of a predicate-scheme.

The position of the automaton on the retina plays the role of *one* of the two print indices I and J remembered by the Turing machine. To give the machine the effect of the second point index, it can be provided with a pebble that can be left anywhere on the retina and retrieved later. We leave to readers the extremely tricky exercise of translating the Turing machine algorithm into a form suitable for an automaton with one pebble. Can connectedness be recognized without using the pebble? Surely not, but we have not proved it! Still unproved, May '72!

9.3 Memory-Tape Requirements for ψ_{CONVEX}

For convexity we can also get a bound on the tape memory. However, since convexity is a metric property, one must face the problem of precision of measurement vis-à-vis the resolution of the finite lattice of R. It seems reasonable to ask that the figure have no indentations larger than the order of the size of a lattice square. One way to verify this is to check, for each pair (a, b) of boundary points, that there is no such indentation:

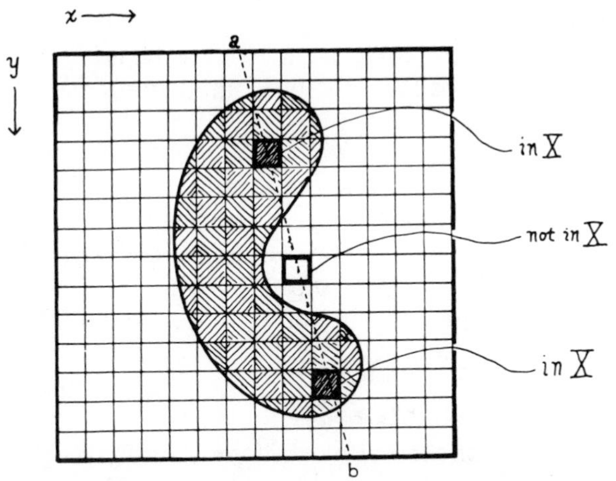

To make this test seems to require the equivalent of scanning the squares close to the ideal line from a to b, and some memory is required to stay sufficiently close to its slope. For each increment in (say) y one must compute for x the largest integer in

$$a + y \cdot \frac{b - a}{n},$$

and the remainder, with its $\log_2 n$ digits must be saved for the iterative computation. Thus the computation can be done if one stores $\log_2 n$ digits for each of a, b, x, y, and r, where

$$r(y) = \text{the remainder of } \frac{r(y - 1) + b - a}{n}$$

which can be obtained from a register containing x and r by adding $b - a$ at each step:

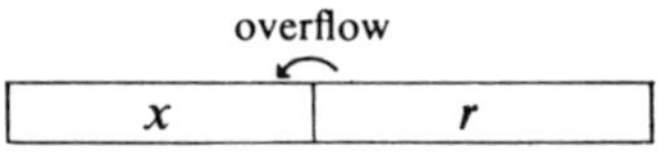

Thus one can test for convexity by using the order of $\frac{5}{2} \log_2 |R|$ squares. There is an evident redundancy here since (for example) a can be reconstructed from the other four quantities, and this suggests that with some ingenuity one could get by with just $(2 + \epsilon) \log_2 |R|$.

In any case we have no idea of how to establish a lower bound. Although convexity is simpler than connectivity in that it is *conjunctively local*, this is no particular advantage to the Turing machine, which is well suited for recursive computation, and this simplicity is quite possibly balanced by the complication of the metric calculation. So we are inclined to conjecture that both ψ_{CONVEX} and $\psi_{\text{CONNECTED}}$ require about $2 \log_2 |R|$ tape squares for realization by Turing machines. We regard our inability to prove a firm lower bound as another symptom of the general weakness of contemporary computation theory's tools for establishing minimal computational complexity measures on particular algorithms.

9.4 Connectedness and Parallel Machinery

We have seen that there exists a Turing machine that can compute $\psi_{\text{CONNECTED}}$ with very little auxiliary storage in the form of memory tape. The computation requires an appreciable amount of time, or number of steps of machine operation. The number of Turing-machine steps appears to be of the order of $|R| \log |R|$ for reasonably regular figures (for "bad" figures there may be a term of order $|R|^2 \log |R|$). On the other side, the Turing machine requires a remarkably small amount of physical machinery, which is used over and over again in the course of the computation.

If one has more machinery, one should be able to reduce the number of time steps required for a computation, but we know very little about the nature of such exchanges. In the case of realizing $\psi_{\text{CONNECTED}}$, one can gain time by subdividing the space into regions and computing, simultaneously, properties of the connectivity within the regions. For example, suppose that we had machines capable of establishing, in less than the time necessary to compute $\psi_{\text{CONNECTED}}$ for the whole retina, a "connection matrix" for boundary points on each quadrant. In the figure, this means knowing that a is connected to a', b to b', and so on.

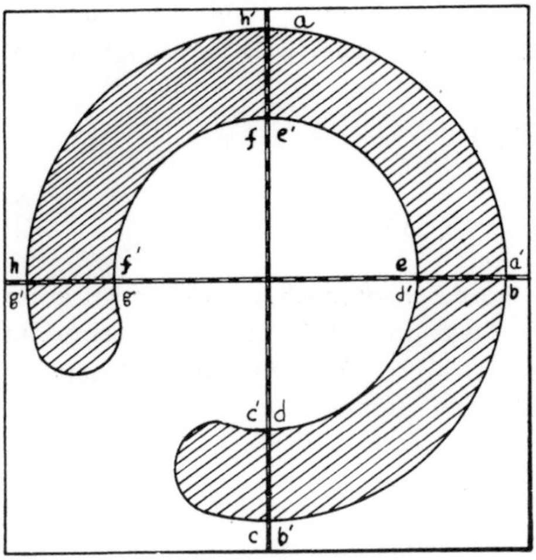

The connectedness of the whole can then be decided by an algorithm that "sews" together these edges.

If the mesh is made finer, the computations within the cells become faster, but the "sewing" becomes more elaborate. On the other hand, the subdivision can probably be applied recursively to the sewing operation also, and we have not studied the possible exchanges. We can find an interesting upper bound for an extreme case: Suppose the machine is composed entirely of Boolean functions of two arguments; then how much time is required for such a machine to compute $\psi_{\text{CONNECTED}}$, assuming that each Boolean operation requires one time unit?

Suppose, for convenience, that R has $|R| = 2^n$ squares (points). Certain pairs of points are considered to be "adjacent," and by chaining this relation we can describe $\psi_{\text{CONNECTED}}$ by a particularly compact inductive definition; we write

$$C^1_{ij}(X) = \lceil x_i \wedge x_j \wedge (x_i \text{ is adjacent to } x_j)\rceil$$

and

$$C^{m+1}_{ij}(X) = \bigvee_{k=1}^{|R|} C^m_{ik}(X) \wedge C^m_{kj}(X). \tag{1}$$

Each point x_i is considered to be connected to itself, so that $C^1_{ii}(X) \equiv \lceil x_i \in X\rceil$. Then it can be seen inductively that $C^m_{ij}(X)$ is true if and only if x_i and x_j are connected by a chain of $\leq 2^m$ of adjacent points, all in X. The whole figure is connected, that is, $\psi_{\text{CONNECTED}}(X) = 1$, if $C^n_{ij}(X) = 1$ for every pair for which $x_i \in X$ and $x_j \in X$. Hence

$$\psi_{\text{CONNECTED}} = \lceil x_i \wedge x_j \Longrightarrow C^n_{ij}(X)\rceil$$

$$= \bigwedge_{i=1}^{|R|} \bigwedge_{j=1}^{|R|} [\bar{x}_i \vee \bar{x}_j \vee C^n_{ij}(X)]. \tag{2}$$

This function can be composed in a machine with a separate layer for each level of C^m_{ij}. To connect C^{m+1}_{ij} to the appropriate C^m_{ij}'s requires bringing together up to $|R|$ terms, using Equation 1, and this requires a tree of *or*'s of at most $n = \log_2 |R|$ layers

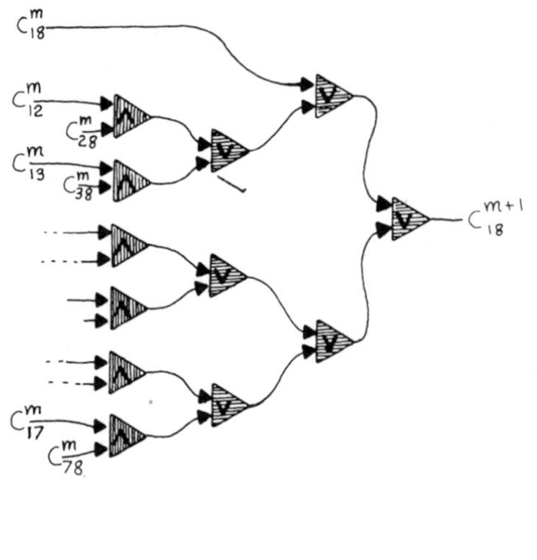

in depth. There are n such layers so the total time to compute C^n_{ij} is of the order of n^2. Using Relation 2, we find the final combination requires about $2n$ layers so we have

$$\text{time}\,(\psi_{\text{CONNECTED}}) \leq (\log |R|)^2 + k \cdot \log |R|,$$

where k is a small constant.*

We doubt that the computation can be done in much less than the order of $(\log |R|)^2$ *units of time, with any arrangement of plausible computer ingredients arranged in any manner whatever.* Notice that we were careful to count the delay entailed by the *or* operations. If this is neglected the computation requires only $\log |R|$ steps, but this is physically unrealistic for large $|R|$. Indeed, we really should prohibit the unlimited "branching" or copying of the *outputs* of the elements; if the amplifiers that are physically necessary for this are counted we have to replace our estimate by $3(\log |R|)^2$. As usual, we have no firm method to establish the lower bound. However, the following pseudoproof seems relevant:

1. *Using more "memory" in the machine doesn't seem to help.* Can the machine be speeded-up by storing a library of connected figures and identifying them rather than working out the definition of connectivity each time? The extreme: build a library of *all* connected figures on R. A tree of binary Boolean operators can be built to match any pattern in just $\log |R|$ time steps. This greatly speeds up the analogue of part 1 above. But there are so many different connected figures that one has now to *or* together of the order of $2^{\theta |R|}$ terms (where θ is some fraction $\frac{2}{3} < \theta < 1$) so the analogue of part 2 takes $\log (2^{\theta |R|}) = \theta\,|R|$ steps, which is worse than $(\log |R|)^2$ for large R. Of course this is not a proof, but we think it is an indication.

2. *Using loops cannot increase speed.* The $(\log |R|)^2$ machine is a loop-free hierarchy of Boolean functions—it has no "serial" computation capacity except that which lies in its layered structure.

One could vastly reduce its number of parts (of which there are the order of $|R|^3 \cdot \log |R|$) by making a network with loops: in-

*This construction was suggested to us by R. Floyd and A. Meyer.

deed we could build a Turing machine that would have only $k \log |R|$ parts, for some modest k. But, for a given computation of bounded lengths, the fastest machine with loops *cannot* be faster than the fastest loop-free machine (ignoring branching costs). For one can always construct an equivalent loop-free machine by making copies of the original machine—one copy for each computation step—with all functions taking arguments from earlier copies.

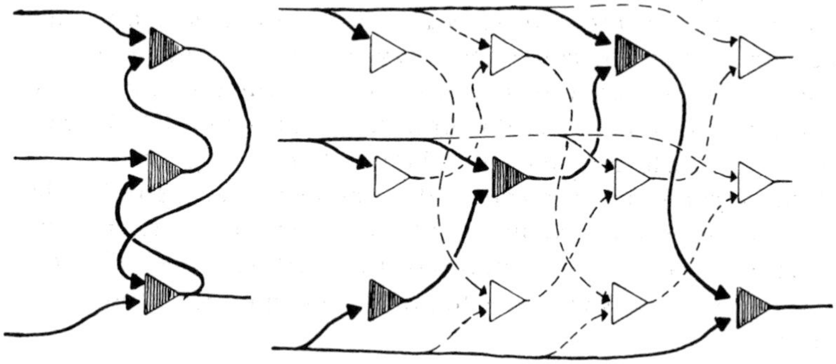

3. *The connection-matrix scheme seems hard to improve.* There exist figures with nonintersecting paths of length the order of $|R|$. It seems clear that any recognition procedure using two-argument functions requires at least $\log |R|$ steps, because one cannot do better than double the path length at each step, as does our C_{ij} connection-matrix method. At each such step there must be of the order of $|R|$ alternative connections that must be *or*-ed together. Perhaps the proof could be completed if one could show that nothing can be gained by postponing these *or*'s, so that each requires $\log |R|$ logic levels.

9.5 Connectedness in Iterative Arrays

Terry Beyer has investigated the time necessary to compute $\psi_{\text{CONNECTED}}$ in a situation that provides a different and perhaps more natural model for parallel geometric procedures. Suppose that each square of a retina contains an automaton able to communicate only with its four neighbors. It can also tell the state (black or white) of its square. The final decision about whether the figure is connected or not is to be made by some fixed automaton, say the one in the top left-hand corner. On the assumption

See Wendell T. Beyer, "Recognitio
Topological Invariants by Iterative
Ph.D. Dissertation, M.I.T., Oct. 1969.

that the states change only at fixed intervals of time, we ask how many time units must pass before the decision can be made. It is obvious that on an $n \times n$ retina this will take at least $2n$ time units, for this is the time required for *any* information to pass from the bottom right corner to the top left. It is not difficult to design arrays of automata that will make the decision in the order of n^2 (that is, $|R|$) time units. Beyer's remarkable result is that $(2 + \epsilon)n$ is sufficient, where ϵ can be made as small as one likes by allowing the automaton to have sufficiently many states.

Thus the order of magnitude of time taken by the array is proportional to $\sqrt{|R|}$, which is (naturally) intermediate between the times taken by the single serial machine ($|R|$) and the unrestricted parallel machine which is known to take $\leq (\log |R|)^2$.

The following gives an intuitive picture of Beyer's (unpublished) algorithmic process. The overall effect is that of enclosing a component in a triangle as shown below, and slowly compressing it into the northwest corner by moving the hypotenuse inward.

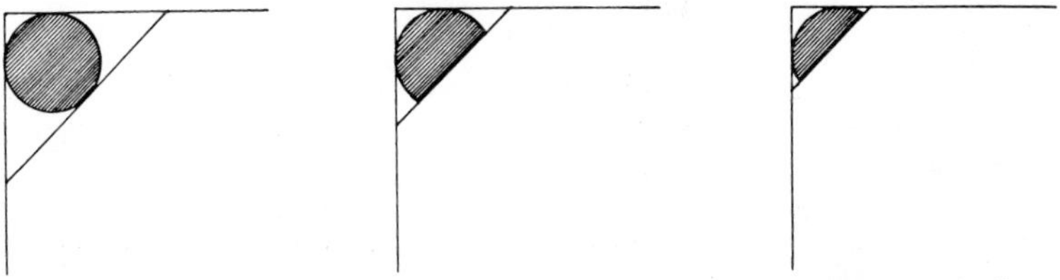

Each component is compressed to one isolated point before vanishing. Whenever this event takes place it can be recognized locally and the information is transmitted through the network to the corner. Thus the connectedness decision is made positively or negatively depending on whether such an event happens once or more than once. More precisely, the compression process starts by finding the set of all "southeast corners" of the figure.

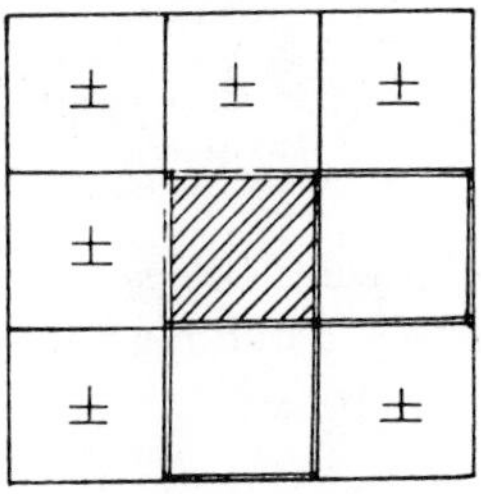

The center square is a SE corner if the South and East are empty. All other squares shown may be empty or full.

In the compression operation, each SE corner is removed, while inserting a new square when necessary to preserve connectedness as shown in the next figure:

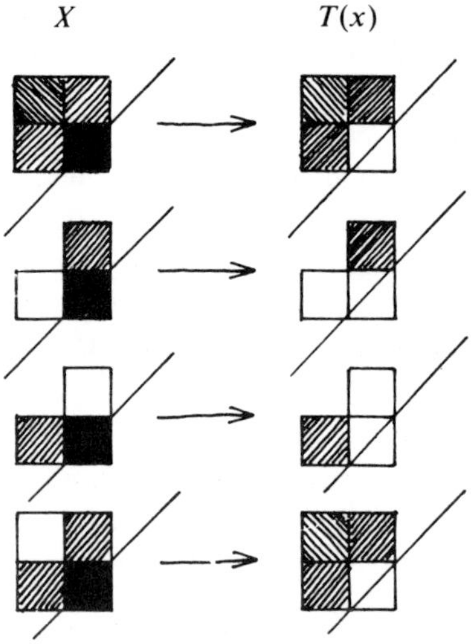

because this would break the connection:

The diagonal lines show how repetition of this local process does squeeze the figure to the northwest.

Repeated applications of T eventually reduce each component to a single point. The next figure shows how it (narrowly but effectively) avoids merging two components.

It is easy to see that a component within a hole will vanish (and be counted) just in time to allow the surrounding component to collapse down. We do not know any equivalent process for three dimensions. (Consider knots!)

LEARNING THEORY

III

Introduction to Part III

Our final chapters explore several themes which have come, in cybernetic jargon, to be grouped under the heading "learning." Up to now we discussed the timeless existence of linear representations. We now ask how to compute them, how long this takes, how big they are, and how efficient they are as a means of storing information. A proof, in Chapter 10, that coefficients can grow much faster than exponentially with $|R|$ has serious consequences both practically and conceptually: the use of more memory capacity to store the coefficients than to list all the figures strains the idea that the machine is making some kind of abstraction.

Chapter 11 clarifies the remarkable *perceptron convergence theorem* by relating it to familiar phenomena associated with finite-state machines, with optimization theory and with feedback as a computational device.

Chapter 12 abandons the strict definition of the perceptron to study a larger family of algorithms based on local partial predicates. These include methods (like Bayesian decisions) used by statisticians, as well as ideas (like hash coding) known only to programmers. Its aim is to indicate an area of computer science encompassing these apparently different processes. We dramatize the need for such a theory by singling out a simply stated unsolved problem about the more direct and commonly advocated methods for the storage and retrieval of information.

10 Magnitude of the Coefficients

10.1 Coefficients of the Parity Predicate

In §3.1 we discussed the predicate $\psi_{\text{PARITY}}(X) = \lceil |X| \text{ is an odd number} \rceil$ and showed that if Φ is the set of masks then all the masks must appear in any $L(\Phi)$ expression for ψ_{PARITY}. One such expression is

$$\psi_{\text{PARITY}}(X) = \lceil \Sigma(-2)^{|S(\varphi)|}\varphi(X) < -1 \rceil$$

which contains all masks of Φ with coefficients that grow exponentially with the support-size of the masks. We will now show that *the coefficients must necessarily grow at this rate*, because the sign-changing character of parity requires that each coefficient be large enough to drown out the effects of the many coefficients of its submasks. In effect, we show that ψ_{PARITY} can be realized over the masks *only* by a stratificationlike technique! So suppose that we have $\psi_{\text{PARITY}} = \lceil \Sigma \alpha_i \varphi_i > 0 \rceil$. Suppose also that the group-invariance theorem has been applied to make equal all α's for all φ's of the same support size, and suppose finally that the discrimination of ψ_{PARITY} is "reliable," for example, that $\Sigma \alpha_i \varphi_i \geq 1$ for odd parity and $\Sigma \alpha_i \varphi_i \leq 0$ for even parity. Then we obtain the inequalities

$$\begin{aligned} \alpha_1 &\geq 1, \\ \alpha_2 + 2\alpha_1 &\leq 0, \\ \alpha_3 + 3\alpha_3 + 3\alpha_1 &\geq 1, \\ \alpha_4 + 4\alpha_3 + 6\alpha_2 + 4\alpha_1 &\leq 0, \\ &\cdots \end{aligned}$$

by applying the linear form to figures with $1, 2, 3, \ldots$ points. The general formula is then obtained by noticing the familiar binomial coefficients, and proving by induction that

$$\sum_{i=1}^{n} \binom{n}{i} \alpha_i \quad \begin{cases} \geq 1 & \text{if } n \text{ is odd,} \\ \leq 0 & \text{if } n \text{ is even.} \end{cases}$$

Next, by subtracting successive inequalities, we define

$$D_n = \sum_{1}^{n+1} \binom{n+1}{i} \alpha_i - \sum_{1}^{n} \binom{n}{i} \alpha_i$$

$$= \alpha_{n+1} + \sum_{1}^{n} \left[\binom{n+1}{i} - \binom{n}{i} \right] \alpha_i = \alpha_{n+1} + \sum_{1}^{n} \binom{n}{i-1} \alpha_i$$

$$= \sum_{0}^{n} \binom{n}{i} \alpha_{i+1}$$

so that for all $n = 0, 1, 2, \ldots$

$$(-1)^n D_n \geq 1.$$

Using these inequalities, we will obtain a bound on the coefficients $\{\alpha_i\}$. We will sum the inequalities with certain positive weights; choose any $M > 0$, and consider the sum

$$\sum_{0}^{M} \binom{M}{i} (-1)^i D_i \geq \sum_{0}^{M} \binom{M}{i} = 2^M.$$

The left-hand side is

$$\sum_{i=0}^{M} \sum_{k=0}^{i} (-1)^i \alpha_{k+1} \binom{i}{k} \binom{M}{i}$$

$$= \sum_{k=0}^{M} \sum_{i=k}^{M} (-1)^i \alpha_{k+1} \binom{i}{k} \binom{M}{i}$$

$$= \sum_{k=0}^{M} \sum_{i=k}^{M} (-1)^i \alpha_{k+1} \left(\frac{i!}{k!(i-k)!} \right) \left(\frac{M!}{i!(M-i)!} \right)$$

$$= \sum_{k=0}^{M} \sum_{i=k}^{M} (-1)^i \alpha_{k+1} \left(\frac{M!}{k!(M-k)!} \right) \left(\frac{(M-k)!}{(i-k)!(M-i)!} \right)$$

$$= \sum_{k=0}^{M} \alpha_{k+1} \binom{M}{k} (-1)^k \sum_{j=0}^{M-k} \left(\frac{(M-k)!}{j!(M-k-j)!} \right) (-1)^j$$

$$= \sum_{k=0}^{M} \alpha_{k+1} \binom{M}{k} (-1)^k (1-1)^{M-k}$$

$$= \alpha_{M+1} (-1)^M,$$

so we obtain

$$|\alpha_{M+1}| \geq 2^M.$$

Theorem 10.1: In any "reliable" realization of ψ_{PARITY} as a linear threshold function over the set of masks, the coefficients grow at least as fast as $2^{|S(\varphi)|-1}$.

These values hold for the average, so if the coefficients of each type are not equal, some must be even larger! This shows that it is impractical to use masklike φ's to recognize paritylike functions: even if one could afford the huge number of φ's, one would have also to cope with huge ranges of their coefficients!

REMARK: This has a practically fatal effect on the corresponding learning machines. At least $2^{|R|}$ instances of just the maximal pattern is required to "learn" the largest coefficient; actually the situation is far worse because of the unfavorable interactions with lower-order coefficients (see §11.4). It follows, moreover, that the information capacity necessary to store the set $\{\alpha_i\}$ of coefficients is as much as would be needed to store the entire set of patterns recognized by ψ_{PARITY}—that is, the odd subsets of $|R|$. For, any uniform representation of the α_i's must allow $|R| - 1$ bits for each, and since there are $2^{|R|}$ coefficients the total number of bits required is $|R| \cdot 2^{|R|-1}$.On the other hand there are $2^{|R|-1}$ odd subsets of R, each representable by an $|R|$-bit sequence, so that $|R| \cdot 2^{|R|-1}$ bits would also suffice to represent the subsets. And the coefficients in §10.2 would require much more storage space.

It should also be noted that ψ_{PARITY} is not very exceptional in this regard because the positive normal-form theorem tells us that all possible $2^{2^{|R|}}$ Boolean functions are linear threshold functions on the set of masks. So, *on the average*, specification of a function will require $2^{|R|}$ bits of coefficient information, and nonuniformity of coefficient sizes would be expected to raise this by a substantial factor.

10.2 Coefficients Can Grow Even Faster than Exponentially in $|R|$

It might be suspected that ψ_{PARITY} is a worst case both because (1) parity is a worst function and (2) masks make a worst Φ. In fact the masks make rather a good base because coefficients over masks never have to be larger than $|\alpha_i| = 2^{|S(\varphi_i)|}$, as can be seen by expanding an arbitrary predicate into positive normal form. We now present a new predicate ψ_{EQ}, together with a rather horrible Φ, that leads to worse coefficients. Let R be a set of points, $y_1, \ldots, y_n, z_1, \ldots, z_n$ and let $\{Y_i\}$ and $\{Z_i\}$ each be enumerations of the 2^n subsets of the y's and z's, respectively. Then any figure $X \subset R$ has a unique decomposition $X = Y_j \cup Z_k$.

We will consider the simple predicate ψ_{EQ},

$$\psi_{EQ}(Y_j \cup Z_k) = \lceil j = k \rceil,$$

which simply tests, for any figure X, whether its Y and Z parts have the same positions in the enumeration. The straightforward geometric example is that in which the two halves of R have the same form, and Y_i and Z_i are corresponding sets of y and z points.

We will construct a very special set Φ of predicates for which $\psi_{EQ} \in L(\Phi)$ and show that any realization of ψ_{EQ} in $L(\Phi)$ must involve incredibly large coefficients!

We want to point out at the start that the Φ we will use was designed for exactly this purpose. In the case of ψ_{PARITY} we saw that coefficients can grow exponentially with the size of $|R|$; in that case the Φ was the set of masks, a natural set, whose interest exists independently of this problem. To show that there are even worse situations we construct a Φ with no other interest than that it gives bad coefficients.

We will define Φ to contain two types of predicates:

$$\psi_i(Y_j \cup Z_k) = \lceil i = k \rceil,$$

$$\chi_i(Y_j \cup Z_k) = \lceil (j = k \wedge i = k) \vee (j = k - 1 \wedge i < k) \rceil,$$

each defined for $i = 1, \ldots, 2^n$. Note that $|S(\psi_i)| = n$ and $|S(\chi_i)| = 2n$. First we must show that $\psi_{EQ} \in L(\Phi)$. But consider the formula

$$\psi_{EQ} = \lceil \Sigma 2^i (\psi_i - \chi_i) < 1 \rceil.$$

Case I: $j = k$
Then $\psi_k = 1$ and $\chi_k = 1$, hence $\psi_{EQ} = \lceil 2^k(1 - 1) < 1 \rceil$ is TRUE.

Case II: $j \neq k$ AND $j \neq k - 1$
Then only $\psi_k = 1$ and $\psi_{EQ} = \lceil 2^k < 1 \rceil$ is FALSE.

Case III: $j = k - 1$
Then $\psi_k = 1$ and $\chi_i = 1$ for $i = 1, \ldots, k - 1$. So

$$\psi_{EQ} = \left\lceil 2^k - \sum_{i=1}^{k-1} 2^i < 1 \right\rceil = \lceil 2 < 1 \rceil \text{ is FALSE.}$$

and the predicate holds only for the $j = k$ case, as it should. So ψ_{EQ} is indeed in $L(\Phi)$.

Now we establish bounds on the coefficients. Consider any expression

$$\psi_{EQ} = \lceil \Sigma \alpha_i \chi_i + \Sigma \beta_i \psi_i > \theta \rceil.$$

Then for sets $Y_{k+1} \cup Z_k$ we get $\beta_k \leq \theta$,
for sets $Y_k \cup Z_k$ we get $\alpha_k + \beta_k \geq \theta + 1$, (*strong separation*)
for sets $Y_{k-1} \cup Z_k$ we get $\alpha_1 + \cdots + \alpha_{k-1} + \beta_k \leq \theta$.

We can set $\theta = 0$ by subtracting it from every β, since just one β appears in each inequality. So $\beta_1 \leq 0$ and $\alpha_1 \geq 1$. And since

$$\alpha_k \geq 1 + \alpha_1 + \cdots + \alpha_{k-1}$$

we have immediately $\alpha_2 \geq 2, \alpha_3 \geq 4, \ldots, \alpha_j \geq 2^{j-1}$. Because the index j runs from 1 to 2^n, the highest α must be at least 2^{2^n-1} times as large as the initial separation term $(\alpha_1 + \beta_1) - \beta_1 = \alpha_1$. This incredible growth rate is based in part on a mathematical joke: we note that an expression "$j = k$" equivalent to that for ψ_{EQ} appears already within the definitions of the χ_i's and it is there precisely to not-quite-fatally weaken their usefulness in $L(\Phi)$.

Ironically, if we write ψ_{EQ} in terms of masks we have

$$\psi_{EQ} = \lceil \Sigma (y_i + z_i - 2y_i z_i < 1) \rceil,$$

and the coefficients are very small indeed!

PROBLEMS: Find a Φ that makes the coefficients of ψ_{PARITY} grow like $2^{2^{|R| \cdot \text{constant}}}$. Solution in §10.3. In §10.1, Φ has $2^{|R|}$ elements and ψ_{PARITY} requires coefficients like $2^{|R|}$. In §10.2 Φ has $2^{\frac{1}{2}|R|}$ elements, but the coefficients are like $2^{2^{|R|}}$. It is possible to make Φ's with up to $2^{2^{|R|}}$ elements. Does this mean there are ψ's and Φ's with coefficients like $2^{2^{2^{|R|}}}$? (We think not. See §10.3.)

Can it be shown that one never needs coefficient ratios larger than $2^{|\Phi|}$ for any Φ? Can we make more precise the relations between coefficient sizes and ratios. Can it be shown that the bounds obtained by assuming integer coefficients give bounds on the precisions required of arbitrary real coefficients? Can you establish linear bounds for coefficients for the predicates in Chapter 7?

The linear threshold predicate

$$\psi_{EQ} = \lceil \Sigma 2^i (\psi_i - \chi_i) > \theta \rceil$$

is very much like those obtained by the stratification-theorem method, in that at each level i the coefficient is chosen to dominate the worst case of summation of the coefficients of preceding levels. The result of theorems of §10.1 and §10.2 is that for those predicates there do not exist any linear forms with smaller coefficients, and this suggests to us that (with respect to given Φ's) perhaps there is a sense in which some predicates are inherently stratified. We don't have any strong ideas about this, except to point out that there is a serious shortage of computer-oriented concepts for classification of patterns. We do not know, for most of the cases in Chapter 7, which of them really require the stratificationlike coefficient growth: that is to say, we don't have any general method to detect "inherent stratification."

10.3 Predicate With Possibly Maximal Coefficients

Define $\|X\|$ to be the index of X in an ordering of all the subsets of R. We will consider the simple predicate $\psi_{\|\text{PARITY}\|} = \lceil \|X\| \text{ is odd} \rceil$ with respect to the following set Φ of predicates:

$$\varphi_i(X) = \begin{cases} 0 \text{ if } \|X\| < i, \\ 1 \text{ if } \|X\| = i, \\ (\|X\| - i) \bmod 2 \text{ if } \|X\| > i. \end{cases}$$

Then $\psi_{\|\text{PARITY}\|}$ is in $L(\Phi)$ and is in fact realized by

$$\psi_{\|\text{PARITY}\|} = \lceil \Sigma (-1)^i f_i \varphi_i < 0 \rceil,$$

where f_i is the ith Fibonacci number ($f_n = f_{n-1} + f_{n-2}$):

$$\{f_i\} = \{1, 1, 2, 3, 5, 8, 13, \ldots\}.$$

Theorem 10.3: Any form in $L(\Phi)$ for $\psi_{\|\text{PARITY}\|}$ must have coefficients at least this large; since the f_i grow approximately as

$$\frac{1}{\sqrt{5}}\left(\frac{\sqrt{5}+1}{2}\right)^i$$

the largest coefficient is then of the order of magnitude of

$$\sim 2^{\alpha \cdot 2^{|R|}}, \text{ where } \alpha = \log_2\left(\frac{\sqrt{5}+1}{2}\right)$$

The proof of the theorem can be inferred by studying the array below:

i	α_i	1	2	3	4	5	6	7	8	9	...
					$\|X_i\|$						
1	−1	**1**	1	0	1	0	1	0	1	0	...
2	+1	0	**1**	1	0	1	0	1	0	1	...
3	−2	0	0	**1**	1	0	1	0	1	0	...
4	+3	0	0	0	**1**	1	0	1	0	1	...
5	−5	0	0	0	0	**1**	1	0	1	0	...
6	+8	0	0	0	0	0	**1**	1	0	1	...
7	−13	0	0	0	0	0	0	**1**	1	0	...
⋮	⋮	⋮	⋮	⋮	⋮	⋮	⋮	⋮	⋮	⋮	⋮

It can be seen that if $\alpha_1 < 0$ and the coefficients are integers then

$$\begin{cases} \alpha_{2i+1} < -\sum_{j=1}^{i} \alpha_{2j} \\ \alpha_{2i} \geq -\sum_{j=1}^{i} \alpha_{2j-1}, \end{cases}$$

and the reader can verify that this implies that for all α_i,

$$|\alpha_i + 1| \geq |\alpha_i| + |\alpha_{i-1}|;$$

hence $|\alpha_i| \geq f_i$.

Discussion and conjecture: This predicate and its Φ have the same quality as that in §10.2—that the φ's themselves are each almost the desired predicate. Note also that by properly ordering the subsets, we can arrange that

$$\psi_{\|\text{PARITY}\|} = \psi_{\text{PARITY}}$$

We conjecture that this example is a worst case: to be precise, if Φ contains $|\Phi|$ elements, the maximal coefficient growth cannot be faster than

$$2^{\left(\frac{\sqrt{5}+1}{2}\right)^{|\Phi|}}$$

where the exponent constant is the Fibonacci, or golden-rectangle, ratio. Our conjecture is based only on arguments too flimsy to write down.*

10.4 The Group-Invariance Theorem and Bounded Coefficients on the Infinite Plane

In §7.10 we noted a counterexample to extending the group-invariance theorem (§2.3) to infinite retinas. The difficulty came through using an infinite stratification that leads to unbounded coefficients. This in turn raises convergence problems for the symmetric summations used to prove equal the coefficients within an equivalence class. If the coefficients are bounded, and the group contains the translation group, we *can* prove the corresponding theorem. (We do not know stronger results: presumably there is a better theorem with a summability-type condition on the coefficients and a structure condition on the group.) The proof uses the geometric fact that for increasing concentric circles about two fixed centers the proportion of area in common approaches unity.

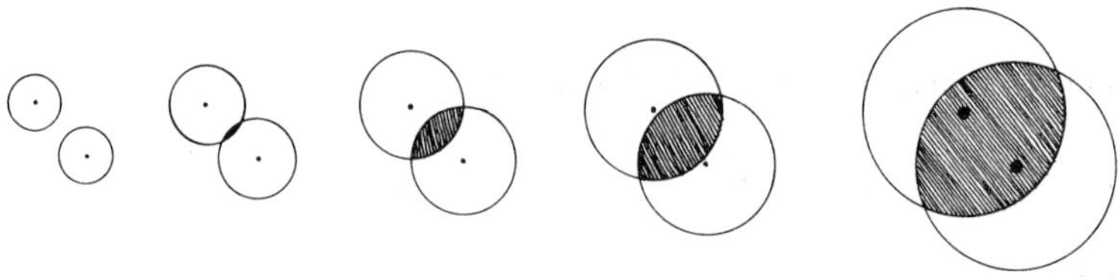

*Such as the fact that $\sqrt{5}$ occurs in upper bounds in the theories of rational approximations and geometry of numbers.

10.4.1 Bounded Coefficients and Group Invariance

Let ψ be a predicate invariant under translation of the infinite plane.

Theorem 10.4.1: If the coefficients of the φ's are *bounded* in each equivalence class, then there exists an equivalent perceptron with coefficients *equal* in each equivalence class.

PROOF: Let T_C be the set of translations with displacements less than some distance C. Let $\psi = \lceil \Sigma\, \alpha(\varphi)\varphi \geq \theta \rceil$. Now define

$$\psi_C(X) = \left\lceil \sum_{g \in T_C} \left(\sum_{\varphi \in \Phi} \alpha(\varphi)\varphi(gX) - \theta \right) \geq 0 \right\rceil$$

$$= \left\lceil \sum_{\Phi} \varphi(X) \sum_{T_C} \alpha(\varphi g^{-1}) \geq \sum_{T_C} \theta \right\rceil$$

$$= \left\lceil \sum_{\Phi} \varphi(X) \sum_{T_C} \alpha(\varphi g) - \sum_{T_C} \theta \right\rceil,$$

because T_C is carried onto itself under the group inverse. By the argument of §2.3 each ψ_C is equivalent to ψ as a predicate. The following lemma shows that we can select an increasing sequence $R_1, R_2, \ldots$ of radii for which the limit

$$\lim_{i \to \infty} \left[\frac{1}{\pi R_i^2} \sum_{g \in T_{R_i}} \alpha(\varphi g) \right]$$

has the same value independent of φ within every equivalence class.

Lemma: Suppose some function $f(x)$ is bounded, that is, $|f(x)| < M$, in E^2. Then there exists a sequence of increasing radii R_i such that for any system of concentric circles with these radii, the value of

$$\lim_{i \to \infty} \frac{1}{\pi R_i^2} \int_{|y-p| < R_i} f(y)\, dA$$

will be the same, independent of the selection of the common center p, ~~if the limit exists for any center at all~~.

PROOF: Let p be the origin. Since all values of the integral lie in the interval [-M, +M], any infinite sequence of them must have an infinite convergent sub-sequence. We can choose such a convergent subsequence from the circles with radii 1, 2, 3, etc. Let $R_1, R_2, \ldots$ be such a sequence.

~~PROOF: Choose as center the origin and any sequence of R_i's increasing without bound.~~ Then for each i we have

$$\left| \frac{1}{\pi R_i^2} \int_{|y| < R_i} f(y)\, da \right| < M.$$

Given any other center p for the circles, note that

$$\left| \int_{|y| < R_i} f(y)\, dA - \int_{|y| < R_i} f(p + y)\, dA \right| < 2 \cdot M \cdot \Delta_i(p),$$

where $\Delta_i(p)$ is the area of nonoverlap between the two disks $|y| < R_i$ and $|y - p| < R_i$. But as the radius grows, for any p

$$\lim_{i \to \infty} \left(\frac{\Delta_i(p)}{R_i^2} \right) = 0$$

so the two sequences approach the same limit ~~(if any)~~. Q.E.D.

To prove the main theorem, we simply choose a representative φ from some equivalent class, and set $f(g) = \alpha(\varphi g)$, regarding g as a translation from the origin.

It follows that the perceptron obtained in §7.4 must have unbounded coefficients, and there is no equivalent representation in $L(\Phi)$ with bounded coefficients.

~~The limit required by the lemma may not exist; in fact it is easy to construct counterexamples. Probably, this means that Theorem 10.4.1 is not strictly true, but we do not think the exceptions are important. We do not know a definite counterexample to the theorem, as stated.~~

Note: The methods of §10.2 and §10.3 are similar to those used by Myhill and Kautz [1961] to find maximal coefficients for the order-1 case. They show that with integer coefficients there is an order-1 predicate for which some coefficient must exceed $2/e \cdot 1/n \cdot 2^n$.

Learning

11

11.0 Introduction

In previous chapters we used no systematic technique to find a representation of a predicate as a member of an $L(\Phi)$. Instead, we always constructed coefficients by specific mathematical analysis of the predicate and the set Φ. These analyses were *ad hoc* to each predicate. In this chapter we study situations in which sets of coefficients can be found by a more systematic and easily mechanized procedure. It is the possibility of doing this that has given the perceptron its reputation as a "learning machine."

The conceptual scheme for "learning" in this context is a machine with an input channel for figures, a pair of YES and NO output indicators, and a *reinforcement* or "reward" button that the machine's operator can use to indicate his approval or disapproval of the machine's behavior (see Figure 11.1). The operator

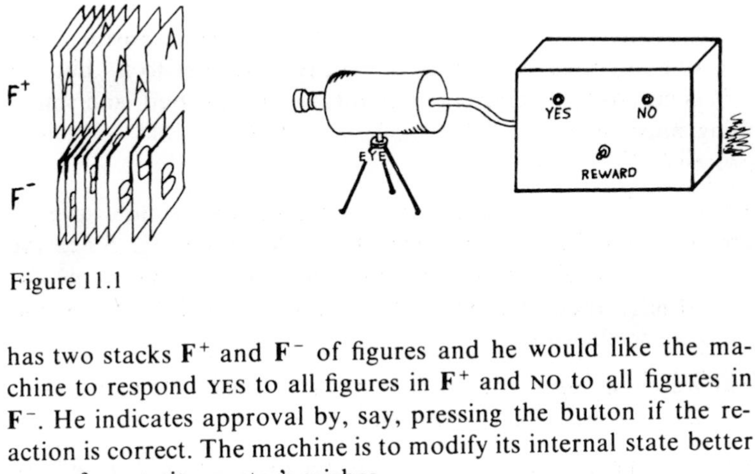

Figure 11.1

has two stacks $\mathbf{F}^+$ and $\mathbf{F}^-$ of figures and he would like the machine to respond YES to all figures in $\mathbf{F}^+$ and NO to all figures in $\mathbf{F}^-$. He indicates approval by, say, pressing the button if the reaction is correct. The machine is to modify its internal state better to conform to its master's wishes.

There are many ways to build such a machine. The most obvious scheme is to have some kind of recording device to store incoming figures in two separate files, for $\mathbf{F}^+$ and $\mathbf{F}^-$. This kind of machine will never make a mistake on a previously seen figure but, along with its never-forgetting, it brings other elephantine characteristics. Another, very different kind of machine would attempt to find descriptive characteristics that distinguish between the figures of the two classes, and to use new figures to sharpen and elaborate these descriptions. This kind of machine would, in the long run, require less memory but its mechanism and its theory are both much more complicated. If the classes $\mathbf{F}^+$ and $\mathbf{F}^-$ are very large then the first machine is disbarred; if there is no description within the practical repertoire of the second machine, it will fail.

The perceptron, as a pattern-discriminating machine, lies between these two paradigms. It is not a pure memory-matching machine, for it does not store the pictures. As a description-machine its repertoire is limited (as we have seen in the previous chapters) to what can be done with "local" features of the patterns and only linear threshold relations between these features. The existence of the simple learning procedures described below results from this restriction on the machine's descriptive power (and could be regarded as a partial compensation for this limitation).

Let us suppose that the machine contains a perceptron with a fixed Φ and adjustable coefficients. When a figure X is presented the sum

$$\Sigma\, \alpha_\varphi \varphi(X)$$

is computed. If X belongs to $\mathbf{F}^+$ and this sum is positive, the machine responds YES and all is well. If X belongs to $\mathbf{F}^+$ but the sum is negative, the machine responds NO. This is bad, and something must be done. What is the simplest possible correction procedure?

The first idea that comes to mind, especially to people who have grown up on the idea of feedback, is the following: Since the sum was too small, let's increase its coefficients. If it had come out too large (namely, response YES for a figure in $\mathbf{F}^-$), we would decrease coefficients.

But we must adjust the coefficients in a reasonable manner, so that the feedback effect is directed properly.

Suppose that $\Sigma\, \alpha_\varphi \varphi(X)$ comes out negative for an X in $\mathbf{F}^+$. In general some φ's give zero values for $\varphi(X)$, and their coefficients clearly cannot be blamed for the bad total. In fact, changing these coefficients might do harm in relation to other X's and does no good in relation to the current X. Thus we should increase α_φ only if $\varphi(X) = 1$. We should like a procedure for doing this whose mathematical form is clear enough to allow simple analysis and whose power is great enough to yield a reasonable success. The procedure given in §11.1 achieves both these goals, but we will first make a few introductory remarks.

11.0.1 Coefficients and Vectors

It is convenient to think of the set of coefficients $\{\alpha_\varphi\}$, ordered in an arbitrary but fixed way, as a vector in $|\Phi|$-dimensional space. Denote this vector by **A**. Similarly the set $\{\varphi(X)\}$, ordered in the same way, can be taken as a vector whose components are the values of the $\varphi(X)$'s. We denote this vector by $\mathbf{\Phi}(X)$. Now the operation of increasing those coefficients that correspond to non-zero values of $\varphi(X)$ is neatly performed by merely adding the vector $\mathbf{\Phi}(X)$ to the vector **A**. If the sum had come out positive for X in $\mathbf{F}^-$, we would subtract $\mathbf{\Phi}(X)$ from **A**.

A priori, any procedure of this sort runs the risk of oscillating wildly. An adjustment of the coefficients in the appropriate direction for one figure might undo the previous adjustment for another figure. Thus our intuition about whether it will work is influenced by two conflicting ideas drawn from experience with cybernetic situations: simple error-correcting feedback does often work; on the other hand, the process involves a search in a $|\Phi|$-dimensional space and our experience with other schemes for "hill-climbing" makes us acutely aware of the dangers that beset such procedures. Close analysis is needed.

This question of whether simple feedback will work can be posed in other words closely related to our main theme. The condition to be satisfied by the set of coefficients $\{\alpha_\varphi\}$ is defined *globally* in relation to the entire set of figures. On the other hand the "correction" procedure is highly local in the sense that each change made to the current values of these coefficients is based on consideration of just one figure. Thus the problem of finding conditions under which the procedure will make the α_φ converge to globally satisfactory values belongs to the study of the relation between apparently global and apparently local computations.

In this chapter we will show that very small refinements will turn the simple feedback principle into a workable "training" or error-correction procedure. The main theorems about this are already fairly well known. Our main concern will be to understand why it works. By analyzing it from several points of view, its mechanism will become transparent and its logic obvious.

In our discussion of recognizability of figures we have tried to replace vague formulations of questions about whether perceptrons are "good" or "bad" recognizers by an analytic theory that shows why perceptrons succeed in some cases and must fail in others. Although we do not have an equally elaborated theory of "learning," we can at least demonstrate that in cases where "learning" or "adaptation" or "self-organization" does occur, its occurrence can be thoroughly elucidated and carries no suggestion of mysterious little-understood principles of complex systems. Whether there are such principles we cannot know. But the perceptron ~~provides no evidence; and our success in analyzing it~~ adds another piece of circumstantial evidence for the thesis that cybernetic processes that work can be understood, and those that cannot be understood are suspect.

11.1 The Perceptron Convergence Theorem

Consider the following program in which the vector notation $\mathbf{A} \cdot \mathbf{\Phi}$ is used in place of our usual "$\Sigma\, \alpha_\varphi \varphi(X)$" notation.

START:	Choose any value for $\mathbf{A}$.
TEST:	Choose an X from $\mathbf{F}^+ \cup \mathbf{F}^-$. If $X \in \mathbf{F}^+$ and $\mathbf{A} \cdot \mathbf{\Phi} > 0$ go to TEST. If $X \in \mathbf{F}^+$ and $\mathbf{A} \cdot \mathbf{\Phi} \leq 0$ go to ADD. If $X \in \mathbf{F}^-$ and $\mathbf{A} \cdot \mathbf{\Phi} < 0$ go to TEST. If $X \in \mathbf{F}^-$ and $\mathbf{A} \cdot \mathbf{\Phi} \geq 0$ go to SUBTRACT.
ADD:	Replace $\mathbf{A}$ by $\mathbf{A} + \mathbf{\Phi}(X)$. Go to TEST.
SUBTRACT:	Replace $\mathbf{A}$ by $\mathbf{A} - \mathbf{\Phi}(X)$. Go to TEST.

We assume until further notice that there exists a vector, $\mathbf{A}^*$, with the property that if $X \in \mathbf{F}^+$ then $\mathbf{A}^* \cdot \mathbf{\Phi}(X) > 0$ and if $X \in \mathbf{F}^-$ then $\mathbf{A}^* \cdot \mathbf{\Phi}(X) < 0$. The *perceptron convergence theorem* then states that *whatever choice is made in START and whatever choice function is used in TEST, the vector **A** will be changed only a finite number of times*. In other words, $\mathbf{A}$ will eventually assume a value $\mathbf{A}^0$ for which $\mathbf{A}^0 \cdot \mathbf{\Phi}(X)$ always has the proper sign, that is, the predicate

$$\psi = \lceil \mathbf{A}^0 \cdot \mathbf{\Phi} > 0 \rceil$$

will have the property:

$X \in \mathbf{F}^+$ implies $\psi(X) = 1$,
$X \in \mathbf{F}^-$ implies $\psi(X) = 0$.

This is often expressed by saying that the predicate $\psi(X)$ **separates** the sets $\mathbf{F}^+$ and $\mathbf{F}^-$. The convergence theorem can be loosely stated as: if the sets are separable (that is, if there exists a "solution" vector $\mathbf{A}^*$), then the program will separate them (that is, it will find a solution vector $\mathbf{A}^0$ which may or may not be the same as $\mathbf{A}^*$).

Because we are now concerned more with the sets of coefficients $\{\alpha_\varphi\}$ than with the nature of Φ itself or the geometry of figures in R, it will be convenient to think of the functions in $L(\Phi)$ as associated with the sets $\{\alpha_\varphi\}$ regarded as vectors whose base vectors are the φ's in Φ. Warning: the vector-space base is the set of φ's, and *not* the points of R! Although in this chapter we will think of the forms $\Sigma\alpha_i\varphi_i$ as elements of a vector space, one should remember that the set $L(\Phi)$ of ψ's *isn't* a vector space, and that each $\psi \in L(\Phi)$ can be represented by many $\mathbf{A}$ vectors.†

In this vector-space context, the classes $\mathbf{F}^+$ and $\mathbf{F}^-$ of figures are mapped into classes of vectors, which we will still call $\mathbf{F}^+$ and $\mathbf{F}^-$.

The mapping from pictures to vectors may, of course, be degenerate, for we could have two figures $X \neq X'$ for which $\Phi(X) = \Phi(X')$: the original figures are "seen" only through the φ's, and some details can be lost.

We will now discard the restriction on the φ's that their values be either 0 or 1. The φ-functions may now take on any real, positive or negative values and, for different X's, each φ may

---

†It may be observed that vector geometry occurs only here and in Chapter 12 of this book. In the general perceptron literature, vector geometry is the chief mathematical tool, followed closely by statistics—which also plays a small role in our development. If we were to volunteer one chief reason why so little was learned about perceptrons in the decade that they have been studied, we would point toward the use of this vector geometry! For in thinking about the $\Sigma\alpha_i\varphi_i$'s as inner products, the relations between the patterns $\{X\}$ and the predicates in $L(\Phi)$ have become very obscure. The $\mathbf{A}$-vectors are not linear operators on the patterns themselves; they are "co-operators," that is, they operate on spaces of functional operators on the patterns. Since the bases—Φ-classes—of their vector spaces are arbitrary, one can't hope to use them to discover much about the kinds of predicates that will lie in an $L(\Phi)$. The important questions aren't about the linear properties of the $L(\Phi)$'s, but about the orders of complexities in computing pattern qualities from the information in the $\{\varphi(X)\}$ set itself.

have any number of different values. So we can think of $\mathbf{F}^+$ and $\mathbf{F}^-$ as two arbitrary clouds of points in Φ-space.

The main danger in allowing this generality is that the feedback procedure might be overwhelmed by vectors too large or stalled by vectors too small, so instead of adding or substracting $\mathbf{\Phi}$ itself, we will later use instead the unit-length vector $\hat{\mathbf{\Phi}}$ in the same direction:

$$\hat{\mathbf{\Phi}} = \frac{\mathbf{\Phi}}{|\mathbf{\Phi}|} \quad \text{so that} \quad |\hat{\mathbf{\Phi}}| = 1.$$

If the sets $\mathbf{F}^+$ and $\mathbf{F}^-$ are infinite the angles between pairs of vectors, one from each set, can have zero as a limit. In that case there is only one solution ~~vector~~ and the program may not find it. The conditions of Theorem 11.1 will exclude this possibility.

The case-analysis in TEST of the program just described is overcomplicated. The following program has the identical behavior:

START: Choose any value for $\mathbf{A}$ ($\neq 0$).

TEST: Choose a $\mathbf{\Phi}$ from $\mathbf{F}^+ \cup \mathbf{F}^-$.
If $\mathbf{\Phi} \in \mathbf{F}^+$ and $\mathbf{A} \cdot \mathbf{\Phi} > 0$ go to TEST.
If $\mathbf{\Phi} \in \mathbf{F}^+$ and $\mathbf{A} \cdot \mathbf{\Phi} \leq 0$ go to ADD.
Replace $\mathbf{\Phi}$ by $-\mathbf{\Phi}$.
If $\mathbf{\Phi} \in \mathbf{F}^-$ and $\mathbf{A} \cdot \mathbf{\Phi} > 0$ go to TEST.
If $\mathbf{\Phi} \in \mathbf{F}^-$ and $\mathbf{A} \cdot \mathbf{\Phi} \leq 0$ go to ADD.

ADD: Replace $\mathbf{A}$ by $\mathbf{A} + \mathbf{\Phi}$.
Go to TEST.

This is equivalent because (1) we have reversed the inequality signs in the part of TEST following changing $\mathbf{\Phi}$, so all decisions will go the same way; (2) the effect of "go to ADD" is the same as "go to SUBTRACT" with reversed sign of $\mathbf{\Phi}$. Now, "replace $\mathbf{\Phi}$ by $-\mathbf{\Phi}$" is executed if and only if $\mathbf{\Phi} \in \mathbf{F}^-$ and since the inequality conditionals now have identical outcomes we can replace the program by the still equivalent program:

START: Choose any value for $\mathbf{A}$.

TEST: Choose a $\mathbf{\Phi}$ from $\mathbf{F}^+ \cup \mathbf{F}^-$;
If $\mathbf{\Phi} \in \mathbf{F}^-$ change the sign of $\mathbf{\Phi}$.
If $\mathbf{A} \cdot \mathbf{\Phi} > 0$ go to TEST;
otherwise go to ADD.

ADD: Replace $\mathbf{A}$ by $\mathbf{A} + \mathbf{\Phi}$.
Go to TEST.

In other words the problem of finding a vector $\mathbf{A}$ *to separate two given sets* $\mathbf{F}^+$ *and* $\mathbf{F}^-$ *is not really different from the problem of finding a vector* $\mathbf{A}$ *that satisfies*

$$\mathbf{\Phi} \in \mathbf{F} \Rightarrow \mathbf{A} \cdot \mathbf{\Phi} > 0$$

for a single given set $\mathbf{F}$, *defined as* $\mathbf{F}^+$ *together with the negatives of the vectors of* $\mathbf{F}^-$.

We use these observations to simplify the program and statement of the convergence theorem: for simplicity we will state a version that uses unit vectors.

Theorem 11.1: Perceptron Convergence Theorem: *Let* $\mathbf{F}$ *be a set of unit-length vectors. If there exists a unit vector* $\mathbf{A}^*$ *and a number* $\delta > 0$ *such that* $\mathbf{A}^* \cdot \mathbf{\Phi} > \delta$ *for all* $\mathbf{\Phi}$ *in* $\mathbf{F}$, *then the program*

START: Set $\mathbf{A}$ to an arbitrary $\mathbf{\Phi}$ of $\mathbf{F}$.

TEST: Choose an arbitrary $\mathbf{\Phi}$ of $\mathbf{F}$, and
if $\mathbf{A} \cdot \mathbf{\Phi} > 0$ go to TEST;
otherwise go to ADD.

ADD: Replace $\mathbf{A}$ by $\mathbf{A} + \mathbf{\Phi}$.
Go to TEST.

will go to ADD *only a finite number of times.*

Some readers might be amused to note that the proof of this theorem does not use any assumptions of finiteness of the set $\mathbf{F}$ or the dimension of the vector space. This will not be true of later sections where the compactness of the unit sphere plays an apparently essential role.

Corollary: We will generally assume that the program is presented a sequence such that each $\mathbf{\Phi} \in \mathbf{F}$ repeats indefinitely often. Then it follows that it will eventually find a "solution" vector **A**, that is, one for which

$$\mathbf{A} \cdot \mathbf{\Phi} > 0 \quad \text{for all } \mathbf{\Phi} \in \mathbf{F}.$$

This will not, of course, necessarily be **A***, because **A*** is an *arbitrary* solution vector. All solution vectors form a "convex cone," and the program will stop changing **A** as soon as it penetrates the boundary of this cone. [Convex cone: a set S of vectors for which (1) $\alpha \in S \Rightarrow k\alpha \in S$ for all $k > 0$, (2) $\alpha \in S$ AND $\beta \in S \Rightarrow (\boldsymbol{\alpha} + \boldsymbol{\beta}) \in S$. It is not a vector subspace because of the $k > 0$ condition.]

11.2 Proof of the Convergence Theorem

11.2.1

Define

$$G(\mathbf{A}) = \frac{\mathbf{A}^* \cdot \mathbf{A}}{|\mathbf{A}|}.$$

It may help some readers to notice that $G(\mathbf{A})$ is the cosine of the angle between **A** and **A***. Because $|\mathbf{A}^*| = 1$, we have

$$G(\mathbf{A}) \leq 1.$$

Consider the behavior of $G(\mathbf{A})$ on successive passes of the program through ADD.

$$\begin{aligned} \mathbf{A}^* \cdot \mathbf{A}_{t+1} &= \mathbf{A}^* \cdot (\mathbf{A}_t + \mathbf{\Phi}) \\ &= \mathbf{A}^* \cdot \mathbf{A}_t + \mathbf{A}^* \cdot \mathbf{\Phi} \\ &\geq \mathbf{A}^* \cdot \mathbf{A}_t + \delta; \end{aligned}$$

hence after the nth application of ADD we obtain

$$\mathbf{A}^* \cdot \mathbf{A}_n \geq n\delta. \qquad \text{THESIS}$$

Thus the numerator of $G(\mathbf{A})$ increases linearly with n, the number of changes of **A**, that is, the number of errors.

As for the denominator, since $\mathbf{A}_t \cdot \mathbf{\Phi}$ must be negative (or the program would not have gone through ADD)

$$\begin{aligned} |\mathbf{A}_{t+1}|^2 &= \mathbf{A}_{t+1} \cdot \mathbf{A}_{t+1} \\ &= (\mathbf{A}_t + \mathbf{\Phi}) \cdot (\mathbf{A}_t + \mathbf{\Phi}) \\ &= |\mathbf{A}_t|^2 + 2\mathbf{A}_t \cdot \mathbf{\Phi} + |\mathbf{\Phi}|^2 \\ &< |\mathbf{A}_t|^2 + 1, \end{aligned}$$

and after the nth application of ADD,

$$|\mathbf{A}_n|^2 < n. \qquad \text{ANTITHESIS}$$

Combining the results THESIS and ANTITHESIS, we obtain

$$G(\mathbf{A}_n) = \frac{\mathbf{A}^* \cdot \mathbf{A}_n}{|\mathbf{A}_n|} > \frac{n\delta}{\sqrt{n}}.$$

But $G(\mathbf{A}) \leq 1$, so this can continue only so long as $\sqrt{n}\,\delta \leq 1$, that is,

$$n \leq 1/\delta^2.$$

This completes the proof.

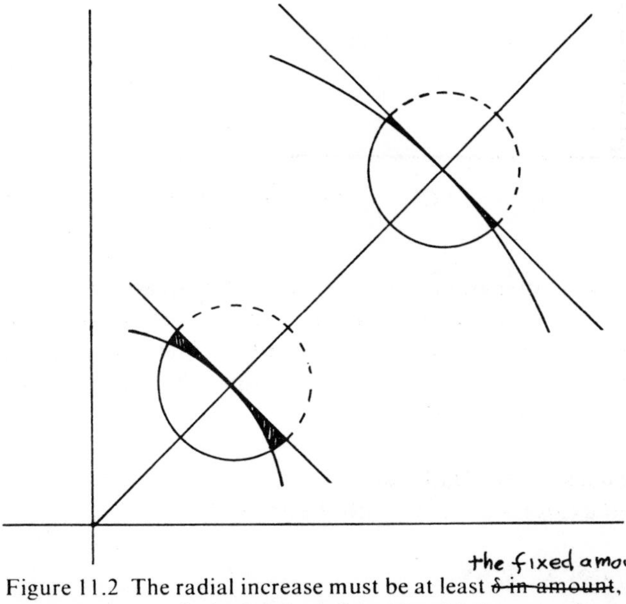

Figure 11.2 The radial increase must be at least ~~δ in amount~~ the fixed amount δ, yet the new vector must remain in the shaded region; this becomes impossible when the region, whose thickness varies inversely with $|A|$, becomes thinner than δ.

Figures 11.2 and 11.3 show some aspects of the geometry of the rate of growth of $|\mathbf{A}|$. They are particularly interesting if one wishes to look at the algebraic proof in the following dialectrical and slightly perverse form. Inequality ANTITHESIS can be read as

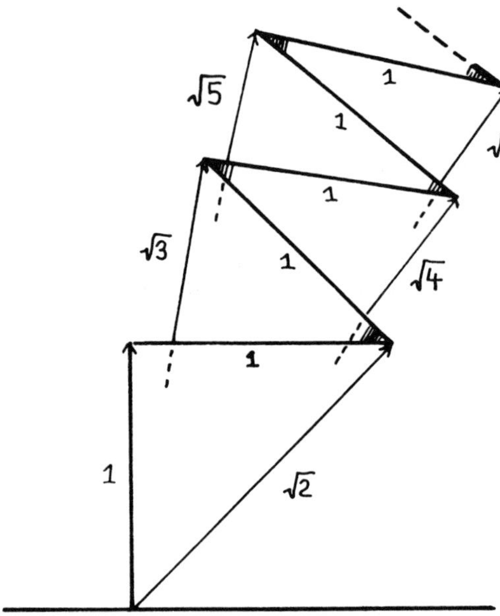

Figure 11.3 The extreme case in which the bound $|A_1| = \sqrt{n}$ is obtained.

saying that $|\mathbf{A}_n|$ increases more slowly then the square root of n. On the other hand Inequality THESIS can be turned (via the Cauchy-Schwartz inequality) into an assertion that $|\mathbf{A}_n|$ grows linearly with n. This leads to a contradiction: $|\mathbf{A}_n|$ must grow, but cannot grow fast enough.

11.3 A Geometric Proof (Optional)
We are given a (unit) vector $\mathbf{A}^*$ with the property

$$\mathbf{A}^* \cdot \mathbf{\Phi} > \delta \quad \text{for all } \mathbf{\Phi} \in \mathbf{F}.$$

This means that every vector $\mathbf{\Phi}$ in $\mathbf{F}$ makes an angle $\theta_{\mathbf{\Phi}}$ with $\mathbf{A}^*$ for which $\cos \theta_{\mathbf{\Phi}} > \delta$. If we choose $\theta^* > 0$ to be smaller than any of the θ_Φ's, then *every* vector **V** within θ^* of **A*** has the property

$$\mathbf{V} \cdot \mathbf{\Phi} > 0 \quad \text{for all } \mathbf{\Phi} \in \mathbf{F}.$$

Therefore any vector **V** *within the circular cone with base angle* θ^* *from* **A*** *will be a solution vector that will cause the program to stop changing.*

Now consider the vector **A** computed within the program. At each stage **A** is a sum of members of **F**. Thus

$$\mathbf{A}^* \cdot \mathbf{A} = \mathbf{A}^* \cdot (\mathbf{\Phi}_1 + \mathbf{\Phi}_2 + \cdots) > 0.$$

Let this page represent the plane containing **A*** and **A**. If we take **A*** as a unit vector oriented vertically, the above inequality shows that **A** must be oriented into the upper half-plane:

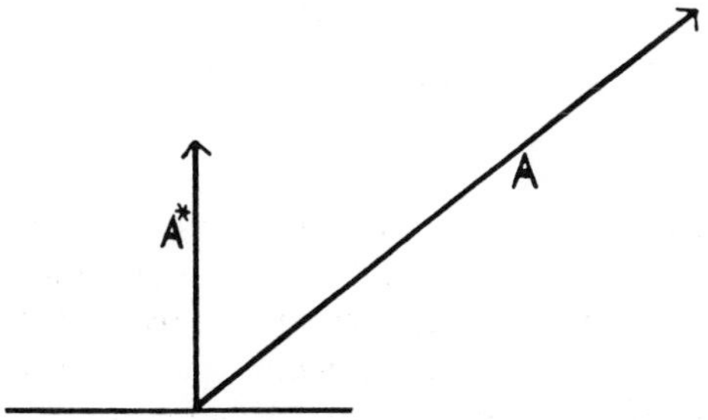

We should like to show that each time the program passes through ADD, **A** is brought closer in direction to **A***. Unfortunately, this is not *strictly* true. Figure 11.4 shows, however, that it will "normally" happen; and we should understand this normal case before closing off the details to obtain a rigorous proof.

When ADD is used a vector **Φ** will be added to the current value of **A**, say $\mathbf{A}_t$, to obtain a new value of **A**, say $\mathbf{A}_{t+1} = \mathbf{A}_t + \mathbf{\Phi}$. We know two facts about **Φ**:

$$\mathbf{A}^* \cdot \mathbf{\Phi} > 0,$$

$$\mathbf{A}_t \cdot \mathbf{\Phi} < 0.$$

Now consider the projection $\mathbf{\Phi}_N$ of $\mathbf{\Phi}$ on the plane of the paper and placed with its origin at the end of $\mathbf{A}_t$ (in preparation for the usual geometric picture of vector addition). The first condition states that the end of $\mathbf{\Phi}_N$ must be above the dotted line and the second condition states that it must be below the dashed line. Thus, it lies as shown and points from the end of $\mathbf{A}_t$ towards the direction of $\mathbf{A}^*$.

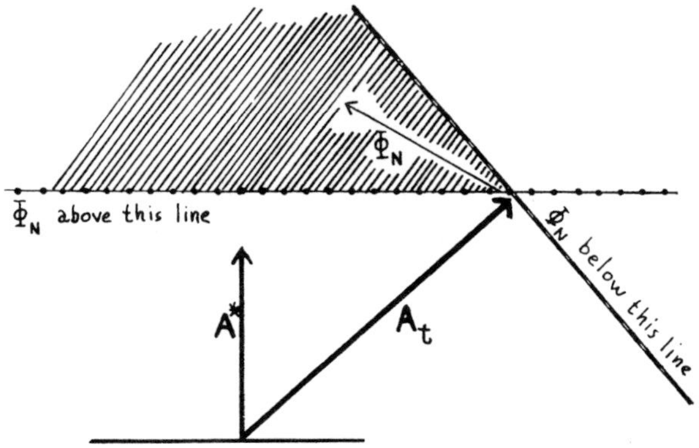

Figure 11.4

If we consider the right cone generated by rotating $\mathbf{A}_t$ about $\mathbf{A}^*$, it is clear that $\mathbf{\Phi}$ itself (of which $\mathbf{\Phi}_N$ is the projection) runs into the cone. The proof of the theorem would be complete except for the observation that $\mathbf{\Phi}$ might leave the cone again and so allow $\mathbf{A}_{t+1}$ to have a larger angular separation from $\mathbf{A}^*$ than did $\mathbf{A}_t$. Figure 11.5 shows how this might happen.

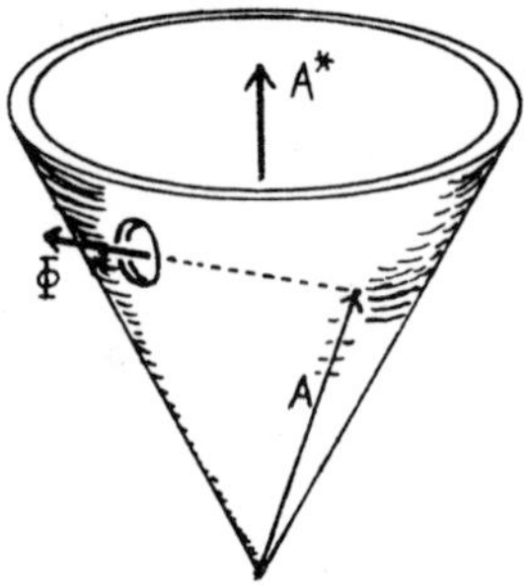

Figure 11.5

But the overshoot phenomenon is not fatal, for it can occur only a limited number of times, depending on θ^*. To prove this consider the cone generated by rotating **A** about **A***. Because $\mathbf{\Phi}$ always has a vertical component $\mathbf{\Phi} \cdot \mathbf{A}^* > \delta$, the height of the cone increases each time **A** is changed. If the angle between **A** and **A*** remains greater than θ^* (and if not, the proof is finished!), the rim of the cone will come to have indefinitely large radii. Now let us look down, along **A***, at the projection $\tilde{\mathbf{\Phi}}$ of $\mathbf{\Phi}$ on the top of the cone: we will show that the end of $\tilde{\mathbf{\Phi}}$ must lie at least a distance d toward **A*** from the tangent line. Also, since $|\mathbf{\Phi}| = 1$, the end of $\mathbf{\Phi}$ must lie inside a unit circle drawn around the end of **A** (see Figure 11.6).

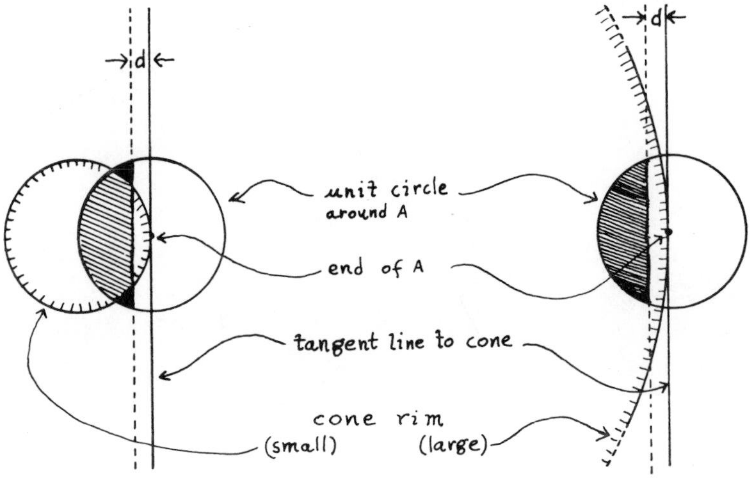

Figure 11.6

Thus the end of $\tilde{\mathbf{\Phi}}$ must lie in the shaded region. When the cone rim gets large enough, the shaded region will lie entirely within the cone, and so will $\tilde{\mathbf{\Phi}}$, and therefore also the end of $\mathbf{\Phi}$ which is directly above it. So it remains only to show where the magic distance d comes from.

To see this, we now look *along* the line tangent to the cone-rim through **A** (see Figure 11.7). Now the end of **Φ** must lie within the shaded region defined by (1) the plane orthogonal to **A**, and (2) a plane orthogonal to **A*** and lying δ above **A** again, because

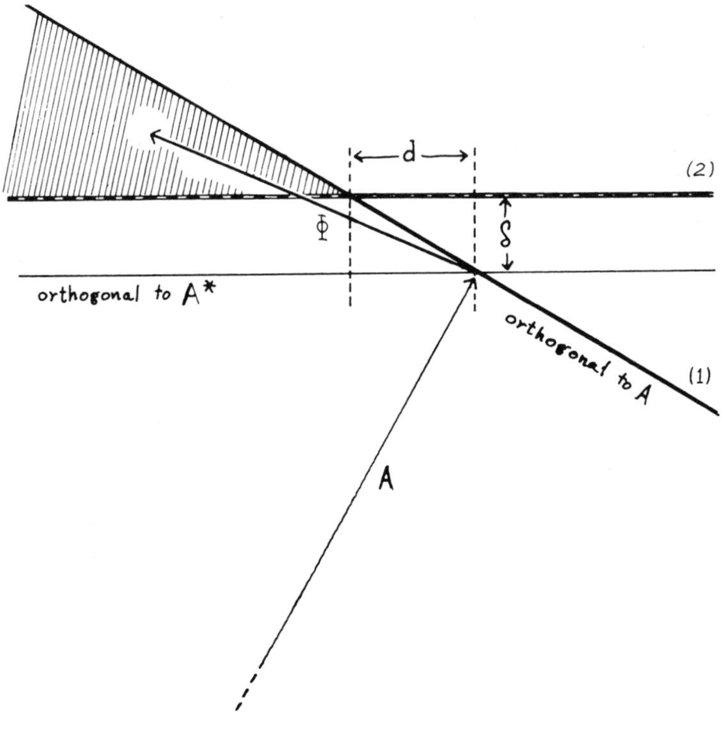

Figure 11.7

A* · **Φ** > δ. Thus, the end of **Φ** cannot come closer than the indicated distance *d* to the tangent. Because **A** is a sum of **Φ**'s it cannot ever make an angle greater than $\frac{1}{2}\pi - \theta^*$ with **A***, and this gives a positive lower bound to *d*. So, after a finite "transient" period, the **A**'s remain in a "vertical" cylinder, which must eventually go inside the acceptance cone around **A***.

This proves that, eventually, **A** must stop changing. Thus Theorem 11.1 is proved.

11.4 Variants of the Convergence Theorem

The convergence theorem has a large number of minor variants. It is easy to adapt our proof to cover any of the following forms in which it occurs in the literature on perceptrons:

(1) Instead of assuming **F** to consist of unit vectors one can assume it to be a finite set, or to satisfy an upper and lower bound on length, that is, $\exists a, b$, such that $0 < a \leq |\mathbf{\Phi}| \leq b$ for all $\mathbf{\Phi} \in \mathbf{F}$.

(2) Instead of replacing **A** by $\mathbf{A} + \mathbf{\Phi}$ one can replace it by $\mathbf{A} + k\mathbf{\Phi}$, where k is a real number chosen by any one of the rules:

k is a constant > 0.
$k = 1/|\mathbf{\Phi}|$, that is, add a unit vector.

$k = c\dfrac{\mathbf{A} \cdot \mathbf{\Phi}}{|\mathbf{\Phi}|^2}$ If $c = 1$ then k is just enough to bring $(\mathbf{A} + k\mathbf{\Phi}) \cdot \mathbf{\Phi}$ out of the negative range. Or, one can use any value for c between 0 and 2. [Agmon, 1954]

These and similar modifications do not change the theorem in the sense that **A** will still ~~become, after a finite number of transfers to ADD, a solution vector. However the actual number of transfers will be altered~~ approach a solution. In the last case, if c<1, the solution is never reached. It would also be interesting to compare the relative *efficiency* of the "local" perceptron convergence program with more "global" analytic methods, for example, linear programming, for solving the system of inequalities in **A**:

$\mathbf{A} \cdot \mathbf{\Phi} > 0$, all $\mathbf{\Phi}$ in **F**.

11.4.1 More Than Two Classes

A more substantial variation is obtained by allowing more than two classes of input figures. Let $\mathbf{F}_1, \mathbf{F}_2, \ldots$ be sets of figures and suppose that there are vectors $\mathbf{A}_i^*$ and $\delta > 0$ such that

$\mathbf{\Phi} \in \mathbf{F}_i$ implies that for all $j \neq i$, $\mathbf{A}_i^* \cdot \mathbf{\Phi} > \mathbf{A}_j^* \cdot \mathbf{\Phi} + \delta$.

The perceptron convergence theorem generalized to this case assures us that vectors with the same property can be found by following the usual principle of feedback: whenever one runs into a figure $\mathbf{\Phi}$ in $\mathbf{F}_i$ for which $\mathbf{A}_i \cdot \mathbf{\Phi} < \mathbf{A}_j \cdot \mathbf{\Phi}$ for some j, $\mathbf{A}_i$ must be "increased" and $\mathbf{A}_j$ "decreased."

This idea is expressed more precisely in the program:

START: Choose any nonzero values for $\mathbf{A}_1, \mathbf{A}_2, \ldots$.

TEST: Choose i, j, and $\mathbf{\Phi} \in \mathbf{F}_i$.
If $\mathbf{A}_i \cdot \mathbf{\Phi} > \mathbf{A}_j \cdot \mathbf{\Phi}$ go to TEST;
otherwise go to CHANGE.

CHANGE: Replace $\mathbf{A}_i$ by $\mathbf{A}_i + \mathbf{\Phi}$.
Replace $\mathbf{A}_j$ by $\mathbf{A}_j - \mathbf{\Phi}$.
Go to TEST.

The generalized theorem states that the program will go to CHANGE only a finite number of times. But this is possible only if the machine eventually stops making mistakes, that is, eventually every $\mathbf{\Phi}$ in $\mathbf{F}_i$ will make

$$\mathbf{A}_i \cdot \mathbf{\Phi} > \mathbf{A}_j \cdot \mathbf{\Phi}, \text{ for all } j \neq i$$

To prove this, let $\mathbf{A}_1^* \ldots \mathbf{A}_i^* \ldots \mathbf{A}_j^* \ldots \mathbf{A}_m^*$ have the required property, and define $\mathbf{A}^*$ to be the vector (in a larger space) defined by stringing together all their coefficients. Also, for each $\mathbf{\Phi}$ define $\mathbf{\Phi}_{ij}$ to be the vector that contains $\mathbf{\Phi}$ and $-\mathbf{\Phi}$ in the ith and jth blocks, with zeros elsewhere. Apply Theorem 11.1 to this large space.

11.5 Application: Learning the Parity Predicate ψ_{PARITY}

As an example to illustrate the convergence theorem, we shall estimate the number of steps required to learn the coefficients for the parity predicate. We have shown in §10.1 that the solution vector with the smallest coefficients can be written

$$\mathbf{A} = (2^{|R|}, \overbrace{2^{|R|-1}, \ldots, 2^{|R|-1}}^{|R| \text{ terms}}, \ldots, \overbrace{2^{|R|-j}, \ldots, 2^{|R|-j}}^{\binom{|R|}{j} \text{ terms}}, \ldots, 1).$$

The length of this vector is given by

$$|\mathbf{A}|^2 = \sum 2^{2(|R|-j)} \binom{|R|}{j} = (1 + 2^2)^{|R|} = 5^{|R|}.$$

The corresponding unit vector is then

$$\mathbf{A}^* = \frac{\mathbf{A}}{5^{|R|/2}}.$$

The analysis of §10.1 shows that $\mathbf{A} \cdot \mathbf{\Phi}$ is 1 or -1. Since $\mathbf{\Phi}$ has $2^{|R|}$ coefficients, each 0 or 1, we have

$$\left| \frac{\mathbf{A}^* \cdot \mathbf{\Phi}}{|\mathbf{\Phi}|} \right| \geq \frac{1}{\sqrt{5^{|R|} \cdot 2^{|R|}}} = \frac{1}{\sqrt{10^{|R|}}}.$$

So we can take $1/\sqrt{10^{|R|}}$ as δ. The number n of corrections is then bounded by

$$n < \frac{1}{\delta^2} \leq 10^{|R|}.$$

We obtain a lower bound of $5^{|R|}$ for n by observing that $|\mathbf{A}_n|$ must be at least $5^{|R|/2}$ and that

$$|\mathbf{A}_n| \leq n.$$

Combining these we have

$$5^{|R|} \leq n \leq 10^{|R|}$$

It is worth observing that if the convergence program had added $\mathbf{\Phi}$ instead of $\hat{\mathbf{\Phi}}$ we would have obtained,

$$\frac{5^{|R|}}{\max |\mathbf{\Phi}|} \leq n \leq 10^{|R|} \text{ that is, } \left(\tfrac{5}{2}\right)^{|R|} \leq n \leq 10^{|R|}.$$

More analysis would be necessary to decide whether this modification would actually result in more rapid learning. In any case it is clear that the learning time must increase exponentially as a function of n.

These inequalities give bounds on the number n of corrections or, what comes to the same thing, of errors. A calculation of the total number of rounds of the program must take account of the decreasing error rate as learning proceeds. It is, however, easy to see that the number $M(r)$ of rounds needed to reduce the proportion of errors to a fraction r should satisfy the inequality $M(r) \leq n/r$ on the assumption that the figures are presented to the machine in random order. Thus it should take something less than $10^{|R|+2}$ rounds to achieve a 1 percent error rate.

11.6 The Convergence Procedure as Hill-Climbing

It is instructive to examine the relation of the convergence procedure to the general problem of "hill-climbing." There, too, one tries to find an apparently globally defined solution (that is, the location of the absolute summit) by local operations (for example, steepest ascent). Success depends, however, on the extent that the summit is not as globally defined as it might appear. In cases where the hill has a complex form with many local relative peaks, ridges, etc., hill-climbing procedures are not always advantageous. Indeed, in extreme cases a random or systematic search might be better than a procedure that relentlessly climbs every little hillock.

In a typical hill-climbing situation one tries to maximize a function $G(\mathbf{A})$ of a point $\mathbf{A}$ in n-dimensional space. The simplest procedure computes the value of the "altitude" function G for a number of points $\mathbf{A}_t + \mathbf{\Phi}_i$ in the vicinity of the current point $\mathbf{A}_t$. On the basis of these experiments, a value $\mathbf{\Phi}$ is chosen and $\mathbf{A}_t + \mathbf{\Phi}$ is taken as $\mathbf{A}_{t+1}$. The algorithm for the choice of $\mathbf{\Phi}$ varies. It might, for example, use unit vectors in the directions of the axes as the $\mathbf{\Phi}_i$, compute the direction of steepest ascent and take $\mathbf{\Phi}$ as the unit vector in this direction. A simpler procedure might take as $\mathbf{\Phi}$ the first unit vector it finds with the property that $G(\mathbf{A}_t + \mathbf{\Phi}) > G(\mathbf{A}_t)$. The choice of the appropriate algorithm will depend on many considerations. If, however, the hill (that is, the surface defined by G) is sufficiently well behaved, any reasonably sophisticated algorithm will work. If the hill is very bad, no ingenious local tricks will do much good. See Figure 11.8.

Now the perceptron convergence procedure can be seen as a hill-climbing algorithm if we define the surface G by

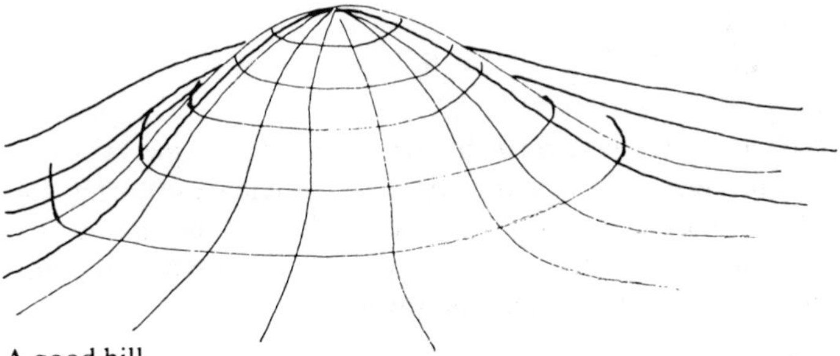

A good hill

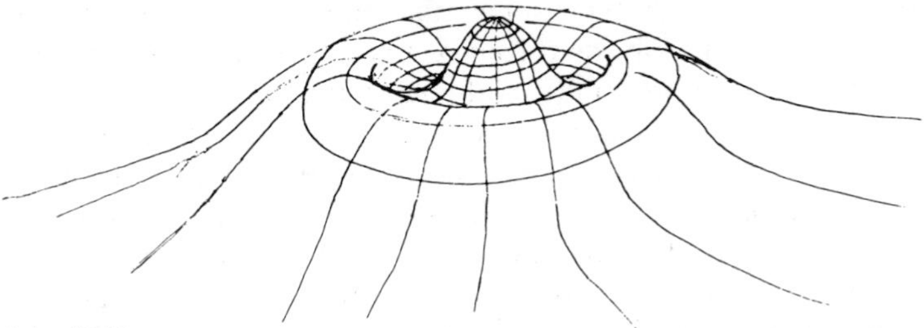

A bad hill

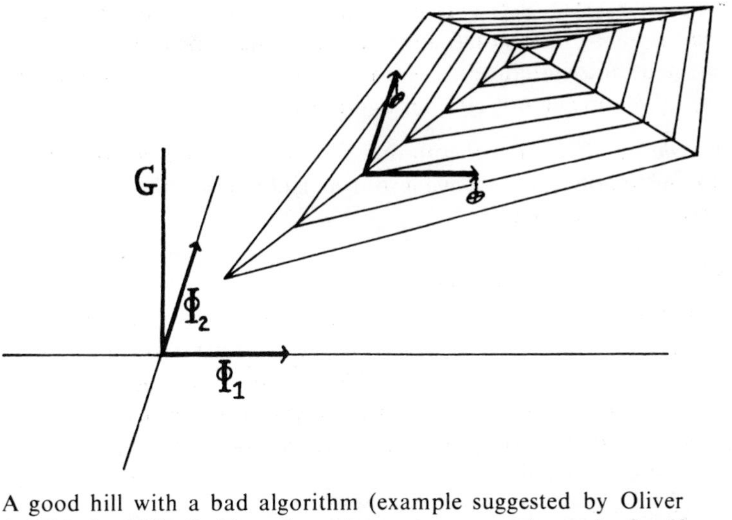

A good hill with a bad algorithm (example suggested by Oliver Selfridge). Hill-climbing along the two axes won't work, for if **A** is a point on the ridge, both $G(\mathbf{A} + \mathbf{\Phi}_1)$ and $G(\mathbf{A} + \mathbf{\Phi}_2)$ are less than $G(\mathbf{A})$. The "resolution" of the test vectors is too coarse for the sharpness of the ridge.

Figure 11.8

$$G(\mathbf{A}) = \frac{\mathbf{A} \cdot \mathbf{A}^*}{|\mathbf{A}|}.$$

It differs from the usual form in two superficial respects. First, the algorithm has no procedure for systematically exploring the effects of moving in all directions from the current point $\mathbf{A}_t$. Second, it never actually has the value of the object function $G(\mathbf{A})$ since $\mathbf{A}^*$ is, by definition, unknown.

Nevertheless, the logic of its operation is essentially like the simpler of the two hill-climbing algorithms mentioned in the previous paragraph: the step from $\mathbf{A}_t$ to $\mathbf{A}_{t+1} = \mathbf{A}_t + \mathbf{\Phi}$ is based on evidence indicating (albeit indirectly) that $G(\mathbf{A}_{t+1})$ is larger than $G(\mathbf{A}_t)$. One would expect its success to be related to the shape of the surface $G(\mathbf{A})$. And, indeed, a little thought will show that this surface has none of the pathological features likely to make hill-climbing difficult: there are *no* false local maxima, no ridges, no plateaus, etc. This is most easily seen by considering the function $G(\hat{\mathbf{A}})$ on the unit sphere, where $\hat{\mathbf{A}} = \mathbf{A}/|\mathbf{A}|$. For $\mathbf{A}$ satisfying $\mathbf{A} \cdot \mathbf{A}^* > 0$ (the only ones we need consider) this surface is an n-dimensional cone. It has a single peak at $\mathbf{A} = \mathbf{A}^*$, connected uniform contours, straight lines of steepest ascent; in short, all features a hill-climber could desire.

Thus, we see, from another point of view, that the convergence theorem is neither as surprising nor as isolated a phenomenon as it might at first appear.

11.7 Perceptrons and Homeostats

The significance of the perceptron convergence theorem must not be reduced (as it often has been, in the literature) to the mere statement: *If two sets of figures are linearly separable then the convergence theorem procedure can find a separating predicate.* For if ~~all one wanted is to find a separating predicate~~, a more trivial procedure would suffice.

one did not care also about practicality

We observe first that if there exists a vector $\mathbf{A}^*$ such that $\mathbf{A}^* \cdot \mathbf{\Phi} > \delta > 0$ for all $\mathbf{\Phi} \in \mathbf{F}$, then there exists a vector $\mathbf{A}'$ with the same property and with integer components. We can therefore find a suitable $\mathbf{A}'$ by the simple program:

START: Set $\mathbf{A}_0 = 0$.

TEST: Choose $\mathbf{\Phi} \in \mathbf{F}$.
If $\mathbf{A} \cdot \mathbf{\Phi} > 0$ go to TEST;
otherwise go to GENERATE.

GENERATE: Replace **A** by $T(\mathbf{A})$ where T is any transformation such that the series $T(0)$, $T(T(0))$, $T(T(T(0)))$, . . . , includes all possible integral vectors.
Go to TEST.

Clearly, the procedure can make but a finite number of errors before it hits upon a solution. It would be hard to justify the term "learning" for a machine that so relentlessly ignores its experience.

The content of the perceptron convergence theorem must be that it yields a better learning procedure than this simple homeostat. Yet the problem of relative speeds of learning of perceptrons and other devices has been almost entirely neglected. There is not yet any general theory of this topic; in §11.5 we discussed some of the problems encountered in estimating learning times. Some other simple methods of "learning" will be discussed in Chapter 12. The logical theory of homeostats, that is, enumerative procedures like the one mentioned just above, is discussed by W. Ross Ashby in the book *Design for a Brain*.

11.8 The Nonseparable Case

There are many reasons for studying the operation of the perceptron learning program when there is no $\mathbf{A}^*$ with the property $\mathbf{A}^* \cdot \mathbf{\Phi} > 0$ for all $\mathbf{\Phi} \in \mathbf{F}$. Some of these are practical reasons. For example, one might want to use the program to *test* whether such an $\mathbf{A}^*$ exists, or one might wish to make a learning machine of this sort and be worried about the possible effects of feedback errors and other "noise." Other motives are theoretical. One cannot claim to have completely *understood* the "separable case" without at least some broader knowledge of other cases.

Now it is perfectly obvious that Theorem 11.1 cannot be true, as it stands, under these more general conditions. It must be possible for **A** to change infinitely often. However, the fate of **A** is not obvious: will $|\mathbf{A}|$ increase indefinitely? Will **A** take infinitely many values or will it cycle through or in some other way remain in some fixed finite set?

In the next sections we shall prove that $|\mathbf{A}|$ remains bounded. To be more precise we introduce the following definitions: *Let* **F** *be a finite set of vectors.* Then

An **F-chain** is a sequence of vectors $\mathbf{A}_1, \mathbf{A}_2, \ldots, \mathbf{A}_n$, for which

$$\begin{cases} \mathbf{A}_{i+1} = \mathbf{A}_i + \mathbf{\Phi}_i \\ \mathbf{\Phi}_i \cdot \mathbf{A}_i \leq 0, \\ \mathbf{\Phi}_i \in \mathbf{F}. \end{cases}$$

An **F**-chain is **proper** if, for all i,

$$|\mathbf{A}_i| \geq |\mathbf{A}_1|.$$

We will prove that **F**-chains beginning with large vectors cannot grow much larger.

11.9 The Perceptron Cycling Theorem

For any $\epsilon > 0$ there is a number $N = N(\epsilon, F)$ such that

$$\text{if} \begin{cases} \mathbf{A}, \ldots, \mathbf{A}' & \text{is a proper F-chain and} \\ |\mathbf{A}| > N, \end{cases}$$

then $|\mathbf{A}'| < |\mathbf{A}| + \epsilon.$

Corollary 1: The lengths $|\mathbf{A}|$ of vectors obtainable by executing the learning program, with a given **F** and a given initial vector, are bounded. If the finite set of vectors in **F** are constrained to have integer coordinates, then the process is finite-state!

The plausibility of these assertions is easily verified by examining Figure 11.10. As $|\mathbf{A}|$ grows it becomes increasingly difficult to find a member of **F** satisfying both $\mathbf{A} \cdot \mathbf{\Phi} \leq 0$ and $|\mathbf{A} + \mathbf{\Phi}| > |\mathbf{A}|$. The formal proof is given in §11.10 and uses induction on the dimension of the vectors in **F**.

Our proof of this theorem is complicated and obscure. So are the other proofs we have since seen. Surely someone will find a simpler approach. Non-specialists should skip to §12.

The theorem (in the form of Corollary 1) was apparently first conjectured by Nilsson, and proved by Efron. Terry Beyer formulated the conjecture quite independently.

11.10 Proof of the Cycling Theorem

The proof depends on some observations about the effect, on the length of an arbitrarily long vector $\mathbf{A}$, of adding to it a short vector $\mathbf{C}$ whose length is fixed.

11.10.1 Lemmas*

If $\mathbf{C}$ is any vector, and $\mathbf{A}$ is very large compared to $\mathbf{C}$, then $|\mathbf{A} + \mathbf{C}| - |\mathbf{A}| \simeq \hat{\mathbf{A}} \cdot \mathbf{C}$.

More precisely, define $\Delta = |\mathbf{A} + \mathbf{C}| - |\mathbf{A}|$. Then for any $\epsilon > 0$, if we choose $|\mathbf{A}| > |\mathbf{C}|^2/\epsilon$ then the difference between Δ and $\hat{\mathbf{A}} \cdot \mathbf{C}$ will be less than ϵ.

It is easy to read from the infinitesimal geometry of Figure 11.9 that $|\hat{\mathbf{A}} \cdot \mathbf{C} - \Delta| < |\mathbf{B}| \sin \theta \simeq |\mathbf{B}|^2/|\mathbf{A}| < |\mathbf{C}|^2/|\mathbf{A}|$, when $|\mathbf{A}| \gg |\mathbf{C}|$.

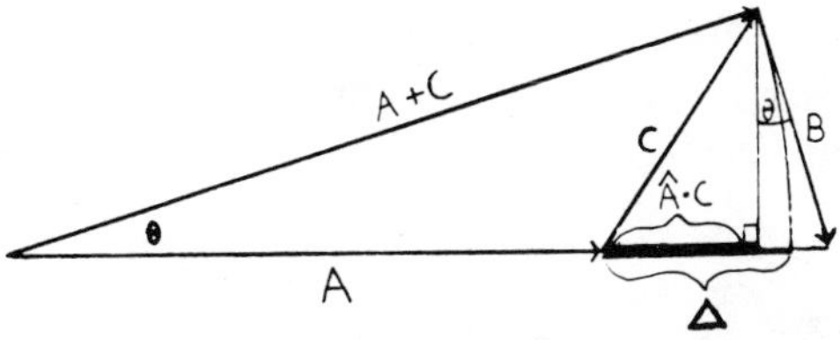

Figure 11.9

A formal proof is hardly necessary, but if we define $x = |\mathbf{A} + \mathbf{C}|$ and $y = |\mathbf{A}|$ we can use the identity

$x^2 - y^2 = 2y(x - y) + (x - y)^2$ to obtain

$2\mathbf{A} \cdot \mathbf{C} + |\mathbf{C}|^2 = 2|\mathbf{A}|\Delta + \Delta^2$; hence

$2|\mathbf{A}|(\hat{\mathbf{A}} \cdot \mathbf{C} - \Delta) = \Delta^2 - |\mathbf{C}|^2$. Since $|\Delta| \leq |\mathbf{C}|$ we then have

$|\hat{\mathbf{A}} \cdot \mathbf{C} - \Delta| < |\mathbf{C}|^2/ |\mathbf{A}|$.

Since this shows that $\Delta \simeq \hat{\mathbf{A}} \cdot \mathbf{C}$ when $|\mathbf{A}| \gg |\mathbf{C}|$ we can conclude that

Lemma 1: We can make Δ as small as we want by setting a lower

*We denote by $\hat{\mathbf{A}}$ the unit length vector along the direction of $\mathbf{A}$.

bound on $|\mathbf{A}|$ and an upper bound on $\hat{\mathbf{A}} \cdot \hat{\mathbf{C}}$, that is, by taking $\mathbf{A}$ large, and nearly orthogonal to $\mathbf{C}$.

Lemma 2: We can make the angle $(\mathbf{A}, \mathbf{A} + \mathbf{C})$ as small as we like by increasing $|\mathbf{A}|$ because $\sin\theta \leq |\mathbf{C}| / |\mathbf{A}|$.

Lemma 3: If a relatively small vector $\mathbf{C}$ is bounded *away from* orthogonal to a very large vector $\mathbf{A}$, with negative inner product, then the Δ is bounded away from (negative) zero. In fact, if $\hat{\mathbf{A}} \cdot \hat{\mathbf{C}} < -\delta < 0$, then if we take $|\mathbf{A}| > (2/\delta)\,|\mathbf{C}|$ we have (because Δ approaches the negative quantity $\hat{\mathbf{A}} \cdot \hat{\mathbf{C}}\,|\mathbf{C}|$),

$$\hat{\mathbf{A}} \cdot \hat{\mathbf{C}}\,|\mathbf{C}| < \Delta < \tfrac{1}{2}\,\hat{\mathbf{A}} \cdot \hat{\mathbf{C}}\,|\mathbf{C}| < 0.$$

Thus $\qquad \Delta < -\tfrac{1}{2}\,\delta\,|\mathbf{C}|.$

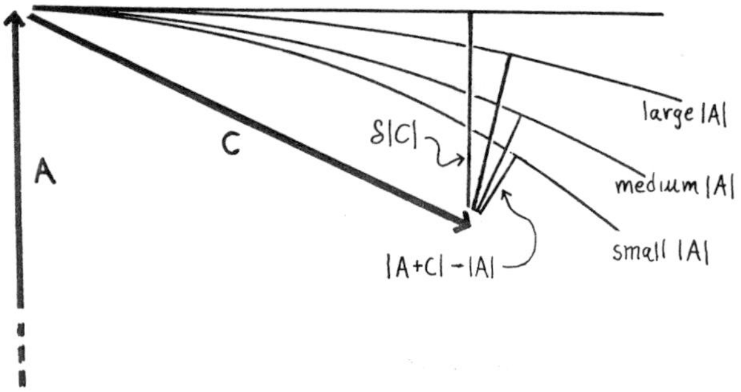

Figure 11.10

Finally, we need one more substantial Lemma:

Lemma 4: *The projection of a proper* **F**-*chain* $\mathbf{A}_1, \ldots, \mathbf{A}_k$ *onto a hyperplane containing* **F** *is a proper* **F**-*chain. Moreover, the increase in length,* $|\mathbf{A}_k| - |\mathbf{A}_1|$ *is not greater than that of the projected chain.*

PROOF: Let $\mathbf{A}_1, \ldots, \mathbf{A}_k$ be a proper chain. Let H be a hyperplane containing $\mathbf{F}$, and $\hat{\mathbf{B}}$ the normal to H. Remember that $\hat{\mathbf{B}} \cdot \mathbf{\Phi} = 0$ for all $\mathbf{\Phi} \in \mathbf{F}$. Write

$\mathbf{A}_i = \tilde{\mathbf{A}}_i + \hat{\mathbf{B}}$. To show $\tilde{\mathbf{A}}_1, \ldots, \tilde{\mathbf{A}}_k$ is an $\mathbf{F}$-chain, let

$$\begin{aligned} \mathbf{A}_{i+1} &= \mathbf{A}_i + \mathbf{\Phi}, \text{ where } \mathbf{A}_i \cdot \mathbf{\Phi} \leq 0. \text{ Now} \\ \mathbf{A}_{i+1} &= \tilde{\mathbf{A}}_{i+1} + x_{i+1}\hat{\mathbf{B}} \\ &= (\tilde{\mathbf{A}}_i + \mathbf{\Phi}) + x_i\hat{\mathbf{B}}. \end{aligned}$$

Then, by the orthogonality of $\hat{\mathbf{B}}$ to all of $\tilde{\mathbf{A}}_i$, $\tilde{\mathbf{A}}_{i+1}$, and $\mathbf{\Phi}$,

$$x_{i+1} = x_i \quad \text{AND} \quad \tilde{\mathbf{A}}_{i+1} = \tilde{\mathbf{A}}_i + \mathbf{\Phi}.$$

Finally, putting $\mathbf{B} = x_i \hat{\mathbf{B}}$ we get

$$0 \geq \mathbf{A}_i \cdot \mathbf{\Phi} = (\tilde{\mathbf{A}}_i + \mathbf{B}) \cdot \mathbf{\Phi} = \tilde{\mathbf{A}}_i \cdot \mathbf{\Phi} + \mathbf{B} \cdot \mathbf{\Phi} = \tilde{\mathbf{A}}_i \cdot \mathbf{\Phi}.$$

To show that the $\tilde{\mathbf{A}}$'s form a proper **F**-chain we must also verify that $|\tilde{\mathbf{A}}_i| \geq |\tilde{\mathbf{A}}_1|$. This follows immediately from

$$\begin{aligned} |\mathbf{A}_i|^2 &= |\tilde{\mathbf{A}}_i|^2 + 2\tilde{\mathbf{A}}_i \cdot \mathbf{B} + |\mathbf{B}|^2 \\ &= |\tilde{\mathbf{A}}_i|^2 + |\mathbf{B}|^2. \end{aligned}$$

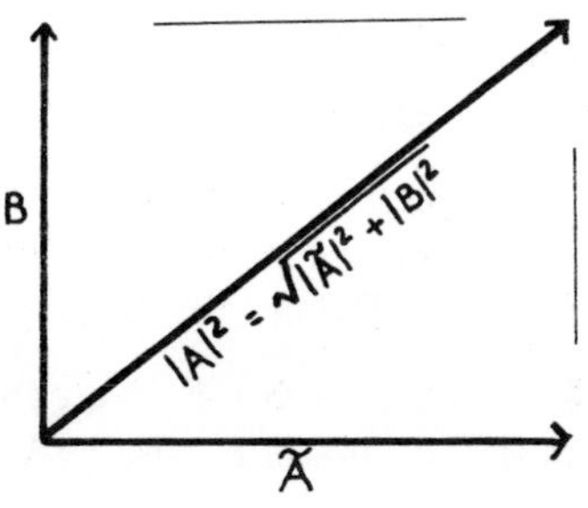

Finally it is easy to see that

$$|\mathbf{A}_k| - |\mathbf{A}_1| = \sqrt{|\tilde{\mathbf{A}}_k|^2 + |\mathbf{B}|^2} - \sqrt{|\tilde{\mathbf{A}}_1|^2 + |\mathbf{B}|^2} < |\tilde{\mathbf{A}}_k| - |\tilde{\mathbf{A}}_1|$$

so the latter must be positive. Q.E.D.

11.10.2 Proof of Cycling Theorem

We prove the theorem by induction on the dimension of the vector space.

BASE: The theorem is obviously true in E_1, the one-dimensional case, for there the vectors are simply real numbers and $\mathbf{\Phi} \cdot \mathbf{A} < 0$ means that $\mathbf{\Phi}$ and $\mathbf{A}$ have opposite signs. If $|\mathbf{A}| > \max_F |\mathbf{\Phi}|$ then $|\mathbf{\Phi} + \mathbf{A}| < |\mathbf{A}|$ for $\mathbf{\Phi} \cdot \mathbf{A} < 0$. So eventually $|\mathbf{A}_t|$ must be less than $\max_F \mathbf{\Phi}$.

INDUCTION: Assume for an inductive proof that the theorem is true in E_{n-1}. Note that this implies the existence of a bound

M_{n-1} such that any **F**-chain, $\mathbf{A}_1, \ldots, \mathbf{A}_m$ in E_{n-1} can grow at most M_{n-1} in length, that is, $|\mathbf{A}_m| < |\mathbf{A}_1| + M_{n-1}$.

Choose any direction (that is, unit vector) $\hat{\mathbf{A}}$ in E_n. Our first subgoal will be to construct an open neighborhood $\mathbf{V}(\hat{\mathbf{A}})$ on the unit sphere from which the growth of chains is bounded; in fact, for any $\epsilon > 0$, there is a bound $N(\hat{\mathbf{A}})$ such that, if $|\mathbf{B}| > N(\hat{\mathbf{A}})$ and $\hat{\mathbf{B}} \in \mathbf{V}(\hat{\mathbf{A}})$ then any proper **F**-chain starting at **B** can grow at most ϵ in length.

Since the open sets $\mathbf{V}(\hat{\mathbf{A}})$ cover the surface of the unit sphere, and since the sphere is compact, it will follow that we can find one N that will work in place of all the $N(\hat{\mathbf{A}})$'s and the theorem will be proved.

Let $\mathbf{H}(\hat{\mathbf{A}})$ be the hyperplane orthogonal to $\hat{\mathbf{A}}$ and let $\overline{\mathbf{H}}(\hat{\mathbf{A}})$ be the complement of $\mathbf{H}(\hat{\mathbf{A}})$, that is, $\overline{\mathbf{H}}(\hat{\mathbf{A}}) = E_n - \mathbf{H}(\hat{\mathbf{A}})$.

Since **F** is finite, there is a number $\delta > 0$ such that $|\mathbf{\Phi} \cdot \hat{\mathbf{A}}| > 2\delta$ for all $\mathbf{\Phi}$ in $\overline{\mathbf{H}}(\hat{\mathbf{A}}) \cap \mathbf{F}$. By continuity there is a neighborhood $\mathbf{V}'(\hat{\mathbf{A}})$ such that if $\hat{\mathbf{B}} \in \mathbf{V}'(\hat{\mathbf{A}})$ and $\mathbf{\Phi} \in \overline{\mathbf{H}}(\hat{\mathbf{A}}) \cap \mathbf{F}$ then $|\mathbf{\Phi} \cdot \hat{\mathbf{B}}| > \delta$.

There is also a number b such that $|\mathbf{\Phi}| < b$ for all $\mathbf{\Phi} \in \mathbf{F}$. We can now deduce from Lemma 3 that there are numbers δ' and $n(\hat{\mathbf{A}})$ such that

$$\text{if} \begin{cases} (1)\ |\mathbf{B}| > n(\hat{\mathbf{A}}) \\ (2)\ \mathbf{\Phi} \in \overline{\mathbf{H}}(\hat{\mathbf{A}}) \cap \mathbf{F} \\ (3)\ \hat{\mathbf{B}} \in \mathbf{V}'(\hat{\mathbf{A}}) \\ (4)\ \mathbf{\Phi} \cdot \mathbf{B} < 0 \end{cases}$$

These are the conditions of Lemma 3, where **B** and **Φ** play the role of **A** and **C** of the lemma. Note that (2) keeps **Φ** from being perpendicular to $\hat{\mathbf{A}}$ and (4) keeps **Φ** from being perpendicular to **B**.

$$\text{then}\quad (5)\ |\mathbf{B} + \mathbf{\Phi}| < |\mathbf{B}| - \delta'.$$

We shall consider a proper **F**-chain,

$$\mathbf{B}_1, \ldots, \mathbf{B}_j, \ldots \quad \text{with} \quad \mathbf{B}_{j+1} = \mathbf{B}_j + \mathbf{\Phi}_j$$

with $\hat{\mathbf{B}}_1$ very near $\hat{\mathbf{A}}$ and $|\mathbf{B}_1| > n(\hat{\mathbf{A}})$. In particular, let $\eta > 0$ be a number such that the diameter of $\mathbf{V}'(\hat{\mathbf{A}})$ is bigger than η. Let $\mathbf{V}(\hat{\mathbf{A}})$ be a neighborhood of $\hat{\mathbf{A}}$ on the unit sphere such that the diameter of $\mathbf{V}(\hat{\mathbf{A}})$ is less than $\eta/2$. So $\mathbf{V}(\hat{\mathbf{A}}) \subset \mathbf{V}'(\hat{\mathbf{A}})$. We now take $\mathbf{B}_1$ such that $\hat{\mathbf{B}}_1 \in \mathbf{V}(\hat{\mathbf{A}})$ and $|\mathbf{B}_1| > n(\hat{\mathbf{A}})$ though we will shortly change this lower bound on the magnitude of $\mathbf{B}_1$ to the desired $N(\hat{\mathbf{A}})$.

By (5) above, the chain cannot be proper unless $\mathbf{\Phi}_1 \in \mathbf{H}(\hat{\mathbf{A}})$. Thus the chain must start growing from $\mathbf{H}(\hat{\mathbf{A}})$. We will see that not only $\mathbf{\Phi}_1$, but all the other $\mathbf{\Phi}$'s must be in $\mathbf{H}(\hat{\mathbf{A}})$; hence the chain's growth is bounded by ϵ. For suppose that

$$\{\mathbf{\Phi}_1, \ldots, \mathbf{\Phi}_j\} \subset \mathbf{H}(\hat{\mathbf{A}}) \quad \text{and} \quad \mathbf{\Phi}_{j+1} \in \mathbf{H}(\hat{\mathbf{A}}).$$

Then $|\mathbf{B}_{j+1}|$ will be less than $|\mathbf{B}_1|$ by at least $\delta'/2$. To see this we use Lemmas 1 and 2 and the inductive assumption. Since the projections $\tilde{\mathbf{B}}_1, \ldots, \tilde{\mathbf{B}}_j$ of $\mathbf{B}_1, \ldots, \mathbf{B}_j$ form a proper **F**-chain in the $(n - 1)$-dimensional space $\mathbf{H}(\hat{\mathbf{A}})$,

$$|\tilde{\mathbf{B}}_j| < |\tilde{\mathbf{B}}_1| + M_{n-1},$$

where M_{n-1} is the bound obtained by the induction assumption for the next lower dimension. Now, if η is chosen small enough and if $N(\hat{\mathbf{A}})$ is chosen large enough the conditions of Lemmas 1 and 2 are satisfied with the following values: we use $\mathbf{\Phi}_1 + \cdots + \mathbf{\Phi}_j$ for "C," so that* $|C| < M_{n-1}$; we use $\mathbf{B}_1$ for "A"; and we use a smaller $\epsilon' = \min(\epsilon, \delta'/2)$ for "ϵ."

It follows from (5) and the fact that $|\mathbf{B}_j| > |\mathbf{B}_1| > N(\hat{\mathbf{A}})$ that $|\mathbf{B}_{j+1}| < |\mathbf{B}_j| - \delta' < |\mathbf{B}_1| - \delta'/2$ so that the jump from $\mathbf{B}_j$ to $\mathbf{B}_{j+1}$ decreased the length of the **B**-vector more than the first j steps increased it! Thus the chain cannot be proper unless *all* the $\mathbf{\Phi}$'s belong to $\mathbf{H}(\hat{\mathbf{A}})$. But in this case the increase in length of the whole chain is bounded by ϵ. This achieves the first subgoal. The surface of the sphere is covered by the $\mathbf{V}(\hat{\mathbf{A}})$'s. By compactness, there is a finite subcovering. Let N be the maximum of the corresponding $N(\hat{\mathbf{A}})$'s. It follows that for *any* proper chain $\mathbf{B}, \ldots, \mathbf{B}'$,

$$|\mathbf{B}| > N \Longrightarrow |\mathbf{B}'| < |\mathbf{B}| + \epsilon.$$

This completes the proof of the cycling theorem.

* There is a gap here, as pointed out and repaired by H.D. Block and S.A. Levin: Proc. Amer. Math. Soc. vol 26, no. 2. pp. 229-235.

12.0 Introduction

The perceptron and the convergence theorems of Chapter 11 are related to many other procedures that are studied in an extensive and disorderly literature under such titles as LEARNING MACHINES, MODELS OF LEARNING, INFORMATION RETRIEVAL, STATISTICAL DECISION THEORY, PATTERN RECOGNITION and many more. In this chapter we will study a few of these to indicate points of contact with the perceptron and to reveal deep differences. We can give neither a fully rigorous account nor a unifying theory of these topics: this would go as far beyond our knowledge as beyond the scope of this book. The chapter is written more in the spirit of inciting students to research than of offering solutions to problems.

12.1 Information Retrieval and Inductive Inference

The perceptron training procedures (Chapter 11) could be used to construct a device that operates within the following pattern of behavior:

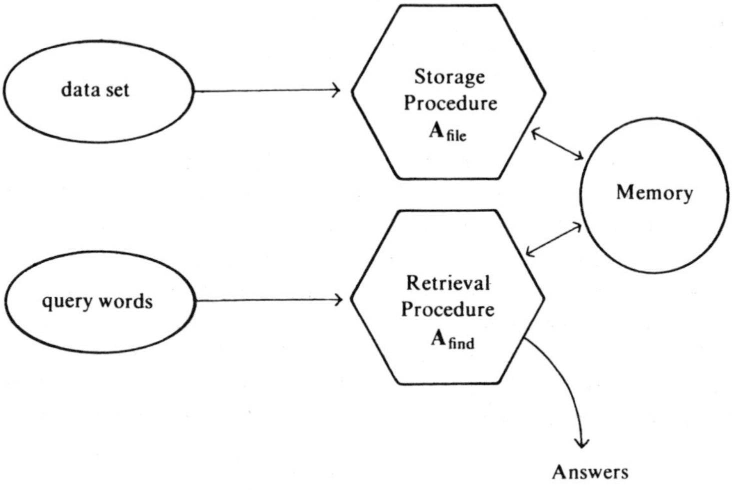

During a "filing" phase, the machine is shown a "data set" of n-dimensional vectors—one can think of them as n-bit binary numbers or as points in n-space. Later, in a "finding" phase, the machine must be able to decide which of a variety of "query" vectors belong to the data set. To generalize this pattern we will use the term $\mathbf{A}_{\text{file}}$ for an algorithm that examines elements of a data set to modify the information in a memory. $\mathbf{A}_{\text{file}}$ is designed to prepare the memory for use by another procedure, $\mathbf{A}_{\text{find}}$, which will use the information in the memory to make decisions about query vectors.

This chapter will survey a variety of instances of this general scheme. We will begin by relating the PERCEPTRON procedure to the simplest such scheme: in the COMPLETE STORAGE procedure $\mathbf{A}_{\text{file}}$ merely copies the data vectors, as they come, into the memory. For each query vector, $\mathbf{A}_{\text{find}}$ searches exhaustively through memory to see if it is recorded there.

12.1.1 Comparing PERCEPTRON with COMPLETE STORAGE

Our purpose is to illustrate, in this simple case, some of the questions one might ask to compare retrieval schemes:

Is the procedure universal? The PERCEPTRON scheme works perfectly only under the restriction that the data set is linearly separable. COMPLETE STORAGE is universal: it works for any data set.

How much memory is required? COMPLETE STORAGE needs a memory large enough to hold the full data set. PERCEPTRON, when it is applicable, sometimes has a summarizing effect, in that the information capacity needed to store its coefficients $\{\alpha_i\}$ is substantially less than that needed to store the whole data set. We have seen (§10.2) that this is not generally true; the coefficients for ψ_{PARITY} may need much more storage than does the list of accepted vectors.

How quickly does $\mathbf{A}_{\text{find}}$ operate? The retrieval scheme—exhaustive search—specified for COMPLETE STORAGE is very slow (usually slower than PERCEPTRON's $\mathbf{A}_{\text{find}}$, which must also retrieve all its coefficients from memory). On the other hand, very similar procedures could be much faster. For example, if $\mathbf{A}_{\text{file}}$ did not just store the data set in its order of entry, but *sorted* the memory into numerical order, then $\mathbf{A}_{\text{find}}$ could use a binary search, reducing the query-answer time to

$$\log_2(|\text{data set}|)$$

memory references. We shall study (in §12.6) $\mathbf{A}_{\text{file}}$ algorithms that sacrifice memory size to obtain dramatic further increases in speed (by the so-called *hash-coding* technique).

Can the procedure operate with some degree (perhaps measured probabilistically) of success even when $\mathbf{A}_{\text{file}}$ *has seen only a subset of the data set—call it a "data sample"?* PERCEPTRON might, but the COMPLETE STORAGE algorithm, as described, cannot make a reasonable guess when presented with a query vector not in the data sample. This deficiency suggests an important modification of the complete storage procedure: let $\mathbf{A}_{\text{find}}$, instead of merely checking whether the query vector is in the data sample, find that member of the data sample *closest* to it. This would lead, on an *a priori* assumption about the "continuity" of the data set, to a degree of generalization as good as the perceptron's. Unfortunately the speed-up procedures such as hash-coding cease to be available and we conjecture (in a sense to be made more precise in §12.7.6) that the loss is irremediable.

Other considerations we shall mention concern the operation of $\mathbf{A}_{\text{file}}$. We note that the PERCEPTRON and the COMPLETE STORAGE procedures share the following features:

They act incrementally, that is, change the stored memory slightly as a function of the currently presented member of the data set.

They operate in "real time" without using large quantities of auxiliary scratch-pad memory.

They can accept the data set in any order and are tolerant of repetitions that cause only delay but do not change the final state.

On the other hand they differ in at least one very fundamental way:

The perceptron's $\mathbf{A}_{\text{file}}$ is a "search procedure" based on feedback from its own results. The complete storage file algorithm is passive. The advantage for the perceptron is that under some conditions it finds an economical summarizing representation. The cost is that it may need to see each data point many times.

12.1.2 Multiple Classification Procedures

It is a slight generalization of these ideas to suppose the data set divided into a number of classes $\mathbf{F}_1, \ldots, \mathbf{F}_k$. The algorithm

$\mathbf{A}_{\text{file}}$ is presented as before with members of the data set but also with indications of the corresponding class. It constructs a body of stored information which is handed over to $\mathbf{A}_{\text{find}}$ whose task is to assign query points to their classes using this information.

Example: We have seen (§11.3.1) how to extend the concept of the perceptron to a multiple classification. The training algorithm, $\mathbf{A}_{\text{file}}$, finds k vectors $\mathbf{A}_1, \ldots, \mathbf{A}_k$, and $\mathbf{A}_{\text{find}}$ assigns the vector $\mathbf{\Phi}$ to $\mathbf{F}_j$ if

$$\mathbf{\Phi} \cdot \mathbf{A}_j > \mathbf{\Phi} \cdot \mathbf{A}_i \qquad (\text{all } i \neq j). \qquad \text{INNER PRODUCT}$$

Example: The following situation will seem much more familiar to many readers. If we think of each class $\mathbf{F}_j$ as a "clump" or "cloud" or "cluster" of points in Φ-space, then we can imagine that with each $\mathbf{F}_j$ is associated a special point $\mathbf{B}_j$ that is, somehow, a "typical" or "average" point. For example, $\mathbf{B}_j$ could be the *center of gravity*, that is, the *mean* of all the vectors in $\mathbf{F}_j$ (or, say, of just those vectors that so far have been observed to be in $\mathbf{F}_j$). Then a familiar procedure is: $\mathbf{\Phi}$ is judged to be in that $\mathbf{F}_j$ for which the Euclidean distance

$$|\mathbf{\Phi} - \mathbf{B}_j|.$$

is the *smallest*. That is, each $\mathbf{\Phi}$ is identified with the nearest $\mathbf{B}$-point.

Now this nearness scheme and the inner-product scheme might look quite different, but they are essentially the same! For we have only to observe that the set of points closer to one given point $\mathbf{B}_1$ than to another $\mathbf{B}_2$ is bounded by a hyperplane (Figure 12.1), and hence can be defined by a linear inequal-

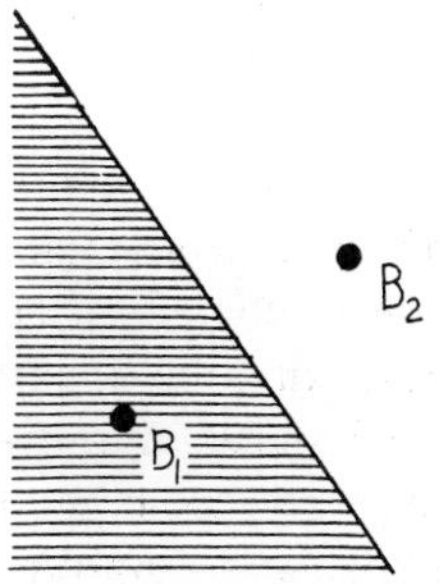

Figure 12.1

ity. Similarly, the points closest to one of a number of $\mathbf{B}_j$'s form a (convex) polygon (Figure 12.2) and this is true in higher dimensions, also.

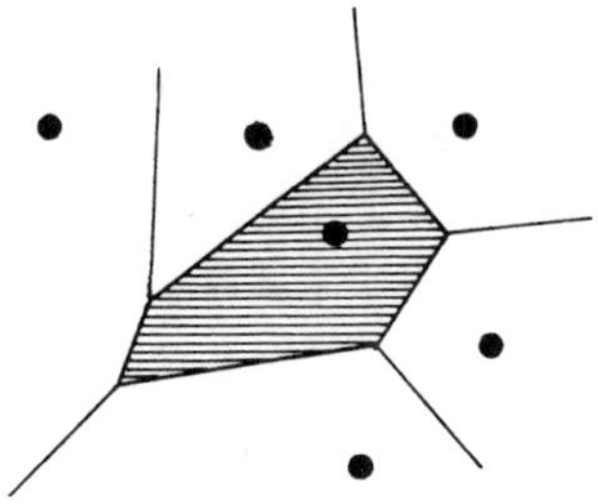

Figure 12.2

Formally, we see this equivalence by observing that

$$|\mathbf{\Phi} - \mathbf{B}_j|^2 = |\mathbf{\Phi}|^2 - 2\mathbf{\Phi} \cdot \mathbf{B}_j + |\mathbf{B}_j|^2.$$

Now, if we can assume that all the Φ's have the same length L then the Euclidean distance (B) will be *smallest* when

$$\mathbf{\Phi} \cdot \mathbf{B}_j - \tfrac{1}{2} |\mathbf{B}_j|^2 \equiv \mathbf{\Phi} \cdot \mathbf{B}_j - \theta_j$$

is largest. But this is exactly the inner-product, if the "threshold" is removed by §1.2.1 (1). To see that the inner-product concept loses nothing by requiring the Φ's to have the same length, we add an extra dimension and replace each $\mathbf{\Phi} = [\varphi_1, \ldots, \varphi_n]$ by

$$\hat{\mathbf{\Phi}} = \left[\varphi_1, \ldots, \varphi_n, \left(n^2 - \sum_1^n \varphi_i\right)^{1/2}\right]$$

so that all $\hat{\mathbf{\Phi}}$'s have length $L^2 = n$. We have to add one dimension to the $\mathbf{B}$'s, too, but can always set its coefficient to zero.

12.2 A Variety of Classification Algorithms

We select, from the infinite variety of schemes that one might use to divide a space into different classes, a few schemes that illustrate aspects of our main subject: computation and linear separation. We will summarize each very briefly here; the remainder of the chapter compares and contrasts some aspects of their algorithmic structures, memory requirements, and commitments they make about the nature of the classes.

Each of our models uses the same basic form of decision algorithm for $\mathbf{A}_{\text{find}}$. In each case there is assigned to each class $\mathbf{F}_j$ one or more vectors $\mathbf{A}_i$; we will represent this assignment by saying that $\mathbf{A}_i$ is associated with $\mathbf{F}_{j(i)}$. Given a vector $\mathbf{\Phi}$, the decision rule is always to choose that $\mathbf{F}_{j(i)}$ for which $\mathbf{A}_i \cdot \mathbf{\Phi}$ is largest. As noted in §12.1.2 this is mathematically equivalent to a rule that minimizes $|\mathbf{\Phi} - \mathbf{A}_i|$ or some very similar formula.

For each model we must also describe the algorithm $\mathbf{A}_{\text{file}}$ that constructs the $\mathbf{A}_i$'s, on the basis of prior experience, or *a priori* information about the classes. In the brief vignettes below, the fine details of the $\mathbf{A}_{\text{file}}$ procedures are deferred to other sections.

12.2.1 The PERCEPTRON Procedure

There is one vector $\mathbf{A}_j$ for each class $\mathbf{F}_j$. $\mathbf{A}_{\text{file}}$ can be the procedures described in §11.1 for the 2-class case and in §11.4.1 for the multi-class case.

12.2.2 The BAYES Linear Statistical Procedure

Again we have one $\mathbf{A}_j$ for each $\mathbf{F}_j$. $\mathbf{A}_{\text{file}}$ is quite different, however. For each class $\mathbf{F}_j$ and each partial predicate φ_i, define

$$w_{ij} = \log\left(\frac{p_{ij}}{1 - p_{ij}}\right),$$

where p_{ij} is *the probability that* $\varphi_i = 1$, *given that* $\mathbf{\Phi}$ *is in* $\mathbf{F}_j$. Then define

$$\mathbf{A}_j = (\theta_j, w_{1j}, w_{2j}, \ldots).$$

We will explain in §12.4.3 the conditions under which this use of "probability" makes sense, and describe some "learning" algorithms that could be used to estimate or approximate the w_{ij}'s.

The BAYES procedure has the advantage that, provided certain statistical conditions are satisfied, it gives good results for classes that are *not* linearly separable. In fact it gives the lowest possible error rate for procedures in which $\mathbf{A}_{\text{file}}$ depends only on conditional probabilities, given that the φ's are statistically independent in the sense explained in §12.4.2. It is astounding that this is achieved by a linear formula.

12.2.3 The BEST PLANES Procedure

In different situations either PERCEPTRON or BAYES may be superior. But often, when the $\mathbf{F}_j$'s are not linearly separable, there will exist a set of $\mathbf{A}_j$ vectors which will give fewer errors than either of these schemes. So define the BEST PLANES procedure to use that set of $\mathbf{A}_j$'s for which choice of the largest $\mathbf{A}_j \cdot \mathbf{\Phi}$ gives the fewest errors.

By definition, BEST PLANES is always at least as good as BAYES or PERCEPTRON. This does not contradict the optimality of BAYES since the search for the best plane uses information other than the conditional probabilities. Unfortunately no practically efficient $\mathbf{A}_{\text{file}}$ is known for discovering its $\mathbf{A}_j$'s. As noted in §12.3, hill-climbing will apparently not work well because of the local peak problem.

12.2.4 The ISODATA Procedure

In the schemes described up to now, we assigned exactly one **A**-vector to each **F**-class. If we shift toward the minimum-distance viewpoint, this suggests that such procedures will work satisfactorily only when the **F**-classes are "localized" into relatively isolated, single regions—one might think of clumps, clusters, or clouds. Given this intuitive picture, one naturally asks what to do if an **F**-class, while not a neat spherical cluster, is nevertheless semilocalized as a small number of clusters or, perhaps, a snake-like structure. We could still handle such situations, using the least-distance $\mathbf{A}_{\text{find}}$, by assigning an **A**-vector to each subcluster of each **F**, and using several **A**'s to outline the spine of the snake. To realize this concept, we need an $\mathbf{A}_{\text{file}}$ scheme that has some ability to analyze distributions into clusters. We will describe one such scheme, called ISODATA, in §12.5.

12.2.5 The NEAREST NEIGHBOR Procedure

Our simplest and most radical scheme assumes no limit on the number of **A**-vectors. $\mathbf{A}_{\text{file}}$ stores in memory every $\mathbf{\Phi}$ that has ever been encountered, together with the name of its associated **F**-class. Given a query vector $\mathbf{\Phi}_0$, we find which $\mathbf{\Phi}$ in the memory is closest to $\mathbf{\Phi}_0$, and choose the **F**-class associated with that $\mathbf{\Phi}$.

This is a very generally powerful method: it is very efficient on many sorts of cluster configurations; it never makes a mistake on an already seen point; in the limit it approaches zero error except under rather peculiar circumstances (one of which is discussed in the following section).

NEAREST NEIGHBOR has an obvious disadvantage—the very large memory required—and a subtle disadvantage: there is reason to suspect that it entails large, and fundamentally unavoidable, computation costs (discussed in §12.6).

12.3 Heuristic Geometry of Linear Separation Methods

The diagrams of this section attempt to suggest some of the behavioral aspects of the methods described in §12.4. To compensate for our inability to depict multidimensional configurations, we use two-dimensional multivalued coordinates. The diagrams may appear plausible, but they are really defective images that do not hint at the horrible things that can happen in a space of many dimensions.

Using this metaphorical kind of picture, we can suggest two kinds of situations which tend to favor one or the other of BAYES or PERCEPTRON (see Figure 12.3).

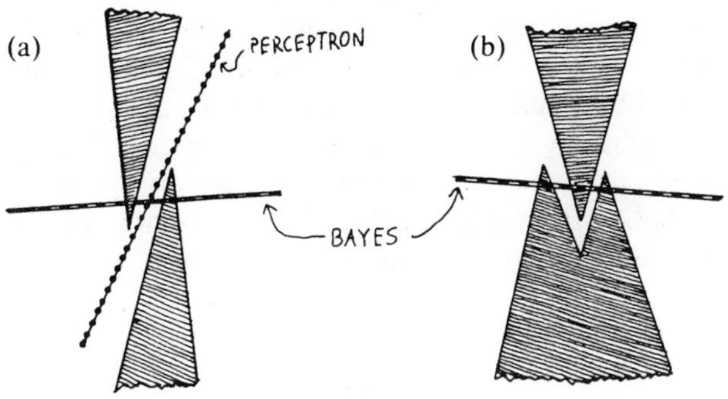

Figure 12.3

The BAYES line in Figure 12.3 tends to lie perpendicular to the line between the "mean" points of $\mathbf{F}_-$ and $\mathbf{F}_+$. Hence in Figure 12.3(a), we find that BAYES makes some errors. The sets are, in fact, linearly separable, hence PERCEPTRON, eventually, makes no errors at all. In Figure 12.3(b) we find that BAYES makes a few errors, just as in 12.3(a). We don't know much about PERCEPTRON in nonseparable situations; it is clear that in some situations it will not do as well as BAYES. By definition BEST PLANE, of course, does at least as well as either BAYES or PERCEPTRON.

From the start, the very suggestion that any of these procedures will be any good at all amounts to an *a priori* proposal that the **F**-classes can be fitted into simple clouds of some kind, perhaps with a little overlapping, as in Figure 12.4. Such an assumption

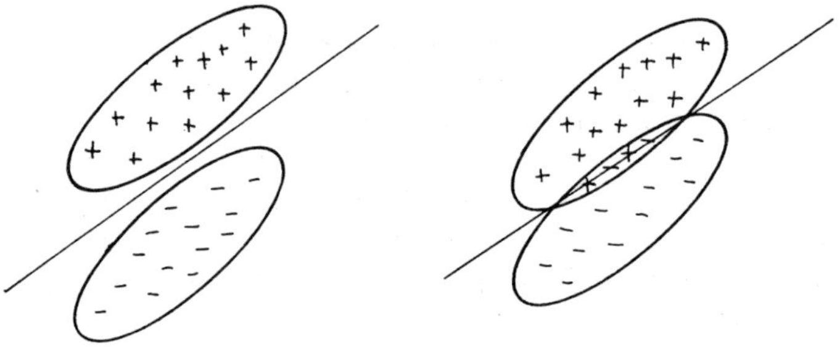

Figure 12.4

could be justified by some reason for believing that the differences between $\mathbf{F}_+$ and $\mathbf{F}_-$ are due to some one major influence plus a variety of smaller, secondary effects. In general PERCEPTRON tends to be sensitive to the outer boundaries of the clouds, and relatively insensitive to the density distributions inside, while BAYES weights all $\boldsymbol{\Phi}$'s equally. In cases that do not satisfy either the single-cloud or the slight-overlap condition (Figure 12.5), we can expect BAYES to do badly, and presumably PERCEPTRON also. BEST PLANE can be substantially better because it is not subject to the bad influence of symmetry. But *finding* the BEST PLANE is

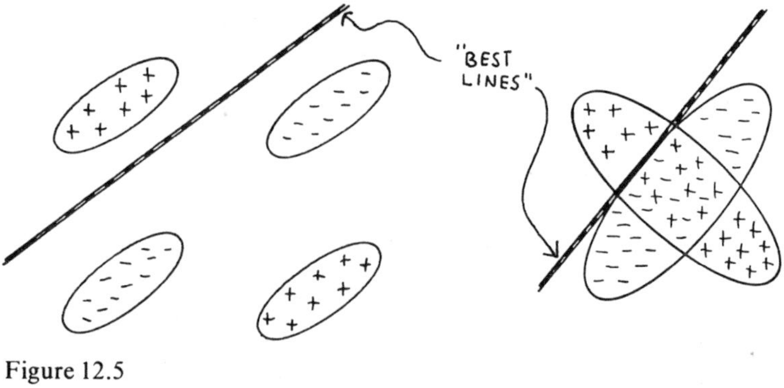

Figure 12.5

likely to involve bad computation problems because of multiple, locally optimal "hills." Figure 12.6 shows some of the local peaks for BEST PLANE in the case of a bad "paritylike" situation. Here, even ISODATA will do badly unless it is allowed to have one **A**-vector for nearly every clump. But in the case of a moderate number of clumps, with an $\mathbf{A}_k$ in each, ISODATA should do quite well. (See §12.5.) Generally, we would expect PERCEPTRON to be slightly better than BAYES because it exploits behavioral feedback, worse because of undue sensitivity to isolated errors.

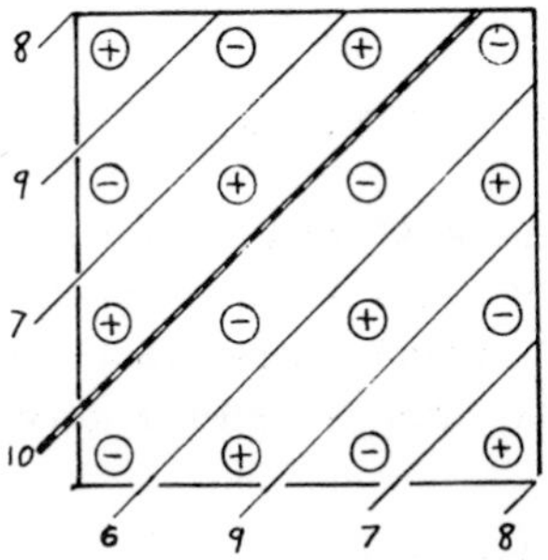

Figure 12.6

One would expect the NEAREST NEIGHBOR procedure to do well under a very wide range of conditions. Indeed, NEAREST NEIGHBOR in the limiting case of recording all **Φ**'s with their class names, will do at least as well as any other procedure. There are conditions, though, in which NEAREST NEIGHBOR does not do so well until the sample size is nearly the whole space. Consider, for example, a space in which there are two regions:

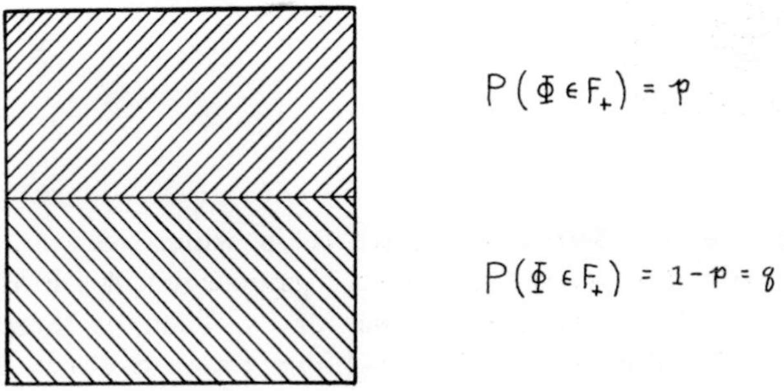

In the upper region a fraction p of the points are in $\mathbf{F}_+$, and these are randomly distributed in space, and similarly for $\mathbf{F}_-$ in the lower region. Then if a small fraction of the points are already recorded, the probability that a randomly selected point has the same $\mathbf{F}$ as its nearest recorded neighbor is

$$p^2 + q^2 = 1 - 2pq,$$

while the probability of correct identification by BAYES or by BEST PLANE is simply p. Assuming that $p > \frac{1}{2}$ (if not, just exchange p and q) we see that

$$\text{Error}_{\text{BEST PLANE}} < \text{Error}_{\text{NEAREST NEIGHBOR}} < 2 \times \text{Error}_{\text{BEST PLANE}}$$

so that NEAREST NEIGHBOR is worse than BEST PLANE, but not arbitrarily worse. This effect will remain until so many points have been sampled that there is a substantial chance that the sampled point has been sampled before, that is, until a good fraction of the whole space is covered.

On the other side, to the extent that the "mixing" of $\mathbf{F}_+$ and $\mathbf{F}_-$ is less severe (see Figure 12.7), the NEAREST NEIGHBOR will converge to very good scores as soon as there is a substantial chance of finding *one* sampled point in most of the microclumps.

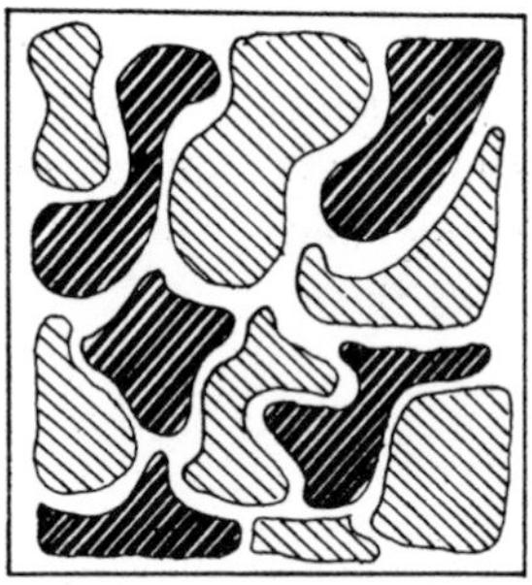

Figure 12.7

A very bad case is a paritylike structure in which NEAREST NEIGHBOR actually does worse than chance. Suppose that $\mathbf{\Phi} \in \mathbf{F}_1$ if and only if $\varphi_i = 1$ for an even number of i's. Then, if there are n φ's, each $\mathbf{\Phi}$ will have exactly n neighbors whose distance d

satisfies $0 < d \leq 1$. Suppose that all but a fraction q of all possible Φ's have already been seen. Then NEAREST NEIGHBOR will err on a given Φ if it has not been seen (probability $= q$) but one of its immediate neighbors has been seen (probability $= 1 - q^n$). So the probability of error is $\geq q(1 - q^n)$, which, for large n, can be quite near certainty.

This example is, of course, "pathological," as mathematicians like to say, and NEAREST NEIGHBOR is probably good in many real situations. Its performance depends, of course, on the precise "metric" used to compute distance, and much of classical statistical technique is concerned with optimizing coordinate axes and measurement scales for applications of NEAREST NEIGHBOR.

Finally, we remark that because the memory and computation costs for this procedure are so high, it is subject to competition from more elaborate schemes outside the regime of linear separation—and hence outside the scope of this book.

12.4 Decisions Based on Probabilities of Predicate-Values

Some of the procedures discussed in previous sections might be called "statistical" in the weak sense that their success is not guaranteed except up to some probability. The procedures discussed in this section are statistical also in the firmer sense that they do not store members of the *data set* directly, but instead store statistical parameters, or measurements, about the data set. We shall analyze in detail a system that computes—or estimates—the conditional probabilities p_{ij} that, for each class $\mathbf{F}_j$ the predicate φ_i has the value 1. It stores these p_{ij}'s together with the absolute probabilities p_j of Φ being in each of the $\mathbf{F}_j$'s.

Given an observed Φ, the decision to choose an $\mathbf{F}_j$ is a typical statistical problem usually solved by a "maximum likelihood" or Bayes-rule method. It is interesting that procedures of this kind resemble very closely the perceptron separation methods. In fact, when we can assume that the conditional probabilities p_{ij} are suitably independent (§12.4.2) it turns out that the best procedure is the linear threshold decision we called BAYES in §12.2.2. We now show how this comes about.

12.4.1 Maximum Likelihood and Bayes Law

In Chapter 11 we assumed that each Φ is associated with a unique $\mathbf{F}_j$. We now consider the slightly more general case in which the same **Φ** could be produced by events in several different **F**-classes. Then, given an observed **Φ** we cannot in general be sure which $\mathbf{F}_j$ is responsible, but we can at best know the associated probabilities.

Suppose that a particular $\mathbf{\Phi}_0$ has occurred and we want to know which **F** is most likely. Now if $\mathbf{F}_j$ is responsible, then the "joint event" $\mathbf{F}_j \wedge \mathbf{\Phi}_0$ has occurred; this has (by definition) probability $\mathcal{P}(\mathbf{F}_j \wedge \mathbf{\Phi}_0)$. Now (by definition of conditional probability) we can write

$$\mathcal{P}(\mathbf{F}_j \wedge \mathbf{\Phi}_0) = \mathcal{P}(\mathbf{F}_j) \cdot \mathcal{P}(\mathbf{\Phi}_0 \mid \mathbf{F}_j). \tag{1}$$

That is, the probability that both $\mathbf{F}_j$ and $\mathbf{\Phi}_0$ will happen together is equal to the probability that $\mathbf{F}_j$ will occur multiplied by the probability that *if* $\mathbf{F}_j$ *occurs so will* $\mathbf{\Phi}_0$.

We should choose that $\mathbf{F}_j$ which gives Formula 1 the largest value because that choice corresponds to the most likely of those events that could have occurred;

$$\mathbf{F}_1 \wedge \mathbf{\Phi}_0 \qquad \mathbf{F}_2 \wedge \mathbf{\Phi}_0 \qquad \cdots \qquad \mathbf{F}_k \wedge \mathbf{\Phi}_0.$$

These are serious practical obstacles to the direct use of Formula 1. If there are many different **Φ**'s it becomes impractical to store all the decisions in memory, let alone to estimate them all on the basis of empirical observation. Nor has the system any ability to guess about **Φ**'s it has not seen before. We can escape all these difficulties by making one critical assumption—in effect, assuming the situation closely fits a certain model—that the partial predicates of $\mathbf{\Phi} = (\varphi_1, \ldots, \varphi_m)$ are suitably independent.

12.4.2 Independence

Up to now we have suppressed the X's of earlier chapters because we did not care where the values of the φ's came from. We bring them back for a moment so that we can give a natural context to the independence hypothesis.

We can evade the problems mentioned above if we can assume that the tests $\varphi_i(X)$ are statistically independent over each **F**-class. Precisely, this means that for any $\mathbf{\Phi}(X) = (\varphi_1(X), \ldots, \varphi_m(X))$ we can assert that, for each j,

$$\mathcal{P}(\mathbf{\Phi} \mid \mathbf{F}_j) = \mathcal{P}(\varphi_1 \mid \mathbf{F}_j) \times \cdots \times \mathcal{P}(\varphi_m \mid \mathbf{F}_j). \tag{2}$$

We emphasize that this is a most stringent condition. For example, it is equivalent to the assertion that:

Given that a Φ *is in a certain* **F**-*class, if one is told also the values of some of the* φ*'s, this gives absolutely no further information about the values of the remaining* φ*'s.*

Experimentally, one would expect to find independence when the variations in the values of φ's are due to "noise" or measurement uncertainties within the individual φ-mechanisms:

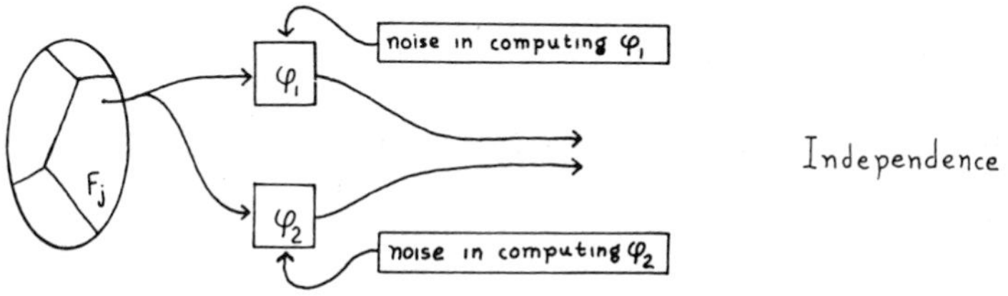

Figure 12.8

For, to the extent that these have separate causes, one would not expect the values of one to help predict the values of another. But if the variations in the φ's are *due to selection of different X's from the same* **F**-*class*, one would *not* ordinarily assume independence, since the value of each φ tells us something about which X in **F** has occurred, and hence should help at least partly to predict the values of other φ's:

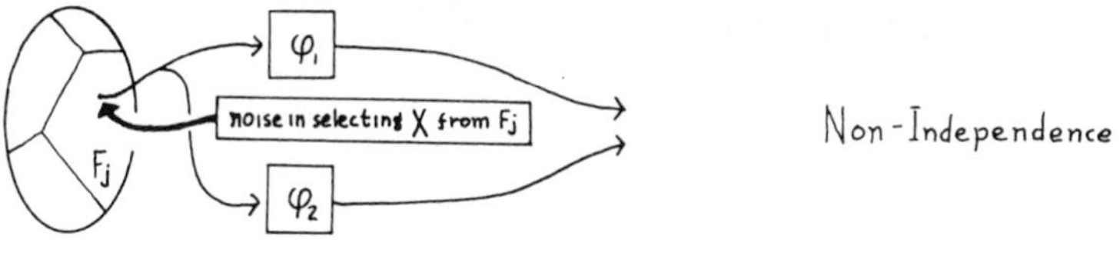

Figure 12.9

An extreme example of nonindependence is the following: there are two classes, $\mathbf{F}_1$ and $\mathbf{F}_2$, and two φ's, defined by

$$\begin{cases} \varphi_1(X) = \text{a pure random variable with } \mathcal{P}(\varphi_1(X) = 1) = \frac{1}{2}. \\ \qquad\qquad \text{Its value is determined by tossing a coin, not by } X. \\ \varphi_2(X) = \begin{cases} \varphi_1(X) \text{ if } X \in \mathbf{F}_1, \\ 1 - \varphi_1(X) \text{ if } X \in \mathbf{F}_2. \end{cases} \end{cases}$$

Then $$\mathcal{P}(\varphi_1 \wedge \varphi_2 | F_1) = \tfrac{1}{2}.$$
But $$\mathcal{P}(\varphi_1 | F_1) \cdot \mathcal{P}(\varphi_2 | F_1) = \tfrac{1}{2} \cdot \tfrac{1}{2}.$$

Notice that *neither* φ_1 *nor* φ_2 *taken alone gives any information whatever about* **F**! Each appears to be a random coin toss. But from both one can determine perfectly which **F** has occured,

for $\varphi_1 = \varphi_2$ implies $\mathbf{F}_1$,
while $\varphi_1 \neq \varphi_2$ implies $\mathbf{F}_2$

with absolute certainty.

REMARK: We assume only independence *within* each class $\mathbf{F}_j$. So if X is not given, then learning one φ-value *can* help predict another. For example, suppose that

$$\varphi_1 = \varphi_2 = 0 \text{ if } X \in \mathbf{F}_1,$$
$$\varphi_1 = \varphi_2 = 1 \text{ if } X \in \mathbf{F}_2.$$

These two φ's are in fact independent on each **F**. But if we *did not know in advance that* $X \in \mathbf{F}_1$ but were told that $\varphi_1 = 0$, we could indeed then predict that $\varphi_2 = 0$ also, without this violating our independence assumption. (If we had previously been told that $X \in \mathbf{F}_1$, then we could *already* predict the value of φ_2; in that case learning the value of φ_1 would have no effect on our prediction of φ_2.)

12.4.3 The Maximum Likelihood Decision, for Independent φ's, Is a Linear Threshold Predicate!

Assume that the φ_i's are statistically independent for each $\mathbf{F}_j$. Define

$$p_j = \mathcal{P}(\mathbf{F}_j),$$
$$p_{ij} = \mathcal{P}(\varphi_i = 1 | \mathbf{F}_j),$$
$$q_{ij} = 1 - p_{ij} = \mathcal{P}(\varphi_i = 0 | \mathbf{F}_j).$$

Suppose that we have just observed a $\mathbf{\Phi} = (\varphi_1, \ldots, \varphi_m)$, and we want to know which $\mathbf{F}_j$ was most probably responsible for this. Then, according to Formulas 1 and 2, we will choose that j which maximizes

$$p_j \cdot \prod_{\varphi_i = 1} p_{ij} \cdot \prod_{\varphi_i = 0} q_{ij}$$

$$= p_j \cdot \prod_i p_{ij}^{\varphi_i} \cdot q_{ij}^{(1-\varphi_i)}$$

$$= p_j \cdot \prod_i \left(\frac{p_{ij}}{q_{ij}}\right)^{\varphi_i} \cdot \prod_i q_{ij}.$$

Because sums are more familiar to us than products, we will replace these by their logarithms. Since log x increases when x does, we still will select the largest of

$$\sum_i \varphi_i \cdot \log \frac{p_{ij}}{q_{ij}} + \left(\log p_j + \sum_i \log q_{ij}\right). \tag{3}$$

Because the right-hand expression is a constant that depends only upon j, and not upon the experimental $\mathbf{\Phi}$, all of Formula 3 can be written simply as

$$\Sigma\, w_{ij} \varphi_i + \theta_j. \tag{3$'$}$$

Example 1: In the case that there are just two classes, $\mathbf{F}_1$ and $\mathbf{F}_2$, we can decide that $X \in \mathbf{F}$ whenever

$$\Sigma\, w_{i1} \varphi_i + \theta_1 > \Sigma\, w_{i2} \varphi_i + \theta_2,$$

that is, when

$$\Sigma\, (w_{i1} - w_{i2}) \varphi_i > (\theta_2 - \theta_1), \tag{4}$$

which has the form of a linear threshold predicate

$$\psi = \lceil \Sigma\, \alpha_i \varphi_i > \theta \rceil.$$

Thus we have the remarkable result that the hypothesis of independence among the φ's leads directly to the familiar linear decision policy.

Example 2 (probabilities of error): Suppose that for all i, $p_{i1} = q_{i2}$. Then p_{i1} is the probability that $\varphi_i(X) = \psi(X)$ and q_{i1} is the probability that $\varphi_i(X) \neq \psi(X)$, that is, that φ_i makes an error in (individually) predicting the value of $\psi = \lceil X \in \mathbf{F}_1 \rceil$.

Then inequality 4 becomes

$$\sum_i w_{i1}(2\varphi_i - 1) > \log \frac{p_2}{p_1}. \tag{4'}$$

Now observe that the $(2\varphi_i - 1)$ term has the effect of *adding* or *subtracting* w_{i1} according to whether $\varphi_i = 1$ or 0. Thus, we can think of the w's as weights to be added (according to the φ's) to one side or the other of a balance:

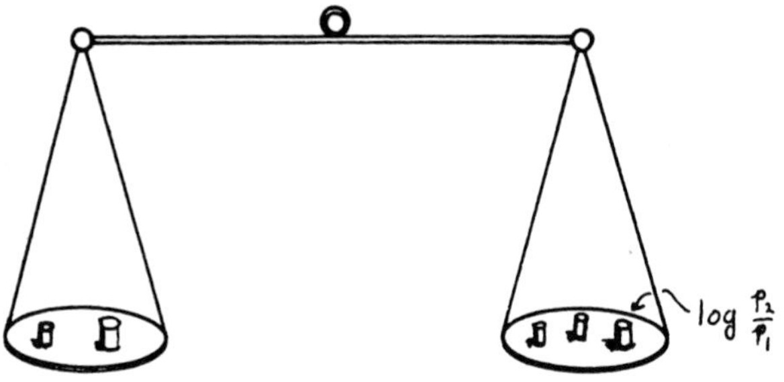

The log (p_2/p_1) is the "*a priori* weight" in favor of $\mathbf{F}_2$ at the start, and each $w_{i1} = \log(p_{i1}/q_{i1})$ is the "weight of the evidence" that $\varphi_i = 1$ gives in favor of $\mathbf{F}_1$.

It is quite remarkable that the optimal separation algorithm—given that the φ-probabilities are independent—has the form (Inequality 4) of a linear threshold predicate. But one must be sure to understand that if $\lceil \Sigma \alpha_\varphi \varphi > \theta \rceil$ is the "optimal" predicate obtained by the independent-probability method, yet does *not* perfectly realize a predicate ψ, this does not preclude the existence of a precise separation $\lceil \Sigma \alpha'_\varphi \varphi > \theta' \rceil$ which always agrees with ψ. [This is the situation suggested by Figure 12.3(a).] For Inequality 4 is "optimal" only in relation to all $\mathbf{A}_{\text{file}}$ procedures *that use no information other than the conditional probabilities* $\{p_j\}$ and $\{p_{ij}\}$, while a perceptron computes coefficients by a nonstatistical search procedure that is sensitive to individual events.

Thus, if ψ is in fact in $L(\Phi)$ the perceptron will eventually perform at least as well as any linear-statistical machine. The latter family can have the advantage in some cases:

1. If $\psi \notin L(\Phi)$ the statistical scheme may produce a good approximate separation while the perceptron might fluctuate wildly.

2. The time to achieve a useful level may be long for the perceptron file algorithm which is basically a serial search procedure. The linear-statis-

tical machine is basically more parallel, because it finds each coefficient independently of the others, and needs only a fair sample of the **F**'s. (While superficially perceptron coefficients appear to be changed individually, each decision about a change depends upon a test involving all the coefficients.)

12.4.4 Layer-Machines

Formula 3′ suggests the design of a machine for making our decision:

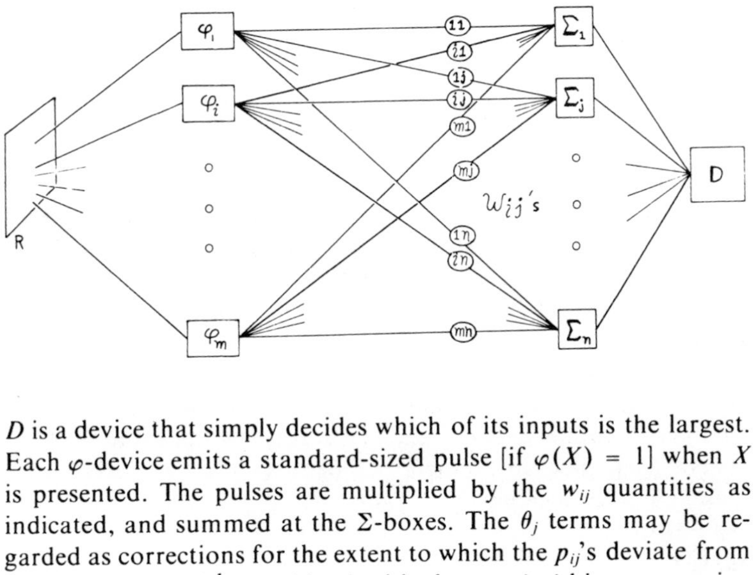

D is a device that simply decides which of its inputs is the largest. Each φ-device emits a standard-sized pulse [if $\varphi(X) = 1$] when X is presented. The pulses are multiplied by the w_{ij} quantities as indicated, and summed at the Σ-boxes. The θ_j terms may be regarded as corrections for the extent to which the p_{ij}'s deviate from a central value of $\frac{1}{2}$, combined with the *a priori* bias concerning $\mathbf{F}_j$ itself.

It is often desirable to minimize the *costs* of errors, rather than simply the chance of error. If we define C_{jk} to be the cost of guessing $\mathbf{F}_k$ when it is really $\mathbf{F}_j$ that has occurred, then it is easy to show that Formulas 1 and 2 now lead to finding the k that minimizes

$$\sum_j C_{jk} \cdot B_j \cdot \prod_i \left(\frac{p_{ij}}{q_{ij}}\right)^{\varphi_i} \cdot P_j$$

where $B_j = \Pi\, q_{ij}$. It is interesting that this more complicated procedure also lends itself to the multilayer structure:

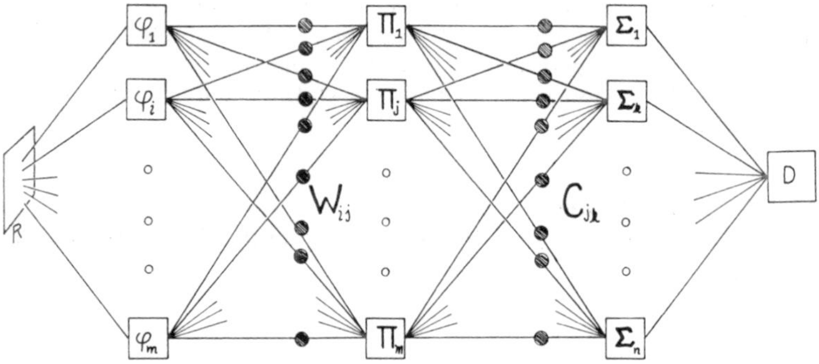

It ought to be possible to devise a training algorithm to optimize the weights in this using, say, the magnitude of a reinforcement signal to communicate to the net the cost of an error. We have not investigated this.

12.4.5 Probability-estimation Procedures

The $\mathbf{A}_{\text{file}}$ algorithm for the BAYES linear-statistical procedure has to compute, or estimate, either the probabilities p_{ij} and p_j of Formula 3 or other statistical quantities such as "weight of evidence" ratios $p/(1 - p)$. Normally these cannot be calculated directly (because they are, by definition, limits) so one must find *estimators*. The simplest way to estimate a probability is to find the ratio H/N of the number H of "favorable" events to the number N of all events in a sequence. If $\varphi^{[t]}$ is the value of φ on the tth trial, then an estimate of $\mathcal{P}(\varphi = 1)$ after n trials can be found by the procedure:

START: Set α to 0.
Set n to 1.

REPEAT: Set α to $\dfrac{(n - 1)\alpha + \varphi^{[n]}}{n}$.
Set n to $n + 1$.
Go to REPEAT.

which can easily be seen to recompute the "score" H/N after each event.

This procedure has the disadvantage that it has to keep a record of n, the number of trials. Since n increases beyond bound, this would require unlimited memory. To avoid this, we rewrite the above program's computation in the form

$$\alpha^{[n]} = \left(1 - \frac{1}{n}\right)\alpha^{[n-1]} + \frac{1}{n}\varphi^{[n]}.$$

This suggests a simpler heuristic substitute: define

$$\begin{cases} \alpha^{[0]} = 0, \\ \alpha^{[n]} = (1 - \epsilon)\alpha^{[n-1]} + \epsilon \cdot \varphi^{[n]}, \end{cases} \tag{5}$$

where ϵ is a "small" number between 0 and 1. It is easy to show that as n increases the *expected* or *mean* value of $\alpha^{[n]}$, which we will write as $\langle \alpha^{[n]} \rangle$, approaches p (that is, $\langle \varphi \rangle$) as a limit. For

$$\begin{aligned} \langle \alpha^{[1]} \rangle &= (1 - \epsilon)\langle \alpha^{[0]} \rangle + \epsilon \langle \varphi^{[1]} \rangle = \epsilon p \\ &= [1 - (1 - \epsilon)]p, \end{aligned}$$

and

$$\begin{aligned} \langle \alpha^{[2]} \rangle &= (1 - \epsilon)(1 - (1 - \epsilon))p + \epsilon p \\ &= (1 - (1 - \epsilon)^2)p, \end{aligned}$$

and one can verify that, for all n,

$$\begin{aligned} \langle \alpha^{[n]} \rangle &= (1 - (1 - \epsilon)^n)p \\ &\to p. \qquad \text{(as } n \to \infty \text{)} \end{aligned}$$

Thus, Process 5 gives an estimation of the probability that $\varphi = 1$. A more detailed analysis would show how the estimate depends on the events of the recent past, with the effect of ancient events decaying exponentially—with coefficients like $(1 - \epsilon)^{(t_0 - t)}$.

Because Process 5 "forgets," it certainly does not make "optimal" use of its past experience; but under some circumstances it will be able to "adapt" to changing environmental statistics, which could be a good thing. As a direct consequence of the decay, our estimator has a peculiar property: its variance "σ^2" does not approach zero. In fact, one can show that, for Process 5,

$$\sigma^2 \to p(1 - p)\frac{e}{2 - \epsilon}$$

and this, while not zero, will be very small whenever ϵ is. The situation is thus quite different from the H/N estimate—whose variance is $p(1 - p)/n$ and approaches zero as n grows.

In fact, we can use the variance to compare the two procedures: If we "equate" the variances

$$p(1 - p) \cdot \frac{\epsilon}{2 - \epsilon} \cong p(1 - p) \cdot \frac{1}{n},$$

we obtain

$$n \sim \frac{2}{\epsilon},$$

suggesting that the reliability of the estimate of p given by Process 5 is about the same as we would get by simple averaging of the last $2/\epsilon$ samples; thus one can think of the number $1/\epsilon$ as corresponding to a "time-constant" for forgetting.

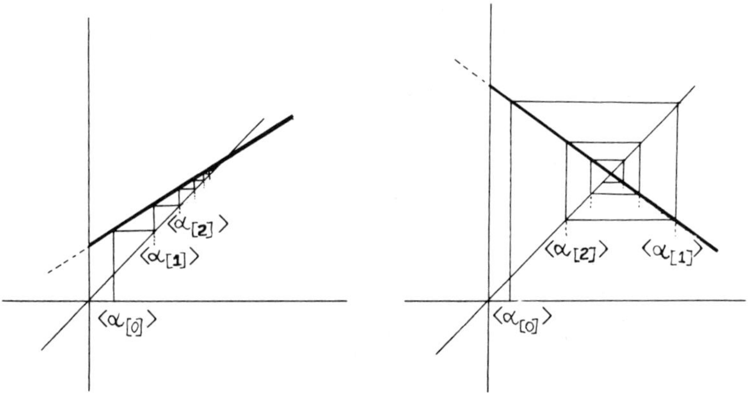

Convergence to the Fixed-Point

Another estimation procedure one might consider is:

START:	Set α to anything.
REPEAT:	If $\varphi = 1$, set α to $\alpha + 1$. If $\varphi = 0$, set α to $(1 - \epsilon)\alpha$. Go to REPEAT.

or, equivalently, one could write

$$\alpha^{[n]} = (1 - \epsilon)\alpha^{[n-1]} + (1 + \epsilon\alpha^{[n-1]})\varphi^{[n]}.$$

It can be shown that this has an expected value, in the limit, of

$$\langle\alpha^{[n]}\rangle \rightarrow \frac{1}{\epsilon} \cdot \left(\frac{p}{1 - p}\right).$$

It is interesting that a direct estimate of the likelihood ratio is obtained by such a simple process as *if* $\varphi = 1$ *add* 1, *otherwise multiply by* $(1 - e)$. The variance, in case anyone cares, is

$$\sigma^2 = \frac{p}{(1 - p)^2} \cdot \frac{1}{1 - (1 - \epsilon)^2}.$$

12.4.6 The Samuel Compromise

In his classical paper about "Some Studies in Machine Learning using the Game of Checkers," Arthur L. Samuel uses an ingenious combination of probability estimation methods. In his application it occasionally happens that *a new evidence term* φ_i *is introduced* (and an old one is abandoned because it has not been of much value in the decision process). When this happens there is a problem of preventing violent fluctuations, because after one or a few trials the term's probability estimate will have a large variance as compared with older terms that have better statistical records. Samuel uses the following algorithm to "stabilize" his system: he sets $\alpha^{[0]}$ to $\frac{1}{2}$ and uses

$$\alpha^{[n+1]} = \left(1 - \frac{1}{N}\right)\alpha^{[n]} + \frac{1}{N}\varphi^{[n+1]},$$

where N is set according to the "schedule":

$$N = \begin{cases} 16 & \text{if } n < 32, \\ 2^m & \text{if } 2^m \leq n < 2^{m+1} \text{ and } 32 \leq n \leq 256, \\ 256 & \text{if } 256 \leq n. \end{cases}$$

Thus, in the beginning the estimate is made as though the probability had already been estimated to be $\frac{1}{2}$ on the basis of several, that is, the order of 16, trials. Then in the "middle" period, the algorithm approximates the uniform weighting procedure. Finally (when $n \sim 256$) the procedure changes to the exponential decay mode, with fixed N, so that recent experience can outweigh earlier results. (The use of the powers of two represents a convenient computer-program technique for doing this.)

In Samuel's system, the terms actually used have the form we found in Inequality 4′ of §12.4.3

$$2\varphi^{[t]} - 1$$

so that the "estimator" ranges in the interval $-1 \leq \rho^{[t]} \leq +1$ and can be treated as a "correlation coefficient."

12.4.7 A Simple "Synaptic" Reinforcer Theory

Let us make a simple "neuronal model." The model is to estimate $p_{ij} = P(\varphi_i \mid \mathbf{F}_j)$, using only information about occurrences of $\lceil \varphi_i = 1 \rceil$ and of $\lceil \Phi \in \mathbf{F}_j \rceil$. Our model will have the following "anatomy":

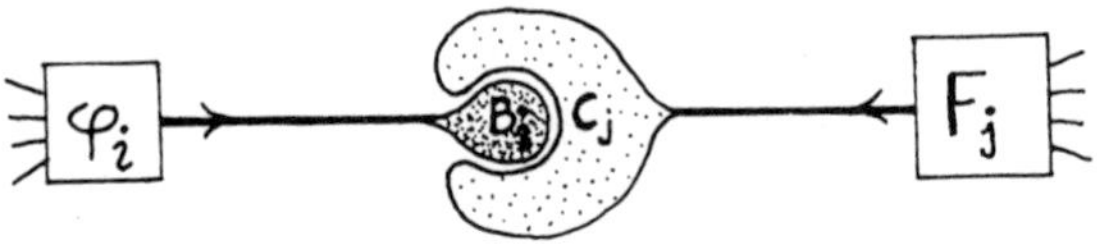

The bag B_i contains a very high and constant concentration of a substance E. When φ_i or $\mathbf{F}_j$ occur—or "fire"—the walls of the corresponding bags B_i and/or C_j become "permeable" to E for a moment. If φ_i alone occurs, nothing really changes, because B_i is surrounded by the impermeable C_j. If $\mathbf{F}_j$ alone occurs, C_j loses some E by diffusion to the outside: in fact, if α is the amount of E in C_j it may be assumed (by the usual laws of diffusion and concentration) to lose some fraction ϵ of α:

$$\alpha' = (1 - \epsilon)\alpha \quad \text{if} \begin{cases} \mathbf{F}_j \text{ occurs and} \\ \varphi_i = 0. \end{cases}$$

If *both* φ_i and $\mathbf{F}_j$ occur then approximately the same loss will occur from C_j. Simultaneously, an essentially constant amount b will be "injected" by diffusion from B_i to C_j. So

$$\alpha' = (1 - \epsilon)\alpha + b \quad \text{if} \begin{cases} F_j \text{ occurs and} \\ \varphi_i = 1. \end{cases}$$

(We can assume that b is constant because the concentration of E is very high in B_i compared to that in C_j. One can invent any number of similar variations.) In either case we get

$$\alpha' = (1 - \epsilon)\alpha + \varphi b \qquad \frac{b}{\epsilon} \cdot p$$

so that in the limit the mean of α approaches ~~$b \cdot p$~~ (as can be seen from the analysis in §12.4.5). This is proportional to, and hence an estimator of $p_{ij} = P(\varphi_i \mid \mathbf{F}_j)$.

Thus the simple anatomy, combined with the membrane becoming permeable briefly following a nerve impulse, could give a quantity that is an estimator of the appropriate probability.

How could this representation of probability be translated into a useful neuronal mechanism? One could imagine all sorts of schemes: ionic concentrations—or rather, their logarithms!—could become membrane potentials, or conductivities, or even probabilities of occurrences of other chemical events. The "anatomy" and "physiology" of our model could easily be modified to obtain likelihood ratios. Indeed, it is so easy to imagine variants—the idea is so insensitive to details—that we don't propose it seriously, except as a family of simple yet intriguing models that a neural theorist should know about.

12.5 A file Algorithms for the ISODATA Procedure

In this section we describe a procedure proposed by G. Ball and D. Hall to delineate "clusters" in an inhomogeneous distribution of vectors. The idea is best shown by a pictorial example: imagine a two-dimensional set of points $\{\mathbf{\Phi}\}$ that fall into obvious clusters, like

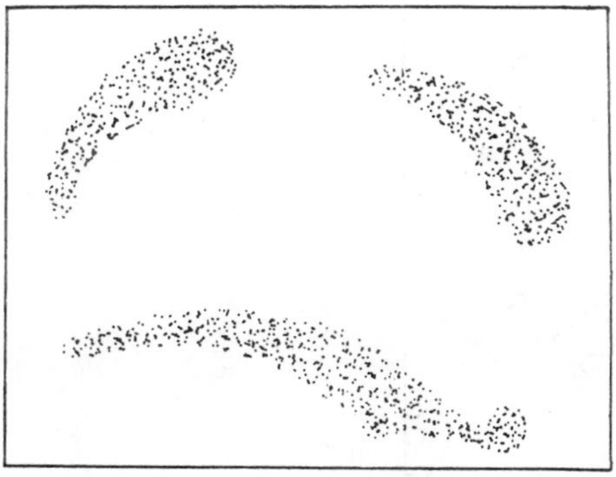

Begin by placing a few "cluster-points" $\mathbf{A}_i^{[1]}$ into the space at some arbitrary locations, say, near the center. We then divide the set of $\mathbf{\Phi}$'s into subsets $\mathbf{R}_i$, assigning each $\mathbf{\Phi}$ to the *nearest* $\mathbf{A}_i^{[1]}$ point:

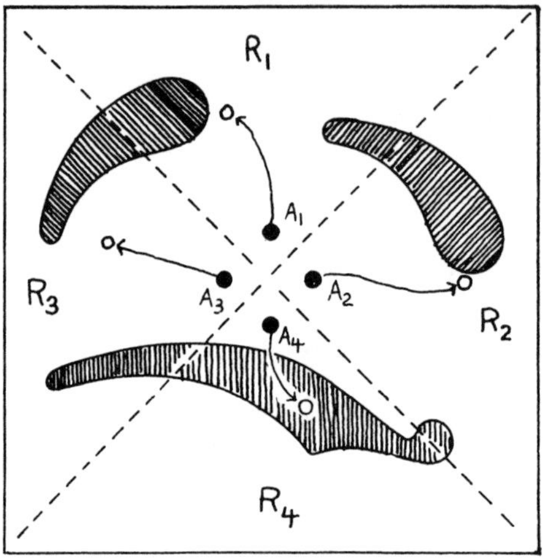

Next, we replace each $\mathbf{A}_i^{[1]}$ by a new cluster-point $\mathbf{A}_i^{[2]}$ which is the *mean* or center-of-gravity of the $\mathbf{\Phi}$'s in $\mathbf{R}_i$, and then define $\mathbf{R}_i^{[2]}$ to be the set of $\mathbf{\Phi}$'s nearest to $\mathbf{A}_i^2$:

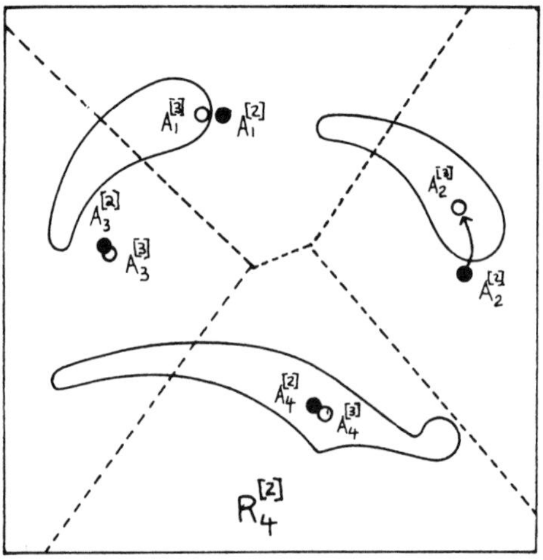

Repeating, we get a new set of $\mathbf{A}_i$'s and $\mathbf{R}_i$'s:

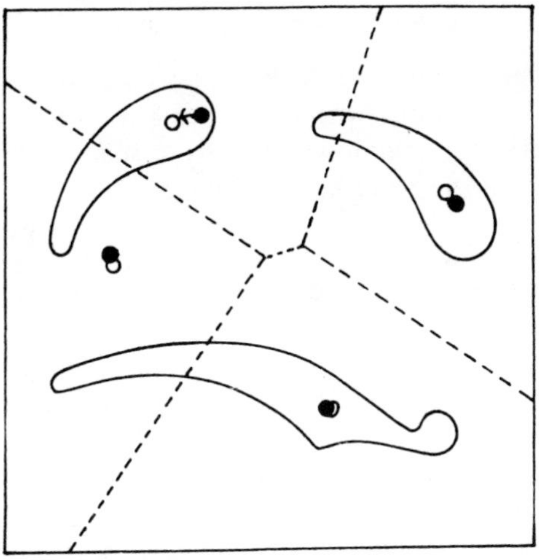

and next

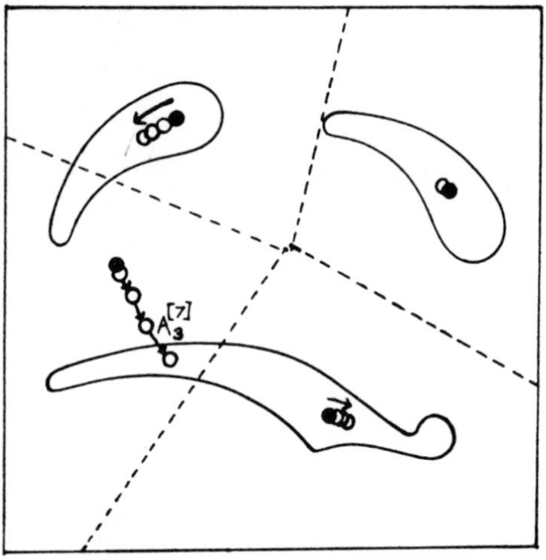

From now on, there is little or no change; the cluster-points have "found the clusters."

Ball and Hall give a number of heuristic refinements for creating and destroying additional cluster points; for example, to add one if the variance of an **R**-set is "too large" and to remove one if two are "too close" together. Of course, one can usually "see" two-dimensional clusters by inspection, but ISODATA is alleged to give useful results in n-dimensional problems where "inspection" is out of the question.

To use this procedure, in our context, we need some way to combine its automatic classification ability with the information about the **F**-classes. An obvious first step would be to apply it separately to each **F**-class, and assign all the resulting **A**'s to that class. We do not know much about more sophisticated schemes that might lead to better results in the $\mathbf{A}_{\text{find}}$ stage.

12.5.1 An ISODATA Convergence Theorem

There is a theorem about ISODATA (told to us by T. Cover) that suggests that it leads to some sort of local minimum. Let us formalize the procedure by defining

$$\mathbf{A}^{[n]}(\mathbf{\Phi}) = \text{the } \mathbf{A}_i^{[n]} \text{ that is nearest to } \mathbf{\Phi}.$$

(If there are several equidistant nearest $\mathbf{A}_i$'s, choose the one with the smallest index.)

$$\mathbf{R}_i^{[n]} = \text{the set of } \mathbf{\Phi}\text{'s for which } \mathbf{A}^{[n]}\mathbf{\Phi} = \mathbf{A}_i^{[n]}.$$

$$\mathbf{A}_i^{[n+1]} = \text{mean}\langle \mathbf{R}_i^{[n]} \rangle.$$

Finally define a "score":

$$S^{[n]} = \sum_{\text{all } \Phi} |\mathbf{\Phi} - \mathbf{A}^{[n]}(\mathbf{\Phi})|^2.$$

Theorem: $S^{[1]} > S^{[2]} > \ldots > S^{[n]} \ldots$

until there is no further change, that is, until $\mathbf{A}_i^{[n]} = \mathbf{A}_i^{[n+1]}$ for all i.

PROOF:

$$S^{[n]} = \sum_j \sum_{\mathbf{R}_j^{[n]}} |\mathbf{\Phi} - \mathbf{A}_j^{[n]}|^2$$

$$> \sum_j \sum_{\mathbf{R}_j^{[n]}} |\mathbf{\Phi} - \mathbf{A}_j^{[n+1]}|^2$$

because the mean ($\mathbf{A}_j^{[n+1]}$) of any set of vectors ($\mathbf{R}_j^{[n]}$) is just the point that minimizes the squared-distance sum to all the points (of $\mathbf{R}_j^{[n]}$). And this is, in turn,

$$\geq \sum_i \sum_{\mathbf{R}_i^{[n+1]}} |\mathbf{\Phi} - \mathbf{A}_i^{[n+1]}|^2 = S^{[n+1]}$$

because each point will be transferred to an $\mathbf{R}_i^{[n+1]}$ for which the distance is minimal, that is, for all j,

$$|\boldsymbol{\Phi} - \mathbf{A}_j^{[n+1]}| \geq |\boldsymbol{\Phi} - \mathbf{A}_i^{[n]}|.$$

Corollary: *The sequence of decreasing positive numbers,* $\{s^{[n]}\}$ *approaches a limit. If there is only a finite set of* $\boldsymbol{\Phi}$*'s, the* **A***'s must stop changing in a finite number of steps.*

For in the finite case there are only a finite number of partitions $\{\mathbf{R}_i\}$ possible.

12.5.2 Incremental Methods

In analogy to the "reinforcement" methods in §12.4.5 we can approximate ISODATA by the following program:

START: Choose a set of starting points $\mathbf{A}_i$.

REPEAT: Choose a $\boldsymbol{\Phi}$.
Find $\mathbf{A}(\boldsymbol{\Phi})$; the $\mathbf{A}_i$ nearest to $\boldsymbol{\Phi}$.
Replace $\mathbf{A}(\boldsymbol{\Phi})$ by $(1 - \epsilon)\mathbf{A}(\boldsymbol{\Phi}) + \epsilon \cdot \boldsymbol{\Phi}$.
Go to REPEAT.

It is clear that this program will lead to qualitatively the same sort of behavior; the **A**'s will tend toward the *means* of their **R**-regions. But, just as in §12.4, the process will retain a permanent sampling-and-forgetting variance, with similar advantages and disadvantages. In fact, all the $\mathbf{A}_{\text{file}}$ algorithms we have seen can be so approximated: there always seems to be a range from very local, incremental methods, to more accurate, somewhat less "adaptive" global schemes. We resume this discussion in §12.8.

12.6 Time vs. Memory for Exact Matching

Suppose that we are given a body of information—we will call it the *data set*—in the form of 2^a binary words each b digits in length (Figure 12.10); one can think of them as 2^a points chosen at random from a space of 2^b points. (Take a million $\cong 2^{20}$ words of length 100, for a practical example.) We will suppose that the data set is to be chosen at random from all possible sets so that one cannot expect to find much redundant structure within it. Then the ordered data set requires about $b \cdot 2^a$ bits of binary information for complete description. We won't, however, be in-

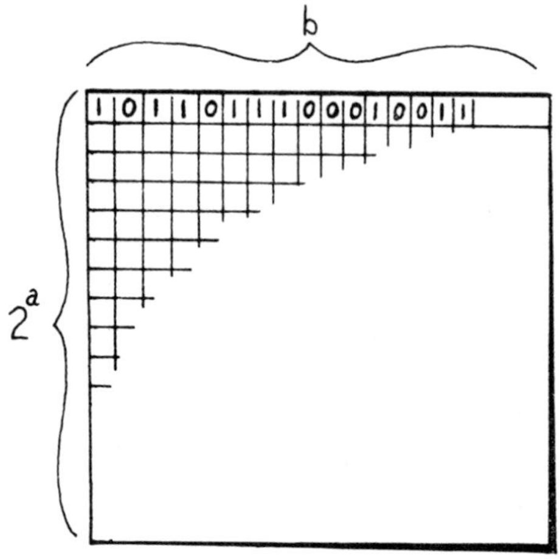

Figure 12.10

terested in the order of the words in the data set. This reduces the amount of information required to store the set to about $(b - a) \cdot 2^a$ bits.

We want a machine that, when given a random b-digit word w, will answer

QUESTION 1. Is w in the data set?*

and we want to formulate constraints upon how this machine works in such a way that we can separate computational aspects from memory aspects. The following scheme achieves this goal well enough to show, by examples, how little is known about the conjugacy between time and memory.

We will give our machine a memory of M separate bits—that is, one-digit binary words. We are required to compose—in advance, before we see the data set—two algorithms $\mathbf{A}_{\text{file}}$ and $\mathbf{A}_{\text{find}}$ that satisfy the following conditions:

1. $\mathbf{A}_{\text{file}}$ is given the data set. Using this as data, it fills the M bits of memory with information. Neither the data set nor $\mathbf{A}_{\text{file}}$ are used again, nor is $\mathbf{A}_{\text{find}}$ allowed to get any information about what $\mathbf{A}_{\text{file}}$ did, except by inspecting the contents of M.

*We will get to Question 2 in about fifteen minutes.

2. $\mathbf{A}_{\text{find}}$ is then given a random word, w, and asked to answer Question 1, using the information stored in the memory by $\mathbf{A}_{\text{file}}$. We are interested in how many bits $\mathbf{A}_{\text{find}}$ has to consult in the process.

3. The goal is to optimize the design of $\mathbf{A}_{\text{file}}$ and $\mathbf{A}_{\text{find}}$ to minimize the number of memory references in the question-answering computation, averaged over all possible words w.

12.6.1 Case 1: Enormous Memory

It is plausible that the larger be M, the smaller will be the average number of memory-references $\mathbf{A}_{\text{find}}$ must make. Suppose that

$$M \geq 2^b.$$

Let m_i be the ith bit in memory; then there is a bit m_w for each possible query word w, and we can define

$$\begin{cases} \mathbf{A}_{\text{file}}\text{: set } m_w \text{ to 1 if } w \text{ is in the data set} \\ \mathbf{A}_{\text{find}}\text{: } w \text{ is in the data set if } m_w = 1. \end{cases}$$

Thus, with a huge enough memory, only *one* reference is required to answer Question 1.

12.6.2 Case 2: Inadequate Memory

Suppose that

$$M < (b - a)2^a.$$

Here, the problem cannot be solved at all, since $\mathbf{A}_{\text{file}}$ cannot store enough information to describe the data set in sufficient detail.

12.6.3 Case 3: Binary Logarithmic Sort

Suppose that

$$M = b \cdot 2^a.$$

Now there is enough room to store the ordered data set. Define

$$\begin{cases} \mathbf{A}_{\text{file}}\text{: store the words of the data set in ascending numerical order.} \\ \mathbf{A}_{\text{find}}\text{: perform a binary search to see first which half of memory might contain } w\text{, then which quartile, etc.} \end{cases}$$

This will require at most $a = \log_2 2^a$ inspections of b-bit words, that is, $a \cdot b$ bit-inspections.

This is not an optimal search since, (1) one does not always need to inspect a *whole* word to decide which word to inspect next, and (2) it does not exploit the uniformity of distribution that the first a digits of the *ordered* data set will (on the average) show. Effect 1 reduces the required number from $a \cdot b$ to the order of $\frac{1}{2} a \cdot b$ and effect 2 reduces it from $a \cdot b$ to $a \cdot (b - a)$. We don't know exactly how these two effects combine.

12.6.4 Case 4: Exhaustive Search

Consider

$$M = (b - a)2^a.$$

This gives just about enough memory to represent the *unordered* data set. For example we could define

$\mathbf{A}_{\text{file}}$: First put the words of the data set in numerical order. Then compute their successive *differences*. These will require about $(b - a)$ bits each. Use a standard method of information theory, Huffman Coding (say), to represent this sequence; it will require about $(b - a) 2^a$ bits.

But the only retrieval schemes we can think of are like

$\mathbf{A}_{\text{find}}$: Add up successive differences in memory until the sum equals or exceeds w. If equality occurs, then w is in the data set.

And this requires $\sim \frac{1}{2}(b - a) 2^a$ memory references, on the average. It seems clear that, given this limit on memory, no $\mathbf{A}_{\text{file}}$ – $\mathbf{A}_{\text{find}}$ pair can do much better. That is, we suspect that

If no extra memory is available then to answer Question 1 one must, on the average, search through half the memory.

One might go slightly further: even Huffman Coding needs some extra memory, and if there is none, $\mathbf{A}_{\text{file}}$ can only store an efficient "number" for the whole data set. Then the conjecture is that $\mathbf{A}_{\text{find}}$ must almost always look at almost all of memory.

12.6.5 Case 5: Hash Coding

Consider

$M = b \cdot 2^a \cdot 2.$

Here we have a case in which there is a substantial margin of extra memory—about twice what is necessary for the data set. The result here is really remarkable—one might even say counter-intuitive—because the mean number of references becomes *very* small. The procedure uses a concept well known to programmers who use it in "symbolic assembly programs" for symbol-table references, but does not seem to be widely known to other computer "specialists." It is called **hash coding**.

There are many variants of this idea. We discuss a particular form adapted to a redundancy of two.

In the hash-coding procedure, $\mathbf{A}_{\text{file}}$ is equipped with a subprogram $R(w,j)$ that, given an integer j and a b-bit word w, produces an $(a + 1)$-bit word. The function $R(w,j)$ is "pseudorandom" in the sense that for each j, $R(w,j)$ maps the set of all 2^b input words with uniform density on the 2^{a+1} possible output words and, for different j's, these mappings are reasonably independent or orthogonal. One could use symmetric functions, modular arithmetics, or any of the conventional pseudorandom methods.*

Now, we think of the $b \cdot 2^{a+1}$-bit memory as organized into b-bit registers with $(a + 1)$-bit addresses: Suppose that $\mathbf{A}_{\text{file}}$ has already filed the words $w_1, \ldots, w_n$, and it is about to dispose of w_{n+1}.

$\mathbf{A}_{\text{file}}$: Compute $R(w_{n+1}, 1)$. If the register with this address is *empty* put w_{n+1} in it. If that register is occupied do the same with $R(w_{n+1}, 2)$, $R(w_{n+1}, 3), \ldots$ until an unoccupied register $R(w_{n+1}, j)$ is found; file w_{n+1} therein.

$\mathbf{A}_{\text{find}}$: Compute $R(w, 1)$. *If this register contains* w, *then* w is in the data set. If $R(w, 1)$ is empty, *then* w *is not in the data set*. If $R(w, 1)$ contains some other word not w, then do

---

*There is a superstition that $R(w, j)$ requires some magical property that can only be approximated. It is true that any particular R will be bad on *particular* data sets, but there is no problem at all when we consider average behavior on *all* possible data sets.

the same with $R(w, 2)$, and if necessary $R(w, 3)$, $R(w, 4)$, . . . , until either w or an empty register is discovered.

On the average, $\mathbf{A}_{\text{file}}$ *will make less than 2b memory-bit references*! To see this, we note first that, on the average, this procedure leads to the inspection of just 2 registers! For half of the registers are empty, and the successive values of $R(w,j)$ for $j = 1, 2, \ldots$ are independent (with respect to the ensemble of all data sets) so the mean number of registers inspected to find an empty register is 2.

Actually, the mean termination time is slightly *less*, because for w's in the data set the expected number of inspected registers is < 2. The procedure is useful for symbol-tables and the like, where one may want not only to know if w is there, but also to retrieve some other data associated (perhaps again by hash coding) with it.

When the margin of redundancy is narrowed, for example, if

$$M = \frac{n}{n-1} \cdot b \cdot 2^a,$$

then only $(1/n)$th of the cells will be empty and one can expect to have to inspect about n registers.

Because people are accustomed to the fact that most computers are "word-oriented" and normally do inspect b bits at each memory cycle the following analysis has not (to our knowledge) been carried through to the case of 1-bit words. When we program $\mathbf{A}_{\text{find}}$ to match words *bit by bit* we find that, since half the words in memory are zero, matching can be speeded up by assigning a special "zero" bit to each word.

Assume, for the moment, that we have room for these 2^a extra bits. Now suppose that a certain w_0 is *not* in the data set. (This has probability $1 - 2^{a-b}$.) First inspect the "zero" bit associated with $R(w_0,1)$. This has probability $\frac{1}{2}$ of being zero. If it is not zero, then we match the bits of w_0 with those of the word associated with $R(w_0,1)$. These cannot all match (since w_0 isn't in the data set) and in fact the mismatch will be found in (an average of) $2 = 1 + \frac{1}{2} + \frac{1}{4} + \ldots$ references. Then the "zero" bit of $R(w_0,2)$ must be inspected, and the process repeats. Each repeat has probability $\frac{1}{2}$ and the process terminates when the "zero" bit of some $R(w_0,j) = 0$. The expected number of references can be counted then as

$$\tfrac{1}{2}(1 + 2 + \tfrac{1}{2}(1 + 2 + \tfrac{1}{2}(\ldots))) + 1 = 3 + 1 = 4.$$

If w_0 *is* in the data set (an event whose probability is 2^{a-b}) and we repeat the analysis we get $4 + b$ references, because the process must terminate by matching all b bits of w_0.

The expected number of bit-references, overall, is then

$$4(1 - 2^{a-b}) + (4 + b)2^{a-b} = 4 + b \cdot 2^{a-b} \sim 4$$

since normally 2^{a-b} will be quite tiny. We consider it quite remarkable that so little redundancy—a factor of two—yields this small number!

The estimates above are on the high side because in the case that w_0 is *in* the data set the "run length" through $R(w_0, j)$ will be shorter, by nearly a factor of 2, than chance would have it just because they were put there by $\mathbf{A}_{\text{file}}$. On the other hand, we must pay for the extra "zero" bits we adjoined to M. If we have $M = 2b \cdot 2^a$ bits and make words of length $b + 1$ instead of b, then the memory becomes slightly *more* than half full: in fact, we must replace "4" in our result by something like $4[(b + 1)/(b - 1)]$. Perhaps these two effects will offset one another; we haven't made exact calculations, mainly because we are not sure that even this $\mathbf{A}_{\text{file}}$-$\mathbf{A}_{\text{find}}$ pair is optimal.

It certainly seems suspicious that half the words in memory are simply empty! On the other hand, the best one could expect from further improving the algorithms is to replace 4 by 3 (or 2?), and this is not a large enough carrot to work hard for.

12.6.6 Summary of Exact Matching Algorithms

To summarize our results on Question 1 we have established upper bounds for the following cases: We believe that they are close to lower bounds also but, especially in cases 3 and 4, are not sure.

Case	Memory size	Bit-references	Method
2	$<(b - a)2^a$	∞	(impossible)
4	$(b - a)2^a$	$\tfrac{1}{2}(b - a)2^a$	(search all memory)
3	$b \cdot 2^a$	$\tfrac{1}{2}b \cdot a$	(logarithmic sort)
5	$2b \cdot 2^a$	$4 + \epsilon$	(hash coding)
1	$\geq 2^b$	1	(table look-up)

12.7 Time vs. Memory for Best Matching: An Open Problem

We have summarized our (limited) understanding of "Question 1" —the exact matching problem—by the little table in §12.6.6. If one "plots the curve" one is instantly struck by the effectiveness of small degrees of redundancy. We do not believe that this should be taken too seriously, for we suspect that when the problem is slightly changed the result may be quite different. We consider now

QUESTION 2: Given w, exhibit the word $\hat{w}$ closest to w in the data set.

The ground rules about $\mathbf{A}_{\text{file}}$ and $\mathbf{A}_{\text{find}}$ are the same, and *distance* can be chosen to be the usual metric, that is, the number of digits in which two words disagree. If $x_1, \ldots, x_b$ and $\hat{x}_1, \ldots, \hat{x}_b$ are the (binary) coordinates of points w and $\hat{w}$ then we define the *Hamming* distance to be

$$d(w, \hat{w}) = \sum_{i=1}^{b} |x_i - \hat{x}_i|.$$

One gets exactly the same situation with the usual *Cartesian* distance $C(w, \hat{w})$, because

$$[C(w, \hat{w})]^2 = \Sigma\, |x_i - \hat{x}_i|^2 = \Sigma\, |x_i - \hat{x}_i| = d(w, \hat{w})$$

so both $C(w, \hat{w})$ and $d(w, \hat{w})$ are minimized by the same $\hat{w}$.

12.7.1 Case 1: $M = 2^b \cdot b$.

$\mathbf{A}_{\text{file}}$ assigns for every possible word w a block of b bits that contain the appropriate bits of the correct $\hat{w}$.

$\mathbf{A}_{\text{find}}$ looks in the block for w and writes out $\hat{w}$. It uses b references, which seems about the smallest possible number.

12.7.2 Case 2: $M < (b - a)2^a$.

Impossible, for same reason as in Question 1.

12.7.3 Case 3: $M = b \cdot 2^a$

No result known.

12.7.4 Case 4: $M = (b - a)2^a$

This presumably requires $(b - a) \cdot 2^a$ references, that is, all of memory, for the same reason as in Question 1.

12.7.5 Case 5: $(b - a)2^a < M < b \cdot 2^b$

No useful results known.

12.7.6 Gloomy Prospects for Best Matching Algorithms

The results in §12.6.6 showed that relatively small factors of redundancy in memory size yield very large increases in speed, for serial computations requiring the discovery of exact matches. Thus, there is no great advantage in using parallel computational mechanisms. In fact, as shown in §12.6.5, a memory-size factor of just 2 is enough to reduce the mean retrieval time to only slightly more than the best possible.

But, when we turn to the *best match* problem, all this seems to evaporate. In fact, we conjecture that even for the best possible $\mathbf{A}_{\text{file}}$-$\mathbf{A}_{\text{find}}$ pairs, the speed-up value of large memory redundancies is very small, and for large data sets with long word lengths there are no practical alternatives to large searches that inspect large parts of the memory.

We apologize for not having a more precise statement of the conjecture, or good suggestions for how to prove it, for we feel that this is a fundamentally important point in the theory of computation, especially in clarifying the distinction between serial and parallel concepts.

Our belief in this conjecture is based in part on experience in finding fallacies in schemes proposed for constructing fast best-matching file and retrieval algorithms. To illustrate this we discuss next the proposal most commonly advanced by students.

12.7.7 The Numerical-Order Scheme

This proposal is a natural attempt to extend the method of Case 3 (12.6.3) from exact match to best match. The scheme is

$\mathbf{A}_{\text{file}}$: store the words of the data set in numerical order.

$\mathbf{A}_{\text{find}}$: given a word w, find (by some procedure) those words whose first a bits agree most closely with the first a bits of w. How to do this isn't clear, but it occurs to one that (since this is the same problem on a smaller scale!) the procedure could be recursively defined. Then see how well the other bits of these words match with w. Next, . . . (?) . . . .

The intuitive idea is simple: the word $\hat{w}$ in the data set that is closest to w ought to show better-than-chance agreement in the first a bits, so why not look first at words known to have this property. There are two disastrous bugs in this program:

1. When can one stop searching? What should we fill in where we wrote "Next ...(?)...." We know no nontrivial rule that *guarantees* getting the best match.

2. The intuitive concept, reasonable as it may appear, is not valid! It isn't even of much use for finding a *good* match, let alone finding the best match.

To elaborate on point 2, consider an example: let $a = 20$, $b = 10{,}000$. Let w, for simplicity, be the all-zero word. A typical word in the data set will have a mean of 5000 *one*'s, and 5000 *zero*'s. The standard deviation will be $\frac{1}{2}(10{,}000)^{1/2} = 50$. Thus, less than one word in $2^a = 2^{20}$ can be expected to have fewer than 4750 *one*'s. Hence, the closest word in the data set will (on the average) have at least this many *one*'s. That closest word will have (on the average) $> 20 \cdot (4750/10{,}000) = 9.5$ *one*'s among its first 20 bits! The probability that w will indeed have very few *one*'s in its first 20 bits is therefore extremely low, and the slight favorable bias obtained by inspecting *those* words first is quite utterly negligible in reducing the amount of inspection. Besides, objection 1 still remains.

The value of ordering the first few bits of the words is quite useless, then. Classifying words in this way amounts, in the n-dimensional geometry, to breaking up the space into "cylinders" which are not well shaped for finding nearby points. We have, therefore, tried various arrangements of spheres, but the same sorts of trouble appear (after more analysis). In the course of that analysis, we are led to suspect that there is a fundamental property of n-dimensional geometry that puts a very strong and discouraging limitation upon all such algorithms.

12.7.8 Why is Best Match so Different from Exact Match?

If our unproved conjecture is true, one might want at least an intuitive explanation for the difference we would get between §12.6.3 and §12.7.3. One way to look at it is to emphasize that, though the phrases "best match" and "exact match" sound similar to the ear, they really are very different. For in the case of exact match, *no* error is allowed, and this has the remarkable effect of *changing an n-dimensional problem into a one-dimensional problem!* For best matching we used the formula

$$\text{Error} = \sum_{i=1}^{b} |x_i - \hat{x}_i| = \sum_{i=1}^{b} 1\ |x_i - \hat{x}_i|,$$

where we have inserted the coefficient "1" to show that all errors, in different dimensions, are counted equally. But for exact match, since *no* error can be tolerated, we don't have to weight them equally: any positive weights will do! So for exact match we could just as well write

$$\text{Error} = \sum_{i=1}^{b} 2^i |x_i - \hat{x}_i| \quad \text{or even} \quad \text{Error} = \sum_{i=1}^{b} 2^i (x_i - \hat{x}_i)$$

because either of these can be zero only when all $x_i = \hat{x}_i$. (Shades of stratification.) But then we can (finally) rewrite the latter as

$$\text{Error} = (\Sigma\, 2^i x_i) - (\Sigma\, 2^i \hat{x}_i)$$

and we have mapped the n-dimensional vector $(x_1, \ldots, x_b)$ into a single point on a one-dimensional line. Thus these superficially similar problems have totally different mathematical personalities!

12.8 Incremental Computation

All the $\mathbf{A}_{\text{file}}$ algorithms mentioned have the following curiously local property. They can be described roughly as computing the stored information M as a function of a large data set:

$$M = \mathbf{A}_{\text{file}}(\text{data set})$$

Now one can imagine algorithms which would use a vast amount of temporary storage (that is, *much* more than M or much more than is needed to store the data set) in order to compute M. Our $\mathbf{A}_{\text{file}}$ algorithms do not. On the contrary, they do not even use significantly more memory capacity than is needed to hold their final output, M. They are even content to examine just one member of the data set at a time, with no control over which they will see next, and without any subterfuge of storing the data internally.

It seems to us that this is an interesting property of computation that deserves to be studied in its own right. It is striking how many apparently "global" properties of a data set can be computed "incrementally" in this sense. Rather than give formal definitions of these terms, we shall illustrate them by simple examples.

Suppose one wishes to compute the median of a set of a million distinct numbers which will be presented in a long, disordered list. The standard solution would be to build up in memory a copy of the entire set in numerical order. The median number can then be read off. This is *not* an incremental computation because the temporary memory capacity required is a million times as great as that required to store the final answer. Moreover it is easy to see that there is no incremental procedure if the data is presented only once.

The situation changes if the list is repeated as often as we wish. For then two registers are enough to find the smallest number on one pass through the list, the second smallest on a second pass, and so on. With an additional register big enough to count up to half the number N of items in the list, we can eventually find the median.

It might seem at first sight, however, that an incremental computation is precluded if the numbers are presented in a random sequence, for example by being drawn, with replacement, from a well-stirred urn. But a little thought will show that an even more profligate expenditure of time will handle this case incrementally provided we can assume (for example) that we know the number of numbers in the set and are prepared to state in advance an acceptable probability of error.

What functions of big "data sets" allow these drastic exchanges of time for storage space? Readers might find it amusing to consider that to compute the BEST PLANE (§12.2.3), given random presentation of samples, and bounds on the coefficients, requires only about three solution-sized memory spaces. One predicate we think cannot be computed without storage as large as the data set is:

⌈the numbers in the data set, concatenated in numerically increasing order, form a prime number⌉.

In case anyone suspects that all functions are incrementally computable (in some sense) let him consider functions involving decisions about whether concatenations of members of the data set are halting tapes for Turing machines.

Perceptrons and Pattern Recognition

13

13.0 Introduction

Many of the theorems show that perceptrons cannot recognize certain kinds of patterns. Does this mean that it will be hard to build machines to recognize those patterns?

No. All the patterns we have discussed can be handled by quite simple algorithms for general-purpose computers.

Does this mean, then, that the theorems are very narrow, applying only to this small class of linear-separation machines?

Not at all. To draw that conclusion is to miss the whole point of how mathematics helps us understand things! Often, the main value of a theorem is in the discovery of a *phenomenon* itself rather than in finding the precise conditions under which it occurs.

Everyone knows, for example, about the "Fourier Series phenomenon" in which linear series expansions over a restricted class of functions (the sines and cosines) are used to represent all the functions of a much larger class. But only a very few of us can recall the precise conditions of a theorem about this! The important knowledge we retain is heuristic rather than formal—that a fruitful approach to certain kinds of problems is to seek an appropriate base for series expansions.

That sounds very sensible. But how might it apply to the theorems about perceptrons?

For example, the *stratification theorem* shows that certain predicates have lower order than one's geometric intuition would suggest; one can *encode* information in a "nonstandard" way by using very large coefficients. The conditions given for Theorem 7.2 are somewhat arbitrary, and many predicates can be realized in similar ways without meeting exactly these conditions. The theorem itself is just a vehicle for thoroughly understanding *an instance of* the more general encoding phenomenon.

Does it apply also to the negative results?

Yes, although it is harder to tell when "phenomena of limitations" will extend to more general machine-schemas. After we circulated early drafts of this book, we heard that some perceptron advocates made statements like "Their conclusions hold only if their conditions are exactly satisfied; our machines are not exactly the same as theirs." But consider, for example, the kind of limitation demonstrated by the And/Or theorem. Although the limitation as stated could be circumvented by adding another layer of logic to the machine scheme to permit "and"-ing two perceptrons together, this would certainly miss the point of the phenomenon. To be sure, the new machine will realize some predicates that the simpler machines could not. But if the and/or phenomenon is understood, then the student will quickly ask: Is the new machine itself subject to a similar closure limitation? We expect that no moderate extension of the machine-schema in such a direction would really make much difference to its ability to handle context-dependence.

We believe (but cannot prove) that the deeper limitations extend also to the variant of the perceptron proposed by A. Gamba. We discuss this in the next section.

13.1 Gamba Perceptrons and other Multilayer Linear Machines

In a series of papers (1960, 1961), A. Gamba and his associates describe experiments with a type of perceptron in which each φ is itself a thresholded *measure*, that is, a perceptron of order 1:

$$\varphi_i = \left[\sum_j \beta_{ij} x_j > \theta_i\right],$$

$$\psi = \left[\sum_i \alpha_i \left[\sum_j \beta_{ij} x_j > \theta_i\right] > \theta\right].$$

This scheme lends itself to physically realizable linear devices. For example, each φ could be realized by an optical filter and threshold photodetector (Figure 13.1).

Filters have been proposed that range from completely random patterns to carefully selected "feature detectors," moment integrals, and templates. One can even obtain complex values for the β_{ij}'s by using paired masks, or phase-coherent optics. We would like to have a good theory of these machines, especially because very large arrays can be obtained so economically by optical and similar techniques.

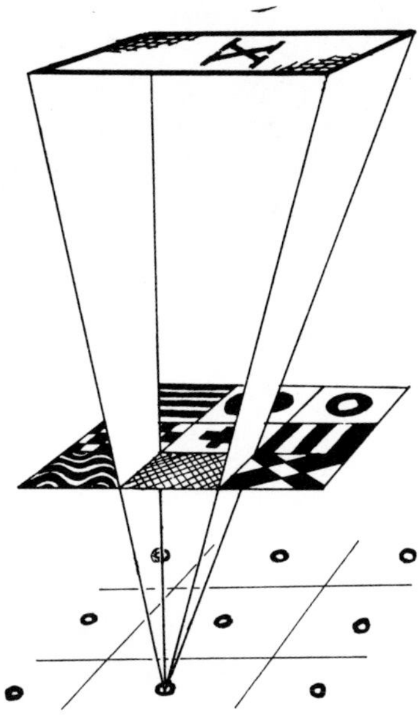

Figure 13.1

Unfortunately, we do not know how to adapt the algebraic methods that worked on order-limited perceptrons, nor have we found any other analytic techniques. We can thus make only a few observations and ask questions. Note first that if the inner threshold operations are eliminated, we have simply an order-1 perceptron:

$$\left\lceil \sum_i \alpha_i \sum_j \beta_{ij} x_j > \theta \right\rceil = \left\lceil \sum_j \left(\sum_i \alpha_i \beta_{ij} \right) x_j > \theta \right\rceil = \left\lceil \sum_j \alpha'_j x_j > \theta \right\rceil.$$

That the nonlinear operations have a real effect is shown by the fact that a simple Gamba machine *can* recognize the predicate

$$\psi_{ABC}(X) = \lceil (|X \cap A| > |X \cap B|) \vee (|X \cap C| > |X \cap B|) \rceil$$

that was shown in Chapter 4 to be not of finite order. For if we define

$$\beta_{1j} = \begin{cases} 1 & \text{if } x_j \epsilon A \\ -1 & \text{if } x_j \epsilon B \\ 0 & \text{otherwise} \end{cases} \qquad \beta_{2j} = \begin{cases} 1 & \text{if } x_j \epsilon C \\ -1 & \text{if } x_j = B \\ 0 & \text{otherwise} \end{cases}$$

then it follows that $\psi_{ABC} = \lceil \varphi_1 + \varphi_2 > 0 \rceil$ is recognizable by a Gamba machine.

Another predicate of unbounded order, ψ_{PARITY}, can be realized by simple Gamba machines; in fact any predicate $\psi(X) = \psi(|X|)$ that depends only on $|X|$ can be realized as follows: define

$$\varphi_{(n)}(X) = \lceil |X| > n \rceil = \lceil \Sigma x_i > n \rceil$$

and define

$$\begin{aligned} \alpha_0 &= \psi(0), \\ \alpha_1 &= \psi(1) - \alpha_0, \\ &\vdots \\ \alpha_{n+1} &= \psi(n+1) - \sum_{i=0}^{n} \alpha_i. \end{aligned}$$

Then we can write

$$\psi(X) = \left\lceil \sum_{i=1}^{|R|} \alpha_i \varphi_{(i)} > 0 \right\rceil.$$

If we place no limitation on the number of Gamba-masks, then the machines can recognize *any* pattern, since we can define, for each figure F, a template that recognizes exactly that figure:

$$\varphi_F = \left\lceil \sum_{x_i \in F} x_i - \sum_{x_i \notin F} x_i \geq |F| \right\rceil.$$

Then any class $\mathbf{F}$ of figures is recognized by

$$\psi_{\mathbf{F}} = \left\lceil \sum_{F \in \mathbf{F}} \varphi_F > 0 \right\rceil.$$

This is *not* an interesting result, for it says only that any class has a disjunctive Boolean form, and can be recognized if one allows as many Gamba masks as there are figures in the class. But it *is* interesting that the area-dependent classes like ψ_{PARITY} and ψ_{ABC} require at most $|R|$ masks, as shown above. It is not hard to prove that ψ_{PARITY} requires at least $\log |R|$ Gamba masks, but it would be nice to have a sharper result. We are quite sure that for predicates involving more sophisticated relations between subparts of figures the Gamba machines, like the order-limited machines, are relatively helpless, but the precise statement of this conjecture eludes us. For instance, we think that $\psi_{\text{CONNECTED}}$ would require an enormous number of Gamba-masks—perhaps nearly as many as the class of connected figures. Such conjectures, stated in terms of the *number* of φ's in the machine, seem harder to deal with than the simpler categorical impossibility of recognition with *any* number of masks of bounded order.

13.2 Other Multilayer Machines

Have you considered "perceptrons" with many layers?

Well, we have considered Gamba machines, which could be described as "two layers of perceptron." We have not found (by thinking or by studying the literature) any other really interesting class of multilayered machine, at least none whose principles seem to have a significant relation to those of the perceptron. To see the force of this qualification it is worth pondering the fact, trivial in itself, that a universal computer could be built entirely out of linear threshold modules. This does not in any sense reduce the theory of computation and programming to the theory of perceptrons. Some philosophers might like to express the relevant general principle by saying that the computer is so much more than the sum of its parts that the computer scientist can afford to ignore the nature of the components and consider only their connectivity. More concretely, we would call the student's attention to the following considerations:

1. Multilayer machines with loops clearly open all the questions of the general theory of automata.
2. A system with no loops but with an *order restriction at each layer* can compute only predicates of finite order.
3. On the other hand, if there is *no* restriction except for the absence of loops, the monster of vacuous generality once more raises its head.

The problem of extension is not merely technical. It is also strategic. The perceptron has shown itself worthy of study despite (and even because of!) its severe limitations. It has many features to attract attention: its linearity; its intriguing learning theorem; its clear paradigmatic simplicity as a kind of parallel computation. There is no reason to suppose that any of these virtues carry over to the many-layered version. Nevertheless, we consider it to be an important research problem to elucidate (or reject) our intuitive judgment that the extension is sterile. Perhaps some powerful convergence theorem will be discovered, or some profound reason for the failure to produce an interesting "learning theorem" for the multilayered machine will be found.

13.3 Analyzing Real-World Scenes

One can understand why you, as mathematicians, would be interested in such clear and simple predicates as ψ_{PARITY} *and* $\psi_{\text{CONNECTED}}$. *But what if one wants to build machines to recognize chairs and tables or people? Do your abstract predicates have any relevance to such problems, and does the theory of the simple perceptron have any relevance to the more complex machines one would use in practice?*

This is a little like asking whether the theory of linear circuits has relevance to the design of television sets. Absolutely, some concept of connectedness is required for analyzing a scene with many objects in it. For the whole is just the sum of its parts and their interrelations, and one needs some analysis related to connectedness to divide the scene into the kinds of parts that correspond to physically continuous objects.

Then must we conclude from the negative results of Chapter 5 that it will be very hard to make machines to analyze scenes?

Only if you confine yourself to perceptrons. The results of Chapter 9 show that connectivity is not particularly hard for more serial machines.

But even granting machines that handle connectivity, isn't there an enormous gap from that to machines capable of finding the objects in a picture of a three-dimensional scene?

The gap is not so large as one might think. To explain this, we will describe some details of a kind of computer program that can do it. The methods we will describe fall into the area that is today called "heuristic programming" or "artificial intelligence."*

*See, for example, *Computers and Thought* (Feigenbaum and Feldman, 1963) and *Semantic Information Processing* (Minsky, 1968).

Consider the problem of designing a machine that, when presented with a photograph, will be capable of *describing* the following scene.

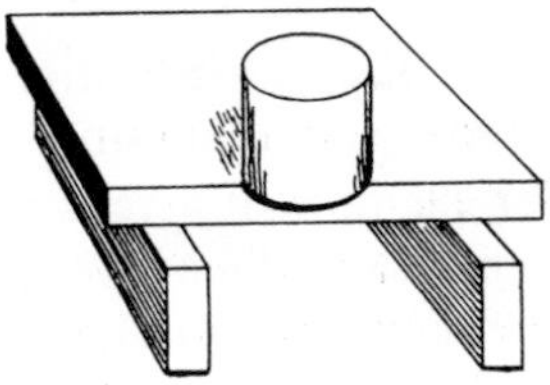

One would want the machine to say, at least, that this scene shows four objects—three of them rectangular and the fourth cylindrical—and to say something about their relative positions.

The tradition of heuristic programming would suggest providing the machine with a number of distinct abilities such as the following:

1. The ability to detect points at which the light conditions change rapidly enough to suggest an edge.

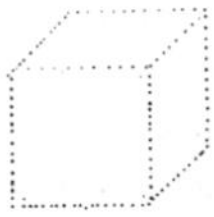

2. The ability to "cluster" the set of proposed edge-points into subsets that may each be taken as a hypothetical line segment or curve.

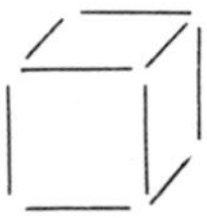

3. The ability to pass from the "line drawing" to a list of connected regions or "faces."

4. The ability to cluster faces into objects. In §13.4, we will describe such a method, developed by one of our students, Adolfo Guzman. This procedure is remarkably insensitive to partial covering of one object by another.

5. The ability to recognize certain features, such as shadows, as artifacts.

Perhaps most important is

6. The ability to make each of the above decisions on a tentative "working" basis and retract them if something "implausible" happens in any phase of the procedure. For example, if a region in Step 3 turns out to have an unusually complicated shape (relative to the class of objects for which it is designed) the existence of some of the lines proposed in Step 2 might be challenged, or others might be proposed, to be verified by re-activating Step 1 with a lower threshold.

7. All these processes might be organized by a supervisory program like the "General Problem Solver" of Newell, Shaw, and Simon (1959) or the executive program of a large programming system.

A system with such a set of abilities is in a very different class from a perceptron, if only because of the variety of operations it performs and forms of knowledge it uses. People often suggest that the methods of artificial intelligence and those associated with the perceptron are not as opposed as we think. For example, they say a perceptronlike algorithm might be used at each "level" to make the separate kinds of distinction. But using a perceptron as a *component* of a highly structured system entirely degrades its pretention to be a "self-organizing" system. If one is going to design such a system, one might as well be pragmatic in choosing an appropriate algorithm at each stage.

The spirit of the approach we have in mind is illustrated by the role in the following example of sequential operations, hypotheses, and hierarchical descriptions.

13.4 Guzman's Approach to Scene-Analysis

In scenes like this,

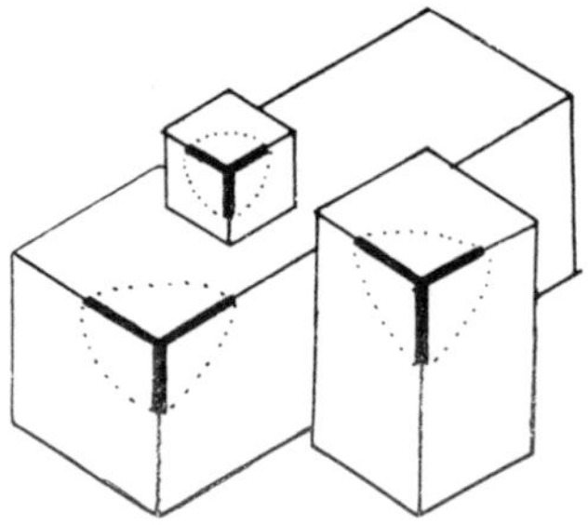

where all the objects are rectangular solids, and do not occlude one another badly, we can discover the objects by the extremely local process of locating all the "Y-joints." Each object contains at most one such distinctive feature. This could, of course, fail because of perspective, as in

which could be a cube, or in

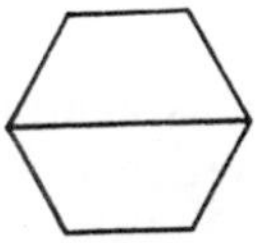

(for we require each of the three angles of a Y-joint to span less than 180 degrees). A more serious failure is in the case of occlusion, as in

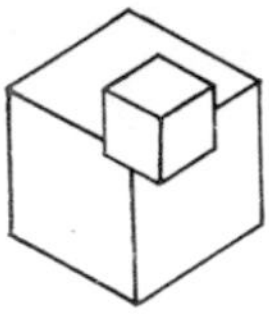

where one of the Y-joints is completely hidden from view. But the great power of programs capable of hierarchical decisions is illustrated by the possibility of first *recognizing the small cube*, then *removing it*, next *extending the hidden lines*, and so discovering the large cube!

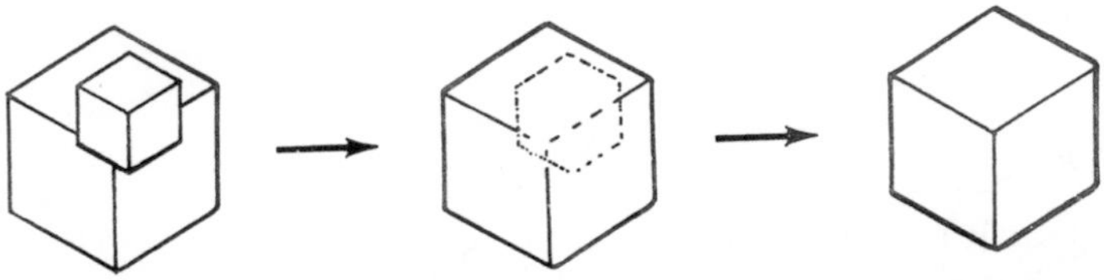

The program developed by Adolfo Guzman proceeds in a rather different way; his idea is to treat different kinds of local configurations as providing different degrees of evidence for "linking" the faces that meet there.

For example, in these three types of vertex configurations

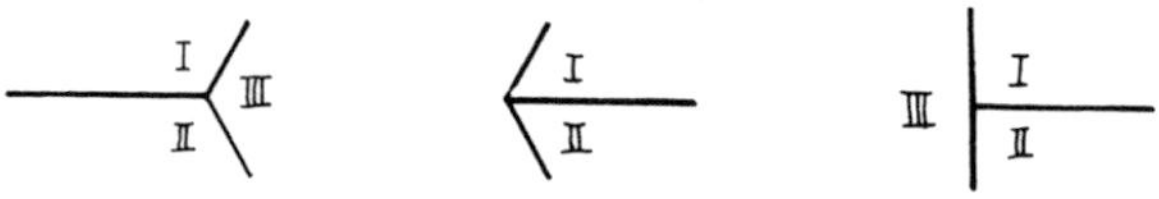

Y arrow T

the "Y" provides evidence for linking I to II, II to III, and I to III. The "arrow" just links I to II. Because a "T" is ordinarily the result of one object occluding part of another, it is regarded as evidence *against* linking I to III or II to III (and it is neutral about I and II). Using just these rules, we can convert pictures into associated groups of faces as follows: we represent Y links by straight lines and arrow links by curves.

(1)

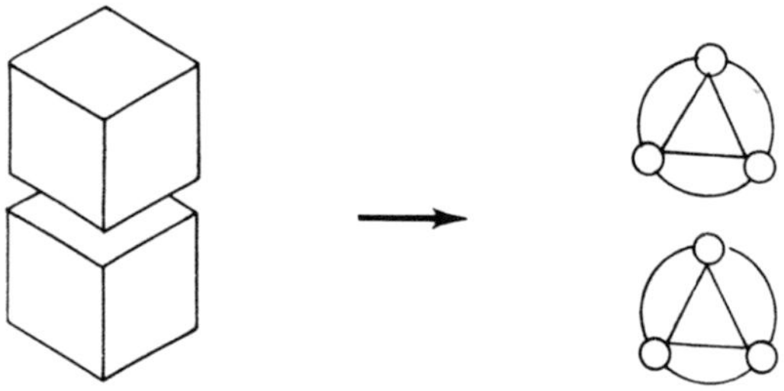

(2)

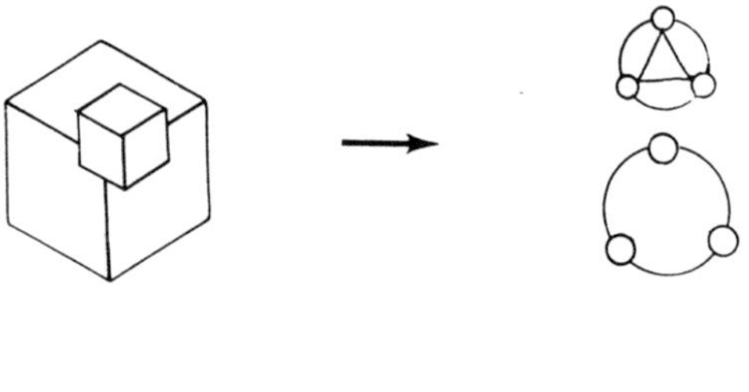

(3)

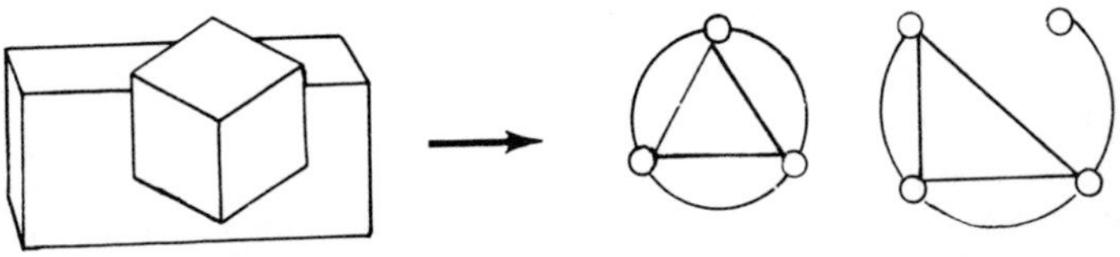

(4)

So far, there has been no difficulty in associating linked faces with objects. The usefulness of the variety of kinds of evidence shows up only in more complicated cases: In this figure

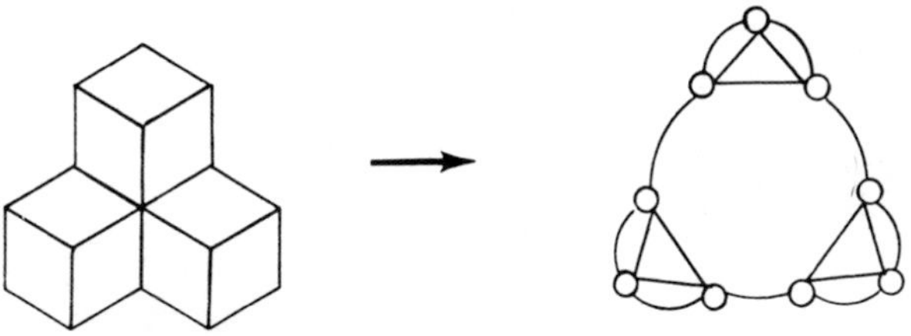

(5)

we find some "false" links due to the merging of vertices on different objects. To break such false connections, the program uses a hierarchical scheme that first finds subsets of faces that are very tightly linked (e.g., by two or more links). These "nuclei" then compete for more weakly linked faces. There is no competition in Examples 1–4, but in 5 the single false links between the cubes are broken by his procedure. In Example 6 the "false" links are broken also. If a very simple "competition" algorithm were not adequate here, one could also take into account the negative evidence the two T-joints provide *against* linking I–III and II–III.

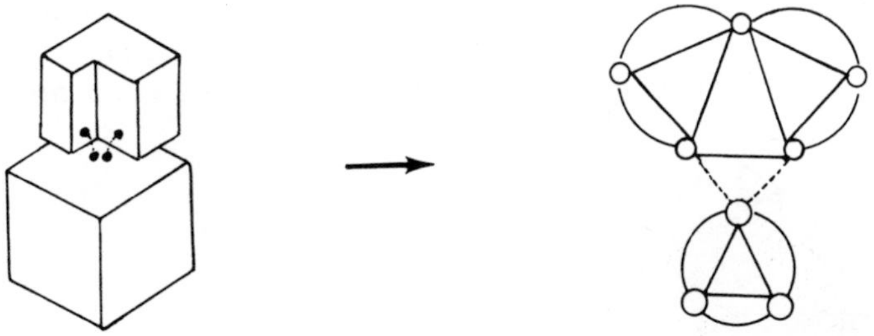

(6)

We have described only the skeleton of his scheme; Guzmán uses several other kinds of links, including evidence from collinear T-joint lines of the form

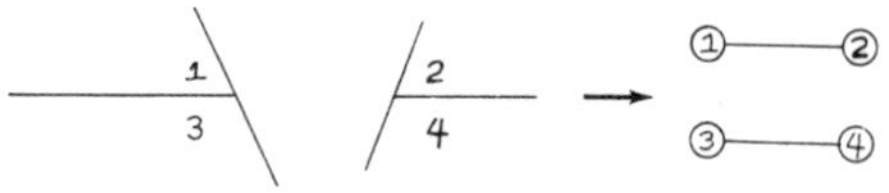

and the effects of some vertices are modified by their associations with others. This variety of resources enables the program to solve scenes like

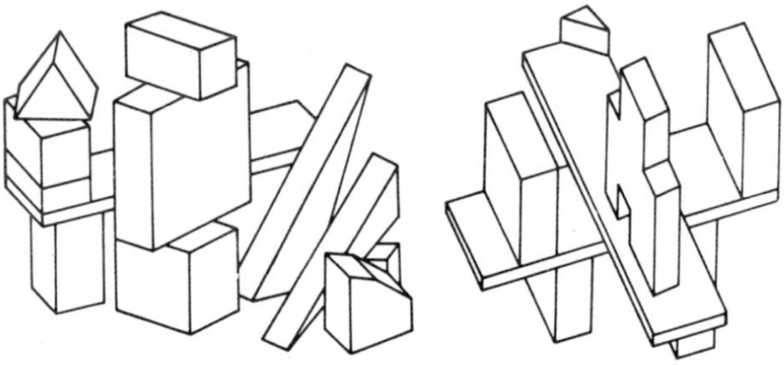

(7)

in which some object faces are completely disconnected.

The method of combining evidence used by this procedure might suggest a similarity to the perceptron's weighting of evidence. However, the local character of this similarity most strongly marks the deep difference between the approaches. For Guzman's algorithm uses this as but a small part of a procedure to evaluate links between abstract entities called faces which in turn have been proposed by another program that uses processes related to connectedness.

In "locally ambiguous" figures, something more akin to reasoning and problem solving is required. For example, the stack of cubes in Figure 13.2 can be falsely structured by the human visual process if one looks only at the center. This structure cannot be extended to the whole figure, suggesting that we, too, use a pro-

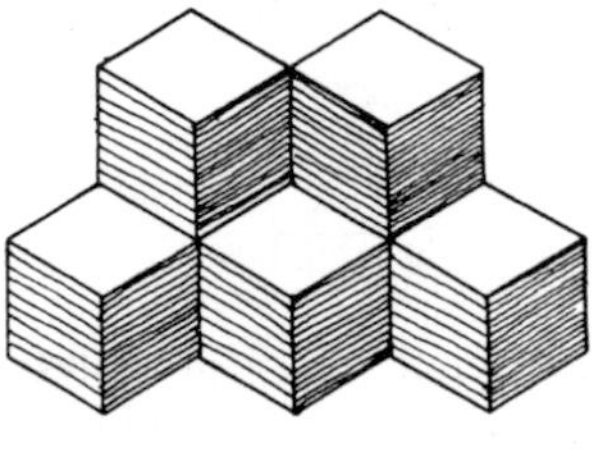

Figure 13.2

cedure that in case of failure can "back up" to a different hypothesis.

It is outside the scope of this book to discuss heuristic programming in further detail. Readers who wish for more information should consult the references. The subject of scene-analysis has advanced dramatically. Consult references at end.

13.5 Why Prove Theorems?

Why did you prove all these complicated theorems? Couldn't you just take a perceptron and see if it can recognize $\psi_{\text{CONNECTED}}$?

No.

13.6 Sources and Development of Ideas

Our debts to previous work and to other people, places, and institutions can best be described by a brief historical sketch of our work. Our collaboration began in 1963 when we were brought together by Warren S. McCulloch. We have a special debt to him not only because of this but because he was the first to think seriously about the problems we have studied.

13.6.1 The Group-Invariance Theorem

We had both been interested in the perceptron since its announcement by Rosenblatt in 1957. In fact we had both presented papers related to its "learning" aspect at a symposium on information theory in London in 1960. Our serious attack on its geometric problems started in the spring of 1965. At that time, it was generally known that order-1 perceptrons could not compute translation-invariant functions other than functions of $|X|$, but there was no hint as to how this might generalize.

In retrospect the most obvious obstacle was the lack of a concept of *order*. Earlier studies on the power of perceptrons were based on Φ-sets of partial functions defined by stochastic generative processes or subject to irrelevant conditions such as that they themselves be linear threshold functions of a small number of variables. Such limitations (as opposed to our $|S(\varphi)| \leq k$) seemed always to produce mathematically intractable situations and so reinforced the dominant tendency to approach the problem as one of statistics rather than algebra. In making the shift, we feel most closely anticipated by Bledsoe and Browning (1959) who considered a pure order limitation on a type of conjunctively local machine.

With the concept of order in mind, the general form of the group-invariance theorem became possible. But we first had to overcome at least four other obstacles of heuristically different kinds.

1. We had to accept the value of studying the geometrically trivial predicate ψ_{PARITY}. No reference to this predicate is *logically* necessary (or even helpful) in proving the group-invariance theorem, the And/Or theorem, or in explaining the principle of stratification. But we are convinced that its *heuristic* role was critical. Its very geometric triviality enabled us to see the algebraic principles in all these situations. The same comment applies to the role of the positive normal form: all our results can be proved without it. But at a time when we were thoroughly confused about everything, it allowed us to replace the bewildering variety of the set of all possible logical functions by the combinatorial tidiness of the masks.

2. The idea of averaging had been in our minds ever since reading Pitts and McCulloch (1947). It was reinforced by a fine proof offered by Tom Marill in response to an exposition, at an M.I.T. seminar, of our early thoughts on the subject. Marill observed that for any φ, if $|S(\varphi)| < |R|$ then $\{X \mid \varphi(X)\}$ contains the same number of even- and odd-sized X's. It follows immediately that for any set Φ of such φ's, the sets of vectors

$$\{\Phi(X) \mid |X| \text{ even}\} \quad \text{AND} \quad \{\Phi(X) \mid |X| \text{ odd}\}$$

must have the same center of gravity. They therefore cannot be separated by a hyperplane!

Although highly suggestive, this proof is still marked by the basic weakness of all early thinking about perceptrons, that is, the preoccupation with the image of predicates as sets of points in the $|\Phi|$-dimensional Euclidean space. To obtain the group-invariance theorem, we had to break away from this image. Marill's proof averages over a set of $|\Phi|$-points; ours averages over a set of functionals defined on the subsets of $|R|$.

3. An "obstacle" of a very different sort was lack of contact with classical mathematical methods of proven depth. The proximity of fundamental properties of polynomials, irreducible curves, Haar integrals, etc., brought the feeling of "real mathematics" as opposed to the "purely combinatorial" methods of earlier papers on perceptrons. This is still sufficiently rare in computer science to be significant. We are convinced that respect for "real mathematics" is a powerful heuristic principle, though it must be tempered with practical judgment.

4. We were reluctant to attach the condition to the group-invariance theorem that Φ *be closed under the group*, for this seemed like a strong restriction. It took us a while to realize that this made the group-invariance theorem stronger rather than weaker! For the theorem is used mainly to show that various predicates *cannot* be realized by various perceptrons. The closure condition then says that such a predicate cannot be realized *even* by a perceptron that has *all* the appropriate φ's of each type. Therefore, it cannot be realized by any smaller perceptron, say, one with a random selection from such partial predicates.

13.6.2 $\psi_{\text{CONNECTED}}$

Our first gropings were driven largely by frustration at not being able to prove, even heuristically, the "obvious" fact that this predicate is not of finite order. The diversion to ψ_{PARITY} was partly motivated by wanting a simpler case for study, partly by the hope of finding a reduction through a switching argument similar to that used to prove the diameter-limited theorem. Our first theorem about the order of $\psi_{\text{CONNECTED}}$ came by a different route, via the one-in-a-box theorem. Although this solved our original problem (in a logical sense) we continued exploring switching arguments, following an intuition which later paid dividends in ways we cannot pretend to have explicitly anticipated.

While we were developing the rather complex switching circuits explained in Chapter 5 we entirely missed the simpler argument suggested to us by David Huffman (§5.5). Although Huffman's construction gives only a weak lower bound to the growth rate of the order of $\psi_{\text{CONNECTED}}$, it provides sufficient proof that the predicate is not of finite order. Moreover, it shows how *any* predicate on a retina of $|R|$ points can be reduced to computing $\psi_{\text{CONNECTED}}$ on a retina of about $2^{|R|}$ points. Thus this predicate is shown formally to have a kind of universality for these parallel machines akin to that possessed by tree-search in the usual serial machine (and also to suffer from similar exponential disasters).

13.6.3 More Topology

A by-product of work on connectedness was the pleasing (and perhaps puzzling) positive result about the Euler predicate. In an early draft of the book we appended to this a mildly false proof that no other topological invariants could be in

$$L\left(\varphi_{\square}, \varphi_{\begin{smallmatrix} & \square \\ \square & \end{smallmatrix}}, \varphi_{\begin{smallmatrix} \square & \\ & \square \end{smallmatrix}}, \varphi_{\begin{smallmatrix} \square \\ \square \end{smallmatrix}}, \varphi_{\begin{smallmatrix} \square & \square \end{smallmatrix}}, \varphi_{\begin{smallmatrix} \square & \\ \square & \square \end{smallmatrix}}, \varphi_{\begin{smallmatrix} \square & \square \\ \square & \end{smallmatrix}}, \varphi_{\begin{smallmatrix} \square & \square \\ & \square \end{smallmatrix}}, \varphi_{\begin{smallmatrix} & \square \\ \square & \square \end{smallmatrix}}, \varphi_{\begin{smallmatrix} \square & \square \\ \square & \square \end{smallmatrix}}\right).$$

When we discovered the correct proof of the theorem (§8.4) that there were no other diameter-limited topological predicates we firmly conjectured that quite different proof methods would be necessary to prove this for the order-limited case. So we were astonished when Mike Paterson, a young British computation theorist who had offered to criticize the manuscript, showed how the ideas in §5.7 could be used to reduce this to the parity switching net, and thus to prove the theorem of §5.9.

13.6.4 Stratification

This is the area in which our early intuitions proved most disastrously wrong.

Our first formal presentation of the principal results in this book was at an American Mathematical Society symposium on Mathematical Aspects of Computer Science in April 1966. At this time we could prove that $\psi_{\text{CONNECTED}}$ was not of finite order and conjectured that the same must be true of the apparently "global" predicates of *symmetry* and *twins* described in §7.3.

For the rest of 1966 the matter rested there. We were pleased and encouraged by the enthusiastic reception by many colleagues at the A.M.S. meeting and no less so by the doleful reception of a similar presentation at a Bionics meeting. However, we were now involved in establishing at M.I.T. an artificial intelligence laboratory largely devoted to real "seeing machines," and gave no attention to perceptrons until we were jolted by attending an I.E.E.E. Workshop on Pattern Recognition in Puerto Rico early in 1967.

Appalled at the persistent influence of perceptrons (and similar ways of thinking) on *practical pattern recognition*, we determined to set out our work as a book. Slightly ironically, the first results obtained in our new phase of interest were the pseudo-positive applications of stratification.

Our first contact with the phenomenon was when our student John White showed the predicate $\psi_{\text{HOLLOW SQUARE}}$ to have order three. We had believed it to be order four for reasons the reader will see if he tries to realize it with coefficients bounded independently of the size of the square. Perhaps we were so convinced of the extreme parallelism of the perceptron that we resisted seeing how certain limited forms of serial computation could be encoded into the perceptron algorithm by constructing a size-domination hierarchy.

Whatever the reason, it took us many months to isolate the stratification principle and so understand why we had failed to prove the group-invariance theorem for infinite retinas. It is clear that stratification is not a mere "trick" that can reduce the order of a predicate, but that unbounded coefficients admit an essentially wider range of sequential (conditional) computations, although at such a price that this is of only mathematical interest. We are convinced that most of the predicates in Chapter 7 have, under the bounded condition, *no* finite orders, and stratification makes the difference between finite and infinite. We have not actually proved this, however.

13.6.5 Learning and Memory

The spirit of the theory in Chapters 11 and 12 is very different from that of our geometric theory. To begin with, the research objectives seem to face in an opposite direction: learning theorems have statements like "*If a given predicate is in an* $L(\Phi)$ then a certain procedure will find a set of coefficients to represent it." Whereas, in the main part of our work the main questions were directed towards understanding *when* and why certain predicates are in certain $L(\Phi)$'s. Also the proper context for the learning theory seems indeed to be the n-dimensional coefficient-space in which figures and predicates become points and hyperplanes (or dually). We have emphasized several times that progress towards the geometric theory seemed to come only when we could break away from this representation. However, we decided to discuss the convergence theorem at first mainly because we felt dissatisfied with the uncritical form of all previous presentations. In particular, it was customary to ignore such questions as

Is the perceptron an efficient form of memory?

Does the learning time become too long to be practical even when separation is possible in principle?
How do the convergence results compare to those obtained by more deliberate design methods?
What is the perceptron's relation to other computational devices?

As time went on, the last question became more and more important to us. The comparison with the homeostat reinforced our interest in the perceptron as a good object for study in the mathematical theory of computation rather than as a practical machine, and we became interested in such questions as: Could we see the perceptron convergence theorem as a manifestation of a finite state situation? How is it related to hill climbing and other search techniques? Does it differ fundamentally from other methods of solving linear inequalities?

We rather complacently thought that the first question would have an easy answer until our student, Terry Beyer, drew our attention to some difficulties and soundly conjectured that the way out would be to prove something like what eventually became Theorem 11.6. A concerted effort to settle the problem with the help of Dona Strauss led to an interesting but unpublishable proof. Soon after this we heard that Bradley Efron had proved a similar theorem and found that by borrowing an idea from him we could generate the demonstration given in §11.6. Efron, who did not publish his proof, credits Nils Nilsson with the conjecture that led him to the theorem.

We now see the perceptron learning theorem as a simple example of a larger problem about memory (or information storage and retrieval), much as the nonlearning perceptron is a paradigm in the theory of parallel computation. Chapter 12 can be regarded as a manifesto on the importance of this problem.

13.7 Computational Geometry

We like to think that the perceptron illustrates the possibility of a more organic interaction between traditional mathematical topics and ideas of computation. When we first talked about $\psi_{\text{CONNECTED}}$ we thought we were studying an isolated fact about a type of computer device. By the time we had conjectured and started to prove that the Eulerian predicates were the only topological ones of finite order, we felt we were studying geometry.

This might represent a bad tendency of people trained in classical mathematics to drag the new subject of computation back into their familiar territory. Or it could prefigure a future of computational thought not just as a new and separate autonomous science but as a way of thinking that will permeate all the other sciences.

The truth must lie between these extremes. In any case, we are excited to see around us at M.I.T. a steady growth of research whose success is a confirmation of the value of the concept of "computational geometry" as well as of the talent of our colleagues and students.

Manuel Blum and Carl Hewitt obtained the first new result by studying the geometric ability of finite-state machines. More recently, Blum, Bill Henneman, and Harriet Fell have found interesting properties of the relations induced on Euclidean figures by the imposition of a discrete grid. Terry Beyer has discovered very surprising algorithms for geometric computation in iterative arrays of automata. Needless to say, these people have contributed to the work described in this book as much by their indirect influence on the intellectual atmosphere around us as by many pieces of advice, comment, and criticism of which only a small proportion is reflected in direct acknowledgments in the text. Many points of mathematical technique and exposition were improved by suggestions from W. Armstrong, R. Beard, L. Lyons, M. Paterson, and G. Sussman.

13.8 Other People

In addition to those already mentioned, we owe much to

W. W. Bledsoe,
Dona Strauss,
O. G. Selfridge,
R. J. Solomonoff,
R. M. Fano.

13.9 Other Places

For political and heuristic reasons, we mention that most of the new ideas came in new environments: beaches, swamps, and mountains.

13.10 Institutions

Even if we had not been supported by the Advanced Research Projects Agency we would have liked to express the debt owed by computer science to its Information Sciences branch and to the imaginative band of men who built it:

J. R. Licklider,
I. E. Sutherland,
R. W. Taylor,
L. G. Roberts.

In fact, ARPA has supported most of our work, through M.I.T.'s Project MAC and the Office of Naval Research.

Epilogue: The New Connectionism

When perceptron-like machines came on the scene, we found that in order to understand their capabilities we needed some new ideas. It was not enough simply to examine the machines themselves or the procedures used to make them learn. Instead, we had to find new ways to understand the problems they would be asked to solve. This is why our book turned out to be concerned less with perceptrons per se than with concepts that could help us see the relation between patterns and the types of parallel-machine architectures that might or might not be able to recognize them.

Why was it so important to develop theories about parallel machines? One reason was that the emergence of serial computers quickly led to a very respectable body of useful ideas about algorithms and algorithmic languages, many of them based on a half-century's previous theories about logic and effective computability. But similarly powerful ideas about parallel computation did not develop nearly so rapidly—partly because massively parallel hardware did not become available until much later and partly because much less knowledge that might be relevant had been accumulated in the mathematical past. Today, however, it is feasible either to simulate or to actually assemble huge and complex arrangements of interacting elements. Consequently, theories about parallel computation have now become of immediate and intense concern to workers in physics, engineering, management, and many other disciplines—and especially to workers involved with brain science, psychology, and artificial intelligence.

Perhaps this is why the past few years have seen new and heated discussions of network machines as part of an intellectually aggressive movement to establish a paradigm for artificial intelligence and cognitive modeling. Indeed, this growth of activity and interest has been so swift that people talk about a "connectionist revolution." The purpose of this epilogue, added in 1988, is to help present-day students to use the ideas presented in *Perceptrons* to put the new results into perspective and to formulate more clearly the research questions suggested by them. To do this succinctly, we adopt the strategy of focusing on one particular example of modern connectionist writing. Recently, David Rumelhart, James McClelland, and fourteen collaborators published a two-volume work that has become something of a connectionist manifesto: *Parallel Distributed Processing* (MIT Press, 1986). We shall take this work (henceforth referred to as *PDP*) as our connectionist text. What we say about this particular text will not, of course, apply literally to other writings on this subject, but thoughtful readers will seize the general point through the particular case. In most of this epilogue we shall discuss the examples in *PDP* from inside the connectionist perspective, in order to flag certain problems that we do not expect to be solvable within the framework of any single, homogeneous machine. At the end, however, we shall consider the same problems from the perspective of the overview we call "society of mind," a conceptual framework that makes it much more feasible to exploit collections of specialized accomplishments.

PDP describes *Perceptrons* as pessimistic about the prospects for connectionist machinery:

". . . even though multilayer linear threshold networks are potentially much more powerful . . . it was the limitations on what perceptrons could possibly learn that led to Minsky and Papert's (1969) pessimistic evaluation of the perceptron. Unfortunately, that evaluation has incorrectly tainted more interesting and powerful networks of linear threshold and other nonlinear units. As we shall see, the limitations of the one-step perceptrons in no way apply to the more complex networks." (vol. 1, p. 65)

We scarcely recognize ourselves in this description, and we recommend rereading the remarks in section 0.3 about romanticism and rigor. We reiterate our belief that the romantic claims have been less wrong than the pompous criticisms. But we also reiterate that the discipline can grow only when it makes a parallel effort to critically evaluate its apparent accomplishments. Our own work in *Perceptrons* is based on the interaction between an enthusiastic pursuit of models of new phenomena and a rigorous search for ways to understand the limitations of these models.

In any case, such citations have given our book the reputation of being mainly concerned with what perceptrons cannot do, and of having concluded with a qualitative evaluation that the subject was not important. Certainly, some chapters prove that various important predicates have perceptron coefficients that grow unmanageably large. But many chapters show that other predicates can be surprisingly tractable. It is no more apt to describe our mathematical theorems as pessimistic than it would be to say the same about deducing the conservation of momentum from the laws of mechanics. Theorems are theorems, and the history of science amply demonstrates how discovering limiting principles can lead to deeper understanding. But this happens only when those principles are taken seriously, so we exhort contemporary connectionist researchers to consider our results seriously as sources of research questions instead of maintaining that they "in no way apply."

What Perceptrons Can't Do

To put our results into perspective, let us recall the situation in the early 1960s: Many people were impressed by the fact that initially unstructured networks composed of very simple devices could be made to perform many interesting tasks—by processes that could be seen as remarkably like some forms of learning.

A different fact seemed to have impressed only a few people: While those networks did well on certain tasks and failed on certain other tasks, there was no theory to explain what made the difference—particularly when they seemed to work well on small ("toy") problems but broke down with larger problems of the same kind.

Our goal was to develop analytic tools to give us better ideas about what made the difference. But finding a comprehensive theory of parallel computation seemed infeasible, because the subject was simply too general. What we had to do was sharpen our ideas by working with some subclass of parallel machines that would be sufficiently powerful to perform significant computations, that would also share at least some of the features that made such networks attractive to those who sought a deeper understanding of the brain, and that would also be mathematically simple enough to permit theoretical analysis. This why we used the abstract definition of *perceptron* given in this book. The perceptron seemed powerful enough in function, suggestive enough in architecture, and simple enough in its mathematical definition, yet understanding the range and character of its capabilities presented challenging puzzles.

Our prime example of such a puzzle was the recognition of connectedness. It took us many months of work to capture in a formal proof our strong intuition that perceptrons were unable to represent that predicate. Perhaps the most instructive aspect of that whole process was that we were guided by a flawed intuition to the proof that perceptrons cannot recognize the connectivity in any general or practical sense. We had assumed that perceptrons could not even detect the connectivity of hole-free blobs—because, as we supposed, no local forms of evidence like those in figure 5.7 could correlate with the correct decision. Yet, as we saw in subsection 5.8.1, if a figure is known to have no holes, then a low-order perceptron can decide on its connectivity; this we had not initially believed to be possible. It is hard to imagine better evidence to show how artificial it is to separate "negative" from "positive" results in this kind of investigation. To explain how this experience affected us, we must abstract what we learned from it.

First we learned to reformulate questions like "Can perceptrons perform a certain task?" Strictly speaking, it is misleading to say that perceptrons cannot recognize connectedness, since for any particular size of retina we can make a perceptron that will recognize any predicate by providing it with enough φs of sufficiently high order. What we did show was that the general predicate requires perceptrons of unbounded order. More generally, we learned to replace globally qualitative questions about what perceptrons cannot do with questions in the spirit of what is now called computational complexity. Many of our results are of the form $M = f(R)$, where R is a measure of the size of the problem and M is the magnitude of some parameter of a perceptron (such as the order of its predicates, how many of them might be required, the information content of the coefficients, or the number of cycles needed for learning to converge). The study of such relationships gave us a better sense of what is likely to go wrong when one tries to enlarge the scale of a perceptron-like computation. In serial computing it was already well known that certain algorithms depending on search processes would require numbers of steps of computation that increased exponentially with the size of the problem. Much less was known about such matters in the case of parallel machines.

The second lesson was that in order to understand what perceptrons can do we would have to develop some theories of "problem domains" and not simply a "theory of perceptrons." In previous work on networks, from McCulloch and Pitts to Rosenblatt, even the best theorists had tried to formulate general-purpose theories about the kinds of networks they were interested in. Rosenblatt's convergence theorem is an example of how such investigations can lead to powerful results. But something qualitatively different was needed to explain why perceptrons could recognize the connectedness of hole-free figures yet be unable to recognize connectedness in general. For this we needed a bridge between a theory about the computing device and a theory about the content of the computation. The reason why our group-invariance theorem was so useful here was that it had one foot on the geometric side and one on the computational side.

Our study of the perceptron was an attempt to understand general principles through the study of a special case. Even today, we still know very little, in general, about how the costs of parallel computation are affected by increases in the scale of problems. Only the cases we understand can serve as bases for conjectures about what will happen in other situations. Thus, until there is evidence to the contrary, we are inclined to project the significance of our results to other networks related to perceptrons. In the past few years, many experiments have demonstrated that various new types of learning machines, composed of multiple layers of perceptron-like elements, can be made to solve many kinds of small-scale problems. Some of those experimenters believe that these performances can be economically extended to larger problems without encountering the limitations we have shown to apply to single-layer perceptrons. Shortly, we shall take a closer look at some of those results and see that much of what we learned about simple perceptrons will still remain quite pertinent. It certainly is true that most of the theorems in this book are explicitly about machines with a single layer of adjustable connection weights. But this does not imply (as many modern connectionists assume) that our conclusions don't apply to multilayered machines. To be sure, those proofs no longer apply unchanged, because their antecedent conditions have changed. But the phenomena they describe will often still persist. One must examine them, case by case. For example, all our conclusions about order-limited predicates (see section 0.7) continue to apply to networks with multiple layers, because the order of any unit in a given layer is bounded by the *product* of the

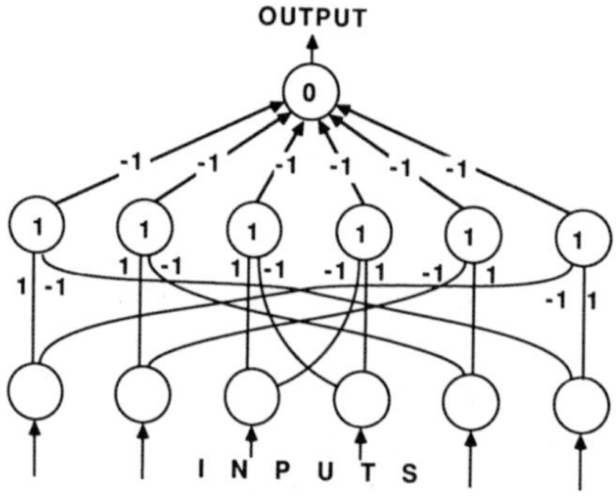

Figure 1 Symmetry using order-2 disjunction.

orders of the units in earlier layers. Since many of our arguments about order constrain the representations of group-invariant predicates, we suspect that many of those conclusions, too, will apply to multilayer nets. For example, multilayer networks will be no more able to recognize connectedness than are perceptrons. (This is not to say that multilayer networks do not have advantages. For example, the product rule can yield logarithmic reductions in the orders and numbers of units required to compute certain high-order predicates. Furthermore, units that are arranged in loops can be of effectively unbounded order; hence, some such networks *will* be able to recognize connectedness by using internal serial processing.)

Thus, in some cases our conclusions will remain provably true and in some cases they will be clearly false. In the middle there are many results that we still think may hold, but we do not know any formal proofs. In the next section we shall show how some of the experiments reported in *PDP* lend credence to some such conjectures.

Recognizing Symmetry

In this section we contrast two different networks, both of which recognize symmetrical patterns defined on a six-point linear retina. To be precise, we would like to recognize the predicate *X is symmetric about the midpoint of R*. Figure 1 shows a simple way to represent this is as a perceptron that uses R φ units, each of order 2. Each one of them will locally detect a deviation from symmetry

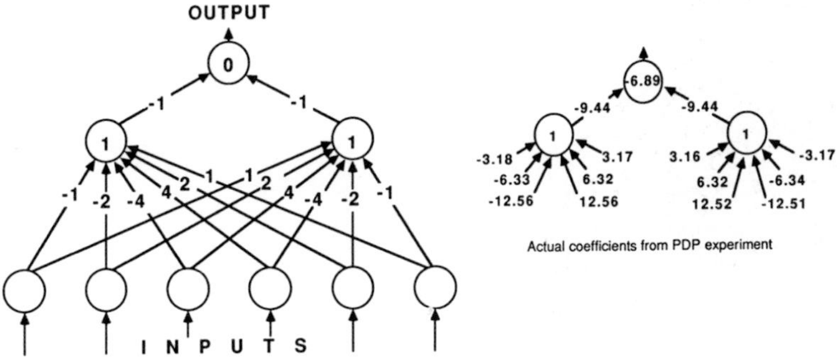

Figure 2 Symmetry using order-R stratification.

at two particular retinal points. Figure 2 shows the results of an experiment from *PDP*. It depicts a network that represents ψ_{SYMMETRY} in quite a different way. Amazingly, this network uses only two φ functions—albeit ones of order R.

The weights displayed in figure 2 were produced by a learning procedure that we shall describe shortly. For the moment, we want to focus not on the learning problem but on the character of the coefficients. We share the sense of excitement the *PDP* experimenters must have experienced as their machine converged to this strange solution, in which this predicate seems to be portrayed as having a more holistic character than would be suggested by its conjunctively local representation. However, one must ask certain questions before celebrating this as a significant discovery. In *PDP* it is recognized that the lower-level coefficients appear to be growing exponentially, yet no alarm is expressed about this. In fact, anyone who reads section 7.3 should recognize such a network as employing precisely the type of computational structure that we called stratification. Also, in the case of network 2, the learning procedure required 1,208 cycles through each of the 64 possible examples—a total of 77,312 trials (enough to make us wonder if the time for this procedure to determine suitable coefficients increases exponentially with the size of the retina). *PDP* does not address this question. What happens when the retina has 100 elements? If such a network required on the order of 2^{200} trials to learn, most observers would lose interest.

This observation shows most starkly how we and the authors of *PDP* differ in interpreting the implications of our theory. Our "pes-

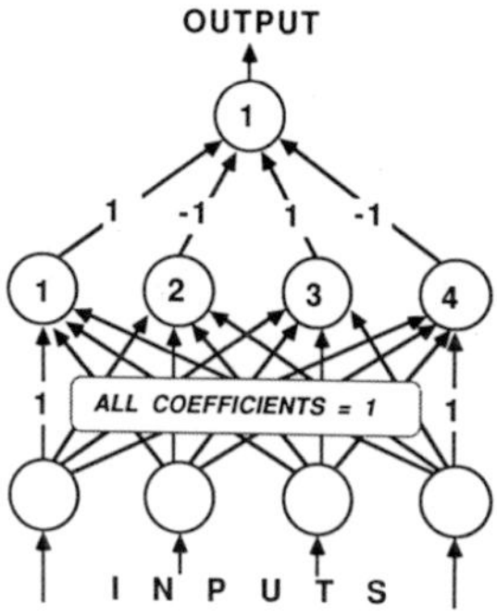

Figure 3 Parity using Gamba masks.

simistic evaluation of the perceptron" was the assertion that, although certain problems can easily by solved by perceptrons on small scales, the computational costs become prohibitive when the problem is scaled up. The authors of *PDP* seem not to recognize that the coefficients of this symmetry machine confirm that thesis, and celebrate this performance on a toy problem as a success rather than asking whether it could become a profoundly "bad" form of behavior when scaled up to problems of larger size.

Both of these networks are in the class of what we called Gamba perceptrons in section 13.1—that is, ordinary perceptrons whose φ functions are themselves perceptrons of order 1. Accordingly, we are uncomfortable about the remark in *PDP* that "multilayer linear threshold networks are potentially much more powerful than single-layer perceptrons." Of course they are, in various ways—and chapter 8 of *PDP* describes several studies of multilayer perceptron-like devices. However, most of them—like figure 2 above—still belong to the class of networks discussed in *Perceptrons*.

Also in chapter 8 of *PDP*, similar methods are applied to the problem of recognizing parity—and the very construction described in our section 13.1, through which a Gamba perceptron can recognize parity, is rediscovered. Figure 3 here shows the results. To learn these coefficients, the procedure described in *PDP* required 2,825 cycles through the 16 possible input patterns, thus consuming 45,200 trials for the network to learn to compute the parity predicate for only four inputs. Is this a good result or a bad result? We cannot tell without more knowledge about why the procedure requires so many trials. Until one has some theory of that, there is no way to assess the significance of any such experimental result; all one can say is that 45,200 = 45,200. In section 10.1 we saw that if a perceptron's φ functions include only masks, the parity predicate requires doubly exponential coefficients. If we were sure that *that* was happening, this would suggest to us that we should represent 45,200 (approximately) as 2^{2^4} rather than, say, as 2^{16}. However, here we suspect that this would be wrong, because the input units aren't masks but predicates—apparently provided from the start—that already know how to "count." These make the problem much easier. In any case, the lesson of *Perceptrons* is that one cannot interpret the meaning of such an experimental report without first making further probes.

Learning

We haven't yet said how those networks learned. The authors of *PDP* describe a learning procedure called the "Generalized Delta Rule"—we'll call it GD—as a new breakthrough in connectionist research. To explain its importance, they depict as follows the theoretical situation they inherited:

"A further argument advanced by Minsky and Papert against perceptron-like models with hidden units is that there was no indication how such multilayer networks were to be trained. One of the appealing features of the one-layer perceptron is the existence of a powerful learning procedure, the perceptron convergence procedure of Rosenblatt. In Minsky and Papert's day, there was no such powerful learning procedure for the more complex multilayer systems. This is no longer true. . . . The GD procedure provides a direct generalization of the perceptron learning procedure which can be applied to arbitrary networks with multiple layers and feedback among layers. This procedure can, in principle, learn arbitrary functions including, of course, parity and connectedness." (vol. 1, p. 113)

In Minsky and Papert's day, indeed! In this section we shall explain why, although the GD learning procedure embodies some useful ideas, it does not justify such sweeping claims. But in order to explain why, and to see how the approach in the current wave of connectionism differs from that in *Perceptrons*, we must first examine with some care the relationship between two branches of perceptron theory which could be called "theory of learning" and "theory of representation." To begin with, one might paraphrase the above quotation as saying that, until recently, connectionism had been paralyzed by the following dilemma:

Perceptrons could learn anything that they could represent, but they were too limited in what they could represent.

Multilayered networks were less limited in what they could represent, but they had no reliable learning procedure.

According to the classical theory of perceptrons, those limitations on representability depend on such issues as whether a given predicate P can be represented as a perceptron defined by a given set Φ on a given retina, whether P is of finite order, whether P can be realized with coefficients of bounded size, whether properties of several representable predicates are inherited by combinations of those predicates, and so forth. All the results in the first half of our book are involved with these sorts of representational issues. Now, when one speaks about "powerful learning procedures," the situation is complicated by the fact that, given enough input units of sufficiently high order, even simple perceptrons can represent—and therefore learn—arbitrary functions. Consequently, it makes no sense to speak about "power" in absolute terms. Such statements must refer to relative measures of sizes and scales.

As for learning, the dependability of Rosenblatt's Perceptron Convergence theorem of section 11.1—let's call it PC for short—is very impressive: If it is possible at all to represent a predicate P as a linear threshold function of a given set of predicates Φ, then the PC procedure will eventually discover some particular set of coefficients that actually represents P. However, this is not, in itself, a sufficient reason to consider PC interesting and important, because that theorem says nothing about the crucial issue of efficiency. PC is not interesting merely because it provides a systematic way to find suitable coefficients. One could always take recourse, instead, to simple, brute-force search—because, given that some solution exists, one could simply search through all possible integer coefficient vectors, in order of increasing magnitude, until no further "errors" occurred. But no one would consider such an exhaustive process to be an interesting foundation for a learning theory.

What, then, makes PC seem significant? That it discovers those coefficients in ways that are intriguing in several other important respects. The PC procedure seems to satisfy many of the intuitive requirements of those who are concerned with modeling what really happens in a biological nervous system. It also appeals to both our engineering aesthetic and our psychological aesthetic by serving simultaneously as both a form of guidance by error correction and a form of hill-climbing. In terms of computational efficiency, PC seems much more efficient than brute-force procedures (although we have no rigorous and general theory of the conditions under which that will be true). Finally, PC is so simple mathematically as to make one wish to believe that it reflects something real.

Hill-Climbing and the Generalized Delta Procedure

Suppose we want to find the maximum value of a given function $F(x,y,z,\ldots)$ of n variables. The extreme brute-force solution is to calculate the function for all sets of values for the variables and then select the point for which F had the largest value. The approach we called hill-climbing in section 11.3 is a local procedure designed to attempt to find that global maximum. To make this subject more concrete, it is useful to think of the two-dimensional case in which the x–y plane is the ground and $z = F(x,y)$ is the elevation of the point (x,y,z) on the surface of a real physical hill. Now, imagine standing on the hill in a fog so dense that only the immediate vicinity is visible. Then the only resort is to use some diameter-limited local process. The best-known method is the method known as "steepest ascent," discussed in section 11.6: First determine the slope of the surface in various directions from the point where you are standing, then choose the direction that most rapidly increases your altitude and take a step of a certain size in that direction. The hope is that, by thus climbing the slope, you will eventually reach the highest point.

It is both well known and obvious that hill-climbing does not always work. The simplest way to fail is to get stuck on a local maximum—an isolated peak whose altitude is relatively insignificant. There simply is no local way for a hill-climbing procedure to be sure that it has reached a global maximum rather than some local feature of topography (such as a peak, a ridge, or a plain) on which it may get trapped. We showed in section 11.6 that PC is equivalent (in a peculiar sense) to a hill-climbing procedure that works its way to the top of a hill whose geometry can actually be proved not to have any such troublesome local features—provided that there actually exists some perceptron-weight vector solution A^* to the problem. Thus, one could argue that perceptrons "work" on those problems not because of any particular virtue of the perceptrons or of their hill-climbing procedures but because the hills for those soluble problems have clean topographies. What are the prospects of finding a learning procedure that works equally well on all problems, and not merely on those that have linearly separable decision functions? The authors of *PDP* maintain that they have indeed discovered one:

"Although our learning results do not guarantee that we can find a solution for all solvable problems, our analyses and results have shown that, as a practical matter, the error propagation scheme leads to solutions in virtually every case. In short, we believe that we have answered Minsky and Papert's challenge and have found a learning result sufficiently powerful to demonstrate that their pessimism about learning in multilayer machines was misplaced." (vol. 1, p. 361)

But the experiments in *PDP*, though interesting and ingenious, do not actually demonstrate any such thing. In fact, the "powerful new learning result" is nothing other than a straightforward hill-climbing algorithm, with all the problems that entails. To see how GD works, assume we are given a network of units interconnected by weighted, unidirectional links. Certain of these units are connected to input terminals, and certain others are regarded as output units. We want to teach this network to respond to each (vector) input pattern $\mathbf{X}_p$ with a specified output vector $\mathbf{Y}_p$. How can we find a set of weights $w = \{w_{ij}\}$ that will accomplish this? We could try to do it by hill-climbing on the space of **W***s*, provided that we could define a suitable measure of relative altitude or "success." One problem is that there cannot be any standard, universal way to measure errors, because each type of error has different costs in different situations. But let us set that issue aside and do what scientists often do when they can't think of anything better: sum the squares of the differences. So, if **X(W,X)** is the network's output vector for internal weights **W** and inputs **X**, define the altitude function $E(\mathbf{W})$ to be this sum:

$$E(\mathbf{W}) = -\sum_{\substack{\text{all input} \\ \text{patterns } p}} [\mathbf{Y}_p - \mathbf{Y}(\mathbf{W}, \mathbf{X}_p)]^2.$$

In other words, we compute our measure of success by presenting successively each stimulus $\mathbf{X}_p$ to the network. Then we compute the (vector) difference between the actual output and the desired output. Finally, we add up the squares of the magnitudes of those differences. (The minus sign is simply for thinking of climbing up instead of down.) The error function E will then have a maximum possible value of zero, which will be achieved if and only if the machine performs perfectly. Otherwise there will be at least one error and $E(\mathbf{W})$ will be negative. Then all we have to is climb the hill $E(\mathbf{W})$ defined over the (high-dimensional) space of weight vectors $\mathbf{W}$. If our paths reaches a $\mathbf{W}$ for which $E(\mathbf{W})$ is zero, our problem will be solved and we will be able to say that our machine has "learned from its experience."

We'll use a process that climbs this hill by the method of steepest ascent. We can do this by estimating, at every step, the partial derivatives $\partial E/\partial w_{ij}$ of the total error with respect to each component of the weight vector. This tells us the direction of the gradient vector $dE/d\mathbf{W}$, and we then proceed to move a certain distance in that direction. This is the mathematical character of the Generalized Delta procedure, and it differs in no significant way from older forms of diameter-limited gradient followers.

Before such a procedure can be employed, there is an obstacle to overcome. One cannot directly apply the method of gradient ascent to networks that contain threshold units. This is because the derivative of a step-function is zero, whenever it exists, and hence no gradient is defined. To get around this, *PDP* applies a smoothing function to make those threshold functions differentiable. The trick is to replace the threshold function for each unit with a monotonic and differentiable function of the sum of that unit's inputs. This permits the output of each unit to encode information about the sum of its inputs while still retaining an approximation to the perceptron's decision-making ability. Then gradient ascent becomes more feasible. However, we suspect that this smoothing trick may entail a large (and avoidable) cost when the predicate to be learned is actually a composition of linear threshold functions. There ought to be a more efficient alternative based on how much each weight must be changed, for each stimulus, to make the local input sum cross the threshold.

In what sense is the particular hill-climbing procedure GD more powerful than the perceptron's PC? Certainly GD can be applied to more networks than PC can, because PC can operate only on the connections between one layer of φ units and a single output unit. GD, however, can modify the weights in an arbitrary multilayered network, including nets containing loops. Thus, in contrast to the perceptron (which is equipped with some fixed set of φs that can never be changed), GP can be regarded as able to change the weights inside the φs. Thus GD promises, in effect, to be able discover useful *new* φ functions—and many of the experiments reported in *PDP* demonstrate that this often works.

A natural way to estimate the gradient of $E(W)$ is to estimate $\partial E/\partial w_{ij}$ by running through the entire set of inputs for each weight. However, for large networks and large problems that could be a horrendous computation. Fortunately, in a highly connected network, all those many components of the gradient are not independent of one another, but are constrained by the algebraic "chain rule" for the derivatives of composite functions. One can exploit those constraints to reduce the amount of computation by applying the chain-rule formula, recursively, to the mathematical description of the network. This recursive computation is called "back-propagation" in *PDP*. It can substantially reduce the amount of calculation for each hill-climbing step in networks with many connections. We have the impression that many people in the connectionist community do not understand that this is merely a particular way to compute a gradient and have assumed instead that back-propagation is a new learning scheme that somehow gets around the basic limitations of hill-climbing.

Clearly GD would be far more valuable than PC if it could be made to be both efficient and dependable. But virtually nothing has been proved about the range of problems upon which GD works both efficiently and dependably. Indeed, GD can fail to find a solution when one exists, so in that narrow sense it could be considered *less* powerful than PC.

In the early years of cybernetics, everyone understood that hill-climbing was always available for working easy problems, but that it almost always became impractical for problems of larger sizes and complexities. We were very pleased to discover (see section 11.6) that PC could be represented as hill-climbing; however, that very fact led us to wonder whether such procedures could *dependably* be generalized, even to the limited class of multilayer machines that we named Gamba perceptrons. The situation seems not to have changed much—we have seen no contemporary connectionist publication that casts much new theoretical light on the situation. Then why has GD become so popular in recent years? In part this is because it is so widely applicable, and because it does indeed yield new results (at least on problems of rather small scale). Its reputation also gains, we think, from its being presented in forms that share, albeit to a lesser degree, the biological plausibility of PC. But we fear that its reputation also stems from unfamiliarity with the manner in which hill-climbing methods deteriorate when confronted with larger-scale problems.

In any case, little good can come from statements like "as a practical matter, GD leads to solutions in virtually every case" or "GD can, in principle, learn arbitrary functions." Such pronouncements are not merely technically wrong; more significantly, the pretense that problems do not exist can deflect us from valuable insights that could come from examining things more carefully. As the field of connectionism becomes more mature, the quest for a general solution to all learning problems will evolve into an understanding of which types of learning processes are likely to work on which classes of problems. And this means that, past a certain point, we won't be able to get by with vacuous generalities about hill-climbing. We will really need to know a great deal more about the nature of those surfaces for each specific realm of problems that we want to solve.

On the positive side, we applaud those who bravely and romantically are empirically applying hill-climbing methods to many new domains for the first time, and we expect such work to result in important advances. Certainly these researchers are exploring networks with architectures far more complex than those of perceptrons, and some of their experiments already have shown indications of new phenomena that are well worth trying to understand.

Scaling Problems Up in Size

Experiments with toy-scale problems have proved as fruitful in artificial intelligence as in other areas of science and engineering.

Many techniques and principles that ultimately found real applications were discovered and honed in microworlds small enough to comprehend yet rich enough to challenge our thinking. But not every phenomenon encountered in dealing with small models can be usefully scaled up. Looking at the relative thickness of the legs of an ant and an elephant reminds us that physical structures do not always scale linearly: an ant magnified a thousand times would collapse under its own weight. Much of the theory of computational complexity is concerned with questions of scale. If it takes 100 steps to solve a certain kind of equation with four terms, how many steps will it take to solve the same kind of equation with eight terms? Only 200, if the problem scales linearly. But for other problems it will take not twice 100 but 100 squared.

For example, the Gamba perceptron of figure 2 needs only two φ functions rather than the six required in figure 1. In neither of these two toy-sized networks does the number seem alarmingly large. One network has fewer units; the other has smaller coefficients. But when we examine how those numbers grow with retinas of increasing size, we discover that whereas the coefficients of figure 1 remain constant, those of figure 2 grow exponentially. And, presumably, a similar price must be paid again in the number of repetitions required in order to learn.

In the examination of theories of learning and problem solving, the study of such growths in cost is not merely one more aspect to be taken into account; in a sense, it is the only aspect worth considering. This is because so many problems can be solved "in principle" by exhaustive search through a suitable space of states. Of course, the trouble with that in practice is that there is usually an exponential increase in the number of steps required for an exhaustive search when the scale of the problem is enlarged. Consequently, solving toy problems by methods related to exhaustive search rarely leads to practical solutions to larger problems. For example, though it is easy to make an exhaustive-search machine that never loses a game of noughts and crosses, it is infeasible to do the same for chess. We do not know if this fact is significant, but many of the small examples described in *PDP* could have been solved as quickly by means of exhaustive search—that is, by systematically assigning and testing all combinations of small integer weights.

When we started our research on perceptrons, we had seen many interesting demonstrations of perceptrons solving problems of very small scale but not doing so well when those problems were scaled up. We wondered what was going wrong. Our first "handle" on how to think about scaling came with the concept of the order of a predicate. If a problem is of order N, then the number of φs for the corresponding perceptron need not increase any faster than as the Nth power of R. Then, whenever we could show that a given problem was of low order, we usually could demonstrate that perceptron-like networks could do surprisingly well on that problem. On the other hand, once we developed the more difficult techniques for showing that certain other problems have unbounded order, this raised alarming warning flags about extending *their* solutions to larger domains.

Unbounded order was not the only source of scaling failures. Another source—one we had not anticipated until the later stages of our work—involved the size, or rather the information content, of the coefficients. The information stored in connectionist systems is embodied in the strengths of weights of the connections between units. The idea that learning can take place by changing such strengths has a ring of biological plausibility, but that plausibility fades away if those strengths are to be represented by numbers that must be accurate to ten or twenty decimal orders of significance.

The Problem of Sampling Variance

Our description of the Generalized Delta Rule assumes that it is feasible to compute the new value of $E(\mathbf{W})$ at every step of the climb. The processes discussed in chapter 8 of *PDP* typically require only on the order of 100,000 iterations, a range that is easily accessible to computers (but that might in some cases strain our sense of biological plausibility). However, it will not be practical, with larger problems, to cycle through all possible input patterns. This means that when precise measures of $E(\mathbf{W})$ are unavailable, we will be forced to act, instead, on the basis of incomplete samples—for example, by making a small hill-climbing step after each reaction to a stimulus. (See the discussion of complete versus incremental methods in subsection 12.1.1.) When we can no longer compute $dE/d\mathbf{W}$ precisely but can only estimate its components, then the actual derivative will be masked by a certain amount of sampling noise. The text of *PDP* argues that using sufficiently small steps can force the resulting trajectory to come arbitrarily close to that which would result from knowing $dE/d\mathbf{W}$ precisely. When we tried to prove this, we were led to suspect that the choice of step size may depend so much on the higher derivatives of the smoothing functions that large-scale problems could require too many steps for such methods to be practical.

So far as we could tell, every experiment described in chapter 8 of *PDP* involved making a complete cycle through all possible input situations before making any change in weights. Whenever this is feasible, it completely eliminates sampling noise—and then even the most minute correlations can become reliably detectable, because the variance is zero. But no person or animal ever faces situations that are so simple and arranged in so orderly a manner as to provide such cycles of teaching examples. Moving from small to large problems will often demand this transition from exhaustive to statistical sampling, and we suspect that in many realistic situations the resulting sampling noise would mask the signal completely. We suspect that many who read the connectionist literature are not aware of this phenomenon, which dims some of the prospects of successfully applying certain learning procedures to large-scale problems.

Problems of Scaling

In principle, connectionist networks offer all the potential of universal computing devices. However, our examples of order and coefficient size suggest that various kinds of scaling problems are likely to become obstacles to attempts to exploit that potential. Fortunately, our analysis of perceptrons does not suggest that connectionist networks need always encounter these obstacles. Indeed, our book is rich in surprising examples of tasks that simple perceptrons can perform using relatively low-order units and small coefficients. However, our analysis does show that parallel networks are, in general, subject to serious scaling phenomena. Consequently, researchers who propose such models must show that, in their context, those phenomena do not occur.

The authors of *PDP* seem disinclined to face such problems. They seem content to argue that, although we showed that single-layer networks cannot solve certain problems, we did not know that there could exist a powerful learning procedure for multilayer networks—to which our theorems no longer apply. However, strictly speaking, it is wrong to formulate our findings in terms of what perceptrons can and cannot do. As we pointed out above, perceptrons of sufficiently large order can represent *any* finite predicate. A better description of what we did is that, in certain cases, we established the computational costs of what perceptrons can do as a function of increasing problem size. The authors of *PDP* show little concern for such issues, and usually seem content with experiments in which small multilayer networks solve particular instances of small problems.

What should one conclude from such examples? A person who thinks in terms of *can* versus *can't* will be tempted to suppose that if toy machines can do something, then larger machines may well do it better. One must always probe into the practicality of a proposed learning algorithm. It is no use to say that "procedure *P* is capable of learning to recognize pattern *X*" unless one can show that this can be done in less time and at less cost than with exhaustive search. Thus, as we noted, in the case of symmetry, the authors of *PDP* actually recognized that the coefficients were growing as powers of 2, yet they did not seem to regard this as suggesting that the experiment worked only because of its very small size. But scientists who exploit the insights gained from studying the single-layer case might draw quite different conclusions.

The authors of *PDP* recognize that GD is a form of hill-climber, but they speak as though becoming trapped on local maxima were rarely a serious problem. In reporting their experiments with learning the XOR predicate, they remark that this occurred "in only two cases . . . in hundreds of times." However, that experiment involved only the toy problem of learning to compute the XOR of two arguments. We conjecture that learning XOR for larger numbers of variables will become increasingly intractable as we increase the numbers of input variables, because by its nature the underlying parity function is absolutely uncorrelated with any function of fewer variables. Therefore, there can exist no useful correlations among the outputs of the lower-order units involved in computing it, and that leads us to suspect that there is little to gain from following whatever paths are indicated by the artificial introduction of smoothing functions that cause partial derivatives to exist.

The *PDP* experimenters encountered a more serious local-maximum problem when trying to make a network learn to add two binary numbers—a problem that contains an embedded XOR problem. When working with certain small networks, the system got stuck reliably. However, the experimenters discovered an interesting way to get around this difficulty by introducing longer chains of intermediate units. We encourage the reader to study the discussion starting on page 341 of *PDP* and try to make a more complete theoretical analysis of this problem. We suspect that further study of this case will show that hill-climbing procedures can indeed get multilayer networks to learn to do multidigit addition. However, such a study should be carried out not to show that "networks are good" but to see which network architectures are most suitable for enabling the information required for "carrying" to flow easily from the smaller to the larger digits. In the *PDP* experiment, the network appears to us to have started on the road toward inventing the technique known to computer engineers as "carry jumping."

To what extent can hill-climbing systems be made to solve hard problems? One might object that this is a wrong question because "hard" is so ill defined. The lesson of *Perceptrons* is that we must find ways to make such questions meaningful. In the case of hill-climbing, we need to find ways to characterize the types of problems that lead to the various obstacles to climbing hills, instead of ignoring those difficulties or trying to find universal ways to get around them.

The Society of Mind

The preceding section was written as though it ought to be the principal goal of research on network models to determine in which situations it will be feasible to scale their operations up to deal with increasingly complicated problems. But now we propose a somewhat shocking alternative: Perhaps the scale of the toy problem is that on which, in physiological actuality, much of the functioning of intelligence operates. Accepting this thesis leads into a way of thinking very different from that of the connectionist movement. We have used the phrase "society of mind" to refer to the idea that mind is made up of a large number of components, or "agents," each of which would operate on the scale of what, if taken in isolation, would be little more than a toy problem. [See Marvin Minsky, *The Society of Mind* (Simon and Schuster, 1987) and Seymour Papert, *Mindstorms* (Basic Books, 1982).]

To illustrate this idea, let's try to compare the performance of the symmetry perceptron in *PDP* with human behavior. An adult human can usually recognize and appreciate the symmetries of a kaleidoscope, and that sort of example leads one to imagine that people do very much better than simple perceptrons. But how much can people actually do? Most people would be hard put to be certain about the symmetry of a large pattern. For example, how long does it take you to decide whether or not the following pattern is symmetrical?

DB4HWUK85HCNZEWJKRKJWEZNCH58KUWH4BD

In many situations, humans clearly show abilities far in excess of what could be learned by simple, uniform networks. But when we take those skills apart, or try to find out how they were learned, we expect to find that they were made by processes that somehow combined the work (already done in the past) of many smaller agencies, none of which, separately, need to work on scales much larger than do those in *PDP*. Is this hypothesis consistent with the *PDP* style of connectionism? Yes, insofar as the computations of the nervous system can be represented as the operation of societies of networks. But no, insofar as the mode of operation of those societies of networks (as we imagine them) raises theoretical issues of a different kind. We do not expect procedures such as GD to be able to produce such societies. Something else is needed.

What that something must be depends on how we try to extend the range of small connectionist models. We see two principal alternatives. We could extend them either by scaling up small connectionist models or by combining small-scale networks into some larger organization. In the first case, we would expect to encounter theoretical obstacles to maintaining GD's effectiveness on larger, deeper nets. And despite the reputed efficacy of other alleged remedies for the deficiencies of hill-climbing, such as "annealing," we stay with our research conjecture that no such procedures will work very well on large-scale nets, except in the case of problems that turn out to be of low order in some appropriate sense. The second alternative is to employ a variety of smaller networks rather than try to scale up a single one. And if we choose (as we do) to move in that direction, then our focus of concern as theoretical psychologists must turn toward the organizing of small nets into effective large systems. The idea that the lowest levels of thinking and learning may operate on toy-like scales fits many of our common-sense impressions of psychology. For example, in the realm of language, any normal person can parse a great many kinds of sentences, but none of them past a certain bound of involuted complexity. We all fall down on expressions like "the cheese that the rat that the cat that the dog bit chased ate." In the realm of vision, no one can count great numbers of things, in parallel, at a single glance. Instead, we learn to "estimate." Indeed, the visual joke in figure 0.1 shows clearly how humans share perceptrons' inability to easily count and match, and a similar example is embodied in the twin spirals of figure 5.1. The spiral example was intended to emphasize not only that low-order perceptrons cannot perceive connectedness but also that humans have similar limitations. However, a determined person can solve the problem, given enough time, by switching to the use of certain sorts of serial mental processes.

Beyond Perceptrons

No single-method learning scheme can operate efficiently for every possible task; we cannot expect any one type of machine to account for any large portion of human psychology. For example, in certain situations it is best to carefully accumulate experience; however, when time is limited, it is necessary to make hasty generalizations and act accordingly. No single scheme can do all things. Our human semblance of intelligence emerged from how the brain evolved a multiplicity of ways to deal with different problem realms. We see this as a principle that underlies the mind's reality, and we interpret the need for many kinds of mechanisms not as a pessimistic and scientifically constraining limitation but as the fundamental source of many of the phenomena that artificial intelligence and psychology have always sought to understand. The power of the brain stems not from any single, fixed, universal principle. Instead it comes from the evolution (in both the individual sense and the Darwinian sense) of a variety of ways to develop new mechanisms and to adapt older ones to perform new functions. Instead of seeking a way to get around that need for diversity, we have come to try to develop ''society of mind'' theories that will recognize and exploit the idea that brains are based on many different kinds of interacting mechanisms.

Several kinds of evidence impel us toward this view. One is the great variety of different and specific functions embodied in the brain's biology. Another is the similarly great variety of phenomena in the psychology of intelligence. And from a much more abstract viewpoint, we cannot help but be impressed with the practical limitations of each ''general'' scheme that has been proposed—and with the theoretical opacity of questions about how they behave when we try to scale their applications past the toy problems for which they were first conceived.

Our research on perceptrons and on other computational schemes has left us with a pervasive bias against seeking a general, domain-independent theory of ''how neural networks work.'' Instead, we ought to look for ways in which particular types of network models can support the development of models of particular domains of mental function—and vice versa. Thus, our understanding of the perceptron's ability to perform geometric tasks was actually based on theories that were more concerned with geometry than with networks. And this example is supported by a broad body of experience in other areas of artificial intelligence. Perhaps this is why the current preoccupation of connectionist theorists with the search for general learning algorithms evokes for us two aspects of the early history of computation.

First, we are reminded of the long line of theoretical work that culminated in the ''pessimistic'' theories of Gödel and Turing about the limitations on effective computability. Yet the realization that there can be no general-purpose decision procedure for mathematics had not the slightest dampening effect on research in mathematics or in computer science. On the contrary, awareness of those limiting discoveries helped motivate the growth of rich cultures involved with classifying and understanding more specialized algorithmic methods. In other words, it was the realization that seeking overgeneral solution methods would be as fruitless as—and equivalent to—trying to solve the unsolvable halting problem for Turing machines. Abandoning this then led to seeking progress in more productive directions.

Our second thought is about how the early research in artificial intelligence tended to focus on general-purpose algorithms for reasoning and problem solving. Those general methods will always play their roles, but the most successful applications of AI research gained much of their practical power from applying specific knowledge to specific domains. Perhaps that work has now moved too far toward ignoring general theoretical considerations, but by now we have learned to be skeptical about the practical power of unrestrained generality.

Interaction and Insulation

Evolution seems to have anticipated these discoveries. Although the nervous system appears to be a network, it is very far from being a single, uniform, highly interconnected assembly of units that each have similar relationships to the others. Nor are all brain cells similarly affected by the same processes. It would be better to think of the brain not as a single network whose elements operate in accord with a uniform set of principles but as a network whose components are themselves networks having a large variety of different architectures and control systems. This "society of mind" idea has led our research perspective away from the search for algorithms, such as GD, that were hoped to work across many domains. Instead, we were led into trying to understand what specific kinds of processing would serve specific domains.

We recognize that the idea of distributed, cooperative processing has a powerful appeal to common sense as well to computational and biological science. Our research instincts tell us to discover as much as we can about distributed processes. But there is another concept, complementary to distribution, that is no less strongly supported by the same sources of intuition. We'll call it *insulation.*

Certain parallel computations are by their nature synergistic and cooperative: each part makes the others easier. But the And/Or of theorem 4.0 shows that under other circumstances, attempting to make the same network perform two simple tasks at the same time leads to a task that has a far greater order of difficulty. In those sorts of circumstances, there will be a clear advantage to having mechanisms, not to connect things together, but to keep such tasks apart. How can this be done in a connectionist net? Some recent work hints that even simple multilayer perceptron-like nets can learn to segregate themselves into quasi-separate components—and that suggests (at least in principle) research on uniform learning procedures. But it also raises the question of how to relate those almost separate parts. In fact, research on networks in which different parts do different things and learn those things in different ways has become our principal concern. And that leads us to ask how such systems could develop *managers* for deciding, in different circumstances, which of those diverse procedures to use.

For example, consider all the specialized agencies that the human brain employs to deal with the visual perception of spatial scenes. Although we still know little about how all those different agencies work, the end result is surely even more complex than what we described in section 13.4. Beyond that, human scene analysis also engages our memories and goals. Furthermore, in addition to all the systems we humans use to dissect two-dimensional scenes into objects and relationships, we also possess machinery for exploiting stereoscopic vision. Indeed, there appear to be many such agencies—distinct ones that employ, for example, motion cues, disparities, central correlations of the Julesz type, and memory-based frame-array-like systems that enable us to imagine and virtually "see" the occluded sides of familiar objects. Beyond those, we seem also to have been supplied with many other visual agencies—for example, ones that are destined to learn to recognize faces and expressions, visual cliffs, threatening movements, sexual attractants, and who knows how many others that have not been discovered yet. What mechanisms manage and control the use of all those diverse agencies? And from where do those managers come?

Stages of Development

In *Mindstorms* and in *The Society of Mind,* we explained how the idea of intermediate, hidden processes might well account for some phenomena discovered by Piaget in his experiments on how children develop their concepts about the "conservation of quantity." We introduced a theory of mental growth based on inserting, at various times, new inner layers of "management" into already existing networks. In particular, we argued that, to learn to make certain types of comparisons, a child's mind must construct a multilayer structure that we call a "society-of-more." The lower levels of that net contain agents specialized to make a variety of spatial and temporal observations. Then the higher-level agents learn to classify, and then control, the activities of the lower ones. We certainly would like to see a demonstration of a learning process that could spontaneously produce the several levels of agents needed to embody a concept as complex as that. Chapter 17 of *The Society of Mind* offers several different reasons why this might be very difficult to do except in systems under systematic controls, both temporal and architectural. We suspect that it would require far too long, in comparison with an infant's months of life, to create sophisticated agencies entirely by undirected, spontaneous learning. Each specialized network must begin with promising ingredients that come either from prior stages of development or from some structural endowment that emerged in the course of organic evolution.

When should new layers of control be introduced? If managers are empowered too soon, when their workers still are too immature, they won't be able to accomplish enough. (If every agent could learn from birth, they would all be overwhelmed by infantile ideas.) But if the managers arrive too late, that will retard all further growth. Ideally, every agency's development would be controlled by yet another agency equipped to introduce new agents just when they are needed—that is, when enough has been learned to justify the start of another stage. However, that would require a good deal of expertise on the controlling agency's part. Another way—much easier to evolve—would simply enable various agencies to establish new connections at genetically predetermined times (perhaps while also causing lower-level parts to slow further growth). Such a scheme could benefit a human population on the whole, although it might handicap individuals who, for one reason or another, happen to move ahead of or behind that inborn "schedule." In any case, there are many reasons to suspect that the parts of any system as complex as a human mind must grow through sequences of stage-like episodes.

Architecture and Specialization

The tradition of connectionism has always tried to establish two claims: that connectionist networks can accomplish interesting tasks and that they can learn to do so with no explicit programming. But a closer look reveals that rarely are those two virtues present in the same device. It is true that networks, taken as a class, can do virtually anything. However, each particular type of network can best learn only certain types of things. Each particular network we have seen seems relatively limited. Yet our wondrous brains are themselves composed of connected networks of cells.

We think that the difference in abilities comes from the fact that a brain is not a single, uniformly structured network. Instead, each brain contains hundreds of different types of machines, interconnected in specific ways which predestine that brain to become a large, diverse society of partially specialized agencies. We are born with specific parts of our brains to serve every sense and muscle group, and with perhaps separate sections for physical and social matters (e.g., natural sounds versus social speech, inanimate scenes versus facial expressions, mechanical contacts versus social caresses). Our brains also embody proto-specialists involved with hunger, laughter, anger, fear, and perhaps hundreds of other functions that scientists have not yet isolated. Many thousands of genes must be involved in constructing specific internal architectures for each of those highly evolved brain centers and in laying out the nerve bundles that interconnect them. And although each such system is embodied in the form of a network-based learning system, each almost surely also learns in accord with somewhat different principles.

Why did our brains evolve so as to contain so many specialized parts? Could not a single, uniform network learn to structure itself into divisions with appropriate architectures and processes? We think that this would be impractical because of the problem of representing knowledge. In order for a machine to learn to recognize or perform X, be it a pattern or a process, that machine must in one sense or another learn to represent or embody X. Doing that efficiently must exploit some happy triadic relationship between the structure of X, the learning procedure, and the initial architecture of the network. It makes no sense to seek the "best" network architecture or learning procedure because it makes no sense to say that *any* network is efficient by itself: that makes sense only in the context of some class of problems to be solved. Different kinds of networks lend themselves best to different kinds of representations and to different sorts of generalizations. This means that the study of networks in general must include attempts, like those in this book, to classify problems and learning processes; but it must also include attempts to classify the network architectures. This is why we maintain that the scientific future of connectionism is tied not to the search for some single, universal scheme to solve all problems at once but to the evolution of a many-faceted technology of "brain design" that encompasses good technical theories about the analysis of learning procedures, of useful architectures, and of organizational principles to use when assembling those components into larger systems.

Symbolic versus Distributed

Let us now return to the conflict posed in our prologue: the war between the connectionists and the symbolists. We hope to make peace by exploiting both sides.

There are important virtues in the use of parallel distributed networks. They certainly often offer advantages in simplicity and in speed. And above all else they offer us ways to learn new skills without the pain and suffering that might come from comprehending how. On the darker side, they can limit large-scale growth because what any distributed network learns is likely to be quite opaque to other networks connected to it.

Symbolic systems yield gains of their own, in versatility and unlimited growth. Above all else they offer us the prospect that computers share: of not being bound by the small details of the parts of which they are composed. But that, too, has its darker side: symbolic processes can evolve worlds of their own, utterly divorced from their origins. Perceptrons can never go insane—but the same cannot be said of a brain.

Now, what are symbols, anyway? We usually conceive of them as compact things that represent more complex things. But what, then, do we mean by *represent*? It simply makes no sense, by itself, to say that "S represents T," because the significance of a symbol depends on at least three participants: on S, on T, and on the context of some process or user U. What, for example, connects the word *table* to any actual, physical table? Since the words people use are the words people learn, clearly the answer must be that there is no direct relationship between S and T, but that there is a more complex triadic relationship that connects a symbol, a thing, and a process that is active in some person's mind. Furthermore, when the term *symbol* is used in the context of network psychology, it usually refers to something that is reassignable so that it can be made to represent different things and so that the symbol-using processes can learn to deal with different symbols.

What do we mean by *distributed*? This usually refers to a system in which each end-effect comes not from any single, localized element-part, but from the interactions of many contributors, all working at the same time. Accordingly, in order to make a desired change in the output of a distributed system, one must usually alter a great many components. And changing the output of any particular component will rarely have a large effect in any particular circumstance; instead, such changes will tend to have small effects in many different circumstances.

Symbols are tokens or handles with which one specialist can manipulate representations within another specialist. But now, suppose that we want one agency to be able to exploit the knowledge in another agency. So long as we stay inside a particular agency, it may be feasible to use representations that involve great hosts of internal interactions and dependencies. But the fine details of such a representation would be meaningless to any outside agency that lacks access to, or the capacity to deal with, all that fine detail. Indeed, if each representation in the first agency involves activities that are uniformly distributed over a very large network, then direct communication to the other agency would require so many connection paths that both agencies would end up enmeshed together into a single, uniform net—and then all the units of both would interact.

How, then, could networks support symbolic forms of activities? We conjecture that, inside the brain, agencies with different jobs are usually constrained to communicate with one another only through neurological bottlenecks (i.e., connections between relatively small numbers of units that are specialized to serve as symbolic recognizers and memorizers). The recognizers learn to encode significant features of the representation active in the first network, and the memorizers learn to evoke an activity that can serve a corresponding function in the receiving network. But in order to prevent those features from interfering too much with one another, there must be an adequate degree of insulation between the units that serve these purposes. And that need for insulation can lead to genuine conflicts between the use of symbolic and distributed representations. This is because distributed representations make it hard to combine (in arbitrary, learnable ways) the different fragments of knowledge embodied in different representations. The difficulty arises because the more distributed is the representation of each fragment, the fewer fragments can be simultaneously active without interfering with one another. Sometimes those interactions can be useful, but in general they will be destructive. This is discussed briefly in section 8.2 of *The Society of Mind:*

"The advantages of distributed systems are not alternatives to the advantages of insulated systems: the two are complementary. To say that the brain may be composed of distributed systems is not the same as saying that it *is* a distributed system—that is, a single network in which all functions are uniformly distributed. We do not believe that any brain of that sort could work, because the interactions would be uncontrollable. To be sure, we have to explain how different ideas can become connected to one another—but we must also explain what keeps our separate memories intact. For example, we praised the power of metaphors that allow us to mix the ideas we have in different realms—but all that power would be lost if all our metaphors got mixed! Similarly, the architecture of a mind-society must encourage the formation and maintenance of distinct levels of management by preventing the formation of connections between agencies whose messages have no mutual significance. Some theorists have assumed that distributed systems are inherently both robust and versatile but, actually, those attributes are more likely to conflict. Systems with too many interactions of different types will tend to be fragile, while systems with too many interactions of similar types will tend to be too redundant to adapt to novel situations and requirements."

A larger-scale problem is that the use of widely distributed representations will tend to oppose the formulation of knowledge about knowledge. This is because information embodied in distributed form will tend to be relatively inaccessible for use as a subject upon which other knowledge-based processes can operate. Consequently (we conjecture), systems that use highly distributed representations will tend to become conceptual dead ends as a result of their putting performance so far ahead of comprehension as to retard the growth of reflective thought. Too much diffusing of information can make it virtually impossible (for other portions of the brain) to find out how results, however useful, are obtained. This would make it very difficult to dissect out the components that might otherwise be used to construct meaningful variations and generalizations. Of course such problems won't become evident in experiments with systems that do only simple things, but we can expect to see such problems grow when systems try to learn to do more complex things. With highly distributed systems, we should anticipate that the accumulation of internal interactions may eventually lead to intractable credit-assignment problems. Perhaps the only ultimate escape from the limitations of internal interactions is to evolve toward organizations in which each network affects others primarily through the use of *serial* operations and specialized short-term-memory systems, for although seriality is relatively slow, its uses makes it possible to produce and control interactions between activities that occur at different and separate places and times.

The Parallel Paradox

It is often argued that the use of distributed representations enables a system to exploit the advantages of parallel processing. But what *are* the advantages of parallel processing? Suppose that a certain task involves two unrelated parts. To deal with both concurrently, we would have to maintain their representations in two decoupled agencies, both active at the same time. Then, should either of those agencies become involved with two or more subtasks, we would have to deal with each of them with no more than a quarter of the available resources. If that proceeded on and on, the system would become so fragmented that each job would end up with virtually no resources assigned to it. In this regard, distribution may oppose parallelism: the more distributed a system is—that is, the more intimately its parts interact—the fewer *different* things it can do at the same time. On the other side, the more we do *separately* in parallel, the less machinery can be assigned to each element of what we do, and that ultimately leads to increasing fragmentation and incompetence.

This is not to say that distributed representations and parallel processing are always incompatible. When we simultaneously activate two distributed representations in the same network, they will be forced to interact. In favorable circumstances, those interactions can lead to useful parallel computations, such as the satisfaction of simultaneous constraints. But that will not happen in general; it will occur only when the representations happen to mesh in suitably fortunate ways. Such problems will be especially serious when we try to train distributed systems to deal with problems that require any sort of structural analysis in which the system must represent relationships between substructures of related types—that is, problems that are likely to compete for the same limited resources.

On the positive side, there are potential virtues to embodying knowledge in the form of networks of units with weighted interconnections. For example, distributed representations can sometimes be used to gain the robustness of redundancy, to make machines that continue to work despite having injured, damaged, or unreliable components. They can embody extremely simple learning algorithms, which operate in parallel with great speed.

Representations and Generalizations

It is often said that distributed representations are inherently possessed of useful holistic qualities; for example, that they have innate tendencies to recognize wholes from partial cues—even for patterns they have not encountered before. Phenomena of that sort are often described with such words as *generalization, induction,* or *gestalt*. Such phenomena certainly *can* emerge from connectionist assemblies. The problem is that, for any body of experience, there are always *many* kinds of generalizations that can be made. The ones made by any particular network are likely to be inappropriate unless there happens to be an appropriate relationship between the network's architecture and the manner in which the problem is represented. What makes architectures and representations appropriate? One way to answer that is to study how they affect which signals will be treated as similar.

Consider the problem of comparing an arbitrary input pattern with a collection of patterns in memory, to find which memory is most similar to that stimulus. In section 12.7 we conjectured that solving best-match problems will always be very tedious when serial hardware is used. *PDP* suggests another view in regard to parallel, distributed machines: "This is precisely the kind of problem that is readily implemented using highly parallel algorithms of the kind we consider." This is, in some ways, plausible, since a sufficiently parallel machine could simultaneously match an input pattern against every pattern in its memory. And yet the assertion is quaintly naive, since *best match* means different things in different circumstances. Which answers should be accepted as best always depends on the domain of application. The very same stimulus may signify food to one animal, companionship to another, and a dangerous predator to a third. Thus, there can be no single, universal measure of how well two descriptions match; every context requires appropriate schemes. Because of this, distributed networks do not magically provide solutions to such best-match problems. Instead, the functional architecture of each particular network imposes its own particular sort of metrical structure on the space of stimuli. Such structures may often be useful. Yet, that can give us no assurance that the outcome will correspond to what an expert observer would consider to be the very best match, given that observer's view of what would be the most appropriate response in the current context or problem realm.

We certainly do not mean to suggest that networks cannot perform useful matching functions. We merely mean to emphasize that different problems entail different matching criteria, and that hence no particular type of network can induce a topology of similarity or nearness that is appropriate for every realm. Instead, we must assume that, over the course of time, each specialized portion of the brain has evolved a particular type of architecture that is reasonably likely to induce similarity relationships that are useful in performing the functions to which that organ is likely (or destined) to be assigned. Perhaps an important activity of future connectionist research will be to develop networks that can *learn* to embody wide ranges of different, context-dependent types of matching functions.

We have also often heard the view that machines that employ localized or symbolic representations must be inherently less capable than are distributed machines of insight, consciousness, or sense of self. We think this stands things on their heads. It is *because* our brains primarily exploit connectionist schemes that we possess such *small* degrees of consciousness, in the sense that we have so little insight into the nature of our own conceptual machinery. We agree that distributed representations probably are used in virtually every part of the brain. Consequently, each agency must learn to exploit the abilities of the others without having direct access to compact representations of what happens inside those other agencies. This makes direct insight infeasible; the best such agencies can do is attempt to construct their own models of the others on the basis of approximate, pragmatic models based on presuppositions and concepts already embodied in the observing agency. Because of this, what appear to us to be direct insights into ourselves must be rarely genuine and usually conjectural. Accordingly, we expect distributed representations to tend to produce systems with only limited abilities to reflect accurately on how they do what they do. Thinking about thinking, we maintain, requires the use of representations that are localized enough that they can be dissected and rearranged. Besides, distributed representations spread out the information that goes into them. The result of this is to mix and obscure the effects of their separate elements. Thus their use must entail a heavy price; surely, many of them must become "conceptual dead ends" because the performances that they produce emerge from processes that other agencies cannot comprehend. In other words, when the representations of concepts are distributed, this will tend to frustrate attempts of other agencies to adapt and transfer those concepts to other contexts.

How much, then, can we expect from connectionist systems? Much more than the above remarks might suggest, since reflective thought is the lesser part of what our minds do. Most probably, we think, the human brain is, in the main, composed of large numbers of relatively small distributed systems, arranged by embryology into a complex society that is controlled in part (but only in part) by serial, symbolic systems that are added later. But the subsymbolic systems that do most of the work from underneath must, by their very character, block all the other parts of the brain from knowing much about how they work. And this, itself, could help explain how people do so many things yet have such incomplete ideas of how those things are actually done.

The following remarks are intended to introduce the literature of this field. This is not to be considered an attempt at historical scholarship, for we have made no serious venture in that direction.

In a decade of work on the family of machines loosely called perceptrons, we find an interacting evolution and refinement of two ideas: first, the concept of realizing a predicate as a linear threshold function of much more local predicates; second, the idea of a convergence or "learning" theorem. The most commonly held version of this history sees the perceptron invented by Rosenblatt in a single act, with the final proof of the convergence theorem vindicating his insight in the face of skepticism from the scientific world. This is an oversimplification, especially in its taking the concept of perceptron as static. For in fact a key part of the process leading to the convergence theorem was the molding of the concept of the machine to the appropriate form. (Indeed, how often does "finding the proof" of a conjecture involve giving the conjecture a more provable form?)

In the early papers one sees a variety, both of machines and of "training" procedures, converging in the course of accumulation of mathematical insight toward the simple concepts we have used in this book. Students interested in this evolution can read:

Rosenblatt, Frank (1959), "Two theorems of statistical separability in the perceptron," *Proceedings of a Symposium on the Mechanization of Thought Processes*, Her Majesty's Stationary Office, London, pp. 421–456;

Rosenblatt, Frank (1962), *Principles of Neurodynamics*, Spartan Books, New York.

In a variety of contexts, other perceptronlike learning experiments had been described. Quite well-known was the paper of

Samuel, Arthur L. (1959), "Some studies in machine learning using the game of checkers," *IBM Journal of Research and Development*, Vol. 3, No. 3, pp. 210–223

who describes a variety of error-correcting vector addition procedures. In a later paper

Samuel, Arthur L. (1967), "Some studies in machine learning using the game of checkers, Part II," *IBM Journal of Research and Development*, Vol. 11, No. 4, pp. 601–618

he describes studies that lead toward detecting more complex interactions between the partial predicates. The simple multilayer perceptronlike machines discussed in Chapter 13 were described in

Palmieri, G. and R. Sanna (1960), *Methodos*, Vol. 12, No. 48;

Gamba, A., L. Gamberini, G. Palmieri, and R. Sanna (1961), "Further experiments with PAPA," *Nuovo Cimento Suppl.* No. 2, Vol. 20, pp. 221–231.

Some earlier reward-modified machines, further from the final form of the perceptron, are described in

Ashby, W. Ross (1952), *Design for a Brain*, Wiley, New York;

Clark, Wesley A., and Farley, B. G. (1955), "Generalization of pattern-recognition in a self-organizing system," *Proceedings 1955 Western Joint Computer Conference*, pp. 85–111;

Minsky, M. (1954), "Neural nets and the brain-model problem," doctoral dissertation, Princeton University, Princeton, N.J.;

Uttley, A. M. (1956), "Conditional probability machines," in *Automata Studies*, Princeton University, Princeton, N.J., pp. 253–285.

The proof of the convergence theorem (Theorem 11.1) is another example of this sort of evolution. In an abstract mathematical sense, both theorem and proof already existed before the perceptron, for several people had considered the idea of solving a set of linear inequalities by "relaxation" methods—successive adjustments much like those used in the perceptron proceduce. An elegant early paper on this is

Agmon, S. (1954), "The relaxation method for linear inequalities," *Canadian Journal of Mathematics*, Vol. 6, No. 3, pp. 382–392.

In Agmon's procedure, one computes the Φ-vector that gives the largest numerical error in the satisfaction of the linear inequality, and uses a multiple of that vector for correction. (See §11.4.) We do not feel sufficiently scholarly to offer an opinion on whether this paper should deserve priority for the discovery of the convergence theorem. It is ~~quite clear~~ possible that the theorem would have been instantly obvious had the cyberneticists interested in perceptrons known about Agmon's work.

In any case, the first proofs of the convergence theorem offered in cybernetic circles were quite independent of the work on linear inequalities. See, for example

Block, H. D. (1962), "The perceptron: a model for brain functioning," *Reviews of Modern Physics*, Vol. 34, No. 1, pp. 123–135.

This proof was quite complicated. The first use known to us of the simpler kind of analysis used in §11.1 is in

Papert, Seymour (1961), "Some Mathematical Models of Learning," *Proceedings of the Fourth London Symposium on Information Theory*, C. Cherry, Editor, Academic Press, New York.

Curiously, this paper is not mentioned by any later commentators (including the usually scholarly Nilsson) other than Rosenblatt in *Neurodynamics*. The convergence theorem is well discussed, in a variety of settings, by

Nilsson, Nils (1965), *Learning Machines*, McGraw-Hill, New York,

who includes a number of historical notes. Readers who consult the London Symposium volume might also read

Minsky, Marvin, and Oliver G. Selfridge (1961), "Learning in neural nets," *Proceedings of the Fourth London Symposium on Information Theory*, C. Cherry, Editor, Academic Press, New York.

for some discussion of the relations between convergence and hill-climbing. Although Minsky and Papert did not yet know one another, their papers in that volume overlap to the extent of proving the same theorem about the Bayesian optimality of linear separation. This coincidence had no obvious connection with their later collaboration.

As Agmon had clearly anticipated the learning aspect of the perceptron, so had Selfridge anticipated its quality of combining local properties to yield apparently global ones. This is seen, for example, in

Selfridge, Oliver G. (1956), "Pattern recognition and learning," *Proceedings of the Third London Symposium of Information Theory*, Academic Press, New York, p. 345.

Incidentally, we consider that there has been a strong influence of these cybernetic ideas on the trend of ideas and discoveries in the physiology of vision represented, for example, in

Lettvin, Jerome Y., H. Maturana, W. S. McCulloch, and W. Pitts (1959), "What the frog's eye tells the frog's brain," *Proceedings of the IRE*, Vol. 47, pp. 1940–1951 and

Hubel, D. H., and T. N. Wiesel (1959), "Receptive fields of single neurons in the cat's striate cortex," *Journal of Physiology*, Vol. 148, pp. 574–591.

Other ideas used in this book come from earlier models of physiological phenomena, notably the paper of

Pitts, W., and W. S. McCulloch (1947), "How we know universals," *Bulletin of Mathematical Biophysics*, Vol. 9, pp. 127–147

which is the first we know of that treats recognition invariant under a group by integrating or summing predicates over the group. This paper and that of Lettvin *et al.* are reprinted in

McCulloch, Warren S. (1965), *Embodiments of Mind*, The M.I.T. Press, Cambridge, Mass.,

and this book reprints other early attempts to pass from the local to the global with networks of individually simple devices. In a third paper reprinted in *Embodiments of Mind*

McCulloch, W. S., and Walter Pitts (1943), "A logical calculus of the ideas immanent in neural nets," *Bulletin of Mathematical Biophysics*, Vol. 5, pp. 115–137

will be found the prototypes of the linear threshold functions themselves. Readers who are unfamiliar with this theory, or that of Turing machines, are directed to the elementary exposition in

Minsky, Marvin (1967), *Computation: Finite and Infinite Machines*, Prentice-Hall, Englewood Cliffs, N.J.

The local-global transition has dominated several biological areas in recent years. A most striking example is the trend in analysis of animal behavior associated with the name of Tinbergen, as in his classic

Tinbergen, N. (1951), *The Study of Instinct*, Oxford, New York.

Returning to the technical aspects of perceptrons, we find that our main subject is not represented at all in the literature. We know of no papers that either prove that a nontrivial perceptron cannot accomplish a given task or else show by mathematical analysis that a perceptron can be made to compute any significant geometric predicate. There is a vast literature about experimental results but generally these are so inconclusive that we will refrain from citing particular papers. In most cases that seem to show "success," it can be seen that the data permits an order-1 separation, or even a conjunctively local separation! In these cases, the authors do not mention this, though it seems inconceivable that they could not have noticed it!

The approach closest to ours, though still quite distant, is that of

Bledsoe, W. W., and I. Browning (1959), "Pattern recognition and reading by machine," *Proceedings of the Eastern Joint Computer Conference, 1959*, pp. 225–232.

Another early paper that recognizes the curiously neglected fact that partial predicates work better when realistically matched to the problem, is

Roberts, Lawrence G. (1960), "Pattern recognition with an adaptive network," *IRE International Convention Record*, Part II, pp. 66–70.

Rosenblatt made some studies (in *Neurodynamics*) concerning the probability that if a perceptron recognizes a certain class of figures it will also recognize other figures that are similar in certain ways. In another paper

Rosenblatt, Frank (1960), "Perceptual generalization over transformation groups," *Self-Organizing Systems*, Pergamon Press, New York, pp. 63–96.

he considers group-invariant patterns but does not come close enough to the group-invariance theorem to get decisive results.

The nearest approach to our negative results and methods is the analysis of ψ_{PARITY} found in

Dertouzos, Michael (1965), *Threshold Logic: A Synthesis Approach*, The M.I.T. Press, Cambridge, Mass.

This is also a good book in which to see how people who are *not* interested in geometric aspects of perceptrons deal with linear threshold functions. They had already been interested, for other reasons, in the size of coefficients of (first-order) threshold functions, and we made use of an idea described in

Myhill, John and W. H. Kautz (1961), "On the size of weights required for linear-input switching functions," *IRE Transactions on Electronic Computers*, Vol. 10, No. 2, pp. 288–290

to get our theorem in §10.1. A more recent result on order-1 coefficients is in

Muroga, Saburo, and I. Toda (1966), "Lower bounds on the number of threshold functions," *IEEE Transactions on Electronic Computers*, Vol. EC-15, No. 5, pp. 805–806,

which improves upon an earlier result in

Muroga, Saburo (1965), "Lower bounds on the number of threshold functions and a maximum weight," *IEEE Transactions on Electronic Computers*, Vol. EC-14, No. 2, pp. 136–148.

These papers also discuss another question: the proportion of Boolean functions (of n-variables) that happens to be first-order. To our knowledge, there is no literature about the same question for higher-order functions.

The general area of artificial intelligence and heuristic programming was mentioned briefly in Chapter 13 as the direction we feel one should look for advanced ideas about pattern recognition and learning. No systematic treatment is available of what is known in this area, but we can recommend a few general references. The collection of papers in

Feigenbaum, Edward A., and Julian Feldman (1963), *Computers and Thought*, McGraw-Hill, New York.

shows the state of affairs in the area up to about 1962, while

Minsky, Marvin (1968), *Semantic Information Processing*, The M.I.T. Press, Cambridge, Mass., 1968

contains more recent papers—mainly doctoral dissertations—dealing with computer programs that manipulate verbal and symbolic descriptions. Anyone interested in this area should also know the classic paper

Newell, Allen, J. C. Shaw, and H. A. Simon (1959), "Report on a general problem-solving program," *Proceedings of International Conference on Information Processing*, UNESCO House, pp. 256–264.

The program mentioned in Chapter 13 is described in detail in

Guzman, Adolfo (1968), "Decomposition of a visual scene into bodies," *Proceedings Fall Joint Computer Conference, 1968*.

Finally, we mention two early works that had a rather broad influence on cybernetic thinking. The fearfully simple homeostat concept mentioned in §11.6 is described in

Ashby, W. Ross (1952), *Design for a brain*, Wiley, New York

which discussed only very simple machines, to be sure, but for the first time with relentless clarity. At the other extreme, perhaps, was

Hebb, Donald O. (1949), *The Organization of Behavior*, Wiley, New York

which sketched a hierarchy of concepts proposed to account for global states in terms of highly local neuronal events. Although the details of such an enterprise have never been thoroughly worked out, Hebb's outline was for many workers a landmark in the shift from a search for a single, simple principle of brain organization toward more realistic attempts to construct hierarchies (or rather *heterarchies*, as McCulloch would insist) that could support the variety of computations evidently needed for thinking.

You might like to compare your reactions to this book with those of other readers. The following are serious discussions of the book and its theoretical approach:

Block, Herbert D: A Review of "Perceptrons". Information and Control vol. 17, 1970, pp. 501-522.

Newell, Allen: A step toward the understanding of Information Processes. Science vol 165, 22 August 1969, pp. 780-782.

Mycielski, Jan: Review of "Perceptrons". Bull. Amer. Math. Soc. vol 78, Jan 1972, pp. 12-15.

Minsky, M. and Papert, S: Re-View of Perceptrons. A.I. Memo 293, Artificial Intelligence Laboratory, M.I.T., Cambridge, Mass. 02139.

The Block review also contains an extensive bibliography.

Index